CARE AND THE PLURIVERSE

Rethinking Global Ethics

Maggie FitzGerald

First published in Great Britain in 2024 by

Bristol University Press
University of Bristol
1–9 Old Park Hill
Bristol
BS2 8BB
UK
t: +44 (0)117 374 6645
e: bup-info@bristol.ac.uk

Details of international sales and distribution partners are available at bristoluniversitypress.co.uk

© Bristol University Press 2024

British Library Cataloguing in Publication Data
A catalogue record for this book is available from the British Library

ISBN 978-1-5292-2011-7 hardcover
ISBN 978-1-5292-2012-4 paperback
ISBN 978-1-5292-2013-1 ePub
ISBN 978-1-5292-2014-8 ePdf

The right of Maggie FitzGerald to be identified as author of this work has been asserted by her in accordance with the Copyright, Designs and Patents Act 1988.

All rights reserved: no part of this publication may be reproduced, stored in a retrieval system, or transmitted in any form or by any means, electronic, mechanical, photocopying, recording, or otherwise without the prior permission of Bristol University Press.

Every reasonable effort has been made to obtain permission to reproduce copyrighted material. If, however, anyone knows of an oversight, please contact the publisher.

The statements and opinions contained within this publication are solely those of the author and not of the University of Bristol or Bristol University Press. The University of Bristol and Bristol University Press disclaim responsibility for any injury to persons or property resulting from any material published in this publication.

Bristol University Press works to counter discrimination on grounds of gender, race, disability, age and sexuality.

Cover design: blu inc, Bristol
Front cover image: Andrey_A / iStock

Bristol Studies in International Theory

Series Editors: **Felix Berenskötter**, SOAS, University of London, UK, **Neta C. Crawford**, Boston University, US and **Stefano Guzzini**, Uppsala University, Sweden, PUC-Rio de Janeiro, Brazil

This series provides a platform for theoretically innovative scholarship that advances our understanding of the world and formulates new visions of, and solutions for, world politics.

Guided by an open mind about what innovation entails, and against the backdrop of various intellectual turns, interrogations of established paradigms, and a world facing complex political challenges, books in the series provoke and deepen theoretical conversations in the field of International Relations.

Also available

Broken Solidarities
How Open Global Governance Divides and Rules
By **Felix Anderl**

Praxis as a Perspective on International Politics
Edited by **Gunther Hellmann** and **Jens Steffek**

The Civil Condition in World Politics
Beyond Tragedy and Utopianism
Edited by **Vassilios Paipais**

Snapshots from Home
Mind, Action and Strategy in an Uncertain World
By **Karin M. Fierke**

What in the World?
Understanding Global Social Change
Edited by **Mathias Albert** and **Tobias Werron**

The Idea of Civilization and the Making of the Global Order
By **Andrew Linklater**

Find out more

bristoluniversitypress.co.uk/
bristol-studies-in-international-theory

International advisory board

Claudia Aradau, King's College London, UK
Jens Bartelson, Lund University, Sweden
Pinar Bilgin, Bilkent University, Turkey
Toni Erskine, Australian National University, Australia
Matthew Evangelista, Cornell University, US
Karin Fierke, University of St Andrews, UK
Kimberly Hutchings, Queen Mary University of London, UK
Peter Katzenstein, Cornell University, US
Gilbert Khadiagala, University of the Witwatersrand, South Africa
Anna Leander, The Graduate Institute, Geneva, Switzerland
Sheryl Lightfoot, The University of British Columbia, Canada
Cecelia Lynch, University of California Irvine, US
Jonathan Mercer, University of Washington, US
Heikki Patomäki, University of Helsinki, Finland
Sergei Prozorov, University of Jyväskylä, Finland
Yaqing Qin, China Foreign Affairs University, Canada
Fiona Robinson, Carleton University, Canada
Justin Rosenberg, University of Sussex, UK
Chih-Yu Shih, National Taiwan University, Taiwan
Jennifer Sterling-Folker, University of Connecticut, US

Find out more

bristoluniversitypress.co.uk/
bristol-studies-in-international-theory

Contents

Acknowledgements		vi
1	The Pluriversal Challenge to Global Ethics	1
2	The Problem of Modernity and the Decolonial Project	29
3	Mapping Global Ethics in the Pluriverse	56
4	A Critical, Political Ethics of Care	104
5	Partial Connections: The Pluriverse, Ethics, and Care	126
6	Vulnerable and Precarious Worlds: A Meta-Theoretical Orientation	146
7	The Political and the Pluriverse: A (Dis)Associative Theory of Care	168
8	Building the Pluriverse with Care	195
9	Rethinking Global Ethics with Care and the Pluriverse	214
References		222
Index		244

Acknowledgements

First and foremost, I wish to thank Dr Fiona Robinson for her endless support and encouragement. Dr Robinson supervised my doctoral project at Carleton University, where my ideas in this book first developed. Her kindness, guidance, and care continue to inspire me. Thank you so very much, Fiona.

Thank you also to Dr Hans-Martin Jaeger and Dr Cristina Rojas, who both challenged me to consider pathways I may have otherwise dismissed. I am truly grateful for their critical and thoughtful feedback, suggestions, and encouragement throughout this project.

Thank you to my many supportive colleagues at Carleton University and the University of Saskatchewan for providing me with friendship and intellectual community. A special thank you to Dr Clinton Westman, who read a draft of Chapter 1 and provided very helpful comments as I finalized the manuscript. Thank you also to two peer reviewers and the series editor for constructive feedback on an earlier version of the manuscript. Thinking through and responding to these comments improved the arguments presented here immensely. The wonderful people at Bristol University Press deserve many thanks for all of their efficient and helpful support throughout the publishing process.

Earlier versions of sections in Chapters 1 and 6 previously appeared as 'Precarious political ontologies and the ethics of care' in *Care Ethics in the Age of Precarity: Resisting Neoliberalism*, ed. by Maurice Hamington and Michael Flower, pp. 191–209. Minneapolis: University of Minnesota Press.

Lastly, thank you to Rob Currie-Wood, Akaysha Humniski, and Sacha Ghandeharian. This book would not exist were it not for your support, intellectual comradery, love, and friendship.

1

The Pluriversal Challenge to Global Ethics

The northern corroboree frog leads a double life. To settler Australians, the northern corroboree frog is an amphibian that largely resides in the seasonal wetlands and surrounding vegetation of the south-western slopes of New South Wales, Australia. The species is identifiable by an alternating pattern of black and yellow, yellowish-green, or lime-green stripes which run longitudinally along its back. They have yellow and white blotches on their underside, and feed primarily on small black ants and other invertebrates. Their bright colours indicate that they are poisonous. The northern corroboree frog is currently designated as 'critically endangered', largely because a multitude of threats have damaged their breeding sites: for instance, the habitat has been damaged by feral pigs, horses, and deer; by the invasion of weeds like blackberry; by the activities and practices of the forestry industry; and by climate change patterns that have resulted in a loss of pools and shallow water spaces that are integral to the reproductive behaviours of the species (New South Wales Government, 2019).

The northern corroboree frog goes by another name as well. For the Wolgalu nation, the northern corroboree frog is called Gyack. Gyack is more than a species of frog for the Wolgalu nation; Gyack is what might more accurately be called a more-than-human being. This is because Gyack is a *present and active* entity in its relationship with the Wolgalu peoples. More precisely, Gyack is present and active in the annual ceremonies of the Wolgalu/Wiradjuri in the New South Wales High Country, and Gyack's 'croak' is more than a call, it is a song (Slater, 2021, p. 2). Held together in this single material being is thus two beings – the corroboree frog, who is enacted in and through a relationship with the ways of being and knowing that comprise the world of settler Australians, and Gyack, who is enacted in and through a relationship with the ways of being and knowing that comprise the world of the Wolgalu nation.

In a reflection on her role in a research project which is working with a variety of stakeholders to reconnect the Wolgalu/Wiradjuri community of Brungle Tumut to the corroboree frog/Gyack, Lisa Slater (2021) directs our attention to some of the implications of the 'double life' of the corroboree frog/Gyack. She writes, 'Gyack is not a frog in the same way a "frog" is a frog to me. How can I [a settler Australian] care for the corroboree frog/Gyack, when we [the Wolgalu/Wiradjuri community and myself] are not caring for the same thing?' While this question is raised in relation to a very particular relation (Slater's relationship, or perhaps non-relationship, with Gyack), the ethico-political tensions foregrounded in this query point directly to the central concern of this book. How can we care – by which I mean, the 'species activity that includes everything that we do to maintain, continue, and repair our "world[s]" so that we can live in [them] as well as possible' (Fisher and Tronto, 1990, p. 40) – for that which we do not, and cannot, know? How can we care for worlds (and the relationships therein) that are not our own?

These questions are, admittedly, thorny and dense. Slater's (2021, pp. 1–2) reflections on trying to hear the corroboree frog/Gyack help demonstrate further the fullness of these questions, and the challenge of 'not knowing' that which one is trying to care for:

> I am listening out for Gyack at Micalong Swamp, on Wolgalu country, in Buccleuch State Forest, east of Tumut. ... Initially I could not tune in to Gyack's call; they sounded like, well, frogs. Not the green trees frogs that are familiar to me from growing up in northern [New South Wales], on Bundjalung country. If I slow down and listen carefully, I hear different calls, like instruments in a small band, but initially I couldn't discern one species from another. After some time and guided by finely tuned ears, I learn to hear Gyack's call. But not their song.

Slater can, of course, hear Gyack. Yet, she cannot hear, she cannot *know*, Gyack's song. This is because the social world she is imbedded within is very different (although not separate from) the world of her Wolgalu/Wiradjuri colleagues. These colleagues have a relation with Gyack; indeed, it is this relationship which motivates the research project in the first place. As trawlwulwuy countrywoman Emma Lee (quoted in Tynan, 2021, p. 601, also see Slater, 2021, p. 2) explains, to protect the corroboree frog is to reclaim Wolgalu/Wiradjuri's web of relationships that are mediated through Country. This research project is thus not simply an ecological conservation project; this is a project that seeks to reclaim and repair relations, and to care for the world which these relations enact – a world which is somewhat paradoxically both inextricably intertwined with, yet in excess of, Slater's world. It is also in this space, a space where (at least) two different worlds are unfolding together but not in identical ways, that we find Slater attempting to care (in her role as a researcher on the project; in her relationship as a collaborator with her Wolgalu/Wiradjuri colleagues; in her critical reflections on what all of this might mean) for Gyack, who she cannot know, for a relationship she cannot access, and for a world of which she is not a part.

The language of the 'pluriverse' (Mignolo, 2013; de la Cadena, 2015) has recently gained currency as a way to conceptualize such ontological multiplicity, exemplified by the 'double life' of the corroboree frog/Gyack. Most simply, the pluriverse is an acknowledgement that we do not live in a single world with different belief systems, paradigms, or cultures; instead, the pluriverse suggests that we live in a world of many worlds. This phrasing, 'a world of many worlds', is important in its formulation: on the one hand, there is one world – we share a material existence, we are connected in and through relations of power, and we also often share concepts, language, practices, and other aspects of our collective forms of life. At the same time, however, there are many worlds; there are different collective worlding practices that enact different worlds, and these worlds are sometimes in excess of each other. 'Difference' thus carries an ontological weight in the pluriversal context: *there are different ways of being/knowing*. Scholarship on the pluriverse seeks to grapple with the ontological, epistemological, and political implications of understanding our shared existence as constituted by such a paradoxical connectedness and excessiveness (see, for example, Rojas, 2016; Escobar, 2018; Jaeger, 2018; Hutchings, 2019; Blaser and de la Cadena, 2021; Slater, 2021). In this book, I aim to contribute to this task by exploring the ethical implications of the pluriverse. I ask: *How can we rethink global ethics in the pluriverse, where differences are at their most deep and pervasive? How might we build a pluriversal ethics? How can we live well with other worlds?* These questions, as should be evident, are inherently tied to the question posed by Slater (2021) when she is considering how to care for the corroboree frog/Gyack. I think that in many ways, this book dwells in that same question, but at the level of different worlds more broadly. *How might we care for worlds that are not our own, and that are, therefore, to some degree unknowable to us?*

Another example will help further demonstrate this notion of multiple distinct, yet intertwined, ontologies or worlds, as well as the stakes involved in these questions. In her book *Earth Beings: Ecologies of Practice across Andean Worlds* (2015), Marisol de la Cadena presents a decade-long dialogue between Mariano and Nazario Turpo, a Quechua father and son, and herself, a Peruvian-born anthropologist living and working in the United States. This dialogue revolves around the ways in which the world of Mariano and Nazario, on the one hand, and the world of de la Cadena on the other, both exceed each other and intertwine in meaningful ways. For instance, in December 2006, 1,000 peasants gathered in the main square of Cuzco, the Plaza de Armas. 'They had travelled from their villages located at the foot of a mountain named Ausangate, well known in Cuzco as a powerful earth-being, the source of life and death, of wealth and misery' (de la Cadena, 2010, p. 338). Ausangate, as an 'earth-being', is more than a mountain for the peasants: Ausangate is an agential being, a more-than-human being, who has relations with the Quechua people, and who is an active participant in the Quechua form of life. 'Obtaining a favorable outcome [thus] requires maintaining proper relationships with [Ausangate] and its surroundings (other mountains, lesser entities)' (de la Cadena, 2010, p. 338). In fact, the reason that the Quechua people, like Nazario, had gathered in the square was to maintain this proper relationship by protesting a prospective concession for a mine located in the Sinakara, one of the peaks of the mountain chain of which Ausangate is a part (de la Cadena, 2010, p. 338). As de la Cadena notes, while the Quechua formed a large part of the gathering, other protesters were also present, including members of the Catholic brotherhood (de la Cadena, 2010, p. 338). On the face of things, these diverse people from diverse backgrounds were all gathering and partaking in the same protest against the development of the mining project.

However, de la Cadena also points out that this surface appearance was misleading, and masked deep ontological differences across protestors – including differences between Nazario's political actions and thoughts and de la Cadena's political actions and thoughts. de la Cadena (2010, pp. 338–9) explains:

> Yet the degree to which this demonstration was different was brought home to me by my friend Nazario, whose village, Pacchanta, is at the foot of the Ausangate. He was there to protest the mining project – in fact he had called to let me know about the event. Initially, while we were demonstrating, I thought we shared a single view against the mine; however, once we debriefed about the meeting, and how it could influence future events, I realized that our shared view was also more than one. My reason for opposing the mine was that it would destroy pastures that families depend on to earn their living grazing alpacas and sheep, and selling their wool and meat. Nazario agreed with me, but said it would be worse: Ausangate would not allow the mine in Sinakara, a mountain over which it presided. Ausangate would get mad, could even kill people. To prevent that killing, the mine should not happen. I could not agree more, and although I could not bring myself to think that Ausangate would kill, I found it impossible to consider it a metaphor. Preventing Ausangate's ire was Nazario's motivation to participate in the demonstration and therefore it had political import.

What de la Cadena realizes is that while Nazario and herself are together engaging in a political act to protect (and, I would suggest, therefore care for) Ausangate, their understanding and stake in this political act is radically different. In Nazario's world, Ausangate is not a belief or metaphor – rather, 'Ausangate *is*, period' (de la Cadena, 2015, p. 26, emphasis in original). More specifically, Ausangate is an ontological being, a being that is enacted and real in Nazario's ontological and epistemological frame. In de la Cadena's world, Ausangate is a mountain – one that may impact the lives of others – but not an agential being itself. Nonetheless, despite these differences, Nazario and de la Cadena were, in that moment, together residing in a common political space. This example thereby again points to the existence of deep ontological differences, and illustrates that such differences, like those between Nazario and de la Cadena, cannot be subsumed or reduced to a singular ontology. Instead, as de la Cadena (2015, p. 4) explains, 'my world was included in the world that my friends inhabited and vice versa, but their world could not be reduced to mine, or mine to theirs'. The notion of the pluriverse, of a matrix of connected yet distinct worlds, has grown from ethnographic accounts like this one, which demonstrate deep and pervasive ontological difference(s).

Mario Blaser (2016) uses a different term to refer to the pluriverse: according to Blaser (2009, p. 877), the term 'political ontology' captures two distinct but inter-related processes:

> On the one hand, it refers to the politics involved in the practices that shape a particular world or ontology. On the other hand, it refers to a field of study that focuses on the conflicts that ensue as different worlds or ontologies strive to sustain their own existence as they interact and mingle with each other.

Each of these points merits some discussion. First, thinking about political ontology as the politics involved in the practices that shape a particular world requires thinking about ontology more generally, and then ontological practices. Ontology is most commonly understood as a way of understanding the world that involves the making of assumptions, either implicitly or explicitly, about what kinds of things do or can exist, and their conditions of existence (Scott and Marshall, 2005). More simply, ontology refers to the assumptions and framings through which we understand the world and conditions of being. Ontology is thus tied to epistemology – how we know what we know. An understanding of the world requires an epistemic framework or set of criteria from which to determine the validity of said understanding of the world (Hutchings, 2001). At the same time, our ontological assumptions influence our epistemic positionalities. The notion of political ontology described by Blaser, however, expands this understanding of ontology by focusing on the politics involved in the practices through which 'ontologies perform themselves into worlds' (2009, p. 877): 'An ontology is a way of worlding, it is a form of enacting a reality' (Blaser, 2013, p. 23). Ontologies in this sense are not simply claims about the world, or framings for understanding the world, but instead, consist of the continual processes and (political) practices which bring worlds into existence, and through which we come to know the world itself; political ontology in particular is meant to distinguish the political aspects of these practices.

Second, Blaser also argues that political ontology refers to a research agenda which aims to explore and understand the ways in which worlds conflict and interact. This dimension of political ontology stems from the two characteristics of political ontology described earlier. If ontology is understood as the way we see the world, the ways in which we claim authority for that viewpoint, and the practices that enact this world, then research, as a practice and an act (Aradau and Huysmans, 2014), is a part of the enactment of ontologies. Research on political ontology cannot be divorced from the ontologies that are examined, nor can it be divorced from the world of which the researcher is a part. As Claudia Aradau and Jef Huysmans (2014) explain, 'Understood as devices, [research and] methods are seen to enact social and political worlds. Understood as acts, methods can become disruptive of social and political worlds' (p. 598) because 'if methods enact particular worlds, their experimental connecting and assembling can also create ruptures in these worlds' (p. 608). Research is both performative, in that it enacts certain worlds, and political, in that the ways in which our research enacts these worlds has (unequal) material and ideological consequences for our ontologies/worldings. Research, as a site of ontological struggle, is necessarily implicated in the very concept of political ontology.

Given this, I suggest that the relation between ontology and epistemology, as explicated earlier, is even more primary from a political ontological perspective. On the one hand, it is through acts of worlding that we not only enact reality but also that we come to know reality. On the other hand, the frames we use to validate how we know reality likewise construct that reality. For this reason, this book suggests that the understanding of ontology implicit in the concept of political ontology may therefore be better captured by the term onto-epistemology, as it prioritizes the *co-constitutive relationship* between how we see and understand the world and the ways in which we claim authority for that particular understanding of the world. Onto-epistemology emphasizes the indivisibility of these two moves: seeing the world in a particular way cannot be separated from the framing used to claim validity for that world, nor can the framework used to validate a world view be separated from broader acts and practices which bring worlds – and ergo our understandings of worlds – into existence. The framework used to validate a world view is, itself, an enactment of worlds, and the world it enacts simultaneously constitutes the framework for validating said world. Throughout this book, the term onto-epistemology[1] (instead of just ontology) is therefore used interchangeably with 'worlds'; a world is defined according to a particular co-constitutive and continually enacted ontology and epistemology and can thus be conceived of as such.

It is based on this understanding of worlds, or onto-epistemologies, that we are able to conceive of a pluriverse. Worlds do not pre-exist our human interactions; they are an outcome of our relations, our interactions, our practices, our knowledge, and our political conflicts revolving around these issues. Given the multiplicity of these relations and practices, a single onto-epistemological standpoint (a single world) is not possible. Instead, there are multiple worlds (Agathangelou and Ling, 2009) or a pluriverse (de la Cadena, 2015): a matrix of entangled worlds that are connected through relations of power (Mignolo, 2013). This connectivity is important: as Walter Mignolo explains, 'pluriversality is not cultural relativism' (2013, np); it is not a world of independent units. Instead, the pluriverse is 'more than one, but less than many' (Blaser, 2018, p. 47); it is an acknowledgement that while we reside in the same present, our worlds can be very different. Marilyn Strathern's (2004) concept of 'partial connections' captures this relationality by foregrounding that these worlds are not singular units; rather, relations are always 'integrally implied' (Rojas, 2016, p. 379). While differences across worlds may be deep and pervasive (onto-epistemic), and thus not necessarily reducible or translatable, they do not limit our interactions, nor do they negate the significance of the ways in which the global order – meaning, the partial connections between worlds – come to shape particular worlds, and often unevenly so. Instead, these differences, and the notion of the pluriverse, demand that we dwell in the messy entanglements that connect worlds and pay attention to the ways in which the enactments of certain worlds are prevented or disparaged through these entanglements.

This idea of the pluriverse thus presents a more expansive political landscape as compared to mainstream conceptualizations of the 'global'. In particular, the notion of multiple worlds does not simply ground the political in competing perspectives, interests, viewpoints, or goals within a singular world, but rather, locates politics as the very processes through

---

[1] This term is not new, although this particular use of it is perhaps novel. For instance, Cristina Rojas (2016) uses the term onto-epistemic to refer to a world which has deep relations with nature; in other words, it refers to a particular characteristic or quality of certain worlds. Karen Barad (2008, p. 147) uses onto-epistem-ology to refer to the study of practices of knowing in being. The use of the term onto-epistemology, or onto-epistemic framings, here, however, is not a description of a quality of a particular relational world, nor does it refer to a field of study; rather, the claim is that all worlds are onto-epistemologies, a co-constitutive continually enacted ontology and epistemology.

which multiple worlds are both deeply intertwined and radically different, creating the very boundaries of what is knowable and speakable. Simply put, in the pluriverse, 'differences' are at their most deep and pervasive; what is at stake in the pluriverse are different worlds/worldings, different onto-epistemologies. These 'differences' fracture prevalent notions of the 'global' as a shared and common world, and of 'global politics' as contestations over different ideologies, values, and interests within this common world.

The pluriverse and the political

The work of Jenny Edkins (1999), and her distinction between 'politics' and 'the political' is useful for understanding further the pluriversal landscape. In contrast to 'politics', which can be understood as the political reality as it is already described and acknowledged, '"the political" has to do with the establishment of that very social order which sets out a particular, historically specific account of what counts as politics and defines other areas of social life as *not* politics' (Edkins, 1999, p. 2, emphasis in original). In other words, the political represents a moment of 'ungrounding' and 'grounding', in which a socio-symbolic order (that is, an order which delineates what is thinkable, knowable, and speakable) is ruptured, reconfigured and shifted, and instantiated anew. In the pluriverse, worlds or onto-epistemologies are connected (partially) through relations of power; the differentials in these power relations situate certain worlds 'above' and 'below' others, resulting in a configuration of worlds that may be thought of as a social order, albeit one that is contingent, fluid, and shifting. When this relational web of onto-epistemologies is arranged as a hierarchy of domination, certain worlds exist outside of 'politics'; they are rendered invisible or incomprehensible by the logic of the dominant world. At the same time, when these relations of power shift, and the marginalized worlds illuminate, and perhaps even reconfigure, the boundaries of the dominant world, there is a political moment which may redefine the pluriversal order itself and, in so doing, redefine what counts as politics. In this way, I assert that the pluriverse is always operating at the level of the political.

Another pluriversal example will help to illustrate this assertion. In March 2017, the local Māori tribe of Whanganui in the North Island of New Zealand/Aotearoa, the Whanganui Iwi, won recognition for the Whanganui River as their ancestor, meaning that the river must be treated as a living entity. The Whanganui River, or Te Awa Tupua (a term which emphasizes the Māori way of knowing the river as an indivisible whole), was granted this recognition, formalized in the Te Awa Tupua (Whanganui River Claims Settlement) Act, and the same legal rights as a human being, after 140 years of struggle by the Whanganui Iwi. Importantly, the scope of this struggle should not be underestimated. As the Whanganui River

Māori Trust Board (2010; see also Hsiao, 2012) clearly documents, the Whanganui Iwi's relentless assertion of their customary rights on behalf of the Whanganui River, through a variety of strategies and means, comprises the longest-standing legal battel in New Zealand's history. And while, of course, this legal decision is not fully reflective of these customary rights or Māori law (a point discussed more fully in Chapter 7), this granting of legal personhood is a positive development in this conflict: in granting legal personality to the Whanganui River, the New Zealand legal system sees no differentiation between harming the tribe and harming the river 'because they are one and the same' (Roy, 2017).

This case, from a pluriversal standpoint, is an example of a conflict between two worlds.[2] On the one hand, the New Zealand Government – constituted by the modern world, which in its current manifestation is premised on thick individualism, private property, and a clear distinction between Humans and Nature – constructs the river as property. On the other hand, the Whanganui Iwi know the river as ancestor and still-living kin. More specifically,

> the Whanganui Iwi share two ancestors, Paerangi and Ruatipua. It is said that Ruatipua 'draws lifeforce from the headwaters of the Whanganui River on Mount Tongariro and its tributaries which stretch down to the sea.' The river itself mirrors the extension of the descendants of Paerangi and Ruatipua. '*Ko au te awa, Ko te awa ko au* – I am the river and the river is me.' As such, the Whanganui Iwi recognize the Whanganui River as their ancestor, as a treasured thing (*taonga*), and as a living being, Te Awa Tupua. (Hsiao, 2012, p. 371, emphasis in original, citing WAI 167, 1999)

This understanding of and relationship with the Whanganui River is key to the enactment of the Whanganui Iwi's relational onto-epistemology, which is devoid of the Human/Nature and living/non-living binaries that constitute the modern world (Povinelli, 2016). However, under the current

---

[2] Some may suggest that this is simply a conflict between cultures, as opposed to a conflict between worlds. However, the concept of the pluriverse, and of multiple worlds, is, in part, a response to the tendency to devalue certain ways of being as simply 'beliefs', 'traditions', or 'culture', while other ways of being are viewed as 'true' or inherently valid. In naming the Māori world a world, and describing this conflict as a conflict between worlds, the aim is to give full ontological weight (Holbraad et al., 2014) to the practices and relations that constitute their way of being and knowing. Further, giving this ontological weight to non-modern ways of being is a necessary step towards decolonization, and towards destabilizing the hierarchies of power which render some ways of being as 'true' and others as less legitimate. Such destabilization is a key political task for the pluriversal literature, as discussed more fully throughout the remainder of this book.

configuration of the pluriverse, whereby the modern world dominates and marks the boundaries of 'legitimate' politics, the Māori world was rendered unintelligible for over 140 years. The river was not viewed by the state as kin, or as a living entity, but rather was treated as property. Moreover, even the Whanganui Iwi's own view of the river as kin was not acknowledged by the state. As a result, the reproduction of the Whanganui Iwi's world was undermined, as the river was both treated in a way that violated the logic of their world and denied a subject status that is key to their broader onto-epistemology.

The 140-year struggle to recognize the river as a living entity, then, is an example of the enactment of the political as defined by Edkins (1999). In this case, the Whanganui Iwi fought to bring into relationship two incommensurable logics: their own knowledge of the river as kin and the view of nature as property that in part constitutes modernity. In so doing, the Whanganui Iwi made visible that which was invisible, namely, their relationship with the river, and more fundamentally, the world which this relationship in part enacts. Importantly, in bringing together these two incommensurable logics, equivocation was not overcome. The New Zealand Government does not see the river as a human in a literal sense, nor do the Māori fully embody the legal human rights framework which facilitated this recognition. Rather, in bringing together these two logics, a tentative reconfiguration of the pluriversal order was achieved, one in which 'the [characteristically political] contradiction of two worlds in a single world' (Rancière, 1999, p. 27) is foregrounded. As this example shows, the pluriverse, as the landscape comprised of multiple connected yet often contradicting worlds, must be thought of as political.

A decolonial project

Lastly, it is important to emphasize that pluriversal scholarship is firmly embedded in a decolonial project, particularly as represented by the Latin American research programme modernity/coloniality/decoloniality (MCD), subsequent literature critiquing and expanding upon this programme (described as the 'ontological turn' [Rojas, 2016]), and related decolonial anthropological literature (see, for example, Blaser, 2009; 2013; de la Cadena, 2014; 2015). That is, the notion of the pluriverse is not an apolitical abstract concept; rather, as Mignolo (2018, p. x) argues, pluriversality is tied to a specific commitment:

> [P]luriversality as a universal project means that the universal cannot have one single owner: the universal can only be pluriversal, which also corresponds with the Zapatistas' vision of a world in which many worlds coexist. All of us on the planet have arrived at the end of the

era of abstract, disembodied universals – of universal universality. Western universalism has the right to coexist in the pluriverse of meaning. Stripped of its pretended uni-versality, Western cosmology would be one of many cosmologies, no longer the one that subsumes and regulates all the others.

The pluriversal project is inherently a critique of the modern world which, through ongoing processes of colonialism (discussed in detail in the next chapter), has posited itself as the one true and legitimate world, the world of 'universal universality'. Simultaneously, pluriversality is also a normative call to envision a world in which multiple worlds are possible as *worlds*, as 'universals' in their own right, as opposed to different beliefs, traditions, or paradigms within a one 'true' world. As Hans-Martin Jaeger (2018, p. 228) summarizes, this 'ontological turn seeks to take seriously the multiplicity of being (alternatively designated as radical alterity or pluriversality) by overturning the Western philosophical presupposition of one ontology ("reality" or "nature") and multiple epistemologies ("representations" or "cultures").' Taking this seriously, for example, involves heeding the call of anthropologists like Paul Nadasdy (2007) and Zoe Todd (2014, p. 222, emphasis in original) who urge us 'to treat Indigenous people's human-animal engagements [for example, the relationship between Gyack and the Wolgalu/Wiradjuri community] and ontological assumptions [for instance, that Ausangate is an agential being] as *literal* rather than only *symbolic* matters'. In so doing, the notion of the pluriverse, and the ontological turn in the decolonial project, seeks to substantiate every world's right to its own universality.

The 'ontological turn' is subsequently often distinguished from the epistemological research programme (see, for example, Mignolo, 2012a; 2012b) in decolonial theory, which is viewed as consisting of these two moments: the 'epistemological' moment versus the 'ontological' moment (Rojas, 2016). Cristina Rojas (2016, p. 374; quoting Escobar, 2007, p. 180) explains:

> The first targets the epistemic logic of modernity–coloniality by making visible the mechanisms through which modern rationality manages the world and legitimizes the universality of modern knowledge. Scholars forming part of the modernity/coloniality/decoloniality (MCD) research program commit to 'an other way of thinking' that counters the main narratives of modernity (Christianity, liberalism, and Marxism). … The 'ontological' moment, on the other hand, aims to interrupt the modern commitment to the existence of one world.

While these two moments do point to different literatures, and different framings of the problem of difference, I would, however, like to suggest that it is important to move beyond such a binary. This is part of the reason why I believe that conceiving of worlds or 'universals' – to borrow Mignolo's language – as 'onto-epistemologies' is useful. Thinking about onto-epistemologies situates us to move beyond such an epistemological/ontological debate by foregrounding the fact that any attempt to restructure the world order so that multiple worlds may co-exist must simultaneously attend to the co-constitutive nature of ontology and epistemology, to the ways in which every world is a co-constitutive onto-epistemology.

The pluriversal challenge to global ethics

The notion of the pluriverse, of a matrix of interconnected worlds, thus poses a significant challenge to the ways in which we study, theorize, and practise global ethics. Global Ethics, as a field of research, is concerned with theoretical inquiry that seeks to analyse and address moral and ethical[3] questions and issues that arise from our global interconnectedness. While there are a multitude of approaches to ethical theorizing in Global Ethics, Kimberly Hutchings (2010) provides a useful schematic that outlines the contours of the field. On the one hand, 'rationalist' approaches to global ethics, such as contractualism, utilitarianism, deontological ethics, and discourse ethics, are united in their assertion that reason is the 'basis for the authority for ethical claims' and that 'the foundations of ethics can be discovered and explained through the exercise of reason by the ethical theorist, in abstraction from the contexts and concerns of actual ethical debates' (2010, pp. 28–9). As a result, rationalist approaches to global ethics reject the idea that context, embodiment, or emotion are of moral salience; ethical theorizing is seen as an individualized task, in which moral philosophers use transcendental reason to grapple with abstracted ethical issues. This attempt to eschew positionality allows the moral theorist to make universalizing claims from an 'objective' vantage point via the exercise of a particular type of reasoning. The moral 'epistemological emphasis [is] on the atomised reasoning individual' (Beattie and Schick, 2013, pp. 3–4), who can access universal moral principles which can then be applied to our political situations and conflicts (Tronto, 1993).

---

[3] Importantly, while some literature distinguishes between ethics and morality – with ethics representing the 'right' and morality representing the 'good' (Benhabib, 1992) – these terms are used interchangeably throughout this book, which rejects this separation. More precisely, this book departs from the idea that what is right is necessarily underpinned by a conception of what is good and vice versa (Geras, 1999). When drawing directly upon a piece of scholarship which upholds the distinction, however, the terms are used in a way that reflects the cited work.

For example, utilitarian and contractualist ethical theories presume that all humans are instrumentally rational in that they can derive, assess, and rank their interests, and then calculate the ways in which to maximize these interests. This entails a universal view of human nature – above all else, humans seek to maximize their interests – and a particular notion of rationality based on the capacity to identify and rank these interests (Hutchings, 2010, p. 38). Ethical deliberation, from these perspectives, involves the exercise of this rationality so as to accumulate a particular kind of moral knowledge which can then be applied to the separate sphere of politics so as 'to create a world marked by predictability, order and stability' (Beattie and Schick, 2013, p. 1). Deontological moral approaches rely on deduction to identify rules and principles consistent with the laws of reason. These rules and principles are viewed as transcending emotion, relationality, community, history, and socio-political-economic context (Beattie and Schick, 2013); they are seen as universally prescriptive in form (Hutchings, 2010). For these approaches, a particular notion of reason/rationality, and an emphasis on reason/rationality as the means through which ethical deliberation should rightly unfold, orients the 'disembodied' moral philosopher, and provides universal foundations for the authority of the moral claims made by this impartial moral judge.

Situated in opposition to mainstream rationalist theories in the field of Global Ethics, according to Hutchings's (2010) schematic, are 'alternative' approaches to ethical deliberation, such as feminist ethics and postmodernist ethics. While the alternative approaches discussed by Hutchings are distinct in various ways (some of which will be discussed later in this book), what they have in common is their rejection of the privileging of abstract, impartial, and/or universal rationality as the means through which we can solve and/or attend to the ethical and moral dilemmas which arise as a result of our global interconnectedness (Hutchings, 2010, pp. 58–72). Instead, the alternative approaches foreground the moral salience of context, where context refers to a variety of factors, including community, social relations, emotions, embodiment, and the ways in which power permeates all these things. They also reject 'the idea that ethics can be given a rational grounding, that moral claims can have the status of truths, and that there are certain fixed, essential properties associated with being "human"' (Hutchings, 2010, p. 67). In so doing, the alternative approaches are united in that they critique the rationalist approaches for their separation of ethics and politics, and for the related assertion that the rationalist perspective is the sole, unbiased, and 'true' approach to contemplating global ethical dilemmas. More simply, the alternative approaches highlight that in failing to foreground the ways in which any and all moral claims are always embedded in and co-constitutive of socio-political-economic contexts, the rationalist approaches involve an unexamined 'privileging of white Western approaches to global ethics ... that not only neglects but actively oppresses alternative voices and perspectives' (Beattie and Schick, 2013, p. 2).

According to this schematic, then, the field of Global Ethics can broadly be understood as divided by a debate over the moral (im)possibility of universality and, by extension, different understandings of the relationship between ethics/ethical knowledge and politics. On the one hand, rationalist approaches valorize a 'universal' reason in an attempt to make or locate universal moral principles which can then be mobilized across various contexts. This involves an understanding of ethics as a realm separate from the socio-political; ethical knowledge is accessed by the impartial, apolitical moral philosopher, and this knowledge is then applied to the realm of politics. On the other hand, alternative approaches highlight the particularity of knowledge, and therefore of ethical knowledge, by understanding that ethics and the socio-political are deeply intertwined and co-constituted. More to the point, the alternative approaches see ethics as operating in and through (relations of) power. In so doing, alternative approaches foreground not only the impossibility of asserting universal authoritative standards in forming moral judgements, but also the dangers of attempting to do so (Robinson, 2006, p. 227): 'the radical privileging of moral rationalism as neutral and universal smuggles in unexamined moral hierarchies that shut down other voices' (Beattie and Schick, 2013, p. 9), both reflecting and reproducing global hierarchies of power.

Finally, it is important to highlight that implicit in this debate regarding the (im)possibility of universal claims are contestations over the nature of difference, and the significance of difference, for moral deliberation. For example, the rationalist approaches ultimately attest that difference (for instance, cultural, social, material, political) can be separated out from moral deliberation, and/or subsumed and transcended via higher-level reasoning and universal moral principles. In taking context seriously, and in asserting the inseparability of politics and ethics, the alternative approaches, on the other hand, foreground that while we share an interconnected world, differences across social groups within that world are morally significant. In fact, for the alternative approaches, differences in and across culture, economy, religion, politics, knowledges, and other identity categories take moral primacy when navigating ethical issues, as these differences comprise the very context in and through which moral dilemmas arise, and shape the ways in which we understand, dialogue about, and deliberate on these dilemmas. While each particular approach will differ in terms of how they conceive the nature of 'difference', and in terms of how they propose we navigate differences, the alternative approaches share a commitment to interrogating the ways in which 'difference' is morally salient when grappling with ethical dilemmas in our shared and interconnected world.

Yet, the notion of the pluriverse poses a fundamental challenge to both of these approaches. As just outlined, Global Ethics can be characterized by a debate regarding the (im)possibility of universality. On the one hand, rationalist approaches purport a thick universality (what Mignolo might call a universal-universality), while alternative approaches – via various critiques – question the very possibility of a universal ethics at all. The pluriverse ruptures this bifurcation. In giving 'full ontological weight' (Holbraad et al., 2014, np) to other ways of being/knowing, the pluriverse puts forth a compelling normative claim: every world has the right to claim their own universality. The pluriverse thereby poses a normative challenge that requires *a multiplication of universality*, as opposed to either a single universal or a multiplicity of contingent particularities. What meta-ethical orientations can theoretically accommodate the multiplication of universality? At the same time, how do such meta-ethical orientations provide us with practical guidance in terms of dealing with ethical issues that cross worlds, and the universals within? *More simply, how can we rethink global ethics in the pluriverse, where differences are at their most deep and pervasive? How might we build a pluriversal ethics? How can we live well with other worlds? How can we care for worlds that are not our own?*

The ethics of care and building a pluriversal ethics

The argument in this book is that a critical, feminist ethics of care is a normative orientation conducive to building an ethics for the pluriverse because it demands that we dwell in the vulnerability that arises from our relational being. On the one hand, in foregrounding our relationality and giving moral weight to the practices that sustain relational selves, the ethics of care is attuned to the multiplication of worlds; on the other hand, in foregrounding our mutual vulnerability which arises from our relationality, the ethics of care simultaneously highlights the impossibility of one moral voice, and orients us to attend critically to relations of power which suppress different moral voices, and by extension, suppress and devalue certain ways of being in and seeing the world more broadly.

The literature on the ethics of care can most accurately be traced back to psychological theory (Gilligan, 1993) and feminist philosophy (Ruddick, 1989), which identified an approach to moral reasoning based on the relational self and the enhancement and preservation of specific relationships. As Carol Gilligan (1993) argued, this relational approach or 'voice' differed from the rationalist voice that dominated moral psychology at the time (more accurately, the rationalist voice was presented as *the* definition of morality); notably, this rational voice is the same voice underpinning the rationalist approaches in Global Ethics discussed earlier. Whereas the rationalist voice conceives of morality as the impartial application of rules and principles to abstracted ethical dilemmas, the relational voice constructs moral problems 'as a problem of responsibility in relationships' (Gilligan, 1993, p. 73). As a result, moral selves emerge through relations of responsibility and care for particular others (Robinson, 1999), and morality is understood as practices – that is, as present in and a feature of almost everything we do (Walker, 2007) – and specifically the practices that emerge in and through our relations with others (Robinson, 2011c).

Accordingly, an ethics of care approach also changes our conceptualization of moral agents, who are now understood to be dependent and vulnerable beings, constituted by relations and their positionality in various relations and systems of power, as opposed to autonomous and independent liberal subjects (see, for example, Hekman, 1995; Kittay, 2002; Kittay *et al.*, 2005). We are embedded in complex relations of power; our moral relations are themselves characterized by these same relations. Because of this recognition, care ethics prioritizes a sensitivity to the political, social, and economic contexts (see, for example, Tronto, 1993; 2013) that shape morality. Furthermore, given that contexts are multiple, and that moral agents are constituted by their unique context, the ethics of care also suggests a multiplicity of relational moral selves. Specifically, subsequent work on the ethics of care built on this 'discovery' of a different voice to highlight the heterogeneity of moral subjects, and, correspondingly, the multiplicity of moral voices/epistemologies/theories. As Susan Hekman (1995, p. 30) writes:

> The epistemology implicit in [Gilligan's] work replaces the disembodied knower with the relational self. The knowledge constituted by this relational self is a very different kind of knowledge. The relational self produces knowledge that is connected, a product of discourses that constitute forms of life; it is plural rather than singular. Gilligan hears moral voices speaking from the lives of connected, situated selves, not the single truth of disembodied moral principles. She hears these voices because she defines morality and moral knowledge as plural and heterogenous.

The plurality of moral knowledge, as suggested by care ethics, implies that the ways in which we make ethical claims, or knowledge claims more generally, are vulnerable and cannot be taken as unassailable. Rather, there are limits to knowing, and knowledge itself is always situated and thereby insecure. The ethics of care thus encourages an orientation towards vulnerability; the moral self must prioritize the limits of their knowing, the uncertainty of ethical claims, and the reality that 'all moral judgement is unsafe' (Hutchings, 2013, p. 26). This is important for engaging in ethical deliberations across difference because it reminds ethical actors of the critical task of questioning their own assumptions and biases and interrogating how power operates in and through moral judgements and knowledge claims. A disposition towards vulnerability, as espoused by the ethics of care, also inherently involves a radical recognition of alterity: foregrounding our vulnerability which stems from our relational being is an implicit acknowledgement of the limits to knowing across deep differences (which are themselves the product of our relational being).

With this understanding of care ethics in mind, this book argues that the ethics of care provides a useful orientation for building a pluriversal ethics. The ethics of care conceives of agents as relational selves constituted by their unique and particular contexts. As a result, moral agents and moral knowledge are multiple and heterogeneous. At the same time, a relational ontology, of course, prioritizes our interconnections. Thus, morality as such is always situated and connected. This understanding of morality, I suggest, echoes much of the pluriversal project, which seeks to bring to the fore a multiplicity of worlds that are deeply connected, but also differently situated, within relations of power. Further, a care ethics approach is committed to interrogating relations of power which render certain moral voices less legitimate than others and that come to frame ethics more fundamentally. Again, this parallels the pluriversal project of deconstructing the notion of a universal-universality, and the relations of power that uphold the modern world as the 'legitimate' arbitrator of truth and knowledge.

In prioritizing the vulnerability of all moral judgement, the ethics of care requires us to pause and consider how our ethical judgements are always vulnerable; it also requires us to consider how moral dilemmas, and the ways in which moral dilemmas come to be understood across difference, arise from our material vulnerabilities situated in relations of power. An approach to morality built on the ethics of care therefore pays close attention to how our moral judgements themselves (re)produce and are co-constitutive of worlds, and therefore may be culpable in the (re)production of certain harms. Finally, because the ethics of care conceives of morality as practice, the moral task is no longer one of determining abstract rules and principles for governing ethical dilemmas; rather, care ethics orients us to focus instead on the practices which allow moral selves and, by extension, worlds to reproduce and sustain themselves.

In these ways, the ethics of care provides us with a different understanding of morality, and a different orientation to contemplating and addressing ethical dilemmas. Expanding on the ways in which the ethics of care reconceptualizes morality and demonstrating how this different approach to ethics can help us build a pluriversal ethics, and thus the pluriverse itself, is the central task of this book.

Notes on methodology

As discussed in a previous section, Blaser (2009, p. 877) uses the term political ontology to refer also to a research agenda that investigates the conflicts that arise and unfold as different onto-epistemologies or worlds interact. From a pluriversal perspective, researchers do not exist outside of worlds; they enact and are enacted by worlds. By extension, research is implicated in the enactment and disruption of worlds. Research, as a practice and an act (Aradau and Huysmans, 2014), is a part of the enactment of onto-epistemologies. Understanding that research is both performative – in that it enacts certain worlds – and political – in that the ways in which our research enacts these worlds has material and ideological consequences across onto-epistemologies – is central to the pluriversal project.

Accordingly, I see research – and specifically the Global Ethics literature that is interrogated in this book, as well as my own theoretical contributions developed here – as a part of the worlding process, as part of the practices through which worlds are enacted (Blaser, 2009). The literature examined here is not simply a representation of an externally given world; rather, the literature is co-constitutive of the world which it alternatively (re)produces or disrupts. Similarly, I do not conceive of methods as techniques of representation that simply extract information from externally given worlds while leaving the worlds they represent untouched; rather, the device of extraction enacts worlds in the sense that it is an active force that is part of a process of continuous production and reproduction of relations, an endless process of bringing worlds into being. It is with this general disposition that I have undertaken this theoretical study, which develops conceptual and theoretical tools to build a pluriversal ethics. More precisely, as I have developed the argument presented here, I have made every attempt to engage with the relevant literatures critically and reflexively, and in a way that allows me to foreground the productive nature of my argument, that is, the type of world(s) my research enacts. Moreover, this process is an ongoing one and, as I hope the argument in this book makes clear, a task which must become central in the field of Global Ethics more generally.

Language has also proven to be somewhat of a methodological obstacle in developing the argument contained in this book. While I have made every attempt to capture the notion that worlds or onto-epistemologies are performative, enacted, and unfolding, there are some discursive limitations that arise when speaking of worlds, and when attempting to develop broader concepts and theoretical tools to analyse worlds and their unfolding. As Lesley Green (2013a, p. 562) writes, '[f]inding a grammar for emergence, in a language that is attuned to objects or subjects, is indeed challenging'. In grappling with this challenge here, I suspect that at times my language around worlds fluctuates between sometimes treating them as objects and sometimes treating them as subjects, when they are, instead, relational unfoldings. In some ways, I do not think I can overcome this challenge entirely (without getting unproductively bogged down in the process), and so I hope that the reader will bear with me as I attempt to think pluriversally with an imperfect language. To be sure, when I refer to a world or onto-epistemology, I mean neither to personify nor objectify it: a world, in this argument, should be understood as a complex and emerging web of practices and relations.

I would be remiss if I did not also emphasize that I owe a great amount of gratitude to various ethnographic scholarship. As previously mentioned, the pluriversal project is intimately tied to the field of anthropology, and examples of the deep and pervasive differences that characterize the pluriverse are most often seen (that is, made visible) through rich ethnographies that cross worlds. As will become apparent later in the book, I also believe that moral philosophy can only be undertaken in dialogue with contextually specific and detailed analysis of how people live their lives. More simply, I see ethics as 'a continuing negotiation *among* people' (Walker, 2007, p. 67, emphasis in original). Accordingly, moral claims can only be made by looking at how people live their lives, the struggles they face, and the ways in which their lived experiences align or conflict with their needs, desires, and interests (Robinson, 2015). Following from this, my theoretical work here relies heavily upon five ethnographic examples which I think through in different ways throughout this book. I wish to express my sincere thanks to anthropologists Marisol de la Cadena (2015), Mario Blaser (2016; 2018), and Zoe Todd (2014; 2016b; 2018), whose ethnographic work I use here continually to ground my theoretical thinking. My hope is that this argument demonstrates the fruitfulness of thinking about questions of global ethics in a way that does not lose hold of our material reality and the ways in which we *actually do ethics*. For this reason, I extend Ulrich Oslender's (2019, p. 1703) 'impassioned plea for greater consideration and application of ethnographies in decolonial debates', and, I would add, moral philosophy.

I also wish to make clear that, in making my argument, the point of advocating a care ethics approach to moral deliberation across deep and pervasive difference is not to suggest that others must adopt this approach, and particularly not others outside of my world. This argument is not a universal roadmap for a pluriversal ethics, nor is it a thick prescription for ethical deliberation in the pluriverse. I believe that pluriversal ethics must be plural in the fullest sense: there are likely multiple ways to approach, understand, and build ethics in the context of multiple worlds, given the very onto-epistemic multiplicity that comprises the pluriverse. In putting forth my argument, I do not wish to obfuscate this plurality, and I am not attempting to insist that the meta-ethical tools developed here must be the ethical tools used by others in different worlds. Instead, I see this argument as specifically addressing actors in my own world, which I call modernity. I believe that the modern world has been unable to recognize its own vulnerability; instead, modernity is premised on universal truths and one 'right' way of being in the world. This, as I argue in Chapter 2, has resulted in many historic and ongoing harms. Increasingly, albeit in different degrees, we are also hearing a desire from within the modern world (and certainly from those other than us) to address these issues. In order to take responsibility for these harms, I believe the modern world needs to develop new tools and orientations, or new 'forms of moral life' (Walker, 2007, p. 105), from which to engage in and across difference in ways that dismantle hierarchies of power, as opposed to deriving authority from them.

It is, in part, for this reason that I assert a care ethics approach to building a pluriversal ethics: the ethics of care provides a vantage point from which to foreground and flesh out the importance of vulnerable existence – at the onto-epistemological level – in the pluriverse, and particularly for modernity. Vulnerable existence challenges the logic of rationalism which so fundamentally shapes the modern world, and which involves the mastery of mind over body, culture over nature, and certainty over uncertainty. In so doing, I believe that the ethics of care creates an openness to multiple ways of knowing/being (as opposed to asserting a different way of knowing/being meant to replace modern rationalism); this openness can, I believe, help us build a pluriversal ethics without precluding the possibility of a multiplicity of pluriversal ethics.

And finally, I wish to acknowledge that I do not think that caring – thinking with care, practising care, dwelling in the vulnerability of our relational being – will be easy for the modern world. That is, many people in the modern world do not care in the sense that is employed throughout this book. How can modern agents orient themselves towards care and think relationally, particularly when their world, as I argue more fully in Chapter 2, is constituted by various mutually reinforcing binaries that obfuscate relationality? Why should modern subjects acknowledge the vulnerability of their judgement, especially if modernity occupies a hegemonic position in the pluriverse and holds so much power? Why should the modern world care? The literature on the ethics of care has grappled with these questions, and in so doing, has sought to illuminate the political reasons why many modern subjects suppress relationality and vulnerability, and do not act on their caring responsibilities. Joan Tronto (2013), for example, argues that certain people are given a 'pass' from thinking about or thinking with care because of the ways in which patriarchy codes the world and upholds certain masculinist norms and values while devaluing feminine norms and values. For instance, under patriarchy, protection is coded in a way that separates it from care, which is instead understood as the narrower activities of caring for certain peoples, people who are 'needy' and 'dependent'. As a result, this splitting of care and protection, or perhaps more accurately, this obfuscation of the caring dimensions of protective work, 'allows those who are in control of protective work to earn themselves the "protection pass" out of responsibility for other, more feminized forms of care work' (Tronto, 2013, p. 79). Other passes, like the 'productive pass', likewise allow some to shirk their caring responsibilities. These passes give certain people 'privileged irresponsibility', the privilege not to care (Tronto, 1993).

Carol Gilligan and Naomi Snider (2018) provide another explanation for why modern subjects do not think relationally or act with care, although this time from a different vantage point. While Gilligan and Snider (2018, p. 6) note that patriarchy has a strong socio-cultural component, in that it 'exists as a set of rules and values, [or] codes and scripts that specify how men and women should act and be in the world', they also argue that patriarchy 'exists internally'. This internalized and psychological functioning of patriarchy helps to explain why patriarchy persists – and why it is so difficult for subjects to think relationally. Specifically, Gilligan and Snider argue that our relational being renders us vulnerable and opens us up to harm. In order to avoid this harm, we repress our relationality, and sacrifice 'relationship', by which Gilligan and Snider mean an authentic connection to self and other. At the same time, suppressing our relational selves allows us to act and behave such that we can 'have "relationships," meaning a place within the patriarchal order' (Gilligan and Snider, 2018, p. 14). Because patriarchy values independence and codes this as masculine, men are 'rewarded' for repressing their relationality, for achieving what Gilligan and Snider call pseudo-independence (2018, p. 72). Conversely, because patriarchy codes care as feminized, women are 'rewarded' for repressing their relationality (their connection to their self, and their authentic connection with others), and 'caring' for others through inauthentic and anxious attachment, for enacting what Gilligan and Snider (2018, pp. 71–2) call pseudo-relationships. In both cases, the suppression of relationship feels rewarding because it provides a defence against the trauma of a loss of relationship, albeit in different, gendered ways. Yet, in moving away from our relationality, and detaching from ourselves and therefore from meaningful relationship with others, Gilligan and Snider (2018, p. 14) suggest that we also lose our capacity to repair relations, to care. The psychological and socio-cultural aspects of patriarchy play in a feedback loop, suppressing relational thinking, preventing us from acting to repair our relations, and impeding our ability to respond to unjust relationships.

These arguments demonstrate that there are many reasons why people do not care. As a result, it seems likely that at least some modern subjects will resist the meta-ethical orientation I propose here. They may resist relational thinking and acting with care, and they may refuse to acknowledge the vulnerability of their moral judgement. These are difficult issues, and while it is beyond the scope of this investigation to develop fully an argument as to how we can change the ways in which people reject relationality, I wish to point to some reasons as to why modern subjects should care, in the care ethical sense mobilized in this book.

First, as developed more fully in both Chapter 2 and Chapter 4, subjects of the modern world are already implicated in relations of power via the historical unfolding and present-day manifestation of social structures. As Iris Marion Young argues (2006), several social structures – including the systems of power discussed in Chapter 2, like patriarchy, capitalism, colonialism, and racism – are intimately intertwined and structure social relations for the world's population, albeit in particular ways in particular contexts. Given these relational ties, I believe that subjects of the modern world should think relationally and seek to engage with the responsibilities that we owe one another in/through this interconnectedness (especially the responsibilities we owe others, given the privileges that we modern subjects hold, which can be directly linked to the ways in which modernity was historically, and continues to be, enacted). Importantly, thinking relationally here, while crucial, is also insufficient. Focusing on the practices of care and responsibility that we owe others also requires an acknowledgement of the vulnerability of our moral judgement, and an openness to the fact that our way may not be the right way. Thinking relationally, and foregrounding the vulnerability of judgement, I suggest, would allow us 'to focus on what *we* really owe according to *our* values to others who do not live as we live' (Walker, 2007, pp. 244–5, emphasis in original), but who are nonetheless walking and 'speaking alongside us' (Todd, 2016a, p. 19).

Second, given that worlds, as argued throughout this book, are connected through (partial) relations, changes in the relations and practices that form a particular world can also have direct implications for our world. The layers of relations that comprise the pluriverse and tie our worlds together mean that the modern world is necessarily vulnerable because of its relations to other worlds (a point I develop more fully in Chapter 6). Ignoring this fact can only result in a failure to understand and grapple with the consequences of the connections between worlds. We can only, however, grapple with such interconnectedness by thinking carefully about our relationality, and by foregrounding the fact that we are always vulnerable as products of relations. Even if modernity occupies a hegemonic position in the current configuration of the pluriverse, modernity is not invincible; as I argue in Chapter 6, other worlds exert power in the ways in which they exceed the onto-epistemology of modernity, and in ways that can have implications for the modern world. These implications, and the potential 'loss' of aspects of our ways of being in and seeing the world that may result as worlds interact in complex ways, cannot be avoided through a suppression of our relational being.

And lastly, as I argue throughout this book, and as Margaret Urban Walker (2007, p. 261) beautifully shows, 'Morality is truly a collective and collaborative work'. Morality emerges in and through practices and forms of life:

These forms of living acquire their authority (as distinct from, but not opposed to, what other powers hold them in place) by its being and seeming worthwhile to live like that. ... What is in question here are the general contours of a shared life, not anything one person does now, but a set of practices that keep people mutually accountable and important things accounted for. Is it worthwhile to live as we, or as others, do? Is how some of us live 'how to live?' (Walker, 2007, pp. 247–8)

Certainly, pursuing such questions will always be an enormous undertaking, particularly in the pluriverse, constituted by radically different ways of being in and seeing the world. Yet, I contend that this undertaking is nearly impossible if we refuse to think relationally, if we deny the vulnerability of our moral judgement, and if we fail to attend to the ways in which power, politics, and morality are intertwined. The ethics of care, as the arguments made subsequently in this book illustrate, provides an orientation which attunes us to these three things. In so doing, the ethics of care also orients us towards a pluriversal ethics, and positions us to build the pluriverse itself. In demonstrating these points more fully, my hope is that this book thereby also offers a compelling argument for why the modern world should, in fact, care.

Outline of the book

This book proceeds as follows. Chapter 2 continues to lay out the central research problem just described via a discussion of the problem of modernity. More exactly, this argument departs from the premise that the central obstacle to rethinking global ethics in the context of the pluriverse (or to put it differently, the central obstacle which prevents much of the field of Global Ethics from thinking pluriversally) is modernity. The purpose of this chapter is to delineate my understanding of modernity, building particularly upon postcolonial and decolonial schools of thought, and to demonstrate why modernity is an obstacle to building a pluriversal ethics.

In short, this book argues that modernity is a world, a collective thinking/being/doing, an onto-epistemology; it is an ideology and political philosophy, an understanding of subjectivity and the world, and then a normative commitment to ordering the world according to these premises. Modernity is therefore also a set of practices and social relations; it is a continual enactment and reproduction of a particular order. Importantly, this enactment and reproduction does not occur within a vacuum. As such, modernity, as a world, is also always implicated with and in other worlds. It is demarcated by other worlds, and it interacts with other worlds in various material and symbolic ways. Understanding modernity as connected to other worlds foreshadows why this particular definition of modernity is useful in the context of the pluriverse, that is, a matrix of worlds connected through/by relations of power.

This chapter also defines power and politics in the context of modernity. Specifically, this chapter argues that power here can be understood as the ability to claim itself as the universal world (that is, the only world), and politics is the technical and calculated task of ordering global social relations in the image of that world. More concretely, I argue that the historical unfolding of modernity was such that modernity was/is able to (re)make social relations in its image through both material and symbolic means. At the same time, however, the modern world fails to see how this (re)making of social relations is very much the product of political processes and relationships of power. Instead, the modern world mistakes its hegemonic position in the global order for abstract and universal rightness. This chapter concludes with a brief overview of the ways in which postcolonial scholarship, critical theories from within Europe, and decolonial literature have sought to illuminate and decentre modernity's assertion of itself as the whole of the real.

Chapter 3 continues the broader discussion about modernity by linking the Global Ethics literature to the modern world. This chapter argues that this literature has been complicit in reproducing the binaries and hierarchies that underpin modernity – modernity and the Global Ethics literature are co-constitutive. As a result, this chapter contends that much of the Global Ethics literature is premised on the same assumptions and binaries as modernity. Because of these theoretical underpinnings, much of this literature is not equipped to contemplate ethical horizons in the pluriverse.

To make this argument, Chapter 3 draws again upon Hutchings's (2010) rationalist/alternative framework, with a particular focus on moral cosmopolitanism, discourse ethics (both rationalist approaches to global ethics), and variants of postmodernist ethics (one of the alternative approaches). I also review the decolonial praxis of Silvia Rivera Cusicanqui (2012; 2015; 2018), particularly as it has been presented by Marcos Scauso (2021). In this discussion, I return to two of the case studies introduced in this chapter (the ongoing dialogue between de la Cadena and Nazario, and the Whanganui Iwi's struggle to protect the Whanganui River) and use these empirical examples to develop and justify my conclusion that, ultimately, all of these approaches are unable to offer a useful vantage point from which to contemplate ethics in/for the pluriverse (particularly an ethics for the pluriverse from the perspective of the modern world). In demonstrating why these approaches fail to offer us tools for a pluriversal ethics, however, this chapter is able to highlight further the normative challenge of the pluriverse. Ultimately, I contend that the challenge for building an ethics for the pluriverse is characterized by a distinct combination of (1) the need to attend to our shared material existence while simultaneously (2) foregrounding the multiple and actually existing 'universals' or onto-epistemologies which comprise the pluriverse. Furthermore, pluriversal ethics must also be able to navigate (3) the problem of incommensurability across difference, and the limits of knowing when differences are at their deepest and most pervasive, or onto-epistemic. It must also, I believe, deal with this problem of incommensurability in a way that is attuned to the potential harms of appropriating other ways of knowing/being that are not our own. To attend to the unique challenges posed by these three attributes, this chapter concludes, requires a different orientation to ethics, a different understanding of morality, and a different set of tools than those offered us by moral cosmopolitanism, discourse ethics, and postmodernist ethics.

Chapter 4 begins theorizing such an orientation and toolkit, drawing upon feminist ethics and particularly the ethics of care. More specifically, this chapter reviews the literature on the ethics of care (see, for example, Gilligan, 1993; Hekman, 1995; Robinson, 1999), with a particular emphasis on its feminist relational ontology, situated epistemology, the ways in which this ontology and epistemology foreground vulnerability, and the broader ways in which the ethics of care reconceptualizes ethics and morality. This chapter also responds to three charges often raised against the ethics of care: (1) that the ethics of care essentializes women and cannot attend to difference; (2) that the ethics of care is only useful for particularistic and close relations, and therefore offers little value for navigating global ethical issues; and (3) that the ethics of care is not a political ethic. In so doing, Chapter 4 develops my understanding of the ethics of care as a critical and political theory that is attuned to differences all the way down. It is also because of this formulation of the ethics of care that I assert that care ethics must engage with the pluriverse. As a political-ethical framework deeply concerned with difference, scholarship on the ethics of care, I propose, must begin to contemplate seriously the conceptual and practical implications of the pluriverse, a landscape where differences are their most deep and pervasive and which, as I have argued in this chapter, operates at the level of the political.

Chapter 5 builds on the theoretical groundwork laid in the preceding discussion and begins to draw out partial connections between the pluriverse, care, and ethics more generally. I argue that when morality is understood in a care ethical sense, the pluriverse can be fruitfully conceived of as a meta-world defined by a co-constitutive relational ontology, situated epistemology, and axiology of partial connections. Further, from this definition, the pluriversal project must then also be fundamentally acknowledged as a normative project, and the moral and ethical dimensions of the pluriverse must be made explicit in thinking about and enacting the pluriverse. In this way, I argue that while the Global Ethics literature needs to contend with the pluriversal challenge, the literature on the pluriverse would likewise benefit from a sustained engagement with moral philosophy, like the ethics of care.

This chapter demonstrates further the generative potential of such an engagement by explicating how the ethics of care additionally aligns with, and usefully expands, thinking about the pluriverse as a meta-world defined by a co-constitutive relational ontology, situated epistemology, and axiology of partial connections. The ethics of care, itself defined by a relational ontology and situated epistemology, is well positioned to serve as a lens for understanding the pluriverse, which, I argue, shares these same ontological and epistemological premises. Moreover, the ethics of care normatively values repairing and maintaining our relations of care that allow us to (re)produce ourselves and our worlds as well as is reasonably possible. This normative vantage point amends the pluriversal axiology of valuing partial connections by encouraging us to consider critically which connections are worth maintaining and extending, and which ones are not. In other words, I suggest that thinking about the pluriverse as a meta-world, from an ethics of care perspective, involves rethinking the normative commitment implicit in the pluriversal project so that it is focused on valuing *partial relations of care*, where care in the most general sense is that which contributes to a world's ability to flourish as a world. This rethinking also illustrates how the pluriversal project, care, and ethics are deeply and inescapably intertwined.

Having demonstrated that the pluriversal project demands contending explicitly with questions of normativity and care, and having argued that Global Ethics and specifically the ethics of care must likewise contend with the pluriverse, Chapter 6 presents a care ethical meta-theoretical framework for contemplating ethical horizons in the pluriverse. Using the ethics of care, I make a distinction between vulnerability, understood as an inherent ontological condition of subjects who are embedded in relations of dependency, and precarity, which I argue is *intensified* vulnerability resulting from unequal distributions of power that render certain subjects more or less vulnerable than others. This chapter then develops and mobilizes this understanding of vulnerability and precarity so as to demonstrate how this lens allows us to consider the explicit effects of global material and ideational hierarchies of power – including capitalism, racism, patriarchy, and colonialism – on particular worlds, and the configuration of the pluriverse more generally. This framing, I suggest, redefines ethics in the image of the pluriverse, and foregrounds the ways in which particular ethical dilemmas in the pluriverse always take place within a broader horizon of precarity, whereby certain worlds are rendered 'more' or 'less' vulnerable than others in and through the processes of ethical deliberation that cross worlds.

This meta-orientation, I propose, allows us to attend to two ongoing pressing ethical concerns in the pluriverse. First, it provides a lens to analyse why some worlds are marginalized and made precarious in the pluriverse while others appear more stable or are more easily reproduced. Second, because the configuration of the pluriverse, and the relations of power which shape the relations between worlds, comprises the backdrop against which ethical dilemmas and conflicts between worlds always unfold, this lens also allows us to understand this background, and thereby better understand ethical dilemmas across worlds. Notably, I again return to the case of the Whanganui River to illustrate the ways in which this framing provides a useful meta-theoretical orientation for a pluriversal ethics.

I next attend to the pluriverse as political in Chapter 7. I argue that thinking about the political relationally (as the ethics of care implores us to do) reveals that the political in the context of the pluriverse involves complex layers of socio-symbolic orders (worlds, onto-epistemologies). As such, the political moment may not occur equally for all worlds involved in a conflict between/across worlds. Because of this layered 'politicality', I suggest that thinking about the political in the pluriverse requires foregrounding equally the political as associative (a collective coming together) and as dissociative (agonistic and ruptural) (cf. Marchart, 2007). The ethics of care, as both a critical and productive ethic, is able to hold these two traits of the political at the fore. I ultimately argue that care ethics provides us with tools to contemplate the political (rethought in the context of multiple partially connected vulnerable worlds) as (dis)associative, involving relational layers of onto-epistemic rupture and conflict, on the one hand, *and* onto-epistemic continuity and cooperation, on the other. It is in this chapter that I also introduce two more case studies, which focus on the political assertions of the Yshiro people as they strive to live well with/in *yrmo* (Blaser, 2019) and the creative ways in which Paulatuuqmiut develop solutions to fulfil their obligations to fish while challenging colonial logics (Todd, 2014; 2016b; 2018). Working through these case studies, and walking with these interlocutors, allows me to draw out the implications of the ways in which I define and understand the political as (dis)associative for worlds as well as worlding processes.

Chapter 8 moves from the preceding meta-ethical discussion to a final pluriversal ethical dilemma so as to outline other ways in which the ethics of care can help us deliberate and navigate specific ethical conflicts between worlds. Drawing particularly upon an ethnography regarding a conflict over caring for what the modern world calls caribou and the Innu Nation calls *atîku* (Blaser, 2016; 2018), this chapter first exemplifies how the meta-orientation developed in the previous chapters orients us to contemplate this ethical conflict. Second, and by extension, this chapter also draws out other ways in which the ethics of care can help build a pluriversal ethics. Through this example, Chapter 8 brings this argument full circle: by starting with the ethics of care, it becomes clear that the pluriverse is *constituted* by morality. Because of this, a pluriversal ethics does not simply refer to the application of ethics to a new global context; instead, building a pluriversal ethics, and particularly building one using the ethics of care, is the very means by which the pluriverse may flourish.

Finally, in Chapter 9 I return to the field of Global Ethics, and I offer some concluding thoughts on what the preceding discussion means for researching and doing global ethics in and for the pluriverse. I reiterate that binary thinking – which, as the next chapter illustrates, is key to the modern onto-epistemology – is an insufficient theoretical space from which to contemplate and build pluriversal ethics. Instead, the pluriverse pulls us into an alternative conceptual space, a space of complex relations upon relations, which enact (sometimes radically) different knowings/beings while paradoxically tying them together. And, just as the double life of the corroboree frog/Gyack is brought into being through divergent relational practices, various theories and practices will produce and sustain unique relations and distinct forms of moral life. Scholars and practitioners in the field of Global Ethics must therefore take responsibility for that which our theorizing alternatively (re)produces and disrupts. More simply, we must care about the consequences, the worlding effects, of the ways in which we think and do global ethics.

2

The Problem of Modernity and the Decolonial Project

This book departs from the premise that the central obstacle to rethinking global ethics in the context of the pluriverse is modernity. While it is notable that critiques of modernity are plentiful, it is not always clear what, exactly, is meant by 'modernity'. The purpose of this chapter is to present my particular understanding of modernity, which builds upon postcolonial and decolonial schools of thought. Importantly, this definition of modernity should not be thought of as universal or definitive. Instead, the definition of modernity developed here is a working definition that highlights, as will become evident, the particular aspects of modernity that make it such a formidable foe for pluriversal ethics.

In short, this chapter asserts that modernity is a 'world', a collective thinking/being/doing; it is an ideology and political philosophy, an understanding of subjectivity and the conditions of being, and then a normative commitment to ordering social relations according to these premises. Modernity is therefore also a set of practices and social relations; it is a continual enactment and reproduction of a co-constitutive onto-epistemology. Importantly, this enactment and reproduction does not occur within a vacuum: modernity, as a world, is also inescapably implicated with and in other worlds. Modernity delineates itself in relation to other worlds, while also being shaped by (and shaping) other worlds. This, as may be obvious, foreshadows why this particular definition of modernity is useful in the context of the pluriverse, that is, a matrix of worlds connected through/by relations of power.

To explicate this definition of modernity more fully, this chapter employs a conceptual distinction between 'modernity as thinking' and 'modernity as doing' – although as will become apparent, this thinking and doing are intimately intertwined, and thus constitutive of a world. Distinguishing between the thinking and doing of modernity is therefore simply a heuristic device to help think through the facets of the world called modernity. Using this device, this chapter proceeds as follows. First, modernity 'as thinking' is discussed. This, I suggest, is the way in which modernity sees itself; it is an attempt to describe modernity on its own terms. This narrative has been called 'Intra-European Modernity' by scholars like Arturo Escobar (2008, p. 165) so as to foreground the ways in which this narrative is premised upon a 'view of modernity as essentially an European phenomenon ... [that] can be fully explained by reference to factors internal to Europe'. In this self-narrative, this chapter asserts that modernity can be understood as a particular axiological break from the Ancients in the Western philosophical tradition, and thus as a particular type of thinking and orientation to philosophy. This orientation is best captured by the idea that Man is the orderer of all around him: Man is able to master Nature and order the world according to his needs and desires, or sense of moral rightness.

After reviewing 'modernity as thinking', this chapter next turns to a discussion of modernity 'as doing'. Drawing upon postcolonial, decolonial, Marxist, and feminist scholarship, the historical enactment of the principles derived from modernity 'as thinking' is described so as to demonstrate the relationship between modernity, on the one hand, and colonialism, racism, patriarchy, and capitalism, on the other. This conceptual device of 'modernity as doing' thereby serves to fracture the mirror in which modernity admires itself in, revealing the ways in which the seemingly progressive, rational, and ordered vision supplied by 'modernity as thinking' resulted in and from a 'modernity as doing' comprised of violence, domination, and exploitation.

In the third section, this chapter demonstrates more directly the ways in which 'modernity as thinking' and 'modernity as doing' map on to one another in order to put forth the conclusion that modernity is a world. That is, by demonstrating the ways in which the thinking and doing of modernity are intimately intertwined and co-constitutive (that is, an onto-epistemology), I assert that modernity is more than a paradigm, or philosophical orientation, or moral system, or political arrangement; rather, modernity, as a whole, is a way of thinking/being/doing that, while fluid and changing, is characterized by an ontological distinction between Man and Nature, a rationalist epistemology, and an axiological bent towards 'rationally' ordering the world to meet Man's needs and desires.

In the final section of this chapter, the meaning of 'power' and 'politics' in the context of modernity is discussed. Specifically, it is suggested that power here can be understood as the ability to claim itself as the universal world (more precisely, the only world), and politics is the technical and calculated task of ordering global social relations in the image of that world. More concretely, it is argued that the ontological distinction between Man/Nature, the rationalist epistemology, and the particular axiology of order underpinning modernity resulted in a specific historical situation in which modernity now holds the power to (re)make social relations in its image.

Further, because of modernity's self-narrative ('modernity as thinking'), the modern world fails to see how this (re)making of social relations is very much the product of political processes and relationships of power (that is, 'modernity as doing'); instead, the modern epistemology mistakes modernity's hegemonic position in the global order for abstract and universal rightness. This limited perspective, as decolonial scholars have noted, is Eurocentrism (Dussel, 2000; 2009). This section thus also includes a brief overview of the ways in which postcolonial scholarship, critical theories from within Europe, and decolonial literature have sought to illuminate this Eurocentrism, and decentre modernity's assertion of its reality as the whole of the real. Lastly, this chapter concludes by briefly returning to the pluriverse to decentre modernity further. The pluriversal literature and the 'ontological turn' pose an even greater challenge to modernity, and its view of itself as *the* world; as I ultimately argue, this challenge is so robust that it necessitates a rethinking of dominant approaches to global ethics.

As a final note before proceeding, I wish to reiterate that in building the argument that modernity is a world, I necessarily present an incomplete argument. To recount the entirety of the unfolding of the modern world, and to analyse the various thinkers, texts, and encounters within and of that world, is impossible. The argument put forth here is in no way meant to be totalizing or complete. Rather, in selecting key concepts and counter-concepts, literatures and counter-literatures, and historical moments and counter-moments, my goal is simply to convince the reader that thinking of modernity as either a type of political philosophy, a historical moment, a set of norms, an epistemological orientation, or a political project is insufficient. Instead, it is all of these at once, and more.

Modernity as thinking

Axiology, coming from Greek ἀξία, axia, meaning 'value' or 'worth', refers broadly to the philosophical study of value and goodness of all varieties (Schroeder, 2016).[1] It thus encompasses both ethics and aesthetics, or the philosophical contemplation of both the right and the beautiful, respectively. Axiological questions, at their core, encourage us to contemplate the nature of value. What do we value? Why is it of value? What is the good? What is right? What is just? The answers to these questions are not simply of

---

[1] The term 'axiology' is used in the broadest sense in this book. There are specific philosophical schools that are often referred to as axiological schools: for instance, 'value theory', tied to consequentialism, is often denoted as an axiological school. This argument is not concerned with these particular branches of philosophy. Instead, this argument mobilizes axiology as a fundamental category of contemplation, akin to epistemology and ontology, that normatively orients our thinking/being/doing.

philosophical import; rather, they colour fundamentally how we think of, and act in, the world.

The Western philosophical tradition, this chapter posits, is underpinned by an axiological assumption that 'order' is the right, good, and beautiful. This, of course, is a sweeping claim, one which cannot be defended fully here. At the same time, the claim is thin: what is meant by 'order', what exactly is the source of 'order', and how to achieve this 'order' are questions left open for debate. Nonetheless, thinking of 'order' as a founding axiological assumption of the Western philosophical tradition is useful for theorizing the particular change in philosophical orientation that characterizes modernity. To demonstrate, consider Jane Bennett's (2009, pp. 127–8) summary narrative of the break between the 'pre-moderns' and 'moderns' of Western philosophy:

> Once upon a time there was a (medieval Christian) world where nature was purposive, God was active in the details of human affairs, all things had a place in the order of things, social life was characterized by face-to-face relations, and political order took the form of an organic community experienced as the 'prose of the world' (Foucault, 1970). But this premodern cosmos gave way to forces of scientific and instrumental rationality, secularism, individualism, and the bureaucratic nation state.

Bennett identifies here a fundamental shift that can be thought of as a reorientation towards a *human-centred* order. Premodern Western philosophy, while already oriented towards order, located order outside of – although not apart from – humans. Order, in this view, was a whole, or totality; people were part of this, but not above it, and more importantly, not the creators of it. Order instead existed and was derived from something outside humans; the best people could do was contemplate this order and attempt (always only partially) to find their place in it. As Charles Taylor (1991, p. 3) summarizes: 'People used to see themselves as part of a larger order; ... a cosmic order, a "great chain of Being," in which humans figured in their proper place along with angels, heavenly bodies, and[/or] our fellow earthly creatures.'

The moderns drastically shifted in terms of their conceptualization of order, and more specifically, in terms of their role within this order. Modern political philosophy eschewed the possibility of a source of order 'out there'. Max Weber (1981) famously referred to this as the 'disenchantment of the world', that is, 'the secularization of a traditional order that had been imbued with divine or natural purpose' (Bennett, 2009, p. 128). With this 'disenchantment', humans became the 'orderers'. As Escobar writes, 'Philosophically, one may see modernity ... in terms of the emergence of *the notion of Man as the foundation of all knowledge and order of the world, separate from the natural and the divine*' (2008, p. 166, emphasis added).

This understanding of Man[2] as the source and agent of order can be evidenced in the works of several key political thinkers and is co-constitutive of several ontological and epistemology binaries that are foundational to the modern imaginary. For instance, Niccolò Machiavelli (1998) locates man as the source of morality and thereby simultaneously introduces the concept of will, which man can use to control or tame chance and nature. While Machiavelli certainly does not present a coherent ontology – that is, a cohesive set of claims about what exists in the world – there is an ontological distinction that emerges from his political science. Now that Man is the orderer, Nature (for instance, change, fortune, and the natural world) is that which is to be ordered. Human and Nature thereby come to exist as distinct entities, in opposition to each other. Machiavelli, in other words, exemplifies the philosophical foundations for one of the first fundamental ontological binaries of modernity: Humans/Nature. Moreover, not only is Man distinct and separate from Nature, but human will means that Man can also *act upon* Nature. This gives us the second, but intimately related, ontological binary that is foundational for modernity: Subject/Object. Humans contain the capacity to will, to act upon Nature, which is now to be mastered. The Subject/Object distinction is mapped onto, and co-constitutive of, the Human/Nature binary: Humans are Subjects, while Nature is the Object. Indeed, from these ontological premises, acting upon Nature, as part of ordering, becomes normative in character, as the ability of one's will to master is, for Machiavelli, virtue (*virtù*) (1998, p. 101). Exercising this virtue leads to glory, earned via one's ability to will, that is, to create and maintain order over all around you.

Thomas Hobbes (1985), another central figure in the modern imaginary, similarly mobilizes an ontological distinction between Humans and Nature (Rojas, 2016). Hobbes develops a 'system of politics as a science' (Macpherson, 1985, p. 10), starting from the Galilean assumption that 'everything, including human sensation, is caused by motion, or more accurately by differences of motion' (Macpherson, 1985, p. 18). His scientific method reduces everything to matter in motion. In casting everything, human and non-human nature alike, as matter in motion, Hobbes also implicitly asserts a conquering of nature by reason. In Hobbes's theory, there arises a point where the realities of life in the state of nature lead man to consent to the creation of a sovereign. This sovereign, and the consent which invokes Him, establishes order and frees man from a constant fear of death

---

[2] Man is here used purposively, to emphasize the masculine bias underpinning this type of thought, as is evident in much of the texts most commonly referred to as exemplary of the Western political philosophical tradition. The linkages between patriarchy and modernity are drawn out more fully in subsequent sections.

by creating a more general situation of peace. In this consenting, matter in motion is given (a human) order: Man uses his reason to create a collective that allows him to escape the disorder (danger, chaos, unpredictability) of Nature. In this way, in Hobbesian scientific method and reasoning, Nature, as matter in motion, is mastered; Human becomes ontologically distinct from Nature in Man's capacity to reason and consent to the rule of Leviathan.

The separation of Human/Nature, as an ontological move, comes with and from a corresponding epistemological shift, rooted in empiricism and science (which, as discussed later, eventually culminates as rationalism). Empiricism is an epistemology that asserts that knowledge is gained through sensory perception (Locke, 2009). With the separation of Human/Nature, Nature is completely outside of Man; Man perceives, and comes to know Nature, through the senses. This epistemology, when understood within the axiological context that order is of value and that man is the source of order, suggests science – that is, the systematic study of the structure and behaviour of the physical and natural world through observation and controlled experiment – and the scientific method.

Francis Bacon is often acknowledged as the forefather of science in this tradition. His philosophy of science is premised on induction, which involves the twofold notion that we can determine general laws from particular observations, and that the same causes will have the same effects time and time again. Science further involves an axiological bent towards order, in that establishing order, and particularly an order to benefit humans, intimately shapes the science project for Bacon. Discovering truth and accumulating knowledge through the scientific method is not a neutral activity. Rather, 'one can, in principle, master all things by calculation' (Weber, 1981, p. 139), and 'knowledge itself is power' (coined by Bacon in 1597; quoted in Rodríguez-García, 2001, p. 110), a power exemplified in the mastery of Nature by Man. More simply, science becomes a normative task to improve human ends (Taylor, 1991, p. 104).

The relationship between Man and Nature, and the notion of science and reason, is a pervasive theme in the body of work that constitutes modern political and moral philosophy more generally. John Locke (1980; 2009), for instance, posits that the world has been given to man, who can exercise his scientific and empiricist reason to make use of the world to fulfil his interests and desires; Man thus stands outside of Nature, and further, above it. The natural world is objectified for the comfort of man, most fundamentally in the form of property (Locke, 1980, p. 19). Implicitly, the ontological split between Human/Nature, and the epistemic-normative project of acting upon Nature for the betterment of Man, is again evident here. Immanuel Kant's (2005) aim to affirm human freedom and autonomy in the face of the deterministic natural world likewise assumes that Humans can be above/apart from (that is, free from the determinism found in) Nature. The role of reason, for Kant, is to order sensory perception: epistemological processes do not unfold as sensory experiences which provide man with the raw data that can then be used to inform how he will literally order the world around him. Instead, for Kant, there is an ordering of sense experience itself that occurs with man's engagement with the world. Therefore, while science suggests that Nature is simply mechanistic, and can be known, measured, and ordered by Man, Kant's critical philosophy says that even mechanistic order is, in a sense, a product of our minds.

Importantly, this theoretical move doubles down on the idea of man as separate from/over and above the natural world. Order, in this theory, is not a literal mechanistic ordering produced by man's labour (à la Locke); rather, order is derived wholly from reason located in man's mind which categorizes sensory experience, and thus all of man's encounters with the material world (Kant, 1998, p. 110; see also Sandel, 1998, p. 8). For Kant, 'the onus of epistemological discovery [is therefore located] within the cognitive abilities of the individual' (Beattie, 2013, p. 62). From this epistemological grounding, the world in its entirety is objectified by reasoning man. Reason, for Kant, is universally 'the precondition for humans having any sort of experience, morality, or conception of beauty' (Seth, 2013, p. 140).

With reason as the centre of knowledge/knowledge creation, Kant moves us from an empiricist epistemology to a rationalist epistemology, and employs this rationalism to formulate his moral philosophy, best outlined in *Groundwork to the Metaphysics of Morals* (2005). Here, Kant argues that the moral law is an imperative of reason, and all human action must adhere to the moral law. The moral law, in other words, transcends particular and contextual concerns and interests. Instead, moral actions must eschew context, embodiment, experience, and emotion (Kant, 2005, p. 72; Hutchings, 2013, p. 27), and depart from a commitment to the moral law; this commitment, in essence, provides the action with its moral worth. This commitment to the moral law also ensures that Man is not determined by his Nature; he is not ruled or determined solely by his base interests, desires, and needs. Again, the separation of Human/Nature is normatively significant here. For Kant, the fact that man is able to reason and act morally (that is, in accordance with the moral law) defines his humanity as such. Further, acting in accordance with the moral law is underpinned by the axiological assumption of the value of order: rationalism 'can help to create a world marked by predictability, order and stability' (Beattie and Schick, 2013, p. 1). Kant (2005, p. 92) ultimately asserts that his moral law, derived from a rationalist moral epistemology, results in 'a systematic union of rational beings through common objective laws'.

Lastly, the idea of linear time and the Hegelian idea of history as a progressive unfolding again exemplifies this self-narrative, or 'modernity as thinking'. As Sanjay Seth (2013, p. 141) notes, G.W.F. Hegel (1977;

1991) departs from Kant in that he contends that 'there are no knockdown transcendental argument that will establish the truth of certain categories once and for all, only categories through which historical communities know their world and organize their place in it'. This historicist lens implies that the ontological and epistemological approaches, concepts, themes, values, and morals of modernity are specific to modernity (Hegel, 1991, pp. 21–2). This is a significant step in terms of demonstrating the historical situatedness, as opposed to transcendentality, of all thought. At the same time, however, the significance of context does not lead Hegel to relativism. Instead, Hegel sees context as meaningful within a broader normative understanding of the development of rationality. Thus, while all thought is a product of its context, these contexts, for Hegel, are already normatively situated along a progressive timeline and can therefore be normatively judged against one another. In other words, the reason that Hegel avoids relativism is that situatedness for Hegel is vertical, where some systems of knowledge/ways of being are located beneath others in the ladder of history. This, it is important to emphasize, is a very different orientation to the significance of context than in the case where situatedness is conceptualized horizontally, such that all contexts are seen as creating their own systems of meaning-making, with no prior judgements upon the validity or value of these different systems of meaning-making in relation to one another.

Hegel describes this ladder of history in detail, positing the top of the ladder – constituted as the end goal that all of history is working towards – as absolute knowing or full self-consciousness (Hegel, 1977), that is, consciousness that is in and for itself, or 'Thought, quite freely determining itself' (Hegel, 1988, p. 16). Importantly, however, part of full self-consciousness *being in and for itself* is that this consciousness must not reside solely in the mind; rather, it must be enacted in the world. Thought cannot remain merely abstract; it must become concrete in the world. For Hegel, this concreteness is most fully manifested in the State: 'the State is the realization of freedom, i.e., of the absolute end-goal, and that it exists for its own sake' (Hegel, 1988, p. 41).

To summarize, modernity's self-narrative – constituted by an ontological distinction between Man/Nature, a scientific, rationalist epistemology, and an axiological bent towards man-made order – leads to a conceptualization of 'modernity as a privileged historical moment and a privileged site, one where the facts and processes that have always governed human history finally become discernable, revealing what has always been true but could not be fully grasped until now' (Seth, 2013, p. 142). With this full 'grasping' of consciousness, man is cemented in his position as orderer, and order can be obtained. Man can reflect critically upon the world and his role in it, and via the establishment of institutions (particularly the state) enact order that maximizes human freedom. 'In the State ... freedom attains its objectivity, and lives in enjoyment of this objectivity' (Hegel, 1988, p. 42), and in this world 'human beings, individually and collectively, can and must make their own history' (Amin, 2009, p. 13). As Seth (2013, p. 142) astutely points out, 'modernity's self-understanding is the self-consciousness of this fact [or narrative, as it is called here]'. Hegel's observation that philosophy is its own time epitomised in thought applies equally to his own work; as outlined briefly here, his philosophy can be understood as modernity's progressivist narrative incapsulated in thought.

Modernity as doing

In conceiving of modernity as premised upon an ontological distinction between Man and Nature, a scientific and rationalist epistemology, and a very specific axiological commitment to order, in which Man is the orderer of Nature, modernity also involves a strong normative orientation to 'doing' and enactment. Man as orderer must not simply think and contemplate order; man must call it into being. To explicate this component of modernity – 'modernity as doing' – this section moves away from modernity's 'self-narrative' and towards an exploration of modernity 'from elsewhere'. That is, the self-narrative described in the previous section, as noted by Escobar (2008), is Eurocentric; the thinkers discussed were all European, and were writing *in and of* Europe. In shifting from Europe to a more global perspective, a different narrative (or, more accurately, multiple narratives) of modernity emerge; these narratives complicate the Intra-European narrative of progress as located solely in the development of Western-European self-consciousness, reason, and the state. Instead, these perspectives reveal that which is *hidden* by modernity's self-narrative: the modern colonial world system, 'the ensemble of processes and social formations that encompass modern colonialism and colonial modernities' (Escobar, 2010, p. 39). More simply, it turns out that 'modernity as thinking' is a European narrative that hides its darker side, 'coloniality' (Mignolo, 2011, p. 3). Engagement with histories and theories of colonialism, as well as with critical postmodern theories like Marxism and feminism which further emphasize the ways in which colonialism is co-constitutive of other systems of power (specifically racism, capitalism, and patriarchy), reveals this 'darker' side, and illuminates how modernity is not only a thinking; modernity is also fundamentally characterized by doing, by the (re)arrangement and (re)creation of a variety of social relations, which, while complex and intertwined, may be analytically sorted into four systems of power: colonialism, racism, capitalism, and patriarchy.

To illuminate this 'darker' side – and in contradistinction to European historians and philosophers who have located modernity as arising in seventeenth-century northern Europe (especially France, Germany, and England) around the processes of the Reformation, the Enlightenment, and the French Revolution (Escobar, 2010, p. 35) – Enrique Dussel (1993), along with other decolonial theorists (see, for example, Escobar, 2007), locates the 'birth' of modernity much earlier, in 1492, with the first colonial encounter between Spain and the Americas. This historical moment, when analysed from a world perspective, is significant for Dussel and other decolonial scholars because it marks the first time in history when 'the whole planet became the space of one world history' (Dussel, 2000, p. 470). The conquering of the Atlantic and the emergence of Spain as the first 'modern' nation – characterized by a cohesive and unified peninsula (resulting from the national consensus created by the Inquisition), a national military power, and the subordination of the church to the state – 'allowed Spain to begin the first stage of modernity: world mercantilism' (Dussel, 2000, p. 470). Within this world history, Europe (first Spain and Portugal, later Holland, France, and England) become the centre, and the rest of world, starting with Latin America, became the periphery. The idea of world history, and, more fundamentally, of an interconnected globe, could thus be conceived for the first time with the advent of colonialism (Quijano, 2000).

These new global relations of power allowed the centre to accumulate wealth through its expansion projects and conquests; this accumulation of wealth, and world mercantilism, in part provided the early seeds for the eventual development of capitalism, another system of power which fundamentally restructured social and material life around the globe (Arrighi, 2010, pp. 86–129). In other words, this colonial encounter, and the subsequent ongoing colonialism, fundamentally reshaped social relations between societies across the globe, with some societies positioned as superior (the core, the powerful, the conquerors) and others positioned as inferior (the periphery, the less powerful, those to be conquered). It is noteworthy that this hierarchy also maps on to a Subject/Object distinction, whereby the colonizers were seen as subjects (agents, autonomous, independent) and the colonized were objectified as non-persons or non-agents.

Of course, as many scholars have demonstrated from a variety of vantage points, colonialism, and the consequences of this reordering of the global hierarchy, remain today, although its particular manifestations may have changed. For instance, Glen Coulthard (2014, p. 25, emphasis in original) demonstrates that while colonial rule no longer depends solely on the exercise of state violence in recent times, colonialism is still reproduced in the enticement of 'Indigenous peoples to *identify*, either implicitly or explicitly, with the profoundly *asymmetrical* and *nonreciprocal* forms of recognition either imposed on or granted to them by the settler state and society'. In these cases, Indigenous peoples must internalize colonial logic, and must adopt the colonizer's form of recognition, reproducing the colonial relation. Duane Champagne (2005, p. 5) further illuminates the modern nation-state's commitment to colonialism by pointing out how liberal nation-states fail to 'extend their definitions of inclusion to bring in native communities in a voluntary [and meaningful] manner, ... [and in so doing, therefore actually come to] deny the foundation of consensual inclusion critical to the definition of a democratic state'. In other words, the 'democratic' nation-states' commitment to colonial relations is so pervasive that its failure to address and amend them ends up undermining its very self-understanding as a democratic entity. Humanitarian aid is similarly shaped by colonialism and serves to reproduce colonialism. David Rieff (2002) and Neta Crawford (2002) both illustrate the ways in which the moral and ideological foundations of colonialism underpin humanitarianism, which functions based upon a binary distinction between those who provide aid (generally white wealthy Westerners) and those who receive aid (largely people of colour from the Global South). This 'us' versus 'them' binary (Edkins, 2003, p. 255) mirrors the Subject/Object distinction described previously; those who receive aid 'are treated as lives to be saved, lives with no political voice' (Edkins, 2003, p. 256). Hayden King (2017, np) shows that the dominant understanding of the international relations system as constituted by atomistic nations in a state of anarchy (a view with deep roots in the Hobbesian state of nature) likewise perpetuates colonial relations:

> By continuing to enforce the view of humanity as a set of political states, with Europe at the centre of the planet – as Chickasaw lawyer James Youngblood Henderson once pointed out in his deconstruction of the familiar Mercator world map – foreign policy actively contributes to the erasure of Indigenous political difference conceptually as well as Indigenous bodies physically. ... [This] is a foreign policy that normalizes and affirms settler colonialism.

And, as Linda Tuhiwai Smith (2012, pp. 52–5) illustrates, even things that appear mundane – such as the ways in which modern maps are drawn, and the importance of boundaries to the nation-state – are, in addition to having been among its key 'technologies', remnants of the colonial encounter, in which new lands were 'discovered', renamed, redrawn, and claimed by the colonizers. The hierarchy between colonizer and colonized, and the global ordering that arose from and mirrors this hierarchy, continues to serve as a key axis around which our global social relations function.

With this global hierarchy of core-periphery/conqueror-conquered/colonizer-colonized also emerged racism, a system of categorization which constructs racial difference and then hierarchizes people based on categories of race. More specifically, as Aníbal Quijano (2000, p. 216) argues, categories were needed to codify the relations between conquering and conquered populations, and new social identities, anchored in claims of biology, were formed. The creation of these social identities, and the ordering of these peoples into hierarchy based on these social identities, became possible in the context of colonialism, as racism served to justify the colonial project, and the conquering of some peoples by others.

In addition to justifying the colonial project, however, racism also led to particular manifestations of the conquering of peoples: for instance, the transatlantic slave trade, whereby black Africans were completely dehumanized, violently displaced and taken to the Americas to perform labour under the most brutal conditions, is intimately premised upon and tied to racism. Racism thereby also came to inform relations of production (Rawley, 2005): the transatlantic slave trade involved a division of labour based upon race whereby people of colour were reduced to commodities and white people were the owners of the means of production, including labour and labourers. Racism also became further entrenched through scientific racism, the belief that scientific evidence exists to justify racist beliefs. For instance, in the eighteenth century, the French naturalist Georges-Louis Leclerc, Comte de Buffon, argued that all races had a single Caucasian origin, but that other races came about from a 'deterioration' process – these races were thus framed as lesser, defective versions of the white race (Sloan, 1973). Other scientific racist practices, such as craniometry (the measurement of skulls to prove racial inferiority), the eugenics project (social engineering based on a perceived hierarchy of biological traits), and even in more recent times, IQ testing (Dennis, 1995), flourished for many years, bolstering racism, and ultimately justifying many of the most heinous racial crimes, including slavery in the United States of America, South African apartheid, and the Holocaust.

While scientific racism has been generally rejected, racism as a system of power, and the ideological remnants of scientific racism, continue to shape social relations today. For instance, 'white' and 'black' now serve as signifiers of 'good' and 'evil' or 'clean' and 'dirty'. Ann McClintock's (1995) analysis of soap advertisements in the Victorian era, for example, demonstrates how these meanings were mobilized to sell soap and other cleaning supplies. In these advertisements, 'the whitening agent of bleach promises an alchemy of racial upliftment through historical contact with commodity culture' (McClintock, 1995, p. 220). Robbie Shilliam (2015) explains how racism is now part of 'the institutional bedrock' of criminal justice systems in the United States and New Zealand (and to be sure, elsewhere); this can be seen in the bloated black and Māori prison populations in these countries. Frantz Fanon's (2008) work on how racism affects the psyche of both white people (who are, within the racist system, the superior group) and people of colour (the inferior groups) further demonstrates how racism permeates all aspects of our lives, even in seemingly ordinary encounters. For instance, Fanon writes that 'there is nothing more exasperating [as a black man] than to hear: "How long have you lived in France? You speak such good French"'

(2008, p. 18). This seemingly quotidian exchange, according to Fanon's analysis, reveals that 'the European has a set idea of the black man' (2008, p. 18) – this man cannot be European – and points to the burden the black man experiences as this 'set idea' is constantly projected onto him. Racism, like colonialism, fundamentally restructured, and continues to structure, social relations in complex and specific ways, but always according to a hierarchy with white people at the top.

The social relations of production also underwent a significant transformation in the context of the emergence of the modern world with the development and expansion of capitalism. Capitalism is a political economic system in which the means of production are privately owned (by individuals, corporations) and workers, now divorced from the means of production and the outputs of their work, sell their labour to the owners of the means of production for a wage. According to Karl Marx's (1977, pp. 320–32) analysis of capitalism, this wage relation produces 'surplus-value'; labour-power is a unique commodity that can produce value greater than its own exchange-value (wage). The fact that the organization of production under capitalism produces surplus-value distinguishes it from other modes of production.

While the emergence of capitalism in the sixteenth and seventeenth centuries[3] offered some new possibilities in terms of social relations (for instance, both the end of feudalism and the possibility of accumulating surplus-value created the potential for social mobility), capitalism operates as a distinct system of domination. As a structure, capital functions to produce ever more surplus-value; in this pursuit, capitalism reorganizes the relations of production to maximize the production of surplus-value. As surplus-value is created by the unique commodity labour-power, this reorganization involves separating the worker from their labour and the product of their labour. For Marx, this separation violates 'the species being (*Gattungswesen*), the human essence of real humans: … that they [develop] their potential and ability through labour' (Heinrich, 2004, p. 21). Now, workers are alienated from their work, from that which is their essence, and thus from themselves. In this way, even the 'innovative' aspects of capitalism, whereby technology and knowledge are greatly advanced in the pursuit of surplus-value, end up dominating the worker.

In addition to this dispossession of humans' innermost potentiality, the pursuit of surplus-value under capitalism also involved direct physical harms. For instance, Marx famously discussed the working conditions in

---

[3] The origin of capitalism is much debated, and it is beyond the breadth of this argument to discuss this fully here. This view follows that of Giovanni Arrighi (2010) and other world-systems thinkers.

the factories in England during the Industrial Revolution; these conditions included excessively long shifts, the employment of children, the continual lowering of wages (which drastically affected the worker's ability to provide for themselves), and the ways in which the factory became a 'House of Terror' (Marx, 1977, p. 388). While working conditions in some parts of the world have improved, under capitalism we still see workers struggling to survive on menial wages, working excessively long hours, and facing poor working conditions (see, for example, Ehrenreich, 2001). The emergence of capitalism was also violent and involved what Marx calls 'primitive accumulation' (Marx, 1977, pp. 874–5). Primitive accumulation refers to the processes by which the means of production were seized from the producers, thereby creating the conditions by which people were forced to sell their labour for a wage.[4] Primitive accumulation was enacted both within Europe, for instance, in the enclosure legislation in Britain, and outside of Europe, where it took an even more brutal form, shaped by the colonial project and racism.

Capitalism, like colonialism and racism, continues to organize and shape our social relations – and particularly the social relations which most directly impact our material well-being – at a fundamental level. Workers are still deprived of the surplus-value they accumulate, while ownership of the means of production grows increasingly concentrated in the hands of a small group (Piketty, 2017). Capital has also co-opted new markets, like the so-called knowledge economy (Castro-Gómez, 2007, p. 437). The commodity – which, under capitalism, is fetishized and appears as the form of all value – shapes all aspects of social interactions: under consumer society, the suggestion is that 'consumption itself can provide the meaning and identity that modern humans crave, and that it is largely through this activity that individuals discover who they are, as well as succeed in combating their sense of ontological insecurity' (Campbell, 2004, p. 42). The class hierarchy inherent to the capitalist system, whereby workers face precarity and material insecurity due to the wage relation, is now a global hierarchy; even groups who have different non-capitalist economic systems are constituted, in part, by being *other* than capital.

Lastly, patriarchy – a system of power structured along gendered lines, with men holding the power and women subordinated to men – also manifested in particular ways within modernity.[5] Within the modern context, gender

---

[4] While Marx discusses primitive accumulation as a now passed historical event, more recent scholarship has highlighted the ongoing nature of this dispossession (see, for example, Federici, 2004; Harvey, 2004).

[5] Importantly, this is not to assert that patriarchy originated in modernity, or that patriarchy was essential to the emergence of modernity. This is a debated topic (see, for example, Segato, 2003; Lugones, 2007). Instead, the emphasis here is that within the context of modernity, relations of power were organized along gendered lines in particular

does not refer simply to 'biological' differences; rather, as V. Spike Peterson (2003, p. 31, emphasis in original) explains, 'gender is a systemic *social construction* that dichotomizes not only men – women but also identities, behaviours, and expectations as masculine – feminine'. Those identities, behaviours, and expectations coded as masculine are then valued above those coded as feminine:

>Masculine/Feminine
>Power/Weakness
>Autonomy/Dependence
>Rationality/Emotion
>Public/Private
>Subject/Object
>Human/Nature

Of course, this gender system of codification is not merely symbolic: social relations were, and are, (re)organized along these lines. For instance, in modern societies, women were relegated to the household (the so-called private sphere) and excluded from politics (the public sphere) (Towns, 2013). Labour was also divided according to gendered lines in modernity, with housework, or 'social reproduction', falling primarily under the purview of women's work. This work was not paid and was also symbolically devalued as non-productive, despite the fact that, as many materialist feminists have shown, it is a key component of the capitalist system, as it is social reproduction which reproduces and replenishes new and existing labour (see, for example, Hennessy and Ingraham, 1997; Federici, 2012; James, 2012).

The restructuring of gender relations took on particular forms in the context of colonialism as well. Partha Chatterjee (1990, p. 249) discusses how women in Bengal were relegated to the home during the Bengali nationalist movement in the last decades of the nineteenth century because the nationalist agenda refused to make 'the women's question an issue of political negotiation with the colonial state'. Here, the allocation of women to the 'private' sphere is situated and justified within the nationalist, anti-colonial project. Kiera Ladner (2009, p. 70; see also 2001) draws upon her community-based research on traditional Blackfoot governance and Mi'kmaw constitutional frameworks to show that present-day gender relations in these contexts are 'the result of the masculinist ideas that now dominate Indigenous political organisations ... [which] have been colonized'. More specifically:

---

ways, and this particular organization of gender is constitutive of modernity as it has historically unfolded.

> One has to understand that the position of women in Indigenous society was, by and large, quite unlike that of European women at the time of contact. ... Unlike the way in which European women were regarded by their own society, Indigenous women were considered within Indigenous society as persons; they were not the property of men, nor the drudges of society. As my own research in the case of the Blackfoot confederacy has found, women were integral members of society in the pre-colonial period. Though most women remained in camp and were responsible for camp life, the persistence of this gendered division of labour cannot be equated with inequality, subordination or oppression. Rather, these roles were respected and are recounted with great reverence in the oral tradition. ... [Furthermore, w]omen were not confined by an absolute gender division, as many *ninawaki* or *sakwo'mapiakikiwan* (manly hearted women) pursued more masculine roles as warriors, hunters and leaders. (Ladner, 2009, p. 70, emphasis in original)

However, as Ladner and others (see, for example, Lawrence, 2003; Green, 2007) testify, colonization reorganized gender relations in ways that were and are oppressive to Indigenous women; the houses of many Indigenous groups 'have been ravaged by patriarchy' (Turpel-Lafond, 1997, p. 190). In a different context, Afsaneh Najmabadi (2005) traces how the colonial encounter between Europe and Iran reshaped gender and sexual relations within Iran. [6] 'As "another gaze" entered the scene of desire, Iranian men interacting with Europeans in Iran or abroad became highly sensitized to the idea that their desire was now under European scrutiny. Homoerotic desire had to be covered' (2005, p. 4). Part of this 'covering' involved an entrenchment of gendered beauty norms. In early Qajar Iran, notions of beauty were undifferentiated by gender; by the end of the nineteenth century, beauty was feminized (2005, p. 26). Even when modern gender norms and meanings were not directly imported or enforced, these norms, within the context of colonial encounters, shaped gendered relations in non-European societies as well.

While the particular form of these gender relations has shifted – for instance, women are increasingly gaining access to politics around the world, although not evenly so – the devaluing of that which is coded feminine remains pervasive today. Care work, both coded as feminine and disproportionately done by women of colour, remains undercompensated and undervalued (see, for example, Waring, 1999; Duffy, 2011). Dependency

---

[6] Iran was never colonized by European powers, although the encounter between Iran and Britain in the late nineteenth century is described as a colonial encounter here as it resulted in a great reshaping of Iran, including the implementation of a modern Iranian state.

and vulnerability, also coded feminine and positioned in opposition to masculine independence and autonomy, are likewise seen as something to be overcome and mastered, as opposed to an inherent quality of the human experience (Beattie and Schick, 2013). Emotion, coded feminine, is seen as less than, and even a hindrance to, rationality, which is coded masculine and viewed as the ultimate form of moral reasoning (Gilligan, 1993). Patriarchy continues to serve as a primary organizing principle of our social relations.

Finally, while describing these four systems of power – colonialism, racism, capitalism, and patriarchy – in isolation from one another is analytically useful, it is crucial to emphasize that these systems were, and continue to be, unfolding, interacting, and co-constituting each other all at once. Silvia Federici's rich analysis in *Caliban and the Witch: Women, The Body and Primitive Accumulation* (2004), which explores the history of the body during the transition to capitalism, is an exemplary piece of scholarship that demonstrates some of the integral connections between these different systems of power. Specifically, Federici presents an expanded Marxian analysis of primitive accumulation to include not only the separation of producers from the means of production and subsistence, the colonial conquering of the Indigenous peoples of the Americas, and the racist transatlantic slave trade, but also the transformation of the body itself (and particularly women's bodies) into a work-machine in the sixteenth and seventeenth centuries. The colonial project, the violent expropriation of workers from the means of production, and the slave trade all resulted in mass death, and a subsequent economic and demographic crisis, which peaked in the 1620s and the 1630s. As markets shrank, trade stopped, and unemployment became widespread, the possibility arose that the developing capitalist economy might crash. In this context, Federici argues, reproduction and population growth were turned into a state matter. While a variety of initiatives were used by European states to drive population growth, Federici suggests that the central initiative to restore the desired population ratio, and thereby avoid economic collapse, was to launch a war against women to break the control they had over their bodies and reproduction; this war was waged largely through the witch-hunts that demonized non-procreative sexuality, pleasure, and any form of birth control (Federici, 2004, p. 88). Midwives, who supported women's reproductive health, were cast as 'witches', and women who practised any form of reproductive control were charged with sacrificing their children to the devil. In this context, severe state penalties against contraception, abortion, and infanticide appeared, and women's wombs became 'public territory' (Federici, 2004, p. 89).

The use of 'magic' and 'witch-craft' to justify the witch-hunts, as Federici argues, demonstrates deep connections between colonialism, racism, capitalism, and patriarchy. Women who exercised reproductive control and autonomy were accused of consorting with the devil. The notion of 'magic' worked to justify the European witch-hunts, and thereby control women's reproduction in order to produce more workers. Yet, 'magic' also posed a broader challenge to capitalist logic:

> Aiming at controlling nature, the capitalist organization of work must refuse the unpredictability implicit in the practice of magic, and the possibility of establishing a privileged relation with the natural elements, as well as the belief in the existence of powers available only to particular individuals, and thus not easily generalized and exploitable. Magic was also an obstacle to the rationalization of the work process, and a threat to the establishment of the principle of individual responsibility. Above all, magic seemed a form of refusal of work, of insubordination, and an instrument of grassroots resistance to power. The world had to be 'disenchanted' in order to be dominated. (Federici, 2004, p. 174)

Magic had to be mastered (again, Man must order Nature), as did everyone who was associated with or practised magic (generally meaning, anyone with a deep relation with the natural world). In this way, magic became a useful symbolic device for the demonization of not only women (who practised magic through reproductive health management) but also of Indigenous peoples (who practised magic in their relations to nature) and people of colour (the devil, for instance, was often portrayed as a black man). Equating women, Indigenous peoples, and people of colour with magic located them closer to Nature (the natural, irrational, unpredictable world) and thus beneath 'Man'; this, in turn, justified their domination and naturalized their exploitation, and allowed for the (re)production of capitalism (and colonialism, racism, and patriarchy).[7]

Equally important to understanding the connections between these systems of power, however, are the ways in which the intersections between colonialism, racism, capitalism, and patriarchy also resulted in unique oppressions, dominations, and exploitations of certain groups. Federici's account of the witch hunt is again instructive here, as she (2004, pp. 89–91) points to some important ways in which the capital-based management of women's reproduction was also differentiated along racial lines:

> In [one] sense, the destiny of West European women, in the period of primitive accumulation, was similar to that of female slaves in the American colonial plantations who, especially after the end of the

---

[7] To be sure, other groups of people were also implicated in these systems of domination and exploitation. For instance, people with cognitive disabilities were often conceived of as possessed or manipulated by the devil and accordingly oppressed and marginalized (Goodey, 2012).

slave-trade in 1807, were forced by their masters to become breeders of new workers. The comparison has obviously serious limits. European women were not openly delivered to sexual assaults – though proletarian women could be raped with impunity and punished for it. Nor had they to suffer the agony of seeing their children taken away and sold on the auction block. The economic profit derived from the births imposed upon them was also far more concealed. In this sense, it is the condition of the enslaved woman that most explicitly reveals the truth and the logic of capitalist accumulation. But despite these differences, in both cases, the female body was turned into an instrument for the reproduction of labour and the expansion of the work-force, treated as a natural breeding-machine, functioning according to rhythms outside of women's control.

Here, the connection between colonialism, racism, capitalism, and patriarchy is demonstrated. Capitalism required more labour; the modern logic of the conquering of nature, and the location of certain bodies closer to nature and therefore conquerable, shaped the solution to this problem. Now, certain bodies, specifically women, people of colour, and Indigenous peoples, could be mastered to produce more labour. At the same time, the intricacies of these systems of power also resulted in distinct differences in terms of this labour-producing project. White European women, for instance, were afforded more freedom than African women who were, quite literally, unfree as slaves. Thus, while the combination of colonialism-racism-capitalism-patriarchy ultimately rendered certain people as 'the commons, as their work was defined as a natural resource' (Federici, 2004, p. 97) meant to be exploited and plundered in the name of the economy, the particular form of this exploitation varied as a result of the complex interactions between colonialism-racism-capitalism-patriarchy. Federici's analysis demonstrates, either way, that capitalism is 'necessarily committed to' sexism, racism, and colonialism (2004, p. 17). This commitment is affirmed by scholarship analysing more contemporary manifestations of capitalism. For instance, Rauna Kuokkanen (2008) illustrates that Indigenous women are amongst the most impacted by the violence of more recent economic globalization, once again affirming the entrenched and ongoing ties between these four systems of power.

As the examples here demonstrate, the 'doing' of modernity was, in many ways, the (re)structuring of the world according to colonial-racist-capitalist-gendered hierarchies. Of course, the particular manifestation of these hierarchies, as illustrated by Federici (2004), varied across contexts; it is for this reason that scholars like Dipesh Chakrabarty (2008), Dussel (1993), and Dilip Parameshwar Gaonkar (2001) emphasize a multiplicity of narratives of modernity. Nonetheless, the broad contours of the power relations that are the product of colonialism-racism-capitalism-patriarchy are evident in both the historical constitution, and present-day manifestation, of modernity.

The collapsing of thinking and doing: modernity as world

With this broad tracing of 'modernity as thinking' and 'modernity as doing' complete, it is now fruitful to put forth my definition of modernity: modernity is a world, a thinking/being/doing. In fact, the axiological bent of modernity – towards Man as orderer of Nature – suggests that, from the modern point of view, thinking and doing must collapse. Man, as rational and self-conscious, can, and must, act to master Nature. Modernity is thus the reproduction of a world, the structuring of social relations and material relations of production based upon an ontological distinction between Man and Nature, and a scientific epistemology and rationalist knowledge system, all of which are co-constituted of and by modern subjects.

Linking these two analyses demonstrates this collapsing of thinking and doing. For instance, there are clear connections between Baconian science (the scientific method and empiricism), on the one hand, and racism as a system of classification and hierarchy (insofar as it was located in biological and empirical 'science'), on the other. Locke's political theory and capitalism are intimately linked as both valorize private property. Kantian rationalism can likewise be connected to the patriarchal devaluing of emotion as feminine, whereby emotion is seen as something to be overcome in order to achieve true moral reasoning. More specific examples demonstrate the co-constitutive nature of modernity's thinking and doing as well. Cristina Rojas (2016, p. 371), for instance, discusses how Hobbes had in mind the 'savages' of America in his contemplation of the state of nature. In this state of nature, the people of America had no culture, no knowledge, no economy; rather, their world was the negation of modernity. The people of America provided the historical and empirical evidence for the state of nature for Hobbes, while at the same time his theory constructed and located these same people in the state of nature, and therefore as 'less than' modern subjects. In locating certain people closer to nature, Hobbes simultaneously deprived their lives of value (Rojas, 2016, p. 371); the 'thinking' and 'doing' here are co-constitutive and mutually enforcing. Anthony Pagden (2003) makes a similar point when he argues that Locke justified the destruction of aboriginal peoples who defended unclaimed land by dehumanizing them for not having private property. That is, in Locke's theorization that private property is key to being human – failing to exercise this natural right to 'improve' upon the natural world indicates a fundamental failure of humanness – Locke also provides a justification for violence against those who do not hold private property and locates these people as less-than human. Again, the thinking–doing relation is evident here, with the thinking justifying the doing and the doing serving as evidence to support the claims of the thinking.

Lastly, Dussel makes a related argument when he demonstrates how Hegel draws upon colonial encounters to justify and construct his notion of progress as history and linear time. For instance, when discussing the development of consciousness as world history, Hegel locates the Americas and Africa in a state of immaturity, and therefore inferiority. Europe (specifically, Western Christian Europe), on the other hand, is the end of history, the full realization of self-consciousness, and 'the path of Europe's modern development must be followed unilaterally by every other culture' (Dussel, 1993, p. 68). At the same time, as Dussel points out, Hegel uses this schematic – his location of the Americas and Africa as 'less developed' than Europe – to support his claim that world history is progressing in a linear way towards full self-consciousness. Like Hobbes – who constructs the state of nature in part by locating certain people in the state of nature – and Locke – who postulates private property as key to being human in part by arguing that those who do not treat nature as property are failures as human – Hegel constructs progress as history, unfolding through linear time, by also positing certain cultures as at 'lesser' stages of development than Europe. In these cases, colonial encounters, and the European view of the Other, serve as evidence of those concepts which purport European superiority (self-conscious, industrious, rational, freed from the state of nature) by simultaneously relegating non-Europeans to inferior positions vis-à-vis Europeans. Importantly, these concepts and theories at the same time serve to recast the narrative of the colonial project and provide normative grounds and justification for the violence of colonialism. The thinking and doing collapse to create a singular, although not entirely cohesive, project, with the thinking providing the epistemological justification for the doing, and the doing providing the empirical evidence to support this same epistemological stance.

More simply, the argument here is that the doing of modernity, as the previous examples demonstrate, operates in/through concepts, and these concepts and ways of thinking are developed and justified in/through the doing of modernity. 'Modernity as thinking' and 'modernity as doing' cannot be separated; rather the two are intimately intertwined, and this intertwinement suggests that modernity is more than a paradigm or particular political project. Instead, modernity, as the collapsing of thinking and doing, is a world characterized by an ontological distinction between Man and Nature, a scientific and rationalist epistemology, and an axiology which orients this world to (re)enact this ontology and epistemology so that Man can master and order Nature, and anything and anyone located in Nature, according to his desires.

Power and politics

In defining modernity as a world, the discussion in this chapter so far has reviewed the axiological, ontological, and epistemological premises of this world, and pointed to some of the systems of power which shape the social relations of this world (colonialism, racism, capitalism, patriarchy). As a final component of sketching 'modernity as world', a brief discussion of 'power' and 'politics' in the context of modernity is merited.

The study of power revolves around a series of related questions: what role does power play in the ways in which social relations are organized and ordered? Who are the subjects of power, both in terms of exercising power and in terms of being subjected to power? Are there legitimate and illegitimate exercises of power? What are the criteria for these? How does power operate? Is it individual? Collective? Institutional? Is power distributed equally (or should power be distributed equally)? What are the means (material, ideational, cultural) of exercising power? Are there limits to power? Many scholars, including those discussed thus far, provide various answers to these questions. For instance, Machiavelli and Hobbes locate power in the state or sovereign; the state can exercise direct coercion or even violence so as to order society as it deems fit. Power, here, is direct, hierarchical, and concentrated in the hands of the sovereign. Locke's theory implies a juridical power, which is constitutional and arises from the social contract, in which individuals come together to form a political society and government. Power, in this theory, is based in law, as opposed to granted fully to someone with an inherent right to rule. In this way, Locke's theory legalizes and constitutionalizes power. Kant discusses how we self-legislate – give freely to ourselves the laws that we will follow – according to the imperatives of reason. The legitimacy of these laws, and the corresponding ways in which society is organized according to these laws, is found in reason, which thus serves as a type of power. Hegel discusses how Spirit, *in and for itself*, determines the principles that will justly order society; these principles must become concretized in social and political institutions. In this theory, power is therefore governing norms made concrete in political institutions. Marx, on the other hand, locates power in the capitalist wage relation, which, because of the unequal distribution of the ownership of the means of production, compels workers to sell their labour to sustain their existence. For Marx, power is structural and material.

All these forms of power, I argue, are crucial to the production and reproduction of the modern world. For instance, direct violent coercion, state power, legal power, normative power and material power were all key to the creation of, and now the continuation of, colonialism, racism, capitalism, and patriarchy in a variety of ways (some of which are evident in the earlier discussion of these systems). However, the (re)production of modernity, as defined here, also involves a type of power that is more than just the sum of these systems of power. In particular, as this chapter has argued, modernity is a world. More significantly for this argument, which begins with the notion of the pluriverse (the idea that there are multiple worlds), modernity is one world amongst many. While these different understandings of power are thus all necessary for the (re)production and functioning of the modern world, they are not sufficient for understanding the power of modernity *in the pluriversal matrix*. Rather, in this context, modernity is characterized by a particular form of power that is more than the sum of the parts; this power is the ability to assert itself as *the* world, as opposed to *a* world, one among many. Assertion here is meant both conceptually (through the 'thinking' of modernity) as well as materially (through the 'doing' of modernity). Politics for modernity, therefore, is the myriad techniques and devices that comprise this assertion; politics is the series of ideologies, practices, relationships, and institutions that are deployed to exercise this power and enact the order of modernity.

Antony Anghie's (1996) discussion of the colonial origins of international law helps to demonstrate this power, and the politics that assert this power. Noting that while Hugo Grotius is generally regarded as the founder of international law, Anghie argues that the works of Francisco de Vitoria, a sixteenth-century Spanish jurist and theologian, are particularly important for understanding the colonial biases inherent in international law today. Vitoria, Anghie argues, was concerned with the unique legal issues generated by the encounter between the Spanish and Indigenous people; he wanted to create 'a system of law which could be used to account for relations between societies which he understood to belong to two very different cultural orders, each with its own ideas of propriety and governance' (1996, pp. 321–2). Vitoria thus acknowledged that Indigenous people had reason, politics, and political institutions (Pagden, 1982), although their particular systems differed from those of the Spanish. Yet, in acknowledging Indigenous peoples' capacity to reason, Vitoria also reduces the differences between the Indigenous people and the Spanish, as he then locates Indigenous people as subjects of 'universal' natural law: '*because* the Indians possess reason … they are bound by *jus gentium*' (Anghie, 1996, p. 325, emphasis in original). In this way, Vitoria concluded that natural law – as administered by sovereign states, and specifically the Spanish state – can become the source of law governing Spanish–Indigenous relations; the Indigenous system of governance disappears from the equation. As a result, '*jus gentium* naturalizes and legitimates a system of commerce and Spanish penetration' (Anghie, 1996, p. 326): the particular system of the Spaniards takes on a universal appearance. *Jus gentium* is the Truth, the one right way to be, and it applies to all, including the Indigenous people who seem to be able to participate in this system as equals. Further, as reasoning equals, Vitoria postulated,

Indigenous people not only can but should act according to this universal natural law. If they do not, they are breaking the law, and this act would 'justify Spanish retaliation' (Anghie, 1996, p. 326).

Under this framework, as Anghie argues, Indigenous people are fractured, 'both alike and unlike the Spaniard' (1996, p. 327). On the one hand, Vitoria acknowledges that Indigenous peoples have their own political institutions and systems, and therefore have reason; it thus follows that they belong to the 'universal' realm of the Spanish. However, reason, for Vitoria, is understood in a particular way, although one which is purported to be universally true. As a result, for Vitoria, Indigenous people both belong to the universal world of the Spanish and are apart from this world – or are 'lesser' manifestations of this world. Indigenous people thereby come to form the constitutive outside of the Spanish. On the one hand, the colonial encounter indicates that Indigenous people are the same as the Spanish, as they have reason, which according to modern ideology is the key to being a subject. On the other hand, they are not quite the Spanish, as their cultures and practices do not correspond to the systems of the Spanish, who also have reason. More specifically, the practices of the Indigenous peoples do not involve seeing themselves as the orderer of nature.

The result of this theoretical move is that it casts Indigenous people as both Human and Non-human. Importantly, as Human/Non-human, they have the potential to be fully human or fully realized (like the Spaniards) and so colonial interventions become normatively justified in the name of 'civilizing', and later 'developing', Indigenous people (even to the point of violence). Put differently, while the Indigenous people are Human, they are located in earlier stages of development in history; as such, they need to be brought forward. At the same time, if Indigenous people resist these interventions, they are breaking the 'universal' (Spanish) laws and are therefore Non-human and deserving of violent retribution. As Anghie's (1996) analysis shows, a variety of political tools, and the exercise of various forms of power, are justified to assert the world of modernity as the one true world, and to bring others to the stage of 'civilization' and 'development' already embodied by modernity.

It is important to emphasize two consequences of asserting modernity as *the* world. First, if modernity is the world – the end of history, the full development of human potential – then it is superior to all other cultures, ways of thinking, and societal organizations, because it is the world realized in its 'highest form'. The power of modernity to assert itself as *the* world implies a hierarchy in which different ways of being, thinking, and organizing social relations are necessarily devalued vis-à-vis modernity. More fundamentally, however, the assertion that modernity is the world also necessarily means that modernity cannot contend with radical alterity. Even social groups that are seen by moderns as non-modern are not viewed as radically different;

instead, they are simply conceived of as in earlier stages of history, and the assumption is always that these societies will ultimately culminate in modernity. Difference is inevitably reduced here: if the whole of the world is moving towards a singular end point and reality, already embodied by modernity, different worlds are not possible, and fundamentally different ontologies and epistemologies are not possible. Rather, the whole of the world is, in essence, modern; it is just a matter of bringing everyone to the 'highest' form, or most developed stage of modernity, as exemplified by European modernity. From this vantage point, the horizon of possibility for seeing difference, and particularly for seeing differences at their deepest and most robust (for instance, other worlds), is non-existent. Modernity cannot contemplate deep and pervasive difference; difference, at best, is necessarily reduced to different paradigms, different cultures, or different practices which are conducted by people who are, or who will soon become, essentially modern.

Thus, because of the ways in which modernity asserts itself as *the* world, fundamentally different onto-epistemologies, or different thinkings/beings/doings, are impossible to contemplate. Given this, the definition of power in the context of modernity mobilized here – that is, the ability to assert itself as *the* world – may be better stated as the ability to assert itself as all of reality. Modernity's thinking and doing, as co-constitutive practices that together come to structure a variety of fields, discourses, mechanisms, and practices that form dominant modes of appropriation and representation, enable 'modernity's rule over "the real"' (Vázquez, 2012, p. 242). Moreover, from the perspective of European modernity, the politics that enable modernity's rule over 'the real' are invisibilized and naturalized. In consequence, modernity need not even think of itself as the world, or in terms of worlds at all. Modernity just *is* the totality of the real. The ideological and material ways in which modernity divides thinking/being/doing into existent and non-existent, rendering certain thinkings/beings/doings valid and others as 'not existing in any relevant or comprehensible way of thinking', is an 'abyssal thinking', in which the invisible forms the constitutive-outside of the visible, and in which the co-presence of the two sides of the line is impossible (de Sousa Santos, 2007, p. 45).

Towards the ontological turn

It may now be evident as to why this chapter begins by claiming that the central obstacle to rethinking approaches to global ethics in the context of the pluriverse is modernity. Modernity, as defined here, is an onto-epistemology or a world, characterized by an ontological distinction between Human and Nature, a rationalist epistemology, and an axiology which valorizes and orients Man to order Nature through the use of science and reason. Key to this world is also the idea that modernity is the one true world; the modern world has the hold on the real. The political processes which have often violently ordered global social relations in the image of modernity have only served to bolster the belief that modernity is the one true world. In fact, the ability to claim itself as the one world, and to hold the real exclusively, is one of the modern world's greatest sleight of hands. In failing to see how the (re)making of social relations was/is very much the product of political processes and relationships of power, the modern epistemology mistakes modernity's hegemonic position in the global order for abstract and universal rightness. This serves to bolster its claim that it is the right, true, and universal world, a claim which is a great source of power for modernity as the hegemon in the global socio-political-economic order.

A variety of scholarship has, of course, critically interrogated this sleight of hand, demonstrating that the limited view of modernity from the modern standpoint (Dussel, 2000) is but one perspective among many. Postcolonial scholarship (see, for example, Gaonkar, 2001; Mohanty, 2003; Chakrabarty, 2008; Amin, 2009), decolonial literature (see, for example, Dussel, 2000; Escobar, 2008; 2010), and even critical theories from within Europe (see, for example, Foucault, 1970; 1972; Heidegger, 1977; Adorno and Horkheimer, 2002) have sought to illuminate this Eurocentric perspective and decentre modernity's assertion of its reality as the whole of the real. By pointing to alternative epistemologies (for instance, Lugones, 2010; 2012; Vázquez, 2012) and highlighting the relations and practices of power through which universal claims emerge and are reproduced (for instance, Foucault, 1970; 1972; Mohanty, 2003; Chakrabarty, 2008), these approaches destabilize modernity's power (its ability to claim itself as the whole of the real) and critically reveal the practices (the politics) in and through which this power operates.

The pluriversal literature continues this decentring of modernity, although in an even more fundamental way. By illuminating multiple worlds, this literature completely severs modernity's hold on the real. As John Law (2015, p. 134) writes:

> If reals are contingent and relational enactments, if they are done in performances and rituals in specific locations [as the pluriversal literature shows], then there is no reason to suppose that those performances will all add up to generate a single reality. On the contrary, it seems much more likely that they will fail to fit together. If this is right then we do not live in a single container universe, but partially participate in multiple realities or a fractiverse.[8]

---

[8] Fractiverse is often used synonymously with pluriverse.

While these multiple realities, or multiple onto-epistemologies, challenge one-world claims, they also reveal the catastrophe of 'one-world metaphysics' (Law, 2015, p. 134) in encounters with the Other. As Law (2015, p. 134) continues:

> [One-world metaphysics] reduce difference. They evacuate reality from non-dominant reals. They turn other worlds into the mere beliefs of people who are more or less like you and me – and correspondingly more or less (probably more) mistaken. They insist, in the end, that there is a universe and that we are all inside it, one way or another.

Modernity, committed to a one-world metaphysics, is guilty of such reduction, in which non-dominant reals are reduced to beliefs, viewpoints, traditions, or erased entirely. As a result, the modern onto-epistemology poses two interrelated challenges to conceiving of a pluriversal ethics. First, modernity is unamenable to contemplating how to deal with ethical dilemmas across worlds, because for the modern onto-episteme, the very idea of multiple worlds or realities, and the humble acknowledgement that modernity is not the whole of the real, is unfathomable; instead, difference is conceived of in terms of economics, culture, communities, politics, religion, and so on, but not *worlds* (ontological and epistemological). Second, or perhaps more aptly, by extension, modernity, with its one-world metaphysics, then actually creates what may be thought of as the most pressing ethical dilemma in the context of the pluriverse as it is configured today: in its assertion and enactment of a one-world metaphysics, modernity actually disparages other worlds, to the point where other onto-epistemologies cannot even be acknowledged as worlds. The co-constitutive nature of these two problems is clear. Modernity cannot contemplate other worlds or the ethical dilemmas between worlds; consequently, it erases other worlds as worlds (or equally, modernity cannot contemplate other worlds or the ethical dilemmas between worlds *because* it erases other worlds as worlds). More simply, to paraphrase Sarah Hunt (2014, p. 30), the modern world creates and sustains 'boundaries around what is considered real and, by extension, what is unable to be seen as real (or to be seen at all)'. If one accepts the normative challenge of the pluriverse, which, as Chapter 1 outlines, is a commitment to a multiplication of worlds as worlds, modernity, as enacted today, is, in many ways, the most significant obstacle to realizing a pluriversal ethics.

3

Mapping Global Ethics in the Pluriverse

Implicit in the pluriversal research programme more broadly, as outlined in the introductory chapter, is the idea that research enacts worlds. Research, as a set of (ontological) practices, and as structured by a particular epistemology, is an act of worlding; research both reflects and (re)produces, or perhaps disrupts, the onto-epistemologies from which it comes. For this reason, research cannot be separated from the onto-epistemologies in/through which it emerges, nor can it be separated from the onto-epistemology of which the researcher is a part. This chapter begins from this premise: the literature that comprises the field of Global Ethics is largely a product of, or more precisely, co-constitutive of, the modern world. As a result, much of this literature, both explicitly or implicitly, reflects, (re)produces, and is premised upon some of the key characteristics and assumptions that shape modernity. For this reason, this chapter argues that many of the dominant approaches in the field of Global Ethics prove wanting when contemplating a pluriversal ethics.

This observation about the modern-, Euro-, and Western-centrism of the International Relations and Global Ethics literature is, of course, not new (for a variety of arguments along this line of thinking, see, for example, Bleiker, 2006; Agathangelou and Ling, 2009; Kayaoglu, 2010; Hobson, 2012; Vitalis, 2015; Connell, 2016; Blaney and Tickner, 2017a). Taken together, this scholarship evidences that the historical enactment of modernity/coloniality – and the theoretical and epistemic justification and groundings for such practices, such as the ways in which the modern world draws binaries and boundaries – is reflected in and bolstered by much of the literature that focuses on international relations and global ethics. However, this begs the question: can existing approaches in the field of Global Ethics, so implicated in the modern world, offer us tools or normative orientations from which to contemplate or build a pluriversal ethics? This chapter engages with this question by analysing in depth three approaches to ethics in the Global

Ethics literature – moral cosmopolitanism, discourse ethics, and (variants of) postmodernist ethics – and by assessing whether these approaches may offer us a useful vantage point from which to consider ethical horizons in the pluriverse.

To this end, this chapter begins with an exploration of moral cosmopolitanism, undeniably one of the most prominent approaches in Global Ethics. At its most basic, moral cosmopolitanism is an approach to ethics premised on the assumption of a common humanity; this common humanity provides the basis or grounding for moral obligations which we owe one another (Brown and Held, 2010). Intuitively, then, cosmopolitanism seems incompatible with the pluriverse, which posits multiple onto-epistemologies and subjectivities. Nonetheless, this exploration starts with moral cosmopolitanism for three reasons. First, Global Ethics, as outlined by Kimberly Hutchings (2010) and as has been presented in this book, is characterized by a debate between two approaches: the rationalist approaches and the alternative approaches. While Hutchings does not include cosmopolitanism explicitly in her schematic, the philosophical foundations of moral cosmopolitanism tend to be either utilitarian, contractualist, and/or deontological, three of the specific rationalist approaches Hutchings attends to in her analysis. Moral cosmopolitanism therefore provides a useful example from which to evaluate the rationalist approaches more broadly in terms of their compatibility with the pluriverse. Second, the significance of moral cosmopolitanism in the field of Global Ethics, and in the ways in which global ethics are practised and addressed in real-world global politics, cannot be over-stated. Moral cosmopolitanism, as the normative-philosophical basis for human rights and various global institutions, is the dominant approach to ethics as both theorized and practised in global politics today. To omit moral cosmopolitanism from this analysis would therefore be a glaring omission that fails to acknowledge the present-day reality of global politics. Lastly, there have been attempts to reconcile moral cosmopolitanism with difference, to reorient moral cosmopolitanism so that it can attend to differences between and across people (see, for example, Appiah, 2006). For these reasons, this chapter engages specifically with the work of moral cosmopolitan scholar Onora O'Neill (2000), who has attempted to reconceptualize moral cosmopolitanism in order to foreground the ethical salience of difference, and also briefly touches on human rights, so as to consider whether moral cosmopolitanism can provide an ethical orientation for the pluriverse. Ultimately, it is argued that moral cosmopolitanism is unsuitable for the pluriverse, as it is committed to a pervasive and unshakeable one-worldism.

Next, this chapter turns to an evaluation of discourse ethics. While discourse ethics was formulated by Jürgen Habermas (1987; 1990) as a procedural approach to ethical deliberation for members who share a common lifeworld (*Lebenswelt*) – and therefore it is again intuitively an inappropriate approach to pluriversal ethics, where multiple 'lifeworlds' are at stake – discourse ethics has been posited as a useful ethics for the international sphere by scholars like Andrew Linklater (1996a; 1998; 1999; 2005), and is worth attending to for two reasons. First, as a procedural ethic which rejects questions of metaphysics, discourse ethics 'involves shifting the grounding of all kinds of claims about the world, scientific as well as normative, from an extra-linguistic foundation (empirical, logical or metaphysical) to the procedure of communication itself' (Hutchings, 2010, p. 44). In other words, for discourse ethics, the assumption of successful communication seems to allow us to detach moral deliberation from particular ways of life without thick metaphysical assumptions, claims about human nature, or pre-formed opinions about right or wrong (see also Warnke, 1995). It seems possible that an approach to ethics which attempts to sidestep metaphysical claims might be useful in the pluriverse. Second, as Hutchings (2010, p. 49) notes, discourse ethics also serves as a sort of bridge between the rationalist and alternative approaches (although she ultimately includes it with the rationalist approaches); in challenging the possibility that an impartial and apolitical moral philosopher can derive substantive ethical principles, discourse ethics can be seen as beginning to move us into a kind of ethical theorizing that is distinct from the purely 'rationalist' approach. Nonetheless, despite discourse ethics' attempt to sidestep metaphysical assumptions, I argue that this approach is unamenable to the pluriverse, given its assumption of knowability. Discourse ethics assumes that through dialogue one can come to know the other; however, in the pluriverse, where differences are at their most robust, there will be limits to knowing and commensurability. Discourse ethics can provide little guidance in terms of navigating moral dilemmas where such limits to knowing are present.

This chapter then turns to an exploration of postmodernist ethics, one of the alternative approaches in Hutchings's schematic. While there are a variety of specific conceptualizations of and approaches to postmodern ethics – for instance, poststructuralist ethics, postfoundational ethics, antifoundationalism, and pragmatism – these various approaches are generally united in their rejection of the idea that ethics can be given a rational grounding (thus they are an 'alternative' to the rationalist approaches), and that there are transcendental features or qualities associated with being 'human' (Hutchings, 2010, p. 67). Without these foundational claims, postmodernist ethics seem to be the most compatible with the pluriverse, for this approach does not assert or require a one-world metaphysics or epistemology. At the same time, however, I argue that while this broad approach provides a vantage point from which to think the possibility of the pluriverse, it ultimately does not offer much in terms of theorizing and ethically contemplating the moral relations and dilemmas between temporally simultaneous worlds. Therefore, I conclude that it is not conducive to the task of building a pluriversal ethics. For purposes of scope, this chapter focuses on one particular postmodern approach, postfoundational cosmopolitanism (see, for example, Mignolo, 2002; Caraus and Paris, 2016), while also briefly addressing pragmatism (see, for example, Rorty, 2010).

Lastly, I consider the decolonial praxis of Silvia Rivera Cusicanqui (2012; 2015; 2018), particularly as it has been presented by Marcos Scauso (2021). In this approach, Rivera seeks to find convergences in meaning-making as interlocutors who are differently situated in the global political economy exchange ideas, concepts, and navigate the relations of power that structure global relations. These convergences can serve as a thin (non-foundational, and therefore arguably postmodernist) ethical orientation for condemning colonialism and other systems of power that hierarchialize Othernesss. While Rivera's work is, as I argue later, undeniably in the vein of developing a pluriversal ethics, my concern with this particular approach is that it may not be accessible to modern subjects (or at least, only accessible in a way that risks appropriating ways of being and knowing that are very different from our own). This is, I believe, an important point. When thinking about ethical horizons in the pluriverse for the modern world, I believe that we must be attuned to the potential harms of appropriating ways of knowing/being that are not accessible to us, given the limits of our onto-epistemic framework. As will be explicated more fully later, it is for this reason that I express some wariness over the potential for Rivera's praxis to serve as a pluriversal ethics for the modern world, even though I believe it is fundamentally pluriversal.

In sum, as the arguments that follow substantiate, these approaches are unable to offer a moral understanding of ethics in the pluriverse for the modern world, albeit for different reasons. Yet, in demonstrating why these approaches fail to offer us tools for a pluriversal ethics, the normative challenge of the pluriverse is further illuminated and delineated. In particular, I assert that a pluriversal ethics is characterized by a distinct combination of (1) the need to attend to our shared and entangled material existence while simultaneously (2) foregrounding the multiple and actually existing 'universals' or onto-epistemologies which comprise the pluriverse through partial connections. Furthermore, pluriversal ethics is also characterized by (3) the problem of incommensurability across difference, and the limits of knowing when differences are at their deepest and most pervasive, or onto-epistemic. To attend to these three attributes requires a different orientation to ethics, and a different set of tools than those offered us by moral cosmopolitanism, discourse ethics, or variants of postmodernist ethics. Beginning to theorize such an orientation and toolkit, drawing upon feminist ethics and particularly the ethics of care, is the task of the next chapter.

Moral cosmopolitanism

Most often traced back to Kant's moral philosophy, moral cosmopolitanism, and particularly moral cosmopolitanism as presented in the Global Ethics literature, can most broadly be thought of as 'any form of moral universalism that takes the human individual as the foundation of moral value' (Hutchings, 2010, pp. 10–11). Kant's basic goal, as Garrett Wallace Brown (2009, p. 33) argues, is to provide philosophical meaning to both material experience (the realm of science and empiricism) and to metaphysical concepts such as the notion of morality. As described in the previous chapter, Kant achieves this via independent principles of reason that precede experience and therefore make sense of experience. The fact that humans individually possess reason becomes crucially important for Kantian morality; the ability to self-legislate, via reason, is what renders us autonomous moral agents, and therefore represents the ultimate source of human dignity. Stemming from this fundamental premise, cosmopolitanism, in its most basic form, maintains that individual human beings, as autonomous moral agents, are the ultimate unit of political and moral concern. Further, all human beings possess equal moral status, and this human status has global scope (Held, 2003; Hayden, 2005). More simply, humans belong to a single moral sphere in which all people are of equal worth; this status of equal worth should be acknowledged by all. Thomas Pogge (1994) summarizes these points as individualism (individual humans as the unit of moral concern), universality (this status of moral concern attaches to all humans equally), and generality (this status is of concern for everyone). From this general grounding, scholarship on cosmopolitanism in Global Ethics has been concerned with attempting to define which or what moral obligations we owe one another, and which factors exist and should exist to foster a cosmopolitan condition (Brown and Held, 2010). Most pertinent for the focus of this argument is the literature on 'cultural cosmopolitanism' (Brown and Held, 2010), which prioritizes the cultivation of global justice in a culturally pluralistic world. This literature, in other words, attempts to foreground difference within the cosmopolitan framework (see, for example, Appiah, 2006).

One of the most prominent scholars who has attempted to reconcile the universalizing claims of cosmopolitanism with difference is Onora O'Neill (2000; 2010). She argues that Kant combines his view of the human capacity for autonomy with an insistence that humans are also finite and mutually vulnerable (O'Neill, 2000, p. 138). The finitude and vulnerability of humans, under this conceptualization, points to difference, according to O'Neill: people are different because they are differently located in contexts which render them vulnerable in different ways. It is this very fact through which the universalizability of a claim can be tested. O'Neill (2000, p. 138, emphasis in original) writes:

The picture of human life which Kant assumes is one in which agents with limited capacities and varied vulnerabilities interact; this picture is required if a universalizability criterion is to identify obligations of justice. The easiest way to see why certain principles *cannot* be universally adopted among finite and interacting beings is by a simple *reductio ad absurdum* thought experiment. If certain sorts of principles could (*per impossibile*) be universally adopted by mutually vulnerable interacting beings, then even moderate success in acting on them (at a level any rational being must expect on the assumption that the principle is universally adopted) will render some others victims, and so unable to adopt those principles, which therefore (contrary to hypothesis) cannot be universally adopted. Examples of principles which can be identified as non-universalizable by this strategy include principles of injury, violence, coercion and deception.

Importantly, what constitutes violence and coercion, for O'Neill, is not just literal physical violence, coercion, and harm; rather, 'cultures of intimidation, insecurity, deference and evasiveness' (2000, p. 139), relations of power, and power distributions are also crucially significant. By incorporating vulnerability – and understanding vulnerability as being differently positioned in various contexts with different access to power – O'Neill includes difference in her cosmopolitan theory, and in such a way that difference has direct ethical-political significance.

O'Neill demonstrates the importance of this type of difference in her discussion of gender and justice. Noting that abstracted notions of justice, including cosmopolitanism, often rely on a conceptualization of moral subjects that reflects a masculinist bias, O'Neill argues that women's lives have not been captured by this literature; poor women's lives, in particular, are not well conceived as the lives of abstract individuals. This is, in part, because women are positioned differently in systems of power, made responsible for different types of labour (reproductive labour specifically), and thus experience particular vulnerabilities not captured in the masculinist moral subject who is abstracted, individualistic, and fully autonomous. In other words, O'Neill puts forth a different understanding of moral subjects as finite rational agents as opposed to free and equal individuals (Flikschuh, 2000). As finite and vulnerable, the scope of difference between and amongst people becomes much greater, and these human differences, such as those produced through gendered social relations, matter both politically and ethically. In conceiving of and foregrounding human vulnerability, O'Neill attempts to capture the dynamics and effects of being positioned differently in various systems of power, and therein amend cosmopolitanism so that it can more practically attend to the political and ethical consequences of difference.

Despite this attention to vulnerability, context, and difference, and her critique of the masculinist bias inherent in abstracted notions of moral subjects, O'Neill maintains, however, that abstraction is important. Abstraction, she writes, is necessary for justice to be global in scope; the problem is when 'idealized conceptualizations of certain crucial matters' (O'Neill, 2000, p. 145) are imported or smuggled into the abstraction, such as the idealized masculinist subject critiqued earlier. 'Idealization masquerading as abstraction yields theories that appear superficially to apply widely, but which covertly exclude those who do not match a certain ideal, or match it less well than others' (O'Neill, 2000, p. 152). Instead, O'Neill writes, we must try to abstract without idealization, thereby allowing us to develop principles of justice that allow for a wide range of human agents and institutions.

This perhaps seems like a promising approach to global ethics in the pluriversal context, given that O'Neill attempts to foreground a range of human difference, and to show why human difference is politically and ethically significant. However, while O'Neill arguably allows for greater difference across moral subjects, she ultimately relies upon a single epistemology: rationalism. Her discussion of consent will help to demonstrate this. Once again foregrounding vulnerability and differently positioned moral subjects, O'Neill suggests that principles of justice can be tested for universalizability based upon whether or not the arrangement in question is one in which 'a plurality of interacting agents with finite capacities could consent' (O'Neill, 2000, p. 162). Put differently, ensuring that moral agents are not coerced by a given institutional arrangement is a key test of whether said arrangement is just; an arrangement is only just if all affected by it or implicated in it could consent to it, and consent must be considered in the face of unequal vulnerabilities (O'Neill, 2010, pp. 76–7). But how do we identify when consent is legitimate? O'Neill provides the following answer, 'If those affected by a given set of arrangements *that could in principle be changed* can in fact refuse or renegotiate what affects them, their consent is no mere formality, but genuine, legitimating consent' (2000, p. 163, emphasis in original). The problem with this, however, is that the issue of who gets to decide that an arrangement could, in principle, be changed is not addressed. How do we know that we know an arrangement is negotiable? On what epistemological grounds is something deemed changeable?

O'Neill does not really engage with such questions; rather, a rationalist epistemology is presumed, one which can abstractly answer these questions. It is also in this problem that one can see the limits of O'Neill's attempt to foreground difference in a cosmopolitan framework. While difference is important in the sense that subjects are differently situated, and therefore differently affected by injustices and coercions, differences at the epistemic level are inconceivable. Lois McNay's (2000) distinction between immediate and extended intersubjectivity is useful for understanding this more generally. On the one hand, McNay (2000, p. 12) notes there is 'intersubjectivity understood primarily as immediate interpersonal relations'; on the other hand, 'extended intersubjective relations ... [refer to] relations that are mediated through impersonal symbolic and material structures'. While O'Neill can be thought of as attempting to attend to relations and differences which are of concern to immediate intersubjectivity – the ways in which direct social relations impede one's ability to enact agency – she is unable to attend fully to extended intersubjectivity, which is shaped through a given symbolic and material order and often operates at the level of sub-consciousness. One can easily conceive of ethical dilemmas in which, when extended intersubjectivity is factored in, O'Neill's test for consent proves wanting. For instance, many women in violent relationships feel they are unable to leave their partner, even when they may have familial support, financial means, and the legal protections to do so. By O'Neill's test of consent, in choosing to stay in such a situation, which could in principle be changed (particularly when only considering immediate relations), such women are freely consenting to their abuse. However, this reading of the scenario ignores the ways in which the socio-linguistic order shapes notions of what is possible in complex, often sub-conscious, ways. Affects, feelings of love and obligation, and gendered systems of meaning-making which implicitly valorize loyalty to one's spouse all shape whether someone feels they can reasonably change the situation.

Thus, when O'Neill (2000, p. 167) concludes that 'the most significant features of actual situations that must be taken into account in judgements of justice are the security and entitlements, or insecurity and vulnerability, that determine whether people can dissent from or seek to change alterable aspects of arrangements and activities which structure their lives', she may be attending to difference in terms of vulnerabilities and positions within systems of power, but she fails to engage with the dilemma of how these same systems *shape subjectivity beyond one's literal subject-position*. Yet, differences stemming from relations of power also affect the enactment of subjectivities, epistemologies, and ontologies in a much more fundamental and co-constitutive way. O'Neill is unable to contemplate this fully given her subscription to a singular rationalist epistemology; like moral cosmopolitanism more broadly, radical difference is obfuscated or erased from her theory, and thus it cannot serve as a fruitful orientation for a pluriversal ethics, where differences are deep and pervasive.

Human rights and the pluriverse

Human rights have been the central mode of actualization of moral cosmopolitanism, and thus merit discussion here. Through legal institutions, human rights have come to occupy a hegemonic position within global politics as the key site of moral action. Human rights, like all variants of moral cosmopolitanism, are premised on the universal equal moral status of human subjects (Donnelly, 2007). Because of this, the critique presented earlier regarding whether moral cosmopolitanism can serve as a fruitful ethics for the pluriverse applies to this form of cosmopolitanism as well. Human rights are premised on a singular ontology; hence, they are incompatible with the pluriverse. To be sure, critiques regarding the problems of the universality of human rights have been well-attended to in the literature (see, for example, Pin-Fat, 2000).

This declaration may, on the face of things, seem odd, given that Chapter 1 provides an example of a pluriversal ethical dilemma that is resolved, or at least appears to be resolved, via human rights. After years of struggle, the Whanganui Iwi received recognition of the Whanganui River as a being and their still-living kin; this recognition came in the form of extending human rights protection to the river by the New Zealand state. If human rights served as an effective solution to this pluriversal ethical dilemma, might they not have broader potential for reorienting the field of Global Ethics to the pluriverse more generally?

Sheryl Lightfoot (2016, p. 4), for example, compelling demonstrates that

> while Indigenous peoples are often dismissed as marginal non-state actors [particularly in the field of International Relations], and Indigenous rights are disregarded as merely aspirational and non-binding ... Global Indigenous politics, defined as a project that advances Indigenous peoples' rights, is far from insignificant and is forging major changes in the international system.

More specifically, as Lightfoot shows, Indigenous inclusion and accommodation in the human rights framework necessitates a rethinking of many key concepts that shape our global international order, such as liberalism (which is, in many ways, a key ideology underpinning the human rights framework, given that it is premised on the prioritization of the individual rights of autonomous and independent people). As the work of scholars like Taiaiake Alfred (2005), Audra Simpson (2014), and Rauna Kuokkanen (2009) show, the liberal framework, which seeks to reduce everything to issues of 'equal individuals', obfuscates Indigenous differences and is incompatible with assertions of Indigenous peoples' collective rights. Yet, in asserting Indigenous rights, the global Indigenous rights movement has foregrounded the collective component of Indigenous political frameworks, and the need for collective protections of the rights of groups. This includes the protection of group cultural, linguistic, spiritual, and artistic practices; for example, Leanne Betasamosake Simpson (2014) discusses the importance of language for Indigenous nation-building, while Katherine Walker (2021) demonstrates the significance of the spiritual domain for Cree-ethical practices. In this way, as Lightfoot (2016, p. 12) argues, the struggle to secure

> the right of individual Indigenous nations to exist as self-determining nations within or across the boundaries of existing nation-states … [and] the implementation of [collective rights] … will ultimately create fundamental change in both the structure and practice of global politics. … Thus, global Indigenous politics not only seeks the inclusion of Indigenous rights within the existing body of human rights but, in addition, seeks a set of rights that, if implemented, would ultimately bring legal, political, social, and cultural change to the entire international system.

In other words, the global Indigenous rights movement, in asserting Indigenous rights (as collective, group based, and relational), holds the potential to transform the liberal focus on individual rights which currently underpins the dominant human rights framework. Human rights, as an opening for such insertions which are often driven by and a product of the struggles of people 'from below', could be transformed in ways that can lead to a fruitful orientation for ethics in the pluriverse. As Lightfoot's scholarship demonstrates, Indigenous peoples are effectively mobilizing human rights frameworks to such ends.

Without negating the significance of these movements, I believe there are a few reasons why human rights are still limited as an approach for contemplating a pluriversal ethics for the modern world (which is, as I have noted throughout the book, the focus of my argument here). These reasons are implicitly tied to the problem of the assumption of a singular ontology and epistemology that limits the moral cosmopolitan approach more generally, and which thereby shapes how subjects in the modern world conceive of and enact human rights. For instance, human rights, particularly as conceived of and enacted by the modern world, are anthropocentric. The issue of who is the subject of human rights is uncritically predetermined and pre-decided in mainstream human rights discourse and practice; 'humans' are universally the holders of rights. Yet, such depoliticized framings ignore the fact that in the past, who was considered 'human' was, and continues to be, a deeply political determination, often reflecting and reproducing patriarchal, racist, and colonial structures of power which denied certain people status as people. The transatlantic slave trade, for example, completely dehumanized Africans and African Americans, as they were treated as property and denied personhood. Women were also denied legal personhood, excluded from the political sphere, and again conceived of as their husbands' or fathers' property.

Given that determining who counts as human has historically been shaped by problematic power dynamics, it seems likely that these issues will reoccur in the pluriversal context. For example, where earth-beings like Ausangate and Whanganui are made visible *as beings* (as opposed to simply 'beliefs' held by other cultures), it is unclear how human rights – and their anthropocentric assumptions – will be able to grapple fully with non-human actors (at least, without some additional meta-ethical orientation or tools that would position the modern world to reflect critically upon its onto-epistemology and the ways in which that limits its ability to contend meaningfully with more-than-human beings and earth-beings).

In the case of Whanganui, for instance, it is clear that the river is not treated or seen as a human from the perspective of the modern world; rather, it is granted an exceptional status which allows it to hold the same rights as a human. The anthropocentrism of human rights, however, goes unchallenged; the fundamental assumption that rights belong exclusively to humans, and that by focusing on humans alone we can attend to all moral dilemmas, is held intact, while certain exceptional cases are added as postscripts. This is, of course, not to undermine the potency of including earth-beings or more-than-human beings under human rights protections. (For instance, and again following Lightfoot, as Indigenous groups continue to struggle for their rights, the human rights framework may come to shift from such pressures within. The inclusion of more-than-human beings in human rights frameworks are, without doubt, a part of this struggle.) Nor do I wish to suggest that we should attempt to conceive of earth-beings and more-than-human beings as humans. Rather, my point ultimately is that such *integrations* may at some point be insufficient, or even serve to erase or obfuscate these beings in a way that does harm to them (for they are not, in fact, human, although they are *beings*), as well as harm to the onto-epistemologies which know and live with these beings. The ways in which we name more-than-human beings/earth-beings have direct implications for the relations between that being and the world of which it is a part (Salmond, 2012, p. 132).

Additionally, it is very unclear what this granting of legal personality means in practice. While the New Zealand Government has appointed two guardians to act on behalf of the river (one representing the Whanganui Iwi and one from the Crown) and invested a NZ$1 million contribution towards establishing a legal framework to accommodate the inclusion and protection of Whanganui, the ways in which Whanganui's rights will actually be enforced and respected continue to unfold (Roy, 2017). For example, while the joint guardian role, called Te Pou Tupua, serves the following functions of 'acting and speaking on behalf of Te Awa Tupua; upholding the status of Te Awa Tupua and Tupua te Kawa; [and] promoting and protecting the health and wellbeing of Te Awa Tupua' (Ngā Tāngata Tiaki, 2021), there is still some uncertainty about what each of these functions will entail in practice and through time. If we are going to attend seriously to some of the ethical dilemmas that arise in the pluriverse, such as those regarding the protection of earth-beings, it seems likely that we will ultimately require a rethinking of the anthropocentrism of human rights, and a rethinking of the implicit assumption that humans are the sole area of concern for global ethical deliberation.

Second, and relatedly, the human rights approach often does very little to acknowledge or attend to relations of power in and through which rights are constructed (Stammers, 1993; 1995; Evans, 1998). As Neil Stammers (1995, p. 448) writes, 'ideas and practices concerning human rights are created by people in particular historical, social and economic circumstances.' Who gets to determine who is the subject of rights? Who gets to determine which things count as rights? Can there be positive (for example, the right to food), as well as negative (the right to non-interference), rights? The act of deciding, constructing, and implementing rights is a deeply political act; rights are not transcendental or natural, but rather operate in and through relations of power. Yet, mainstream (modern) human rights discourse and practices often fail to acknowledge and foreground this reality, instead treating rights as self-evident and universally held. It is in part because of this depoliticized framing of rights that the historical and ongoing denial of rights to certain people can fade into the background. Undoubtedly, the very fact that the Whanganui Iwi had to fight for over 140 years to receive this recognition of the Whanganui River's rights attests to the political and power-laden nature of the determination and construction of rights.

This last point leads to the final, and arguably most concerning, reason as to why human rights is problematic as a fruitful starting point for building an ethics for the pluriverse. Without attending to the relations of power which shape both the construction and implementation of rights, human rights fail to provide the tools required to assess and challenge the relations of power which currently uphold the world order. Why is it that some have the power to grant, recognize, and implement rights (in this case, the New Zealand Government), while others (the Whanganui Iwi and Whanganui River) must fight for their rights (or for certain subjects of rights) to be acknowledged at all?

At the heart of this question is a critique of recognition more generally. Charles Taylor (1992) conceives of recognition as 'a vital human need' (p. 26) because of the idea that 'our identity is partly shaped by recognition or its absence, often by the *mis*recognition of others, and so a person or group of people can suffer real damage, real distortion, if the people or society around them mirror back to them a confining or demeaning or contemptible picture of themselves' (p. 25, emphasis in original). More simply, recognition is necessary for the formation and maintenance of flourishing subjectivities, and as a result, is of great political import. The importance of recognition for this reason also generates practical implications. For instance, in the colonial context of Canada, Taylor (1992) argues that Indigenous people are threatened minorities that should be recognized for their cultural distinctiveness; this might require allowing Indigenous groups various types of self-determination or autonomy over governance structures.

At the same time, however, critical scholars have pointed out that recognition itself can be problematic. For instance, as noted in the previous chapter, Glen Coulthard (2014) expands upon Frantz Fanon's (2008) critique of the ways in which the maintenance of settler-state hegemony, particularly when force is not used, requires the production of what Fanon calls 'colonized subjects'. These colonized subjects are 'recognized' by the settler-state *when/if they produce and reproduce specific modes of colonial thought and behaviour.* In such a context, recognition itself is actually harmful. Recognition, when conceived of as something that is ultimately granted to a subaltern or marginalized group by a dominant group 'prefigures its failure to significantly modify, let alone transcend, the breadth of power at play in colonial relations' (Coulthard, 2014, p. 31). Other scholars have made similar critiques of recognition; for instance, Kelly Oliver (2001) and McNay (2008) both point to the limitations of recognition, which cannot attend to the relations of power in and through which recognition operates.

While human rights are not, of course, equivalent to recognition, human rights as an approach to ethics in the pluriverse for the modern world suffers from this same limitation. As historically and currently enacted in/by the modern world, human rights tell us very little about why some are protected, or granted rights, while others are not. Human rights from within the modern onto-epistemic framework also often fail to provide an orientation to reflect adequately on questions regarding who gets to decide who the subject of rights is, and who is responsible for ensuring that the rights of others are respected and upheld. Without providing additional tools for exploring and critically examining these questions, and the ways in which these questions play out 'on the ground', human rights, like other cosmopolitanisms, will be unable to orient the modern world to grapple fully with the complex power relations operating through ethical dilemmas in the context of the pluriverse.

Moral cosmopolitanism: erasing radical difference

As should now be evident, cosmopolitanism, even in its variants that attempt to attend to difference, is unamenable to the task of building a pluriversal ethics, as difference is ultimately conceived of in such a way that it can be subsumed by universal ontological claims about human nature (we share some common humanity), or overcome by an appeal to a universal rationalist epistemology which will (universally) guide moral action and deliberation on moral principles (even when people with different vulnerabilities are involved). In the pluriverse, where different onto-epistemologies are at stake, commitment to this one-world metaphysics is insufficient. The fact that cosmopolitanism fails to hold up as an approach to pluriversal ethics should come as no surprise, given its clear roots in the philosophy of thinkers like Kant, who, as argued in the previous chapter, reflect and (re)produce the very onto-epistemic assumptions that structure the modern world in its current configuration.

While this may be obvious, however, the preceding discussion nonetheless points to the first challenge to conceiving of global ethics in the pluriverse for the modern world: what might global ethics look like when one onto-epistemology cannot be assumed? What orientations allow us to contemplate multiple universals, or worlds, or onto-epistemologies? How do such orientations allow us to deliberate on ethical dilemmas that involve multiple worlds without defaulting to a universal ontology or epistemology? How can modern subjects – subjects of a one-world world – contemplate the ethical implications of multiple worlds?

Discourse ethics and Linklater's post-Westphalian communities

At its core, discourse ethics, as formulated by Jürgen Habermas (1987; 1990), stems from the idea of pure argument, in which actors hope to come together to an uncoerced understanding. Opposing the 'philosophy of the subject' which occupied the intellectual thought of his Frankfurt school predecessors (particularly Adorno) (Habermas, 1990; Baynes, 2004; Haacke, 2005), Habermas moves from a monological approach to enlightenment, whereby individual self-reflection provides the key to emancipation, and thereby refocuses critical theory onto epistemological questions (Weber, 2005, p. 196). In so doing, Habermas develops an intersubjectivist epistemology (Anievas, 2005, p. 140), in which 'the (normative) resources for coordinating social action can be derived from the pragmatic suppositions of "mutual understanding" or communicative action' (Baynes, 2004, p. 212). In other words, Habermas locates emancipation in processes of argumentation and consensus (Haacke, 1996, p. 260) based on the assumption that ordinary language practices offer the resources for apprehending and assessing the growth of knowledge (Weber, 2005, p. 197).

More precisely, Habermas claims that in communicative action, agents are engaged in the assessment and subsequent validation of claims made by other agents. Habermas identifies three basic validity claims that are at stake in communicative action: (a) the claim that the speech act is sincere, truthful, and authentic; (b) the claim that the speech act is socially appropriate or right, and thus the norms of the underlying arguments are right; and (c) the claim that the speech act is factually true based on the perceived facts (Risse, 2000; Bohman and Rehg, 2017). Habermasian discourse ethics is premised on these validity claims as 'the universal rationality structures underpinning communication' (Anievas, 2005, p. 136). Discourse ethics suggests that when agents with the ability to reason (that is, the ability to assess, critique, and validate these claims) and empathize (to see things through the eyes of another) are freed from relationships of power, force, and coercion and share a common lifeworld (*Lebenswelt*), they can reach normative consensuses based on the force of the better argument. In so doing, the agents together uncover the normative resources for strategizing and organizing social action, which may lead to emancipation. On this basis, discourse ethics is a universalist procedural ethic, as opposed to a substantive ethic. It is based on the idea that all those affected by certain norms should have equal voice in the communicative procedures through which decisions and norms are (re)legitimized via rational justification (Linklater, 1996a). Discourse ethics

> sets out the procedures to be followed so that individuals are equally free to express their moral differences, and able to resolve them, if this is possible, through the force of the better argument. It does not provide putative solutions to substantive moral debates, envisage end points or circulate blueprints. (Linklater, 1996a, p. 87)

By contrast, discourse ethics is concerned with questions of the 'right' in the public sphere and attempts to avoid the thicker moral questions of the good life (Shapcott, 2002).

There is a robust literature that draws upon discourse ethics to explore issues in international relations (see, for example, Risse, 2000; Ellis, 2002; Diez and Steans, 2005; Crawford, 2009). Linklater (1996a; 1998; 1999; 2005) specifically inserts discourse ethics into the international sphere by developing 'the case for a multicultural dialogical cosmopolitanism modelled on Habermas's discourse ethics' (Shapcott, 2002, p. 222). Discourse ethics, according to Linklater (1998, p. 92), provides a suitable model of dialogue for 'post-Westphalian' forms of community in which radically different agents are equally free to express their moral claims, explore the possibilities for attending to their moral differences and, significantly, reach a compromise in the absence of consensus. The consequence of using discourse ethics in this way, according to Linklater (1996a, pp. 87–8), is a dual questioning of 'traditional modes of exclusion' – including the exclusions that result from the sovereign state system and its emphasis on national citizenship and boundaries – and an imagining of 'new dialogic possibilities' which involve a greater universality (in that all people are able to participate in the dialogue) as well as openness to difference than the modern state has allowed. Because of this, Linklater sees discourse ethics as providing a fruitful and universal basis for a post-Westphalian cosmopolitan community. The procedure and universal structure of language allows all to be included, and as the theory is not based on a metaphysical postulation of the rational subject, discourse ethics is able to accommodate deep subjective differences.

Discourse ethics, particularly as applied to international politics, has been critiqued on a number of fronts. For instance, the potential to (in)validate empirically the tenets of discourse ethics has been debated (Bohman, 1999; Ellis, 2002; Deitelhoff and Müller, 2005). Discourse ethics, as a procedural ethic concerned with determining the right in the public sphere, has also been critiqued for the assertion that it does not involve substantive moral underpinnings related to, or even concerned with, broader questions of the good life (Benhabib, 1992; Geras, 1999; Linklater, 2005). Perhaps most significant of all, and most pertinent to the critique to follow here, there have been numerous arguments that challenge the universalizing tendencies of discourse ethics, particularly when applied to international relations. Richard Shapcott (2002, p. 222) notes that while 'at first glance such a model fulfils the requirements of a model of communication in which radically different agents engage with each other as equals in a discursively constituted community', there is a tension between the universal and plural in Linklater's formulation that is not fully addressed. Linklater's model requires a degree of homogeneity amongst the participants of the dialogue; discourse ethics presumes that people are at least minimally liberal in the first place or must become so in order to come to partake in such communicative cosmopolitanism (Hopgood, 2000; Shapcott, 2002). Despite the claim that this approach allows for plurality, in that equal voice is given to people despite differences in subjectivity, the fact that discourse ethics requires a common lifeworld – in that others must come to the conversation with an agreed-upon, pre-established notion of what constitutes an ethical conversation in the first place – serves only to undermine pluralism. Discourse ethics also presupposes a great deal about what morality must mean (Hutchings, 2005, p. 165), what constitutes dialogue and discourse in the first place (see, for example, Young, 1997; Dallmayr, 2001; Vaughan-Williams, 2005), and involves a potentially problematic prioritization of discourse – at the exclusion of those things which operate prediscursively, like affects, emotions, senses, desires, and imagination – as the intersubjective site for emancipation (Coole, 1996, p. 239). Together these criticisms all centre on the fact that discourse ethics operates according to a pre-established understanding which supposes that, as just noted, people are at least minimally liberal: they are equal, other-recognizing, and able to distance themselves from their own contexts so that they come to the discussion willing to be persuaded by the force of the better argument (even if, and particularly when, the 'better' argument is not their own). In other words, the theoretical promise that discourse ethics sidesteps questions of subjectivity falls flat (Hopgood, 2000).

The concern here, then, is that discourse ethics theoretically requires an assimilative universalism in which the plurality of being that exists globally becomes subsumed under a Western liberal model of what it means to be human (Hutchings, 2005). Put differently, discourse ethics presupposes liberal subjectivities and is premised on liberal notions of moral communication. While Linklater sees discourse ethics as obliterating exclusions and expanding boundaries by creating a more inclusive, open-to-difference, and universal dialogue (and by extension, political community), discourse ethics actually draws its own boundaries, such that moral subjects must, in at least some broad way, be liberal subjects. The result is that deep ontological differences cannot be accommodated under the discourse ethics framework. Furthermore, given that liberalism is, itself, embedded in hierarchies of power, discourse ethics likewise reproduces these same hierarchies: the rules of the ethical dialogue are premised upon the ideologies (liberalism) that are most powerful in the global political economy today (Hutchings, 2005). In this way, even if subjects are 'assimilated' (Hutchings, 2005, p. 162), and given equal status to participate in the dialogue, the existing power relations may prevent meaningful equality and participation. For example, as Fiona Robinson (2011c) argues, even if people are 'equally' able to speak in political and ethical dialogue, this does not mean that all people will be equally heard, as those with power may not need to listen attentively to those with relatively less power. Clearly, discourse ethics, and its processes for giving all people equal voice in ethical and political dialogues, is an abstract and universalist response which fails to attend to the power relations which inform and shape all our lives. As Hutchings concludes, 'in the end any "dialogue" on Habermasian terms turns out to be one-sided and exclusive' (2005, p. 155).

Discourse ethics and the limits to knowing

While the critiques noted earlier already point to the ways in which discourse ethics is a limited approach for contemplating global ethics in the context of the pluriverse, it is worth considering another anecdote from the ongoing dialogue between de la Cadena and Nazario (who were introduced in Chapter 1) so as to understand further the pluriversal challenge to global ethics. In this dialogue, de la Cadena, a Peruvian-born anthropologist now living in the United States, asks Nazario, a Quechua man, to explain the meaning of the word *pukara*. She (2015, pp. 29–30, emphasis in original) writes:

> Suggesting that the word belonged to a speech regime different from the one I most commonly used, [Nazario] answered: *That way of speaking is very difficult. … You will not understand, and whatever you write on your paper, something else it is going to say.* He went on to tell

me: *Pukara is just pukara. Rock pukara is pukara, soil pukara is pukara, water pukara is pukara. It is a different way of talking. Pukara is not a different person, it is not a different soil, it is not a different rock, it is not a different water. It is the same thing – pukara. It is difficult to talk about. Marisol may want to know where the pukara lives, what its name is – she would say it is a person, an abyss, a rock, a water, a lagoon. It is not. Pukara is a different way of saying; it is hard to understand. It is not easy. Pukara is Pukara!* His tone was impatiently emphatic about the connection; as if he wanted to delete the separation between the word pukara and the entity pukara habitual of my form of understanding.

In this exchange, it is evident that two different onto-epistemological standpoints, or two different worlds, are confronting the limits of mutual intelligibility. de la Cadena, as a liberal subject, resides in an onto-epistemological space in which subject/object distinctions are made, as are distinctions between signifier and signified. In her 'lifeworld', discourse is thus a distinct way of knowing: through dialogue, meaning and understanding about the world manifests. Nazario's world, on the other hand, consists of an onto-epistemological being which he calls *ayllu* (de la Cadena, 2015, p. 101). Being in-*ayllu* is a deeply relational onto-epistemological state, in which there is no separation between *tirakuna* (earth-beings), like Pukara and Ausangate, and *runakuna* (people). Neither is there separation between these beings and place. In Nazario's lifeworld, 'they are all in-ayllu, the relation from which they emerge *being*' (de la Cadena, 2015, p. 101, emphasis in original). In-*ayllu*, knowing and being emerge together and are inseparable. As de la Cadena (2015, p. 30, emphasis in original) explains:

> By saying 'pukara is pukara,' he indicated that *pukara*, the word, is always already with content and, thus, already the entity it names – not different from it. Of course I could understand *the meaning* of pukara. I could write it on paper, but that would not be the same; it would not be pukara. *Something else it is going to say.* ... [O]n successfully crossing the linguistic barriers, [any] translation would leave the earth-being behind and move pukara into a regime where the word stands for the being and allows for its representation (of pukara, for example). ... What is lost is not meaning or the mode of signification; what is lost in translation is the earth-being itself, and with it the worlding practice in which runakuna and tirakuna are together without the mediation of meaning: naming suffices.

In Nazario's lifeworld (to keep with the language of discourse ethics), knowledge is inseparable from practice: naming *pukara* is a worlding practice which enacts *pukara,* Nazario, and their entire onto-epistemology. In this enacting, Nazario simultaneously comes to know *pukara*. His knowledge is completely tied to his being, and to the practices which bring his world into existence; he does not speak *for* the *ayllu*, he speaks *from* it (de la Cadena, 2015, p. 45). de la Cadena cannot, therefore, ever know *pukara* – at least not in the way that Nazario knows *pukara*. She lacks the epistemic tools; as a liberal subject, her onto-epistemological world is one which speaks for objects, as opposed to from relations. Further, no amount of dialogue would allow her to know *pukara*; the onto-epistemological space between speaking for (de la Cadena) and speaking from (Nazario) is too great:

> I could translate them, but that did not mean I knew them. And frequently not knowing was not a question of leaving meaning behind, because for many practices or words there was no such thing as meaning. The practices were what my friends did, and the words were what they said; but what those practices did or what those words said escaped my knowing. Of course I described them in forms that I could understand; but when I turned those practices or words into what I could grasp, *that* – what I was describing – was not what those practices did, or what those words said. (de la Cadena, 2015, p. 3, emphasis in original)

It is this unknowability, this dialogical limit, that I wish to point to in this critique of discourse ethics, and which, I assert, poses a broader challenge to the field of Global Ethics for thinking pluriversally more generally. While others have made forceful critiques of the limitations of the particular *type* of dialogue espoused in discourse ethics, the critique put forth here is of discourse ethics' primordial reliance on discourse, language, and dialogue, in whatever form, as the source of reason, the way to settle normative disputes, and the way to accumulate knowledge for emancipatory purposes. As outlined previously, Habermas locates 'practical reason in the medium of language' (Haacke, 2005, p. 183). In so doing, discourse becomes the tool through which understanding is debated, and, by extension, knowledge claims are validated. This epistemic axiom has a twofold effect. First, it erases or devalues other epistemes, such as the deep relational epistemology of Nazario's world. For Nazario, knowledge is not obtained exclusively through dialogue. Knowledge comes from *being in-ayllu*. Discourse ethics, in locating reason in intersubjective language exchange, renders different knowledges and knowledge claims, such as those based on deep being-in relation, as less-than rational. This epistemic move, in which reason is equated with modern ways of knowing alone, has long been a pillar of Eurocentrism (Amin, 2009) and the colonial project (Said, 1978), as argued in the previous chapter. By extension, given that Habermas locates the development and exercise of reason, and therefore the potential for emancipation, in discourse, subjects like Nazario are rendered unintelligible as subjects of emancipation. The politics these subjects invoke based on being in-*ayllu*, such as Nazario's demonstration to protect Ausungate from the mining development project described in Chapter 1, are likewise rendered unintelligible. The motivation for what is, by all liberal accounts, clearly a political act – a social movement, a protest, a strategic claim-raising against the state – is unintelligible within the modernist onto-epistemological framing at work in Habermasian discourse ethics. Nazario's motivation for his politics comes from a deep being in-relation; the knowledge that he, and his community, must protect Ausungate is not realized through dialogue alone. Yet this knowledge, and the subsequent political action towards emancipation, does not fit within a discourse ethics framework. By extension, Nazario, and subjects like him, are not intelligible as valid subjects of emancipation either. In this way, Habermasian discourse ethics can be thought of as a 'partition of the sensible', that is, an order that defines certain activities as visible and others as invisible (Rancière, 1999, p. 29).

This observation should come as no surprise – the existing critiques of discourse ethics reviewed previously allude to this problem. More concretely, Habermas's discourse ethics is premised on a moral psychology that distinguishes between pre- and post-conventional morality. As Linklater (1996b, p. 286) explains:

> Pre-conventional morality exists when actors obey norms because they fear that non-compliance will be sanctioned by a higher authority; conventional norms are observed because actors are loyal to a specific social group; post-conventional morality occurs when actors stand back from authority structures and group membership and ask whether they are complying with principles which have universal validity.

Under such a scheme, Nazario and his world would be deemed pre-conventional; Habermas argues that such lifeworlds are comprised of a 'mythical' worldview and asserts that discourse ethics is thus not applicable (Rustin, 1999). However, as de la Cadena (2015) emphasizes, *tirakuna* (earth-beings) are not a belief for Nazario; they simply *are*. Reducing them to a myth or belief loses sight of the fact that belief does not mediate the relationship between Ausangate and Nazario; rather, Ausangate is a presence enacted through everyday practices in-*ayllu*. Second, in the context of international relations, and particularly in relation to Linklater's proposal that discourse ethics provide the basis for a universal community in which all actors have a place at the table, this hierarchy of lifeworlds and moral frameworks – a hierarchy which would deem Nazario's world as less than or 'behind' the modern onto-epistemology – is deeply problematic. Beate Jahn (1998, p. 641) captures this concern when she writes: 'How, one wonders, do [those engaged in the critical theory project in International Relations] expect to establish any kind of equal communication with peoples whom they have told beforehand that they, unfortunately, are morally backward?'

Second, the axiomatic status of language as rationality also implicitly asserts that if we just dialogue enough, then we can come to know the other. As Linklater (2005, p. 151) writes, discourse ethics invites moral agents to 'think from the standpoint of others, to place themselves in other's shoes and to test their preferred ethical principles by asking if they would accept them if roles were reversed'. The problem here lies in the assumption that if we just adopt the right disposition, we *can* place ourselves in others' shoes. Put differently, even in the seemingly humble assertion that, above all else, discourse ethics means that 'there is no certainty about who will learn from whom' (Linklater, 1996a, p. 86) lies the grand assumption that someone *can* always or necessarily learn from the other. Attempts to amend discourse ethics by employing a thicker definition of dialogue (see, for example, Young, 1997; Dallmayr, 2001) still assume, at some level, that knowability is guaranteed.

This assumption reflects a failure to recognize the limits of knowing when differences are deep and pervasive, when they are onto-epistemological, when they involve multiple worlds. The literature on the pluriverse, including the example presented previously, highlights the limits of knowability, and thereby deeply challenges the assumption of unfettered mutual understanding and knowing that underpins discourse ethics. To put it differently, from a pluriversal perspective, the metaphor of stepping into someone else's shoes falls incredibly short. What is at stake in the pluriverse is not removable footwear but rather the feet themselves. How can we wear another's feet (knowledge), when they are not separable from the body (the ontology)? Perhaps even more significantly, in assuming ultimate knowability, discourse ethics provides us with little guidance on how to navigate moral dilemmas when knowing the other fully is not possible, as demonstrated in the case of de la Cadena and Nazario. How do we proceed when concepts central to moral dilemmas are not translatable? What do we lose in translation? Are such losses significant enough to matter in terms of navigating moral dilemmas? Perhaps most importantly of all, how do we know when the losses are significant enough? Who gets to determine when the limits to knowing across difference are surmountable and when they are not? How does power shape and impact the answers to these questions, both theoretically and in practice?

Of course, in raising these questions, I do not wish to suggest that we must descend into relativism, in which knowledge across difference is completely inaccessible. In fact, the literature on the pluriverse, the notion of multiple worlds, and the specific examples of de la Cadena and Nazario all provide evidence to reject such a relativist conclusion: while there are multiple onto-epistemologies, the pluriverse emphasizes the connectedness of these onto-epistemologies, the fact that we reside in a common present. The pluriverse is a world of partial relations, albeit ones which do not always map out neatly. The fact that these worlds are related means that navigating moral dilemmas and attempting understanding, even across complex differences, is not only possible but necessary. The example of de la Cadena and Nazario demonstrates this; mutual dialoguing, knowing, and understanding is clearly unfolding in their sustained conversation. However, the type of knowing that results from this dialogue is a far humbler, more vulnerable, and limited knowing than that which is espoused by discourse ethics. It evades one-to-one translation; were de la Cadena to make smooth equivalences between *tirakuna* (earth-beings) and non-humans (nature), for instance, she would 'be ignoring the ontological excesses between each pair' (de la Cadena, 2014, p. 256). These excesses, however, are crucially important: they render *tirakuna as tirakuna* unknowable to de la Cadena, and *non-human nature as an object* unknowable to Nazario.

At the same time, however, in prioritizing these excesses, de la Cadena does not abandon attempting to know *tirakuna*. Rather, she simultaneously pays attention to the part of *tirakuna* that she cannot know. The result, as de la Cadena explains, is that by highlighting these incommensurabilities – the same incommensurabilities that exceed the type of dialogue envisioned by discourse ethics – she is able to bring to the fore the onto-epistemological differences between her and Nazario, allowing them 'to be acknowledged even if not known' (2015, p. 31). In this way, de la Cadena takes difference seriously while still pursuing cross-cultural meaning-making with Nazario; she is able both 'to attend to fractures [the excess] *and* entanglements [the shared]' (Pratt, 2002, p. 25, emphasis added). Thus, via this discussion of discourse ethics, and this pluriversal critique of the assumption of knowability, we can identify another facet of the challenge of building a pluriversal ethics: what tools do we have for ethical deliberation when knowing fully is not possible, when we cannot step outside of our world, when dialogue and knowledge has limits, but when we nonetheless occupy the same present and material reality?

Postmodernist ethics

Postmodernist ethics refers to a variety of ethical frameworks which are united in their rejection of the idea that there are essential features or qualities associated with being 'human', and relatedly, that ethics can be given a rational, universal, transcendental grounding (again, this is why they are one of the 'alternative' approaches to the rationalist approaches in Hutchings's schematic) (Hutchings, 2010, p. 67). In fact, postmodernist ethicists not only assert that such groundings are impossible, but also foreground the dangers of relying on such grounds as providing ultimate authority, as every assertion of a ground necessarily excludes or marks something else as outside the realm of reasonable or politically significant. Because of this, postmodernist ethics prioritize a deconstructivist approach to ethics, in which the assertion of any and all normative grounds must continually be examined and interrogated: 'the task is to interrogate what the theoretical move that establishes foundations *authorizes*, and what precisely it excludes or forecloses' (Butler, 1992, p. 7, emphasis in original). Through such interrogation, postmodernist ethics seeks to 'relieve the category [of universal grounding] of its foundationalist weight in order to render it as a site of permanent political contest' (Butler, 1992, p. 8). Significantly, as was introduced in the introductory chapter and as is discussed more fully later, the term 'political' here connotes something very particular in this tradition.

It is important to emphasize that while the term 'postmodernist ethics' encompasses numerous schools of thought and approaches to ethics, including poststructuralism, postfoundationalism, and pragmatism, there are significant differences between these approaches, despite their mutual commitment to questioning transcendental and universal normative groundings. For purposes of scope, this section focuses on one particular variant of postmodernist ethics, postfoundational cosmopolitanism (see, for example, Caraus and Paris, 2016), and assesses whether a postfoundational cosmopolitanism can orient us to contemplate the ethical landscape of the pluriverse. In order to undertake such an assessment, however, it is important first to discuss the meaning of 'postfoundationalism'.

The term 'postfoundational political thought' was coined by Oliver Marchart (2007) to refer to the collective works of scholars like Jean-Luc Nancy, Ernesto Laclau, Alain Badiou, and Claude Lefort who focus on the political difference, and in so doing, seek to move beyond the antinomy between universal foundations and antifoundationalism. Foundational thought, according to Marchart, refers to 'all theoretical approaches for which the social is grounded on principles that transcend politics and society' (2016, p. 183); for foundational theories, like moral cosmopolitanisms, principles of politics and the social are undeniable and immune to revision. Antifoundationalism, on the other hand, is the rejection of foundationalism and groundings. As Richard Rorty (2010, p. 151) writes, 'On this view ... nothing grounds our practices, nothing legitimizes them, nothing shows them to be in touch with the way things really are.' However, as Marchart (2007, p. 12) points out, this antinomy between foundationalists and antifoundationalists leads to a particular contradiction. Are not antifoundationalists making a foundational claim in their assertion that there are no grounds or universal and transcendent principles? Furthermore, both sides of this binary point to particular, albeit distinct, dilemmas. If one accepts foundations, questions arise regarding how these foundations are determined, the ways in which power shapes such determining, and how we might deal with contestations over the nature of grounds. This has, if somewhat implicitly, been pointed out in the preceding chapter on modernity and the previous sections of this chapter that outline the limitations of the rationalist approaches in the field of Global Ethics: claims regarding universal truths and principles are exclusionary and come to mask the fact that such claims are always made from a particular locatedness that cannot reflect or capture different ways of knowing or being in the world. Antifoundationalism, and the denial of any and all grounds, on the other hand, has its own problem, as it can lead to a sort of nihilism or radical relativism in which normative claims can never be asserted or contested meaningfully.

To resolve this bind, or at the very least, to help us move beyond it, Marchart points to several political theories which could 'be rightfully called a *post*-foundational constellation' (2007, p. 12, emphasis in original). These theories, according to Marchart, posit neither a universal grounding nor do they deny groundings all together. Rather, they assert what Judith Butler (1992) has called 'contingent foundations'. This position, according to Marchart (2007, p. 14, emphasis in original), allows for the foregrounding of the revisability of grounds, while also accepting 'the necessity for *some* grounds'. That is, postfoundational thinkers, 'even as they refute the idea of a single, ultimate ground ... still seek to account for the *dimension of grounding*' (Marchart, 2016, p. 184, emphasis in original), the ways in which the 'social world is characterized by incessant – yet ultimately unsuccessful – attempts at constructing foundations which sooner or later will crumble under the increasing weight of competing attempts at constructing alternative foundations' (Marchart, 2016, p. 184).

While intuitively this makes sense, this postfoundational standpoint raises several other questions, most significant of which is: what, then, is the ontological status of foundations? If foundations are neither 'existing' nor 'not existing', what are they? Marchart compellingly argues that this question calls for a shift in the analysis – 'from "actually existing" foundations to their status', where their status is their condition of possibility (2007, p. 14). Ontologically, what accounts for the condition of possibility through which several (infinite) contingent foundations may emerge?

According to Marchart and other postfoundational political theorists, the condition of possibility for contingent foundations is, perhaps somewhat ironically, the lack of any ultimate or final grounding. It is the impossibility of the final achievement of a totality that makes pluralization itself possible (Marchart, 2007, p. 17); the constant interplay between the grounding and ungrounding of contingent foundations can only emerge from the impossibility of any grounds at all. From this theoretical vantage point, it is this interplay, and this splitting between a purely negative foundation and plural contingent foundations, that becomes significant. Marchart argues that an array of scholars, including those mentioned previously, have attended to this split, which can be conceptualized based on a distinction between 'the political' and 'politics'. 'The political', according to Marchart, refers to the primordial or ontological absence of an ultimate ground; this ultimate absence is itself the grounds of possibility for any grounds to emerge, as just noted. 'Politics', on the other hand, refers to the 'empirical existence' of grounds, 'a specific discursive regime, a particular social system, a certain form of action' (Marchart, 2007, p. 8), that is, most broadly, the socio-symbolic order which structures our lives. Notably, this distinction, between politics and the political, was introduced previously via the work of Jenny Edkins (1999) to argue that the pluriverse is necessarily operating at the level of the political; I return to this distinction again in Chapter 7.

Postfoundational cosmopolitanism(s)

Recently, Tamara Caraus and colleagues (Caraus, 2015; 2016a; 2016b; Caraus and Pârvu, 2015; Caraus and Paris, 2016) have posited 'postfoundational cosmopolitanism' as an approach to ethics based on the legacy of contesting, questioning, challenging and rejecting unjust political regimes or forms of power (Caraus, 2015), while also recognizing 'the contingency of its own conceptual, normative and empirical foundations' (Pârvu, 2016, p. 87). From this broad definition, postfoundational cosmopolitanism may therefore best be thought of as spectrum of cosmopolitanisms that are loosening the hold on the universal claims and foundational groundings inherent to moral cosmopolitanism. For instance, at one end of the spectrum are cosmopolitan variants like 'cosmic cosmopolitanism' (Burke, 2013), 'practical cosmopolitanism' (Dallmayr, 2012), 'critical cosmopolitanism' (Mignolo, 2002; 2010), 'cosmopolitan patriotism' (Appiah, 1998), and 'cosmopolitics' (Cheah, 1998; Robbins, 1998; Ingram, 2013). These approaches to cosmopolitanism all emphasize that 'any cosmopolitanism's normative and idealizing power must acknowledge the actual historical and geographic contexts from which it emerges' (Robbins, 1998, p. 2), while equally arguing that these local attachments and contexts need not preclude the possibility of universal obligations. These approaches have been conceived of as 'new radical cosmopolitanisms from below' (Cheah, 1998, p. 21), whereby particular and situated normative commitments engage in and interact with global relations, vernacularizing both universal normative commitments and more local ethical processes. According to Caraus (2015; 2016b), because these critical 'cosmopolitanisms from below' destabilize, contextualize, and contest the myth of a singular universal foundation for ethics, and in so doing also destabilize the power relations which uphold such a universality, they fall under the postfoundational cosmopolitanism umbrella.

While such tempered cosmopolitan visions provide a more nuanced and located approach to ethics than the traditional moral cosmopolitanism approach, my fear is that these approaches often suffer from the same shortcomings identified previously in my discussion of cosmopolitan approaches that seek to attend meaningfully to difference. For instance, Boaventura de Sousa Santos (2006, p. 397) calls for an 'insurgent cosmopolitanism', which 'consists of the transnationally organized resistance against the unequal exchanges produced or intensified by globalized localism and localized globalisms'. This approach seeks to forge a universal struggle against injustice where various locally situated groups act in solidarity with one another. Different ways of being in and knowing the world can, in this vision, act together for a common good. Walter Mignolo's 'critical' (2002; 2010) or 'decolonial cosmopolitanism' operates similarly, in that it 'dwells in the borders [of] the colonial difference', 'connecting (rather than uniting) many projects and trajectories in a global process of de-colonial cosmopolitanism, toward the horizon of pluri-versality as a universal project' (2010, p. 125). However, it is unclear from both de Sousa Santos's and Mignolo's discussion as to how this organized resistance or 'global process of de-colonial cosmopolitanism' would adjudicate amongst competing claims, identify ally and foe, and determine actions to struggle against (an apparently agreed upon understanding of) global injustice. The identification of 'progressive' struggles, for example, seems self-apparent in de Sousa Santos's formulation; as a result, it seems that despite the local differences that may unite in this struggle, a universal notion of the 'good' is taken as given and largely agreed upon. In the most extreme reading of this approach, difference here is secondary to, or subsumed by, a universal common struggle. A more generous reading, in which this universal common struggle is one that emerges (as opposed to being assumed), still suffers from limitations, as the ways in which an emergent universal common struggle may be/is limited or shaped by the given universality (by which I mean the current configuration of our global social relations) is not sufficiently addressed. Similarly, in Mignolo's approach, the assumption that 'all human beings confronting … the consequences of modern/colonial racism and patriarchy have something in common' (2010, p. 125) – namely, an epistemological position that is a 'privileged source of cosmopolitan orientations' (Leinius, 2014, p. 47) which will help 'materialize' the decolonial option (Mignolo, 2010, p. 125) – is problematic. Theoretically, as Johanna Leinius (2014, p. 48) argues:

> [t]he general tendency of the advocates of [decolonial cosmopolitanism] to attribute cosmopolitan consciousness to people perceived as subaltern creates its own exclusions that, in the end, endanger their emancipatory project. By focusing on those groups that have been able to express political agency, they do not take into account the subaltern – those who have internalized their condition of disenfranchisement

as 'normal', [and/or] who, lacking the resources to form a political consciousness, do not participate in struggles for emancipation.

Furthermore, it is also evident that in practice the 'commonality' between all those confronting the consequences of modern/colonial racism and patriarchy is often not sufficient for building connections across global struggles (see, for example, Ylä-Anttila, 2005; Conway, 2011; 2013; Leinius, 2014).

Lastly, it is unclear as to how these 'cosmopolitanisms from below' draw upon or relate to the postfoundational intellectual tradition reviewed earlier, or even mobilize the politics/political distinction that characterizes postfoundational thinking. Thus, despite nodding to these various approaches in her own overview of postfoundational cosmopolitanism, Caraus aptly concludes that these cosmopolitanisms, while attempting to avoid the 'foundationalist figures of universalism ... by putting the anchor in both the global and the local [or particular,] may not be enough to rid ourselves of foundational thinking' (2016b, p. 5).

Moving along this spectrum, scholars like Caraus (2016a; 2016b) and James Ingram (2013) articulate a more explicitly postfoundational cosmopolitanism. Caraus (2016b, p. 2) specifically links her postfoundational cosmopolitanism to postfoundational thinkers like Badiou, Nancy, Lefort, Laclau, Butler, and Jacques Rancière, arguing that:

> cosmopolitanism cannot be anything other than post-foundational: it cannot be advanced without assuming a universal ground, although the assumed universal ground will fail or will be contingent. At the same time, cosmopolitanism cannot be reduced only to this failed ground; it is co-substantial freedom that makes possible the plural attempts to offer an ultimate cosmopolitan foundation.

In this rethinking of cosmopolitanism in the image of postfoundationalism, Caraus argues that cosmopolitanism is part of the postfoundational process that demonstrates the contingency of all grounds by reminding society 'that it does not fully live up to the condition of the possibility in terms of inclusion, equality or justice' (Caraus, 2016b, p. 14). The possibility of contestation and critique, opened up by the postfoundational perspective, rethinks cosmopolitanism as 'a dynamic vision in a certain agonistic relation with the current order' (Caraus, 2016b, p. 16) – this is in contrast to the vision of a unified world posited in moral cosmopolitan visions. More specifically, the critique of grounds facilitated by postfoundationalism allows for the 'cosmopolitan stance [to emerge] in a certain context and time as an act of distancing from current local practices and in confrontation with the established meanings, requiring a subtraction from one's place and a dis-identification from one particular identity, thus enhancing radicalism' (Caraus, 2016b, p. 16). These last two points are significant, as they help to explain why Caraus sees postfoundational cosmopolitanism as cosmopolitan at all. For Caraus, cosmopolitanism is the interplay between the ideal cosmos and the current order of the polis. This opposition between the cosmos and polis, Caraus claims, is evident in all theories of cosmopolitanism and global justice (2016a, p. 109). What distinguishes her cosmopolitanism as postfoundational, then, is the antagonistic nature of this interaction. The recognition of the absence of grounds and radical contingency of all foundations allows for the very assertion that the world could be otherwise, that the cosmopolitical is possible; this, in turn, creates the possibility for contestation and radical critique of actually existing politics. This contestation, however, is of a more antagonistic nature than the more 'peaceful' coming together of the world based upon common principles that is envisioned in moral cosmopolitanism. Other postfoundational cosmopolitan scholars, like Ingram (2013), articulate a similar stance and argue that this approach allows us to recognize that antagonistic normative reflection is an essential part of political action. It is through normative assertions that antagonistic politics may give rise to the political moment (that is, a fundamental restructuring of a socio-symbolic order).

There are several concerns, however, about this approach to ethics. First, it is unclear as to why these scholars insist upon maintaining the word 'cosmopolitanism' to demarcate this approach, particularly when postfoundationalism is in many ways antithetical to cosmopolitanism.[1] On the one hand, if we take the definition of cosmopolitanism that Caraus puts forth (that is, cosmopolitanism as the literal conflict between the ideal cosmos and the actually existing unjust polis) at face value, one could argue that what she is actually referring to is 'critical thinking', plain and simple. To assert that something 'ought to be' different is always a disruption or critique of the 'actually is'. When authors like Caraus speak of cosmopolitanism as the conflict between ought and an unjust is, it is puzzling as to why they would hold on to such a loaded word, with a very particular and locatable intellectual history, simply to describe critical thought more generally. On the other hand, if these scholars use cosmopolitanism because they are maintaining some hold on universal principles (that is, the 'ought' of which they speak actually holds some pre-existing content for them), then it is unclear how these scholars can assert so fully that this is simultaneously a postfoundational approach. For instance, Caraus begins the introductory

---

[1] Chantal Mouffe (2013, p. 21) briefly makes a similar point vis-à-vis cosmopolitanism, and the various approaches, including those outlined here, which seek to retain the term while foregrounding alterity, locatedness, particularity, and contingency.

chapter to her edited volume on postfoundational cosmopolitanism (with Paris, 2016) with the statement that 'the contingency of grounds opens the potentiality of contestation of the current order towards a more inclusive *cosmos*, with its cosmopolitan ideals of justice, equality and freedom' (2016b, p. 1). Ingram (2013, p. 222) similarly mobilizes equality and freedom in his 'radical cosmopolitics'. However, these cosmopolitan ideals of justice, equality, and freedom are given no explanation. The grounds on which these are asserted as the normative goals to strive towards are not interrogated. Instead, it appears that the ground that needs to be shown to be contingent is the social order itself, and not the ground on which we would assert that a particular value or idea is the vision towards which we should strive. Focusing on the contingency of the grounds of the existing social order while neglecting to interrogate critically the grounds upon which one would claim that we should strive towards cosmopolitan ideals of justice, equality, and freedom involves an odd separation of the ways in which the content of ideals of equality, justice, and freedom have come to shape the socio-political-economic order and the 'injustices' therein (and vice versa). As the previous chapter demonstrates, for instance, many harms were instituted in the name of particular notions of justice, or visions of the 'good' or 'right' way to order society. To assert that there are no grounds more generally, and that this groundlessness allows us to implement normative change, while also mobilizing particular universal values without interrogating their particular groundings, strikes as a disjointed theoretical move which suggests that values and principles somehow emerge from outside a given socio-symbolic order.

For these reasons, these postfoundational cosmopolitan scholars end up in a theoretical bind. Drawing upon postfoundational thought, they argue that any given socio-symbolic order is ungrounded and therefore revisable. The very notion of the cosmos points to this revisability. However, the content of the cosmos, in these theories, is taken as given. The grounds for claims of equality and freedom, and what it means to be equal and free, are presented as largely self-evident and beyond contestation. In other words, the cosmic vision of postfoundational cosmopolitanism serves as a sort of unexamined ground. This type of grounding, as Camil Alexandru Pârvu (2016, p. 97) argues, is necessary if one is to retain the 'cosmopolitan' in this approach: 'There is, I maintain, a constitutive, structural limit within cosmopolitan theory, regarding the degree of contingency that it admits for its foundations. In other words, it cannot renounce a commitment to some universal dimension of human worth without ceasing to be cosmopolitan.'

Such commitments are evident in the postfoundational cosmopolitanisms presented by Caraus and Ingram, if only because of their own turning away from any critical inquiry about the values which are to guide our contestations of the 'actually existing' social order and our identification of possible allies in such struggles. As Chantal Mouffe (2013, p. 21) notes, preoccupying oneself wholly with the recognition of allegiances and lines of solidarity may in some ways actually ignore the political, meaning the radical contingency of the socio-symbolic order, particularly in its antagonistic dimension. These postfoundational approaches prioritize a solidarity-based global justice movement whereby identifying allies and visions of justice are guided by cosmopolitan principles that are not scrutinized. While such an approach seems to hold promise in terms of disrupting 'actually existing' politics, it simultaneously seems to preclude the possibility of contesting and revising, in the political sense, the meaning of justice as such.

Second, there seems also to be a fatal misunderstanding of the postfoundational approach to political theory in the formulations of postfoundational cosmopolitanism reviewed here, particularly with regard to theories of the subject. As Edkins (1999, p. 6) reminds us, in postfoundational thought, 'the constitution of the subject entails and is inextricably linked with the constitution of a particular social or symbolic order'. However, in these postfoundational cosmopolitanism approaches, there seems to be some pre-existing subject, with a pre-existing notion of the ideal cosmos, that will enact contestations and dissent to change the existing socio-symbolic order, ultimately in the hopes of bringing about the political moment. More acutely, this formulation of postfoundational cosmopolitanism can only make sense if the subject is a liberal subject, independent, unencumbered, autonomous, and pre-existing social relations. Such an assumption belies the 'postfoundational' nomenclature of this literature and demonstrates how close this approach actually is to moral cosmopolitanism. More simply, overstating contingency, and separating the socio-symbolic from the subject, such that pre-existing subjects can 'contest' any foundation to enact change, is to underestimate grossly the co-constitutive nature of subjects and socio-political-economic structures (or perhaps more pertinent for this discussion, onto-epistemologies). Susan Marks (2009) employs the useful term 'false contingency' to refer to the ways in which contingency is sometimes mobilized without restraint, or as is suggested here, without accounting fully for the relationship between subject/agency and structure. Without attending to the relationship between the subject and the socio-symbolic order, and by mobilizing a notion of contingency that seems to suggest that the theoretical fact of revisability corresponds equally to empirical revision, the postfoundational cosmopolitanism explored here presents itself as a sort of domesticated postfoundationalism, verging on the simply cosmopolitan, and loses the radicalness of the postfoundational framework in general.

As a final approach to consider, in her discussion, Caraus (2015; 2016b) notes that there are also radical and agonistic political theories at the far end of her spectrum of postfoundational cosmopolitanism. As Caraus acknowledges, the theorists here would be unlikely to identify in any way with cosmopolitanism; for that reason, the term is abandoned now.

However, in moving through postfoundational cosmopolitanism, this section is able to turn more fully to postfoundational political thought so as to consider what it can offer us in terms of moving towards a pluriversal ethics. While Caraus highlights numerous postfoundational thinkers in this part of the spectrum, I focus here on the work of Marchart (2016), who puts forth a postfoundational orientation to ethics. Specifically, while he maintains that the political is distinct from ethics, Marchart (2016) agrees with de Sousa Santos (2006) and Ingram (2013) in their conceptualization of a cosmopolitan democracy of movements, which can be understood as a multiplicity of 'partial struggles against particular forms of hierarchy and exclusion' (Ingram, 2013, p. 143). According to these scholars, these partial struggles, and the multiplied enactment of postfoundational democratic equality, may result in political moments and change. At the same time, Marchart is attuned to the problem highlighted in the critique of de Sousa Santos mentioned earlier: how does one know when a particular movement is an ally, when a movement actually is 'democratic', that is, an enactment of the radical equality that is inherent in the contingency of foundations?[2] Put differently, Marchart is concerned that not every democratization movement is necessarily a democratic movement that instantiates and makes visible the radical equality of all (2016, p. 192). This, according to Marchart, is where ethics comes in. An ethics of democracy allows us to distinguish between non- and anti-democratic politics based on the criteria of self-alienation:

> Constant reflection upon the ultimately ungrounded nature of one's own project and objectives is precisely the sign of an ethics of democracy. The latter stands in an antinomic relation towards the political because from a purely political perspective it would be considered self-defeating to engage in a process of eternal self-questioning. Attesting, in the face of an enemy, to your own weakness and the ungrounded nature of your project is not a political move, it is an ethical move which has nothing to do with pragmatism and a strategic approach to political affairs. ... Democracy, from a purely ethical perspective, would mean the unconditional acceptance of the un-grounded nature of the social. (Marchart, 2016, pp. 193–4)

Therefore, 'struggles for democratization are fully democratic only if their political impetus is supplemented, and baffled, by an ethical acceptance of their abyssal nature. ... [C]osmopolitan democracy confronts every given community with the unconditional demand of *self-alienation*, i.e., of accepting

---

[2] 'Democracy' in this literature refers to enactments of radical equality, as opposed to institutionalized democracy or liberal notions of democratic institutions and procedures.

the impossibility of ever attaining a state of full self-identity' (Marchart, 2016, p. 195, emphasis in original). One consequence of this, as Marchart highlights, is that democracy can only ever be a secular affair – we can only recognize a movement as democratic if it is void of any and all transcendent markers and certainty (2016, p. 196).[3]

From a pluriversal perspective, this ethics, I contend, reads almost as a form of neo-colonialism. One's political practices can only be considered democratic, and by extension, normatively valuable, if one first accepts the notion of radical contingency, and, specifically, the radical contingency of one's own onto-epistemology. One can only be a moral subject if one is self-alienated, which itself is a very particular notion of subjectivity with a long history in modern political thought. Of course, this is not to suggest that people in other worlds cannot self-alienate, or do not have conceptualizations of the contingent nature of their own socio-symbolic orders or worlds. Rather, the point is that to *require* this condition, and to use it to judge whether or not a political act is ethical (democratic in the postfoundational sense) erases or subsumes the possibility that there are other ways of approaching ethics, other ways of being, other onto-epistemologies, including those that may be deeply rooted in transcendental foundations.

Consider once again the example of Nazario's protest against the development of the mining industry on one of the peaks of the earth-being Ausangate. Nazario's motivation to protest the mining project is that he is afraid that Ausangate will get mad, and may even kill people, should mining proceed. Yet, from Marchart's perspective, Nazario's act could only be considered ethically valuable, an act of democratization, if he first admitted that his world – the very thing which motivates his political action – is contingent, and that Ausangate may not be what the Quechua people claim it to be. Nazario would need to be attuned to, and even foreground, the possibility that that which motivated him to act politically (that is, to avoid Ausangate's ire) is a contingent social construct, an unfounded consequence of his socio-symbolic order. While Marchart notes that there is a strategic risk to admitting the contingency of one's own project to 'the enemy', to require all moral subjects to admit the contingency of their onto-epistemologies, and to self-alienate, seems almost perverse in the context of the pluriverse. That is, while Habermasian discourse ethics misses the point – and asks us to swap shoes, when it is, in fact, our feet (our onto-epistemologies) that are at stake – Marchart's postfoundational ethics seems to require subjects to cut off their feet (onto-epistemologies) and offer them to us to show

---

[3] Or perhaps a non-secular movement can be recognized as democratic if is self-reflexive about its transcendent elements, as suggested by Hans-Martin Jaeger (2018), who writes about political theology as a mode of Western self-estrangement.

that they know they can 'remove' them (they are contingent, changeable, not transcendental). Further, this must be done before we will even begin to contemplate and acknowledge that what they are fighting for – in this case, the protection of Ausangate, an earth-being key to the (re)production of Nazario's world – is morally salient and worthwhile.

Were it posited for the pluriverse, such a requirement both asserts a level of homogenization across worlds and subjects of worlds (all subjects must be self-alienating), and perhaps even more importantly, fails to acknowledge that there is a privilege associated with being able to foreground the revisability of one's onto-epistemology. The risk, for example, for a modern subject to assert that modernity is not 'real' seems far less than the risk associated with this same move by subjects who are members of onto-epistemologies that are already marginalized in the global political economy (who are already fighting for their worlds to be taken seriously as worlds). I inherently feel that there is a certain privilege in being able to dwell in contingency when colonial relations of power are at play, when some onto-epistemologies have the power to hold on to their claim on the real without even trying. For these reasons, democratic ethics, like that proposed by Marchart, is antithetical to the pluriversal project of contemplating different worlds and giving weight to worlds as worlds (particularly those that have been rendered invisible as worlds by the power relations that uphold the narrative of modernity as the whole of the real).

Postfoundationalism: theorizing the pluriverse but not an ethics for the pluriverse

In sum, based upon this (necessarily limited) survey, this discussion implies that while the postfoundational literature provides one possible theoretical framework from which modern scholars can theorize the pluriverse, it does not offer an ethics for the pluriverse. Clearly, the postfoundational literature offers a set of concepts that hypothesize the possibility of infinite possibilities for our socio-symbolic orders, or onto-epistemologies, arising from the ground without ground. Sergei Prozorov (2014) summarizes this framework nicely in his term 'void universalism': it is the universal void, the ground without ground and the impossibility of final foundations, that creates the condition of possibility for an infinite horizon of possible foundations, orders, or worlds (albeit ones which can never fully totalize because of the impossibility of foundations). While this theory thus makes an important contribution, in that theorizing radical and infinite possibilities for worlds and orders is particularly significant from a normative standpoint (if things were unchangeable, the very idea of contemplating ethics and morality would be nonsensical), this approach, as the preceding discussion suggests, ultimately offers us little guidance in terms of theorizing and orienting ourselves ethically to *the temporally simultaneous existence of multiple worlds* as stipulated by the pluriverse. That is, theorizing the condition of possibility for multiple worlds, while deeply important, is not the same as attending to and caring for those worlds which exist, and the ethical quandaries that relate and shape them. And positing the radical contingency of all social orders, while certainly relevant, is not quite the same thing as realizing 'other *truths* also exist and have the right to exist' (Tlostanova and Mignolo, 2009, p. 18, emphasis added).

Put differently, the ways in which contingency and universalism have been framed, defined, and debated in the postfoundational thought literature is limiting in the context of the pluriverse. Speaking of multiple worlds as worlds, attending to the ways in which we can give weight to these worlds as worlds, and orienting ourselves to the challenge of traversing political-ethical relations as worlds interact, involves a different orientation to 'universality' and 'contingency' than is present in postfoundational political theory. This different orientation is evident even in the ways in which postfoundational thinkers use terms like 'alternative universals' or 'multiple universals' or 'worlds'. While linguistically, it may seem like these scholars are speaking pluriversally, their use of these words in the context of their work strikes as possessing a qualitatively different meaning than that which is signified by the ways in which the words 'universal', 'world', or as proposed here, 'onto-epistemology', are mobilized in the pluriverse literature. For instance, Prozorov (2014) speaks of multiple 'situations or worlds', implying that worlds are equal to situations. However, it is easy to think of situations that are not worlds in the pluriversal meaning of the word. Likewise, Butler (1992) refers to 'alternative universals', but her discussion focuses on different discursive framings of 'rape' in a legal case in the United States. Again, while different universals may be at play in that example – as in, different normative and socio-symbolic systems which locate and construct rape in different ways – it does not seem like there are different *worlds* (in the most robust sense, different onto-epistemologies) at play here. In part, this is why this book mobilizes the term onto-epistemology to signify and emphasize the qualitatively unique nature of worlds as more than 'universals'[4] (in the particular modern connotation of the word). This is also why this book argues that the anthropology literature which grounds the notion of the pluriverse (and the word 'ground' here is indeed used purposefully) is so crucial to the investigation at hand. It is through this anthropological work that we come to identify different worlds from a bottom-up, deeply relational, and very material vantage point; it is also through this grounded work that we are

---

[4] The word 'universal' is maintained, however, when engaging with those who employ the term in this way.

reminded that what is at stake here are actually existing worlds, and sets of practices and ways of knowing, and the subjects constituted therein.

For this reason, I suggest that from a pluriversal standpoint, the very intonation of words like 'universal' and 'grounds' is shifted. More exactly, in the pluriverse such words come to signify something *in excess of their meaning within the modern socio-symbolic order.* While undoubtedly postfoundational thought provides useful tools for political theorists, like myself, who seek to theorize the condition of possibility of a pluriverse (some of which are drawn upon throughout this argument), I also think that, in its current configuration, its own discursive tools limit the horizons of possibility for thinking through all facets of the pluriverse. In particular, postfoundational thought is not, perhaps, fully amenable to the part of the pluriversal project which seeks to 'multiply universality', in the sense of giving full ontological weight to worlds, and of then orienting ourselves to caring for and living relationally with multiple actually existing and 'grounded' onto-epistemologies.

As a final point, while deconstructing normativity, norms, and other foundational claims is often an important task for challenging hierarchies and relations of power, the focus on contingency that so characterizes the postfoundational literature also sometimes results in an approach that is entirely unable to contemplate ethics, 'as it tends to forget that while there certainly are normative limits we need to criticize and transgress, there are others we need to endorse and refine' (Ruti, 2015, p. 206). In other words, postfoundational thought can suffer from the limitations of a negative ontology, in which one can only assert what is not. Yet, as Mari Ruti (2015, p. 206) states, 'there are times when we need to make decisions about right and wrong, and to act accordingly'. These moments are positive; a decision has to be made, for even not making one turns out to be an ethical decision. Given that the goal of this book is to contemplate and develop tools that can help orient subjects of the modern world towards dealing with and thinking through ethical dilemmas that arise between and across temporally simultaneous and actually existing worlds, deconstruction, or always foregrounding radical contingency – while an important tool, which is mobilized throughout this text – cannot be all that we rely on lest we forgo the ever-important moment of decision and action.

A note on pragmatism: ethics without grounds

While the focus of this section has largely been on postfoundational thought, a brief reflection on antifoundational ethics is merited. Antifoundationalism is often realized in its ethical form as pragmatism. If there are no foundations, then 'instead of accepting the imperatives and laws of traditional epistemology and moral philosophy, one should finally come to understand that our only responsibility is to our fellow human beings in the world of practice (there is no other)' (Schulenberg, 2017, p. 276). Pragmatists try to bypass disputes that may be unresolvable, particularly those regarding questions of ontology and epistemology, and instead focus on possible consequences in concrete situations (Sil and Katzenstein, 2010). In a recent essay, Hutchings (2019, p. 123) has alluded to a pragmatist approach to global ethics in the context of the pluriverse:

> I am suggesting, therefore, that taking pluriversality seriously means shifting our understanding of global ethics away from seeing it as a route to determining answers to questions of global justice and toward seeing it as an embodied, reflective practice contingently attached to specific goals and contexts. This means learning how to live with bracketing ontological and ethical commitments, and learning how to discriminate ethical priorities within complex and power-laden situations. In this respect, it is helpful to remember that such bracketing and discrimination are part of everyday ethical practice everywhere.

On the one hand, I am, to some extent, sympathetic to this viewpoint, in that it does 'ground' our ethical dilemmas in the pluriverse (in the anthropological sense that I use the term). I am ultimately motivated by the actual dilemmas and relations between onto-epistemologies, and I am concerned with developing tools to navigate these relations ethically within/from my onto-epistemology, the modern world. However, I am unsure if a full pragmatic turn is conducive to the pluriverse. Bracketing ontological, epistemological, and ethical commitments, in some ways, seems to miss the very challenge of the pluriverse. It seems to me that a huge part of the pluriversal challenge to existing approaches in Global Ethics is that it foregrounds different ontologies and epistemologies, and therefore ethical commitments, in the most robust sense. Different onto-epistemologies, and the ways these worlds relate and are related through relations of power, constitute the very landscape in and through which practical and grounded ethical dilemmas emerge. Attempting to sidestep such issues strikes me as somewhat impossible, and potentially dangerous. So very often, a commitment to pragmatism ends up as a commitment to the status quo, as what is seen as 'doable' and which consequences are judged to be 'good' are shaped by prevailing logics, epistemes, and ontologies, and particularly those that occupy privileged positions in relations of power.

To be fair, Hutchings highlights that such bracketing is a part of ethical practices that occur everywhere and every day. I agree with this claim: sometimes, perhaps even frequently, the moment of ethical decision ends up being pragmatic, and not premised on some deep onto-epistemic commitment. It is also important to remember that onto-epistemic differences may not be of particular ethical-political significance in every encounter between and across worlds. We must be careful not to (over)project the significance of deep and pervasive differences when they may not be of primary concern. For instance, consider another brief exchange between de la Cadena and Nazario, in which they were discussing the illness of Nazario's grandson: 'Once I asked [Nazario] why he was not able to cure José Hernán, his grandson, who was suffering from stomachaches. He looked at me, and with a you've-got-to-be-kidding-me smile said, *Because up here I do not have antibiotics*' (de la Cadena, 2015, p. xxii, emphasis in original). de la Cadena's orientation towards difference, and towards hearing/seeing the differences that exist between her world and the world of Nazario, including varied healing knowledges and medicinal practices, led her astray in this exchange. Indeed, while Nazario's world certainly involves unique 'know-how', meaning inseparable knowledge and practices (de la Cadena, 2015, p. xx), Nazario himself was aware that 'depending on the circumstances, many knowledges, things, and practices were more effective than what he knew and did' (de la Cadena, 2015, p. xxiii). And incorporating these alternative knowledges did not need to involve some onto-epistemic shift or deep reflection on Nazario's behalf. Instead, these ontological and epistemological concerns could be bracketed, and the medical epistemology of antibiotics could sit alongside Nazario's healing 'know-how' without requiring one to be subsumed or reconciled with the other. 'Learning, in this case about antibiotics, did not replace Nazario's healing practices; rather, it extended his knowledge: knowing about antibiotics meant to know more, not to know better' (de la Cadena, 2015, p. xxii). This 'knowing more' did not require Nazario to shed or question his own practices/knowing. It simply provided a wider breadth of tools on which to draw upon so as to address concerns as best as possible. Such an approach is, I suggest, in line with a pragmatist ethics as outlined by Hutchings. It is also akin (although of course not equivalent) to other approaches advanced by some Indigenous leaders and scholars. For instance, Inuvialuit political leader Rosemarie Kuptana (2014) speaks of the Inuit practice of 'principled pragmatism'. As Zoe Todd explains, Kuptana's principled pragmatism is 'a practice of negotiating across simultaneous sameness and difference in order to contend with the paradoxes and twists of colonialism and the colonial nation-state' (2018, p. 65).[5] This practice of negotiating across sameness and difference also shares certain parallels with the *ch'ixi* realm-based ethical position put forth by Andean intellectual Silvia Rivera Cusicanqui (2012; 2015; 2018) – I discuss this approach more fully in the next section.

---

[5] I return to Todd's work, and her exploration of 'principled pragmatism' (Kuptana, 2014) in Chapter 7.

At the same time, however, I believe that it is important to hold a healthy scepticism of the potentiality of a pragmatist pluriversal ethics, particularly for those of the modern world (which is my primary concern in this text). For instance, in the case of earth-beings or more-than-human beings, like the Whanganui River, the competing ontological commitments between the moral agents (on the one hand, the people of the Whanganui Iwi, who know nature as relational kin, and on the other hand, the modern New Zealand state which constructs nature as property or nature as distinct from humans) form the very basis for the ethical dilemma itself. Sidestepping these issues – pragmatically bracketing onto-epistemic concerns and commitments, and their moral salience – would greatly impede one's ability to understand the moral dilemma, the power relations at play, and the nature of the contestation in ethical quandaries like this. Furthermore, as argued extensively in Chapter 2, it is also clear that modernity has not had to grapple seriously with onto-epistemological differences; it has instead conceived itself the whole of the real, and in so doing, committed violent erasure of other ways of being/knowing. I fear that a pragmatic approach to a pluriversal ethics for the modern world, while perhaps useful in some ethical dilemmas, will make it too easy for the modern world to continue to perpetuate such epistemic and ontological erasures, to be ignorant to the fact that it is not the only world.

The *Ch'ixi* realm and Rivera's decolonial praxis

In this final section, I turn to the decolonial praxis of Aymara sociologist Silvia Rivera Cusicanqui (2012; 2015; 2018), particularly as it has been presented by Marcos Scauso (2021).[6] While Rivera does not in a general sense use the word 'ethics' to describe her approach, I believe that her use of the *ch'ixi* realm (Rivera, 2015) to ground her decolonial praxis is in line with postmodernist approaches to ethics that see cultural and cross-group translation, dialogue, and exchange as 'not about reaching agreement in conditions of fair argumentation but about expanding the range of understandings of the universal and constructing new, always revisable, understandings in the light of interaction with other points of view' (Hutchings, 2018, p. 63). Or, as Scauso (2021, 172) writes, Rivera 'carefully listens to [I]ndigenous insights, finding convergences of voices, which [then] help her to construct another way to think about politics and act in the world' (see also Rivera, 2015). For

---

[6] Most of Rivera's work is published in Spanish; for this reason, much of my engagement with her work is through the careful reading provided by Scauso (2021), although I do consult her articles that are available in English (see, for example, Rivera, 2010; 2012). I very much acknowledge that this is, of course, a limitation of my engagement with her work here.

this reason, I suggest that when read as a decolonial ethics, Rivera's praxis offers a decolonial approach to ethics that could fall into the 'alternative' camp in Hutchings's schematic.

Rivera (2018) develops her praxis starting from the cosmological ideas of Pacha.[7] Fausto Reinaga (2014, p. 234; also cited in Scauso, 2021, p. 84) describes Pachamama as follows:

> Every planet of each system, every system of each galaxy exists inside laws of cohesion and interdependence. From their joined work, or, better yet, from their solidary movement emerges the being and the existence of each galaxy, each system, each planet, each man. ... The Mayan thinker had reached the conclusion that man was created by the same creators of earth and that he was not an exceptional being inside of nature; he is only one part in it. He realized that man, just like nature, had to obey the laws of nature, just like plants, beasts, birds, insects.

Pachamama is an ontology premised on an interconnected cosmos. As Scauso (2021, p. 84) argues, in starting from Pachamama, this cosmology necessarily posits an ontology of equality and difference. On the one hand, all things are connected, sharing matter and/or energy, constituted by shared elements of nature. The very fact that everything shares the elements of the cosmos provides a commonality for every existence. At the same time, the endless possibilities of compositions that might emerge from, or exist in, Pachamama foregrounds difference. The equality inherent to Pachamama does not obfuscate difference, but is rather premised upon it.

> The fact that each entity is different and is a distinct part of the complex aggregate that makes up Pachamama grants equal status to every life or inert existence. Since it is based on the idea that entities are separate and missing something vis-à-vis each other, difference appears as a negative principle of equality. (Scauso, 2021, p. 85)[8]

---

[7] Pacha roughly means earth (world, landscape, soil, time) and Mama roughly translates to mother (soul and essence). Following Scauso (2021), I use Pacha and Pachamama interchangeably to refer to the Andean cosmic vision discussed here.

[8] A notion of radical equality coming from the cosmos clearly shares much overlap with the postfoundational political thought perspective as described earlier at the beginning of the 'Postmodernist ethics' section. This again demonstrates why I think that Rivera's decolonial praxis could arguably be included under the 'postmodernist ethics' umbrella, especially when considered from the vantage point of Hutchings's schematic (2010), which has been used to organize this chapter. However, as discussed later in this section, there is a productive element to Rivera's approach that I think renders it distinct from postmodernist ethics more generally. For this reason, I have included this discussion under its own subheading.

While Rivera's decolonial praxis starts from this ontological premise, it is important to emphasize that she is also careful not to essentialize Pacha as a foundational bedrock (Scauso, 2021, p. 172). Instead, Rivera prioritizes the importance of dialoguing with others and shows how her own position as a co-interpreter in relationships (as she, too, is embedded in the cosmos) enables her to construct a possibility of knowing (Rivera, 2015). This emphasis constitutes an important move. In locating herself as an epistemological resource equal to (and not above) all other entities in the cosmos, knowledge becomes 'the result of a relationship among equal subjects'. There is no longer a 'knower' who 'knows'; knowledge itself comes from equal subjects sharing epistemological equality. 'Due to this de-essentialization of the Cosmos, Rivera moves the possibility of knowing away from the essence of entities and towards experiences of relationships' (Scauso, 2021, pp. 172–3, emphasis in the original), which themselves can be, and often are, experienced differently by different (but equal) subjects. This understanding of multiplicity, as Rivera asserts (2018), emerges from Andean ideas of diversity which are premised on relationships of equality that lead to productive exchange.

Adopting this vantage point, then, involves what Rivera (2015, p. 228) calls 'senti-pensar': 'the possibility of thinking based on complex feelings and to feel based on complex thoughts' (Scauso, 2021, p. 173). This type of thinking is contextual and momentary; it involves the 'inexplicably complex feelings and thoughts that are used by an interpreter to reconstruct experiences of relationships meaningfully'. It requires the thinker (who is equal amongst many other thinkers) to dwell in ongoing exchanges in and through which meaning is weaved together in various ways. And, given that Pacha is not an essentialized bedrock for judgement, these 'weaved narratives' (Scauso, 2021, pp. 173–5) must again *all* be viewed as equally valid. While this may feel counter-intuitive, this also then includes colonial narratives and relationships – these must be viewed as equally valid too. The lack of bedrock means that nothing can be judged a priori. Instead, there is a radical element of uncertainty and incommensurability (Rivera, 2018) that is consistent with Andean cosmological notions of Pacha, and which includes a space called *Khä Pacha*, 'the world of what does not yet exist, of what is unknown, which emerges as a force in permanent displacement, which confronts a permanent disjuction' (Rivera, 2015, p. 212; translated by and cited in Scauso, 2021, p. 177). The cosmological ontology of Pacha, which includes *Khä Pacha,* encompasses all that does exist, and all that might yet come to be. In this space, a space of both endless possible and existing difference, everything must be equal.

As Scauso aptly notes, however, this vantage point seems to lead to a political conundrum. If all voices, narratives, relationships, and knowledges are equally and inherently authorized, on what grounds would one assert that others should transform their oppressive tendencies (2021, p. 176)? This could be extended further: how do we even know that certain tendencies are oppressive?

To respond to this, Rivera asserts a 'profession of faith, which is based on the idea that decolonization can only be realized in practice' (2015, p. 28; translated by and cited in Scauso, 2021, p. 177). That is, Rivera makes a profession of faith, an epistemological wager, that settles (a momentary) classifying boundary which can demand the restructuring of colonial relations. Significantly, this boundary emerges from convergences of narratives, meaning 'the continuities, connections, and sharedness that can be established between meanings throughout space and time' (Scauso, 2021, p. 179). For instance, 'the reality' of multiple decolonial voices, the convergences of experiences of oppressions, and the work of weaving these together, allows for a (momentary, non-transcendental) assertion to be made and sustained, which can then constitute a standpoint in and from which to judge other assertions and relations. These continuities thus 'emphasize the non-arbitrary status of some ways of knowing, being, and enacting' (Scauso, 2021, p. 179); in so doing, the narratives or relationships that emerge from these convergences can serve as an 'ethical compass' (Rivera, 2018, p. 80) that can orient us towards enacting new ethico-political horizons. At the same time, it is crucial to foreground that taking such a profession of faith involves an ongoing reflexivity; the 'moment of elevation, validation, authorization, and legitimation', in which a particular convergence is woven together and foregrounded, is a moment of 'epistemic precarity' (Scauso, 2021, pp. 180–1). This profession of faith, while aware of the impossibilities of foundations more broadly, is therefore a positive orientation that resists the postmodernist tendency towards deconstruction alone. Taking a profession of faith is to orient oneself to the constructive side of meaning, to the ways in which our interweavings can be productive in the creation and recreation of spaces and relationships that serve as sites of solidarity.

In some ways, the productive capacities of this decolonial approach are what bring Rivera to the *ch'ixi* realm (2012; 2015). 'The notion of *ch'ixi*, like many others (*allqa, ayni*), reflects the Aymara idea of something that is and is not at the same time. ... The notion of *ch'ixi* ... expresses the parallel coexistence of multiple cultural differences that do not extinguish but instead antagonize and complement each other' (Rivera, 2012, p. 105, emphasis in original). The world of *ch'ixi* is thus distinct from hybridity, as it does not assume that mixing two things can and will result in a third that is entirely distinct (Rivera, 2012). The *ch'ixi* realm maintains difference but sees difference as complimentary: it works as a metaphorical principle 'which re-organizes life into a logic of equality that is based on the idea *complementarity*' (Scauso, 2021, p. 184, emphasis in original). In this reorganization of life into complements, Rivera's decolonial praxis involves prioritizing confrontations and convergences so as to weave together different narratives, narratives that do not need to be equivalent or map onto one another directly, but that rather serve as complementary resources or stories that broaden the terrains of decolonial struggles (Asher, 2017). These stories, in their complementarity (as opposed to their equivalence), can thereby confront the dominating tendencies of thick universalisms and colonialism in a more fulsome way, but without resorting to grounding the 'truths' of these stories in some new universal narrative. In many ways, I believe that the ongoing dialogue between de la Cadena and Nazario (de la Cadena, 2015), presented throughout this book, demonstrates the fruitfulness of such convergences. Together, de la Cadena and Nazario in and through their relationship alternatively share meaning and contest meaning, and in so doing, construct new connections of meaning that both tie their worlds together without equating them and without losing sight of the differences therein. In the moments of such convergence and confrontation, 'momentary maps of relationships, struggle, and projects' (Scauso, 2021, p. 187) can emerge through narrative weavings, which themselves do not form a superior or pure grounding for knowledge claims. Instead, these confrontations, and momentary maps, can be unsettled by other 'others'; listening to the convergences and meanings that emerge through ongoing confrontations ensures that no particular narrative is 'over-expanded' in a particular context (Scauso, 2021, p. 197).

The consequences of this position, of a decolonial praxis in/from the *ch'ixi* realm, are myriad. First, because it is in the moment of confrontation that momentary boundaries are drawn, the 'real' experience of colonialism, class oppression, gender oppression, and so on, cannot be predetermined or universalized (Scauso, 2021, p. 187). These things must be understood by looking at how they manifest in particular and contextually specific ways in the global political economy (Asher, 2017, p. 521). Such a task is iterative and ongoing; it 'demands a constant return to the possibility of listening for moments and voices of confrontation' (Scauso, 2021, p. 187). Second, it is also for this reason that Rivera's decolonial praxis avoids a romanticization of otherness, or a static conception of what it means to be and know from a particular position. As Scauso notes, this means that ways of being and knowing can be re-valued without claiming to correspond to a 'pure' pre-colonial past, an 'objective' truth, a 'real' human nature, or 'authentic' form of Indigeneity. Instead, 'the profession of faith in the sharedness of convergences epistemically re-values the multiple "impurities" that confront universalisms and domination' (Scauso, 2021, p. 196). It is this position that allows Rivera to maintain some role for colonial entities like the state or development (Asher, 2017), which are now understood as parts of constructing relations, processes, 'habits, gestures, modes of interaction, and ideas about the world' (Rivera, 2012, p. 106). This position thereby also avoids treating the modern world 'as if it were a stadium or a theatre' (Rivera, 2012, p. 106) which people can exit in and out of; it foregrounds the socio-political-economic reality that relations tie worlds together in complex ways, and it highlights the fact that people often 'maintain a double residence [where one residence cannot be subsumed into the other] and live "straddling two worlds"' (Rivera, 2010, p. 41).

I believe that Rivera's decolonial praxis, particularly as presented by Scauso (2021), can certainly be thought of as an ethics for the pluriverse. It is attuned to radical difference as well as the ways in which our differences are complexly intertwined. It foregrounds the importance of deconstruction (unsettling dominant narratives through confrontations with other narratives) while also asserting constructive orientations (that themselves emerge from productive sites of confrontation and meaning-making). It is committed to enacting a decolonial politics while maintaining reflexivity about what that may or may not mean. All of these qualities suggest that it is a fruitful orientation to ethics in the pluriverse. Despite this, however, I have one reservation about the appropriateness of this approach as a pluriversal ethics from the standpoint of my world, modernity. This is perhaps best illustrated by considering Rivera's argument that Pacha, the ontological starting point for this approach, works as both 'an abstract concept of *metaphorical and interpretative* nature, and a practical tool to walk the here/now of daily life' (Rivera, 2015, p. 207; translated by and cited in Scauso, 2021, p. 184, italics in original). According to Rivera, Pacha works as a metaphorical principle that, as noted previously, reorganizes life into a logic of equals that are complementary, and thus can serve as an ethical compass for our actions in the present. My fear, however, is that the modern world, which is premised on a particular understanding of ontology and epistemology, may all too easily warp this understanding of Pacha, and the ways in which it organizes life, *as a metaphor*.

The works of scholars Sarah Hunt (2014), Zoe Todd (2016a) and Vanessa Watts (2013) are instructive on this point. As Hunt (2014, p. 27) writes, 'Ontology is, ironically, not a word that comes to mind when I think of Indigenous ontologies. What comes to mind, instead, are stories.' Yet, stories in this sense are not equivalent to what the modern world understands as stories. Contrasting a Place-Thought frame (Haudenosaunee and Anishnaabe cosmologies) to an epistemological-ontological frame (the modern world), Watts (2013, p. 22) points out that Place-Thought understandings of the world are often easily viewed as 'mythic by "modern" society'; 'our stories are considered to be an alternative mode of understanding and interpretation rather than "real" events'. But these stories, as Watts beautifully illustrates, are not 'alternative modes of understanding and interpretation'; they are 'embodied expressions of stories, laws, and songs' (Todd, 2016a, p. 9) that are bound together in Indigenous self-determination. Stories, from this standpoint, are not interpretative or metaphorical; 'human thought and action are ... derived from a literal expression of particular places and historical events' (Watts, 2013, p. 23) from these cosmological positionalities. As Todd (2016a, p. 9) argues, when Indigenous interlocutors are not present 'to hold the use of Indigenous stories and laws to account [, this] flattens, distorts and erases the embodied, legal-governance and spiritual aspects of Indigenous thinking'. I interpret this to mean that Indigenous stories are all too easily emptied of the embodied/real content when employed in/by the modern world. Because Indigenous thinking is embodied and place specific, Indigenous stories are not stories in the modern sense of the word; Indigenous stories exceed modern understandings of stories as that which are simply metaphorical and interpretive, working to describe something (and therefore existing apart from that thing). In contradistinction, Indigenous stories, and the human and more-than-human agential beings that operate in them, are real. Watts (2013, p. 21) foregrounds this point when recounting the creation story of Sky Woman. '[This event] was not imagined or fantasized. This is not lore, myth or legend. These histories are not versions of "and the moral of the story is...". This is what happened.' I have attempted to emphasize a similar point throughout this book in relation to earth-beings and more-than-human beings. These beings, as agential entities in different worlds, are not metaphors for nature (where nature is understood in the modern sense). Rather, for these different worlds, nature itself is agential in the fullest sense (see also Watts, 2013, for more on this point). Both stories and nature, from these cosmological vantage points, 'are alive and embody legal obligations through which Indigenous people are fighting for self-determination, sovereignty and cultural-political existence' (Slater, 2021, p. 3).

To be sure, I do not think that when Rivera uses the term 'metaphor' she necessarily means it in the modern sense (in fact, I suspect she does not). However, when thinking about how modern subjects can therefore access Pacha and the *ch'ixi* realm as a basis for a pluriversal ethics, I find myself in a bind. On the one hand, I could attempt to access these spaces/places as metaphors. However, as I have learned from the work of scholars like Watts, Todd, and Hunt, as well as from the very concept of the pluriverse more generally, when the modern world casts these worlding practices/relations/ knowings as metaphors it often serves as a kind of violence because the modern world does not know stories in the way that Indigenous communities know/ embody stories. Stories, from the embedded location and epistemological vantage point of the modern world, are easily downgraded to something (perhaps cannot be other than) 'less than real'. I worry that if one was to assert the *ch'ixi* realm as a starting point for a pluriversal ethics for the modern world, there would be a tendency to conceive of this realm as metaphor alone, a theoretical move which fundamentally and directly contradicts the pluriversal project, which seeks to give ontological weight to other onto-epistemologies. On the other hand, I am not entirely sure if modern subjects can access the realness of Indigenous stories and metaphors in a direct sense. For modern subjects to try and directly access the *ch'ixi* realm and Pacha as a starting point for ethics, for example, feels somewhat disingenuous: these are spaces/places and cosmic orientations that exceed the modern onto-epistemic framework. Glossing over this point, I believe, would be a failure to acknowledge fully the limits to knowing that operate in the pluriverse: as a modern subject, I do not know Pacha, and I do not know what it is to reside in the *ch'ixi* realm. As a result, either treating Pacha as metaphor or asserting that modern subjects can know Pacha directly seems problematic. In both instances, there seems to be great potential for distortion, misrepresentation (Todd, 2016a, p. 9), and/or appropriation in using the *ch'ixi* realm as a starting point for a pluriversal ethical approach for the modern world.

I return to this problem time and time again. To be certain, I do not want to overstate the excesses between worlds. I find the work of Rivera to be crucially important in part because of its emphasis on sharedness, convergences, and the ways in which two worlds can (and often do) occupy the same space without being reduced to a sameness. At the same time, I am acutely aware of the unequal ways in which certain people have been, at least implicitly, granted the ability to traverse worlds and boundaries, while others are cast as stuck and timeless. As John Borrows (2009, p. 415) writes: 'We [Indigenous peoples] are told "you can't go there" when we want to trek beyond imposed ideological boundaries, which stereotype us as past-tense peoples. The same restrictions cannot be said to apply to non-Indigenous people.' That is, modern subjects are apparently able to move through time and land (and perhaps worlds?), while Indigenous peoples are often treated as static, unchanging, and stuck. This, on the one hand, is of course absurd in that it denies the fact that Indigenous worlds are not fixed; they are 'active, mobile, relational' (Hunt, 2014, p. 30) and dynamic. On the other hand, however, this uneven distribution of 'movement' is also absurd because the 'ease' with which moderns can supposedly traverse time and place can also implicitly suggest, particularly in the context of the pluriverse, that they can somehow access other worlds in some fulsome sense. This, I believe, is to some extent incorrect. As previously discussed in the section 'Discourse ethics and Linklater's post-Westphalian communities', there are limits to knowing across worlds – this is, in part, what gives worlds such weight. It is also for this reason that I am uncomfortable with suggesting that the modern world could thus access, in some robust way, the *ch'ixi* realm as a basis for a pluriversal ethics, as *ch'ixi* and Pacha are not part of the modern world's onto-epistemic framework.

Thus, while I in no way mean this as a wholesale rejection of Rivera's decolonial praxis (I think rather the opposite, as there is much to learn from Rivera's approach, particularly in terms of strategies for finding convergences), I do have some apprehension about this approach as a way for the modern world to contemplate ethical horizons in the pluriverse, as just outlined. This apprehension, in many ways, also takes us back to the questions raised by the double life of Gyack, or the corroboree frog, which helped me introduce the challenge of the pluriverse in the first chapter of the book. How can we care for that which we do not know? How can we 'create an awareness of different social worlds when all [that is] at one's disposal is terms which belong to one's own' (Strathern, 1987, p. 256)? And of particular import for this discussion, how can we ground (even if it is a thin, tentative, contingent, non-transcendental grounding) our ethical practices in something that we cannot access, something that we cannot know, something that the very onto-epistemic framework of our world cannot accommodate in any direct way? Rivera's decolonial praxis is embedded in Pacha; reconnecting with Pacha offers the possibility of a non-essentialist and de-hierarchical way of conceiving of difference and building connection across difference. Yet, I do not know if the modern world can (re)connect with Pacha, in the way that Rivera asserts it, as Pacha is a cosmology that is distinct from the modern onto-epistemology. Or at the very least (and so as not to preclude the possibility that the modern world itself may fundamentally evolve through its encounters with other worlds), I am not sure if the modern world can (re)connect with Pacha in its current enactment. While worlds are constantly changing and shifting in and through confrontations with one another, and while paying particular attention to convergences can helpfully illuminate how these confrontations are productive for meaning-making, I believe that the modern world, in its current configuration, needs additional tools and resources from which to contemplate, access, or conceive of non-modern entities and spaces – like the *ch'ixi* realm, Pacha, and more-than-human beings – in a way that neither downgrades the onto-epistemic existence of these things nor romantically (and therefore problematically) appropriates them for itself. How can subjects of the modern world contemplate non-modern entities, spaces, and cosmologies while not being able to know them, in that the modern world is not in relation with such entities and spaces?

As the remainder of this book demonstrates, I believe that one possible 'toolkit' to assist in such a task is a critical and political ethics of care. As Chapter 8 in particular shows, care can orient modern subjects towards other onto-epistemologies and the non-modern entities that co-constitute these worlds without requiring modern subjects to *know* these cosmologies and entities. This discussion therefore does not seek to reject the decolonial praxis of the *ch'ixi* realm put forward by Rivera. Instead, I think that an ethics of care, as the subsequent argument shows, can usefully position modern subjects to engage in the type of solidarity-building work that

Rivera's framework points towards. More simply, care ethics can provide a meta-theoretical orientation or framework that can enable modern subjects to begin the type of work that is necessary to weave together narratives at moments of convergence. It can orient modern subjects to listen for other 'others', especially those other 'others' that are outside of the modern world. While it is beyond the breadth of the current discussion to explore this more fully here, a fruitful site for ongoing work in relation to building pluriversal ethics will certainly be investigating further the overlaps, parallels, divergences, and productive potentialities of intertwining narratives of care with the decolonial praxis put forth by Rivera.

The pluriversal challenge to Global Ethics

This chapter has sought to review existing approaches in the field of Global Ethics in order to parse out their compatibility with the pluriverse: can prominent approaches to global ethics, including moral cosmopolitanism, discourse ethics, and ethical approaches related to postmodernist thought, provide useful vantage points from which to contemplate the ethical landscape of the pluriverse, and the particular ethical dilemmas that arise therein? The first two approaches – which fall under the rationalist approaches to global ethics – do not hold up to the pluriversal challenge. Moral cosmopolitanism is unable to contemplate difference at its most deep and pervasive, as is the case in the pluriverse, where there are multiple onto-epistemologies. Discourse ethics is unsuited as a pluriversal ethics due to its implicit assumption of knowability across difference; as the pluriversal anthropological literature demonstrates, knowing fully in the context of the pluriverse is not always possible. There are sometimes ontological and epistemological 'gaps', 'excesses', or 'intranslatabilities' between worlds; no amount of dialogue will close these gaps fully. Postmodernist ethics, I suggest, offers more potential – in that certain concepts like 'the political' provide tools for theorizing the very possibility of a pluriverse – but ultimately fails as an approach to ethics in the pluriverse, a landscape which requires contemplating the existence of a multitude of temporally simultaneous and existing worlds. And finally, while the decolonial praxis of Rivera is undeniably well positioned to contemplate ethical horizons in the pluriverse, I wonder whether it can offer a starting point for the modern world specifically to think/enact a pluriversal ethics given that it departs from a cosmology that is very different from – and perhaps even unknowable to – the modern onto-epistemology.

Nonetheless, interrogating the literature in this way is a necessary step in addressing the pluriversal challenge to Global Ethics. One cannot orient oneself to the pluriverse, as a political landscape, from the perspective of one universal truth, and from the impoverished understanding of difference that such a stance implies (à la moral cosmopolitanism). The pluriverse is the acknowledgement of a multiplicity of worlds, or onto-epistemologies, and differences here are at their most pervasive. The pluriverse is not simply a new multiculturalism; it does not refer to different viewpoints, interests, or claims in a singular world. Rather, the pluriverse refers to multiple worlds in the most robust sense, and difference cannot be glossed over or bracketed away. Relatedly, the pervasiveness of these differences means that we cannot assume knowability or translatability in the context of the pluriverse (à la discourse ethics). There may be an 'excess', or an incommensurability, in terms of dialoguing and understanding between and across worlds. Dealing with such unknowability is a particular challenge in the pluriversal context, when the very ontological, epistemological, and/or axiological significance of someone/something (a river, a mountain, for instance) may be inaccessible to certain groups of people or moral subjects involved in the dilemma. Lastly, while differences are primary in the pluriverse, these differences are not fully contemplatable when the focus is on contingency (postmodernist ethics); they are actually existing, and onto-epistemologies constitute their own internal truths. In this way, the pluriversal project not only orients us towards the idea that there are multiple truths, but further articulates that these truths have the right to their status as truths. Thinking of onto-epistemologies in the pluriversal context as voidal (emerging from the negative, the ground without grounds) or unfounded, even if in terms of a complex interplay between universality and contingency, is not quite in the spirit of the pluriverse. The modern intonation inherent in the terms 'contingency', 'universal', 'ground', and 'foundation' is insufficient, or at the very least limiting, when seeking to imagine ways to grapple with the pluriverse and a pluriversal ethics.

In some ways, to return to the beginning of the chapter, it is perhaps unsurprising that these approaches (with the exception of Rivera's work) – rooted in modernity and its commitment to one-worldism – are unable to attend fully to the political-ethical landscape of the pluriverse. Nonetheless, I believe that there is one approach in the Global Ethics literature that can provide a vantage point from which to contemplate a pluriversal ethics for the modern world. The next chapters turns to this approach, and begins to present the hypothesis that a critical, political, feminist ethics of care can help orient modern ethical theory and modern subjects towards the pluriverse in a way that facilitates ethical reflection and action across worlds, thereby building a pluriversal ethics.

4

A Critical, Political Ethics of Care

Another alternative approach in Global Ethics in Kimberly Hutchings's (2010) schematic is feminist ethics, which most broadly can be understood as arising from a critique of the patriarchal assumptions and traditions underpinning mainstream modernist approaches to ethics. This book argues that a particular approach to feminist ethics, the ethics of care, provides a useful vantage point from which to build a pluriversal ethics. The purpose of this chapter is to introduce the ethics of care, highlight key debates, developments and advances in the literature on care ethics, and describe precisely how I understand care ethics as an approach to moral thinking that is both critical and political. In so doing, this chapter lays the groundwork for the final chapters of this text, in which I rethink global ethics along pluriversal lines using a critical and political ethics of care.

In order to introduce the ethics of care, it is helpful to first begin with a discussion of the feminist critique of moral philosophy and ethics, and to give a general introduction to feminist ethics. As feminists like Seyla Benhabib (1987, p. 158) have argued, dominant moral epistemologies, like the rationalist approaches to global ethics, define the moral domain based on a strong distinction between justice (the right) and the good life (the good). This distinction – and the ways in which this distinction is intimately intertwined with other binaries that constitute the modern world, including the public/private divide, the binary between reason and emotion, and the patriarchal dichotomy of masculine/feminine – 'lead[s] to a *privatization* of women's experience and to the exclusion of its consideration from a moral point of view' (Benhabib, 1987, p. 158, emphasis in original). More specifically, Benhabib argues that 'questions of the good life', including questions about kinship, love, friendship, and virtue, were key to moral thinking in ancient and medieval systems; 'in such moral systems, the rules that govern just relations within the human community are embedded in a more encompassing concept of the good life. This good life, the *telos* of man, is defined ontologically with reference to man's place in the cosmos at large' (1987, p. 159). However, modernity, which is characterized by an axiological shift in which Man sees himself as the master of Nature (as argued in Chapter 2), fundamentally alters this understanding of morality. Now, Man is 'emancipated from cosmology and from an all-encompassing world view that normatively limits man's relation to nature' (Benhabib, 1987, p. 160); Man, as the 'orderer' of the universe, is separate and above Nature and the cosmos, and Man is now responsible for organizing social life. With this separation between Man and Nature, another bifurcation manifests: the distinction between justice and the good life emerges to protect the autonomy of the self as distinct from the cosmos. Justice, as that which will provide the legitimate basis for the social order, becomes the focus of moral theory as atomistic individuals 'become' orderers of their universe.

This shift in orientation to the relationship between Man and Nature, and corresponding bifurcation of justice and the good life, is evident in some of the discussion from the previous two chapters, where morality, and answers to questions of what 'ought' to be done, is either 'defined as what all would have rationally to agree to in order to ensure civil peace and prosperity (Hobbes, Locke); or … is derived from the rational form of moral law alone (Rousseau, Kant)' (Benhabib, 1987, p. 160). Questions of the good life now belong to the individual, who can define the good life for themself *because of justice*: so long as the social contract and rights-claims of individuals are upheld and respected (justice), autonomous moral subjects can pursue their own interests, desires, and live well (the good life). In this way, moral autonomy and personal autonomy are also made distinct; 'people gain moral autonomy when they use their reason to discern which principles ought to be followed; personal autonomy is their entitlement to pursue their own visions of the good in their own way' (Meyers and Kittay, 1987, p. 4).

One of the consequences of this separation between justice and the good life is that a hierarchy emerges, in which justice became the whole of moral theory, while questions of the good life are personalized and relegated to the 'private sphere'. The private sphere, in contrast to the 'public sphere', is a related dichotomy that is of particular significance in dominant modern political thought. The private sphere is the realm of familial relations, while the public sphere is the realm of politics and economics. These spheres, conceived of in this dichotomous manner, are separate and distinct; issues of the home have no place in the public. As feminists have long pointed out, however, the public/private divide is related to another binary, masculine/feminine, which is fundamental to the patriarchal gender-sex system, in which notions of masculinity and femininity serve as a powerful system of codification, which organizes our social lives discursively and materially, and which shapes embodied identity. Importantly, and as noted in Chapter 2, this coding of the world is not neutral; rather, under patriarchy, that which is coded masculine is valued above that which is coded feminine. Mapping the masculine/feminine binary on to the binaries of justice/good life, the right/the good, and public/private reveals a pattern, where those on the left-hand side of the divide are valued above those on the right-hand side:[1]

> Masculine/Feminine
> Justice/Good Life
> The Right/The Good
> Public/Private
> Men/Women

These intimately related binaries create a series of boundaries which serve to exclude women and other feminized actors from moral thinking and public life. These binaries, and related boundaries, are therefore not simply conceptual; they come to shape social relations in very concrete ways.

In addition to excluding women (and the issues that women are often responsible for, given our particular socio-political-economic arrangements) from moral and political considerations, these binaries, and the systems of codification which value one part of the dichotomy over the other, also serve to devalue and even exclude whole ways of moral thinking and deliberation from moral philosophy. For example, Benhabib (1987, p. 163) discusses how the dominant approach to moral thinking, based on rationalism, relies on taking the standpoint of the 'generalized other', 'which requires us to view each and every individual as a rational being entitled to the same rights and duties we would want to ascribe to ourselves'. In assuming this standpoint, evident in many of the approaches described in the previous chapter, we abstract from the 'individuality and concrete identity of the other' (Benhabib, 1987, p. 163). Moreover, in privileging the rationalist approach to ethics, which sees taking the standpoint of the generalized other as the highest form of moral thinking, modern moral philosophy also suppresses other moral voices and lines of moral inquiry, like that which takes the standpoint of the 'concrete other' by locating 'each and every rational being as an individual with a concrete history, identity, and affective-emotional constitution' (Benhabib, 1987, p. 164).

Thinking about the generalized versus the concrete other draws our attention to additional binaries in modern moral philosophy, like the separation of mind and body, and reason and emotion. For instance, contemplating concrete others and their embodied needs, interests, and

---

[1] These binaries were already introduced in Chapter 2, which argues that modernity *as a world* is constituted in part by particular gendered relations and binary thinking; in this discussion, the aim is now to demonstrate specifically how moral philosophy in modernity is characterized by these same relations.

desires means tending to their embodiment, their emotions, and our embodied and emotional relation to them. This type of moral thinking, however, is pitted against, and seen as less morally valuable than, moral theorizing which is concerned with tending to the abstract other, who can only be a disembodied other, separated from their context and contemplated using abstracted reason. Concerns about affects, emotions, bodily needs, and particular hopes and desires – the very fabric of everyday interactions – are coded feminine (as are approaches to moral thinking which foreground such things), relegated to the private sphere, and removed from discussions of justice, moral life, and other public concerns. As Sophie Bourgault (2014, p. 4) writes, from the standpoint of dominant moral political theory, meeting needs (be they emotional or corporeal) and attending to people's different hopes, desires, and interests are 'the plain stuff of everyday life, crude matters tied to necessity. As such needs do not inspire our loftiest theoretical ambitions, nor does their fulfilment seem to represent a fitting (read noble) goal for the sociopolitical creatures that we are.' Through these foundational binaries, it is not just particular gendered bodies which are excluded as legitimate moral agents in dominant approaches to modern moral philosophy: entire ethical concerns and ways of moral thinking are deemed irrelevant or insufficiently sophisticated to constitute morality as such.

More simply, these boundaries operate at the level of the *very conception of morality* and constitute understandings of morality as separate from everyday concerns and the material and relational activities which comprise our interactions. This means that morality is segregated from matters that are most fundamental to living healthy and happy lives. These 'moral boundaries' (Tronto, 1993) also co-constitute and come to define what it means to be a moral agent; masculinist notions of objectivity, reason, and autonomy define moral agents as unencumbered individuals who can access universal truths and principles via abstracted reasoning. They mark certain concerns – such as issues related to care, reproduction, kinship, family, and friends – and certain knowledges – such as those derived from contexts, relations, and emotions – as inferior approaches to moral deliberation. These binaries shape what is seen as legitimate moral epistemology, meaning 'the nature, source, and justification of moral knowledge' (Walker, 2007, p. 4). Thus, while feminist philosophers have argued that women have been, quite literally, excluded from moral philosophizing and from being seen as moral agents, the feminist critique of dominant modern moral theory runs much deeper. Feminist ethics emerged as a field of study dedicated to revealing and critiquing the patriarchal biases and binaries inherent in key theoretical assumptions in moral philosophy, including assumptions about 'the sources and content of moral principles, the process of moral deliberation, and the concept of moral agency' (Meyers and Kittay, 1987, p. 4). Feminist ethics seek to challenge the ways in which these assumptions and binaries shape moral deliberation and impact how decisions unfold in the world. And feminist ethics strive to uncover and critique the exclusions that result from the justice model of morality and moral philosophy. The ethics of care, as a particular approach to feminist ethics and moral philosophy, is exemplary of such scholarship.

The ethics of care

While the ethics of care is most frequently traced back to Carol Gilligan's (1993) work on moral psychology, care ethics has since expanded into a robust interdisciplinary research agenda (Leget *et al.*, 2019), with a range of scholarship on the ethics of care covering a variety of topics, issues, and avenues of inquiry. Despite the significant scholarship on the ethics of care, care ethics is not easily distilled into a set of rules. However, there are some characteristics of the ethics of care that unite the varied scholarship in this field. The purpose of this section is first to provide a brief introduction to the ethics of care. Then, in the following three sections, I explore more fully three debates in the ethics of care literature: the debate on the ethics of care as essentialism; the debate regarding the feasibility of the ethics of care as a 'global' ethic; and the debate over the political nature of care. Through this introductory section and by reviewing the aforementioned debates, I develop and explore my understanding of the ethics of care as a critical and political theory.

A relational ontology

First, and foremost, the ethics of care is premised upon a relational social ontology.[2] As Maurice Hamington (2018, p. 310) writes, 'we are the product

---

[2] It may be of interest to note that some care ethics scholarship has demonstrated linkages between this relational social ontology and non-modern ontologies, like 'the African concept of Ubuntu; *suma qamaña,* a collective concept of well-being that was adopted as a central value in the Bolivian constitution of 2009; and the Māori principles of whanaungatanga or relationship building' (Barnes *et al.*, 2015, p. 11, emphasis in original; see also Boulton and Brannelly, 2015). Aymara intellectual Silvia Rivera Cusicanqui's decolonial praxis (reviewed in Chapter 3), Papaschase Cree scholar Dwayne Donald's (2009) principle of 'ethical relationality', and nehiyaw political theorist Katherine Walker's (2021) recent work on Cree ethics that are based in the wholistic layers of okâwîmâwaskiy (mother earth) could also be read as sharing some key characteristics with the ethics of care as presented here. This affinity rests in how these different ways of relational thinking and knowing challenge the binary thinking and individualistic rationalism that constitute modernity. At the same time, however, I do wish to foreground that I see the ethics of care as a product of the modern world. While some scholarship links care theory more fundamentally to non-modern philosophical traditions, such as Confucianism (Li, 1994), the development of the ethics of care is most generally accredited to American feminist theorists, many of whom are cited in this chapter, who were writing in the early 1980s

of our relationships and cannot shed our social existence'. More specifically, the ethics of care 'starts from the premise that people live in and perceive the world within social relationships; moreover, this approach recognizes that these relationships are both a source of moral motivation and moral responsiveness and a basis for the construction and expression of power and knowledge' (Robinson, 1999, p. 2).

From a care ethics perspective, we are all (re)produced and sustained by our relations, including both close, personal relationships (such as those with family and friends) and broader social relations, such as systems of power and other public, social, and institutional arrangements (Hankivsky, 2004). Significantly, this claim is an ontological claim. The relational social ontology inherent in an ethics of care is not simply saying that we 'have' relations (although this is of course true); rather, the relational claim at the heart of the ethics of care refers to our very being. In a useful distinction, Kelly Oliver (2002, p. 326, emphasis in original) uses the terms '*subjectivity* to mean one's sense of oneself as an "I," as an agent, and *subject position* to mean one's position in society and history as developed through various social relationships'. From a care ethics perspective, both subjectivity and subject position, which are, of course, intimately intertwined, are (re)produced through relations.

Because we are 'inextricably interdependent' (Kittay, 2015, p. 57) in this deep relational sense, the ethics of care also understands humans as vulnerable. As the product of relations, we are always vulnerable to changes in/of relations. Our very moral selves only emerge through a relational processual becoming which is always vulnerable in its becoming. Selves do not exist outside of the shifting and fluid relations that constitute them; selves are only always a vulnerable unfolding through relations, which are themselves vulnerable. From this vantage point, then, (inter)dependence and vulnerability are not qualities possessed by some, such as the sick, poor, or weak, or something to be overcome to achieve the ideal of 'independence'. Rather, vulnerability and dependency are ontological conditions, albeit ones that manifest differently for different people across different contexts. The relational ontology of an ethics of care is therefore diametrically opposed to

---

(Engster and Hamington, 2015, p. 4), and who are themselves subjects of the modern world and trained in an academic tradition that is shaped by modernity. Care ethics, in this sense, is undoubtedly 'modern' – although, as should become apparent throughout the remainder of this chapter, the ethics of care also poses a fundamental challenge to the modern onto-epistemology. To be sure, one of the strengths of the ethics of care, as the basis for a pluriversal ethics for the modern world, is that it challenges the modern world from within, and therefore does not rely on appropriating non-modern onto-epistemologies (see the section 'The *Ch'ixi* realm and Rivera's decolonial praxis' in Chapter 3, Chapter 7, and especially Chapter 8 for more on this).

the ontological assumptions underpinning mainstream approaches to modern moral philosophy, in which humans are atomistic and independent beings who can (and should) abstract themselves from context.

To summarize, the ethics of care, as mobilized in this argument, stems from a twofold socio-ontological claim. First, we are relational beings. Second, this fact makes us vulnerable. If our very existence is relational – dependent on others – we are all susceptible to harms that may emerge through our relations. Our embodied well-being and our very identities are vulnerable and shaped by the shifting and unequal relations that comprise our lives.

A situated epistemology

As Fiona Robinson (2011a, p. 134) notes, while the relational ontology of an ethics of care is generally agreed upon, 'there is rather less agreement regarding epistemological and methodological questions in care ethics'. However, following Robinson, this argument assumes that because of this relational ontology, the ethics of care also 'eschews the epistemological certainty of moral foundationalism' (Robinson, 2011a, p. 128). Instead, like our subjectivity and subject position, knowledge, from a care ethical perspective, is relational, 'an intersubjective product constructed within communal practices of acknowledgement, correction, and critique' (Code, 1991, p. 224). 'All would-be knowers are *situated* in (typically multiple, overlapping) epistemic *communities*' (Walker, 2007, p. 64, emphasis in original). The resources for making knowledge claims, interrogating knowledge claims, and validating knowledge claims can be found in language, symbolisms, and practices which relationally tie us together. Consequently, our judgement, and particularly our moral judgement, is also dependent and vulnerable. There are not principles 'out there' that need to be accessed through rational thought; instead, moral thinking from this vantage point requires understanding how morality is situated and (re)produced in and through different relational webs. It requires critically examining the 'background assumptions working alongside or loaded into the cognitive instruments and practices of communities of inquiry' (Walker, 2007, p. 64). It demands deep examination and consideration of the world we live in, including political, economic, and other social relations and arrangements which are so often 'kept separate' from moral philosophizing. As care ethicists agree, context matters, and we must critically examine contexts in order to understand moral dilemmas and practices (see, for example, Tronto, 1993; Sevenhuijsen, 1998; Hankivsky, 2004). And finally, a care ethics approach to moral thinking means we must foreground the riskiness and vulnerability of our own moral judgement (Hutchings, 2013), which is itself the product of our own relational being and knowing. The 'multiple and ambiguous moral self [must be] aware of his or her own limitations, dependencies, vulnerability and finiteness, and [be] prepared to accept responsibility for these things' (Sevenhuijsen, 1998, p. 57).

Morality as practices

Beginning with this relational ontology and critical situated epistemology thus recasts ethics and morality in radical ways. Instead of the rationalist (or as Benhabib [1987] calls it, justice) approach to and understanding of morality, which sees morality as comprised of universal and transcendental truths that can be accessed by the impartial and rational moral philosopher, and then applied to the messy 'real' world, *morality is now understood as practices – including knowledge practices – which make up the very fabric of our everyday lives*. Of course, simply to say that morality is practices is a sweeping statement; there are many practices, and surely not all of them are about living well and doing right. Yet, by starting with a relational ontology, the ethics of care suggests more specifically that morality is practices, and particularly the practices of responsibility that allow us to maintain and repair our world and relations as well as possible. That is, because we are relational and vulnerable beings, care activities – the 'species activity that includes everything that we do to maintain, continue, and repair our "world" so that we can live in it as well as possible' (Fisher and Tronto, 1990, p. 40) – are the substance of moral practices and are the ways in which we attempt, often through many iterations, to live well, to respond to needs, and to minimize harm and suffering. Responsibility in this sense is therefore distinct from rationalist notions of responsibility or duty, which are conceived of in 'terms of obedience to some higher abstract ideal' (Prattes, 2020, p. 28). Instead, responsibility in care ethics refers to 'who gets to do what to whom and who is supposed to do what for whom' (Walker, 2007, p. 16), and the ways in which these responsibilities are already woven, and unequally distributed, in the fabric of our lives.

In this way, the ethics of care is also a 'material ethics' (Alaimo and Hekman, 2008, p. 7), as it is concerned with the practices that allow for human and non-human flourishing. It is through material practices, and attentiveness to others, that the vulnerable moral thinker comes to make moral claims. Practices of care and responsibility require attentiveness and responsiveness to the needs and vulnerabilities of others (Robinson, 1999, p. 30), particularly when others are very different from ourselves. From a care ethics perspective, the process of care thus becomes a form of enquiry (Hamington, 2018), in which ongoing attentiveness involves a 'conscious effort at de-centring the self and then centring it again' (Confortini and Ruane, 2013, p. 79) as one listens to the other and then responds to their needs. As Catia Confortini and Abigail Ruane (2013, p. 79) write, 'this weaving practice between self and other is a condition of knowing'; it is through attentive, responsive, and often material practices that moral knowledge emerges. Including knowledge practices as moral practices in the care ethical definition of morality presented here points to this intimate relation between our practices and our knowledges: 'knowledge practices are those collective, routine socio-material ways of carrying on that enable people to say "we know" with at least some degree of certainty' (Verran, 2013, p. 155).

From a care ethics perspective, it is also by paying attention to our practices that we can see if the ways in which we organize and live our lives align with our stated values and reflect on whether or not our practices and morals make sense to all those involved (Robinson, 2011b). More simply, it is through practices of care and responsibility that morality is produced and negotiated relationally. From this perspective, as Riikka Prattes (2020, p. 40, emphasis in original) argues, ignorance is an epistemology 'that *structurally* and *violently fails to perceive* existing connections'. Because moral knowledge and moral practices are so fundamentally intertwined, to be inattentive to practices of care is to ignore and neglect our relationality and the moral responsibilities that emerge through it.

Lastly, care ethics is, as just noted, also a materialist ethics as it 'asks after the effects on recipients of our care. It demands to know whether relations of care have in fact been established, maintained, or enhanced, and by extension it counsels us to consider effects on the whole web or network of care' (Noddings, 2002, p. 30). The effects of our caring practices and knowledges are significant, not only because the outcome of care practices matter (which, of course, they do), but also because it is through assessing the outcomes of practices of responsibility and care that moral knowledge and deed are tested, evaluated, and revised. From a care ethics perspective, caring is much more than a concern or sentiment for another; caring entails practices and actions in and through which moral knowledge is evaluated, challenged, and adapted. Accordingly, embodiment and performativity, as the material resources for action and practices, are of great moral significance for the ethics of care (Hamington, 2015a).

A critical ethic

For these reasons, the ethics of care completely challenges the moral boundaries that shape the rationalist model of moral thinking. Treating morality as a sphere separate from politics or social relations makes no sense if morality is the practices that emerge in and through our relations; 'the impossibility of "purifying" morality or moral knowledge or practical reason' (Walker, 2007, p. 17) is revealed by the care ethical approach. Similarly, the 'moral point of view boundary' (Tronto, 1993), which insists that moral philosophizing requires one to eschew their context and embodiment and employ objective and decontextualized thinking, does not make sense. A relational epistemology acknowledges that knowledge emerges through relations, and that things like care, needs, and vulnerabilities (the stuff that comprises our situated and relational being) are central moral-political concerns. Questions of what is 'right' and questions of 'the good life' also cannot be separated from a care ethics perspective, as what is right is in part determined by our notions and practices of the good life, and vice versa. Instead, the ethics of care obliterates this boundary by 'requir[ing] us to change the terms of the discussion' (Tronto, 2017, p. 37). Who is responsible to whom and for what? How are responsibilities distributed? Why are some responsible for certain activities, like care, and why do some have a 'pass' from worrying about such things (Tronto, 2013)? How do our practices of responsibility change in response to changing vulnerabilities? How do relations of power shape all of this? How can we be morally responsible to others so as to foster living well? And crucially, how do our forms of life shape our answers to all of these moral questions?

In these ways, the ethics of care is also a critical ethic. While the moniker of care ethics may conjure up images of sentimental caring, the ethics of care does not prescribe caring in some idealized form. The ethics of care is a critical ethic which 'traces the processes through which patriarchy serves to stifle this relational ethic' (Robinson, 2019, p. 13), and which reveals the harms and exclusions that result from the moral boundaries that constitute the dominant justice approach to morality and moral philosophy. This approach is not thickly prescriptive or based on rules and calculations. 'Care entails a more organic approach to normativity, ... a context driven emergent trajectory of moral standards' (Hamington, 2015b, p. 278). The ethics of care asserts that ethics emerge, are judged, and are revised accordingly, in and through our relations and practices. Consequently, care ethics radically reconceptualizes the entire enterprise of morality and moral philosophy by understanding moral life 'as a continuing negotiation *among* people' (Walker, 2007, p. 67, emphasis in original), a 'cooperative engagement in producing habitable communities, environments, and ways of life' (Code, 2002, p. 160). Care ethics orients us to attend continually to the ongoing negotiations and relational engagements in and through which different moral understandings and practices emerge.

Care as anti-essentialism

One of the earliest concerns regarding the ethics of care rested on the perceived essentialism of care ethics, which was charged with naturalizing women as caring, and reifying gender roles by aiming to replace the 'masculine' approach to ethics with a competing, or perhaps complementary, feminine approach (see, for example, Broughton, 1983; Kerber, 1986;

Senchuk, 1990). Relatedly, many feminist scholars have also expressed concern that some care ethics literature lacks engagement with other perspectives and fails to consider the experiences of women from a variety of positionalities (Stack, 1986; Spelman, 1988; Fraser and Nicholson, 1989; Raghuram, 2012; 2016; 2019), thereby essentializing white women's experiences as the experience of all women. As Robinson (2015, p. 303) writes, 'the ethics of care was damned on both sides – it was seen to reify and essentialize women's roles as carers ... and second, it ignored or wilfully washed over differences among women.'

Yet, as argued in the previous section, the ethics of care hinges on the claim that the self and morality are inextricably linked. 'The relational self produces knowledge that is connected, a product of discourses that constitute forms of life' (Hekman, 1995, p. 30). This knowledge, in turn, forms the subjects' sense of identity and connection to the world, and their moral reasoning. Furthermore, and crucially important for this argument, the understanding of moral selves as relational also implies a plurality of heterogenous moral voices. The relational self, as constituted in/by their unique sets of relations, must be heterogenous and plural; the moral knowledge held by these plural subjects, and the epistemologies which produce such knowledge, must likewise be heterogenous and multiple. For an ethics of care, then, morality and moral theorizing is primarily concerned with the ways in which multiple moral voices and selves *are constituted and interacting* (Hekman, 1995, p. 33). This, as argued in the previous section, offers a different conceptualization of morality than the rationalist model, and opens space for a multiplicity of moral voices to be heard, for other moral practices and understandings to be taken seriously.

By extension, as Robinson (2019, p. 14, emphasis in original) argues, 'the assumption of difference *inheres in the very core of the relational subject of care ethics*'. As relational beings, the self in the ethics of care is conceived of as multiple and heterogeneous; this conceptualization 'gives these "different" voices equal standing and imagines a world in which they would be granted the status "moral"' (Hekman, 1995, p. 159). More generally, the ethics of care – as a framework for critiquing modern moral philosophy and the binaries that constitute it, as a different approach to moral theorizing, and as a series of contextual, attentive, and revisable moral practices – challenges binary thinking, exclusionary categories, and the ways in which power operates through these to marginalize and even erase difference and different moral voices (Robinson, 2019). As a result, the ethics of care is inherently anti-essentialist. It does not locate 'women' as essentialized caregivers; instead, it seeks to provide a lens from which to question and uncover the ways in which women are positioned (both socially and through internalized patriarchy) as caregivers, and to focus on how other axes of oppression, like class and race, further shape the distribution of caring responsibilities. Care ethics also does not treat 'women' as a homogenous category; the ethics of care works in the opposite vein and understands that, as relational selves, 'each subject will possess a particular moral voice, a voice rooted in her social, historical, linguistic, and cultural situation' (Hekman, 1995, pp. 129–30). Understanding these contexts in all their rich and complex difference, and understanding the ways in which these contexts are constitutive of both the moral self and their moral thinking, is a primary task for the ethics of care.

There are two final points I wish to make about the ethics of care and difference. The first pertains to the potential critique that in conceiving of multiple moral selves, with multiple moral voices and understandings, the ethics of care descends into relativism, an approach to morality where 'anything goes' and where no moral judgement can be made. However, such a critique, as Susan Hekman (1995, p. 44) points out, relies on staying in a theoretical terrain which values binaries – such as the one between absolute and relative knowledge/judgement – and which thus fails to offer an alternative to modernist moral theory. In Donna Haraway's (1991, p. 191) words, 'Relativism is the perfect mirror twin of totalization in the ideologies of objectivity; both deny the stakes in location, embodiment, and partial perspective. ... Relativism and totalization are both "god-tricks" promising vision from everywhere and nowhere equally and fully.' The ethics of care is not simply a rejection of universal and absolute moral claims, and it certainly does not assert that we move to the other 'end of the pole' and adopt a relativistic approach to moral thinking. Care ethics instead takes us to a different epistemological space, in which knowledge is always situated (Faur and Tizziani, 2018), contextual, and therefore partial.

How, then, does one make judgements from an ethics of care perspective? As discussed earlier, because a care ethical perspective understands morality as practices, moral judgements can only be made by looking at the practices which sustain, or alternatively harm, ourselves, our communities, and our relations. As Sara Ruddick (1989, p. 16) writes, 'It is only within a practice that thinkers judge which questions are sensible, which answers are appropriate to them, and which criteria distinguish between better and worse answers.' It is through our practices, and particularly our practices of care, that we can come to judge whether something may be morally worthy. By the same token, it is also through examining our practices, and reflecting upon them, that we are able to examine whether certain practices are worth reproducing (Walker, 2007, p. 257). Notably, this iterative process in which practices and knowledges are simultaneously reflected upon must be just that – iterative and ongoing. Because practices themselves are revisable, dynamic, and changing, moral judgement – evaluated in relation to contingent sets of practices, and inherently situated – must also be revisable. Likewise, care practices must be revised when our moral understandings shift.

The second point I wish to address here pertains to empathy. Some care ethicists, like Michael Slote (2007; 2015), argue that an ethics of care requires empathy, a process involving the contemplation of another person; internalizing that other person's experience; experiencing that experience while also experiencing your own in that moment; and moving away from that moment of merger to respond and act (de Meriche, 2015, p. 100). There are some problems, however, with the use of empathy here, as the process of projecting oneself into the other's position contradicts the care ethical assertion of a relational self, a moral subject constituted by relations 'all the way down'.[3] As Nel Noddings (2015, p. 78) argues, advocating the use of 'empathy' in care ethics, which she describes 'as projection into a work of art or another's mind in order to understand it', seems to suggest that one can project into another, and then cognitively absorb that experience in order to know what must be done. This sort of projection seems to involve, for instance, a mind/body split, a subject who can shed their own relations and contexts and step into the 'shoes' of another, and the erasure of difference (how you would feel in a situation might never approximate how another might feel in that situation). In other words, this type of empathy requires a subject more akin to the subject theorized in dominant modern moral theory.

To avoid the connotations associated with empathy – connotations which do not align with an ethics of care approach – I prefer to use the concept of 'attentiveness' (see, for example, Tronto, 1993; Sevenhuijsen, 1998; Robinson, 1999). Attentiveness denotes an openness to the other, a thoroughgoing attempt to understand their different needs, desires, and point of view, a willingness to listen actively to their moral voice, and a commitment to treating their moral voice as a legitimate moral voice. It does not, however, purport to know the other fully or in some final and ultimate sense, particularly through a self-projection which will only ever allow us to 'know' the other as filtered through our own situatedness. Being attentive means that while 'we listen for expressed needs [we] do not assume what the other needs by reference to our own experience' (Noddings, 2015, p. 78). As a result, attentiveness requires a much more difficult, perhaps even agonistic, process; 'if difference is to emerge, there must first be silence, a willing suspension of habitual speech, and then a *patient struggle* requiring of

---

[3] To be fair, and as Slote (2007) points out, the term 'empathy' refers to many different things, and there are other types of empathy that are not premised upon projection. For pragmatic reasons, however, the focus here is specifically on the meaning of the word in the most colloquial sense: the idea of feeling for someone else as if you were in their situation, also called projective empathy in that one projects oneself into the context of another. For a more robust discussion of the concerns surrounding 'empathy' in the ethics of care see Jolanda van Dijke and colleagues (2019).

speaker and listener an attentive respect for different reasonings' (Ruddick, 1987, p. 245, emphasis added). Care ethics, as anti-essentialist through and through, is committed to such 'patient struggle'.

Care as global

Another recurring debate in the ethics of care literature hinges on the usefulness of the ethics of care as a global ethic. Can care ethics respond to global problems? Does an approach to ethics which centres on attentiveness, and which stems from relational thinking and concern for concrete and intimate others, offer a way to contemplate and navigate moral dilemmas at the global scale? As Robinson (1999, p. 43) writes, 'Care does not, at first sight, seem to respond well to distance', especially in comparison to rationalist approaches to moral thinking which valorize 'distance' by abjuring context and employing impartial reasoning.

Following the work of care ethicists like Robinson (1999), I argue that the ethics of care is undoubtedly useful as an ethic for the global sphere for two reasons. First, we are already intimately connected, that is, embedded in relational ties, at the global level via social structures. According to Iris Marion Young (2006), social structures are constellations in which different social positions are connected; these social positions are distributed within a given group of people. 'The "structure" in social structures consists in the connections among these positions and their relationships, and the way the attributes of positions internally constitute one another through those relationships' (Young, 2006, p. 112). Importantly, given that the structure 'exists only in the action and interaction of persons' (Young, 2006, p. 112), structures are not monoliths or static; rather, they are processes. Several social structures (including patriarchy, capitalism, colonialism, and racism) today intertwine and enmesh the global population (even as these same social structures have particular manifestations in and through particular contexts, as noted in Chapter 2). Certain social structures can thus be thought of as global, or perhaps can be understood as 'universality as reality' (Balibar, 2011). Universality as reality, as Cinzia Arruzza (2017) writes, does not refer to transcendental universal truths, a notion of universality that characterizes modernity. Rather, universality as reality acknowledges the ways in which we are entangled in a 'universality' that is socially and historically produced; it 'indicates the actual interdependency between the units that build what we call the world' (Arruzza, 2017, p. 848). Foregrounding these connections is not, of course, meant to obfuscate the deep and pervasive differences that also comprise our world. To be sure, our current global context requires us to 'confront the unique paradox of increasing interrelatedness in the context of profound difference' (Robinson, 1999, p. 45).

Second, and relatedly, care and care relations are now transnational and global, and care and reproductive work, including emotional and affective labour, are now a fundamental component of the global political economy (Robinson, 2011b). 'Vulnerable bodies' exert great power on the state and the global market by demanding care (Vaittinen, 2015). And as the rich literature on global care chains and migrant care labour (see, for example, Peterson, 2003; Chang and Ling, 2011; Prattes, 2020) has demonstrated, care has been increasingly commodified, in highly gendered, racialized, and classed ways, in the wider neoliberal order in response to these demands (Hoppania and Vaittinen, 2015). Migrant labourers from the Global South, for instance, increasingly provide care and reproductive work in the Global North, and 'menial' or 'dirty' reproductive labour is increasingly outsourced from the Global North to the Global South. Many accounts of these global care relations exist in the broader care scholarship (see, for example, Hochschild, 2000; Parreñas, 2015). Care work and reproductive labour are global in this very literal sense.

Yet, there is another way in which care and reproductive work are now intertwined in the global political economy. As Kimberly A. Chang and L.H.M. Ling (2011) argue, recent restructuring of the global political economy has also occurred along a gendered, racialized, and classed division of labour, a division which has had specific consequences for the ways in which care work is organized and valued globally. On the one hand, the rise of 'technomuscular capitalism' refers to the ways in which global finance, technology, production, and trade have been restructured along the lines of 'norms and practices usually associated with modernist capitalist masculinity – "deregulation," "privatization," "strategic alliances," "core regions," "deadlines"' (Chang and Ling, 2011, p. 30). This is the face of global capitalism; finance markets, tech industries, and trade comprise the visible sectors and valued relations of production in the context of the global political economy today. On the other hand, upholding technomuscular capitalism is a 'regime of labour intimacy', a deeply racialized, sexualized, and class-based set of reproductive relations which restructures care and reproductive work as low-wage and low-skilled, to be provided by female migrant workers (Chang and Ling, 2011). This restructuring devalues care and care work and relegates care work and care workers to the margins of the global political economy, at times 'erasing' them from sight all together. This devaluing is done despite the reality that it is this very care work which creates the conditions of possibility for technomuscular capitalism, in that it is this care labour that cares for, reproduces, and sustains the bodies who labour in the technomuscular sectors. According to this understanding of the global political economy, care work has not just become global, in the literal sense that much care labour is now provided through migrant labour or via largescale outsourcing of 'menial' care work from the Global North to the Global South (although this is certainly true). Care is also global in that the current configuration of global capitalism is upheld by and demarcated according to its constitutive outside, its 'intimate other' (Chang and Ling, 2011), the economy of care and reproductive labour.

Given these realities – that we are increasingly connected via social structures at the global scale, that care and care work is quite literally a transnational affair, and that the global political economy, in its current configuration, is upheld by particular gendered, racialized, and classed relations of care which are, at the same time, devalued or even erased – this argument asserts that the ethics of care can absolutely prove useful as a global ethic. More strongly, the relational, contextualized, and vulnerable approach to ethics inherent in the ethics of care is actually necessary if we are to assess and address adequately the types of moral dilemmas that arise in this interconnected and global world. Structural injustices arise when social structures, and the processes that (re)produce social structures, oppress, marginalize, or exploit whole categories or groups of people, while allowing others to dominate (or at the very least, be free from such domination and thereby able to pursue their desires and interests) (Young, 2006, p. 114). Without a relational understanding of such injustices – of the ways in which social structures, and the injustices therein, emerge in and through relations between differently situated people – it becomes impossible to understand how these injustices arise *structurally*.

It also becomes all too easy for those with the power to address such injustices to ignore their role in the situation. That is, 'distance' enables us to ignore our interconnections, and the ways in which we (re)produce and benefit from social structures that harm others. Global problems are easily dismissed as 'problems out there', belonging to other people, and of little concern to us. However, in taking a relational view, the ethics of care foregrounds our already existing connections; this allows us both to examine critically the causes and sources of structural injustices, and to take responsibility for these injustices. As Young (2006, p. 114) writes, 'all the persons who participate by their actions in the ongoing schemes of cooperation that constitute these structures are responsible for them, in the sense that they are part of the process that causes them.' While this does not mean that people are responsible 'in the sense of having directed the process or intended its outcomes' (Young, 2006, p. 114), this understanding of relational responsibility means that it is a moral failing to ignore the harms caused by social structures, even when these harms are directed towards seemingly distant others. It is only in viewing these issues relationally that responsibility can be (re)distributed so that those with relatively more power, or those who benefit most from the social structures, can adopt a sense of responsibility to those who are oppressed by these structures.

For these reasons, an ethics of care for the global sphere is a critical and political ethic. A global ethics of care is not a plea for benevolent care for distant others;[4] it is an ontological claim about the world we inhabit – we are deeply relational and interdependent – and a normative orientation towards assessing those relations and taking responsibility for the harms that emerge through these connections. Understanding these harms, similarly, requires a relational approach, in which we attend patiently, carefully, and with humility to the needs of others. As Robinson (1999, p. 46, emphasis in original) writes, 'an era of global interdependence demands a *relational* ethics which places the highest value on the promotion, restoration, or creation of good social and personal relations and gives priority to the needs and concerns of "concrete" rather than "generalizable" others.'

Care as political

Finally, the ethics of care has been critiqued for valorising a specific notion of 'care' as normatively valuable, or for uncritically romanticizing care as a panacea. From this vantage point, as Fiona Williams (2001, p. 478) writes:

> the very concept of 'care' embodies an oppressive history in which the practices and discourses of paid (particularly professional) and unpaid carers have maintained disabled and older people in a position of, at worst, unwanted dependency, abused and stripped of their dignity, and at best, patronized and protected from exercising any agency over their lives.

Other critical disability scholars similarly point out that care has historically, and continues to be, an oppressive practice (see, for example, Watson *et al.*, 2004; Kröger, 2009; Simplican, 2015; Kelly, 2020). Postcolonial scholars raise similar and important concerns. Uma Narayan (1995, pp. 133–4, emphasis in original), for instance, points out that:

> in general terms, the colonizing project was seen as being *in the interests of, for the good of*, and as *promoting the welfare of* the colonized – notions that draw our attention to the existence of a *colonialist* care discourse whose terms have some resonance with those of some contemporary strands of the ethic of care.

---

[4] As Robinson points out, such benevolent caring approaches are already covered by liberal humanitarianism, 'which call upon the benevolent, autonomous global north to keep peace, build security and "develop" the dependent, impoverished global south' (2013, p. 133). The dangers of romanticized notions of care and paternalism, as often exemplified by humanitarianism, are fleshed out more fully in the next section.

Parvati Raghuram (2012; 2016; 2019) also notes that the ethics of care literature sometimes focuses on particular practices of care (white, bourgeois practices from the Global North), and presents them as the whole of 'care', thereby marginalizing and obfuscating other practices and relations of care from other contexts.

In some ways, the preceding sections have, perhaps, already implicitly addressed these concerns. For instance, as argued in the discussion regarding care and essentialism, the ethics of care, as presented here, conceives of moral selves as relational all the way down, and therefore theorizes a multiplicity of heterogenous moral selves and moral practices of care. Yet, taken more holistically, these critiques raise an important concern. Given that care is contextual and heterogenous, how do we know which practices of care are morally worthy when faced with competing care practices and needs? Who gets to determine which care practices should be reproduced and which should be revised or disposed of? What happens when one normative vision of care conflicts with another? While the answers to these questions have already been alluded to, Kristin G. Cloyes (2002) provides more explicit guidance when she argues that a truly political theory of care requires *agonizing care*. An agonistic theory of care means that care – how it is constructed, how power operates through it, and other related questions – must be agonized, and this process will be a struggle. Further, agonizing care is a political act, which seeks to disrupt the current configurations of power and discourse that 'naturalize' certain care practices.

For a critical and political ethics of care, care itself is contingent; particular practices of care and understandings of care are situated; they are the products of social relations, and they are multiple and revisable. This means that as these multiple and contingent practices and conceptualizations of care come into contact, the potential for conflicting versions of care, struggles over what constitutes care, and the emergence of other productive tensions, is an ever-present reality. When such conflicts and struggles arise, a central task for a critical political ethics of care is to stick with the tension, to consider carefully the different versions of care at stake, to contemplate the ways in which specific practices of care constitute particular moral subjects and their ways of life, and to be open to the possibility that one's vision of 'good' care may need to be revised in light of the needs and ways of life of the other. We also need to be attuned to the power relations at play in such circumstances.

The ethics of care does not uphold a particular version of 'good' care as the normative ideal towards which we all should strive; care ethics is not a thick, prescription of a certain type of care. Nor does a critical and political ethics of care valorize a sanitized caring relationship. Instead, the ethics of care, as conceived here, 'allows the frequently conflict-laden, intense, gritty, and fleshy character of relationships to surface *as care*' (Cooper, 2007, p. 257, emphasis in original); it is only through agonizing care, working through the conflicts that so often arise from our relations, and practising epistemic humility (an often difficult undertaking) that 'good' care can emerge. Questioning practices of (non)care, weighing different caring practices against each other, uncovering the ways in which our hidden assumptions, biases, and privileges increase others' suffering and hardship, being responsible to others, and foregrounding the vulnerability of our moral judgement – all of which are primary moral tasks from a critical ethics of care perspective – will sometimes, and perhaps even frequently, involve conflict. As Amanda Russell Beattie and Kate Schick (2013, p. 12, emphasis in original) argue, these moral tasks take us down 'a difficult path: the journey towards vulnerability and accountability is one beset by *agon*, by struggle'. The ethics of care is a 'tough ethic' (Noddings, 2003, p. 99) and requires hard work.

Put differently, the ethics of care, as presented here, is a political ethic in that it politicizes care. How we organize our lives to care (or not), our understandings and practices of care (and the ways in which dominant notions of care marginalize and erase other practices of care), the distribution of the responsibility for care (often along gendered, racialized, and classed axes), and the ways in which we meet the needs of some groups of people and not others are deeply political concerns that must be deliberated upon collectively and continually. Further, our informal and formal caring arrangements, the distribution of caring responsibilities, the ways in which our needs are viewed socially, and which people, groups, and institutions have a 'pass' from worrying about care (Tronto, 2013) are all intimately tied to social, political, and economic relations of power. Power shapes care, care practices, and caring relations in a fundamental way; the relation between care and power only serves to heighten the political nature of care. A critical and political ethics of care orients us to contemplate and attend to the ways in which care, politics, ethics, and power are all intertwined.

Lastly, there is a second and related way in which the ethics of care is political. Hanna-Kaisa Hoppania and Tiina Vaittinen (2015) make a useful distinction between care as 'politics' and care as 'the political' (and which aligns with the ways in which these terms have been used throughout this book): the 'politics of care' refers to concerns regarding the organization of the resources and relations of care *within* the present social order, while 'care as the political' 'refers to the latent forces of disruption that are imbued in the corporeal character of care relations that challenge the logics of the present order' (Hoppania and Vaittinen, 2015, pp. 77–8). For instance, while care has been increasingly commodified and reorganized within the global political economy, as pointed out in the previous section, care also evades full co-optation by the dominant logic of capitalism. This logic seeks to translate care into a series of linear transactions, in which a need can be unidirectionally met via a quantifiable market exchange.

> The logic of care, by contrast, does not perceive care in terms of singular transactions. Instead, caring means that we interact and shift our actions around, so as to best accommodate the exigencies and specificities of the situation at hand, recognizing the corporeal capacities and limitations of both the one in need and the one who cares. (Hoppania and Vaittinen, 2015, p. 84)

Care is an ongoing process; it takes time, it requires ongoing attentiveness, response, and it must be revised and assessed as needs shift. Care thereby resists capitalist logic, according to which work and production are for profit instead of use. The focus on meeting the needs of vulnerable bodies which cannot, in the end, be controlled or tamed (Hoppania and Vaittinen, 2015) continually confronts capitalist tendencies towards efficiency and profit-maximization. Care is a defining feature of our life, and our political existence, and 'when care is not adequately accounted for in some sphere of life, it starts to challenge that very sphere – it demands to be noticed, thereby opening up a space for "the political", calling for change in the very order in which it is being governed' (Hoppania and Vaittinen, 2015, p. 87).

In sum, then, the ethics of care is political in the fullest sense. It is political, in that as an approach to moral thinking premised on relationality and epistemic humility, it challenges the dominant justice model which touts rationalism and abstraction as the superior form of moral thinking while marginalizing other moral voices. It is political because it does not assert a thick normative ideal of care, but rather locates conflicts and contestations over the meaning of care and 'good' care practices as a collective and political concern. And it is political in that care – as an ever-present corporeal need, as an articulation of the relational moral subject, and as an approach to an epistemology premised on revisability and vulnerable judgement – cannot be mastered or totalized by existing relations of power. Care cannot be divided or sorted into the atomistic categories that constitute modern-patriarchal-colonial-racist-capitalism. Care points to the limits of our current order, and thereby orients us continually towards the possibility of a different world.

Reconceptualizing morality

This chapter has sought to outline my understanding of the ethics of care as a critical and political feminist ethics. The ethics of care, as defined in this book, is premised upon a relational ontology, a situated epistemology, an understanding of morality as practices, and a devastating feminist critique of the moral boundaries that constitute the dominant modernist (justice/rationalist) approach to morality and moral philosophy. Because of these premises, the ethics of care is anti-essentialist and attuned to difference. Care ethics conceives of moral subjects as multiple and heterogeneous; accordingly, there are multiple moral epistemologies and moral practices of care. A central task for ethics, from an ethics of care perspective, is to examine the ways in which our relations constitute moral selves, and to respond to the particular and unique needs of (sometimes radically) different others. The ethics of care is also a global ethic, because in addition to being attuned to difference, a critical care ethics is well positioned to illuminate our global relations and the ways in which care and care practices are shaped fundamentally by global relations of power and the global political economy. Using a care ethics lens allows us to assess and address the moral dilemmas that arise in and through the nexus of our messy and complex global interconnections, on the one hand, and the fact of our deep and pervasive differences, on the other.

Lastly, the ethics of care is political, because it orients us collectively to agonize care and to deliberate on often competing and conflicting notions of care and care practices in an ongoing way. It is also political because care operates in a logic of its own; care is a life-sustaining and life-affirming activity that continually resists domination by modern-patriarchal-colonial-racist-capitalist logic. In resisting these dominant logics, care points towards the limits of these hegemonic systems of power, and towards the possibility of new social orders. The ethics of care orients us towards this fact, provides us with the tools to critique the existing social order, and positions us to prioritize care practices that evade and challenge dominant logics. In this way, the ethics of care, as a productive ethic concerned with creatively building new relations and social arrangements to manifest different visions of the good life, operates at the level of 'the political'. It is also for this reason that I assert that the ethics of care must begin to think with/through/for the pluriverse, which itself operates at the level of the political. As an approach to ethics that is fundamentally concerned with the political and moral salience of difference, the ethics of care must contend with the political landscape of the pluriverse, where differences are at their most deep and pervasive.

As a final note, I wish to acknowledge that there may seem to be some circularity between my arguments that the ethics of care is anti-essentialist, global, and political. Emphatically, that is the point. Just as the binaries that construct the rationalist model of moral theorizing – and the modern world more generally – are mutually reinforcing, in shifting to a different meta-ethical vantage point, and a different meta-theoretical space, *the ethics of care completely changes all aspects of morality in an interrelated way*. The ethics of care, as presented and described here, can only be a critical, global, and political ethic attuned to difference – each of these terms inherently implies the other.

To return, then, to the central concern of this book, which asks: *How can we rethink global ethics in the pluriverse, where differences are at their most deep and pervasive?* The main argument of this book is that the characteristics of a critical and political ethics of care, specifically as outlined in this chapter, provide a unique meta-ethical orientation that can help subjects of the modern world rethink global ethics in the image of the pluriverse. Undertaking such a rethinking and demonstrating how the ethics of care positions us to contemplate better the distinct moral-political landscape of the pluriverse is the task of the remainder of the book.

5

Partial Connections: The Pluriverse, Ethics, and Care

At the beginning of this book, I introduced the field of Global Ethics and, following Kimberly Hutchings (2010), described the various approaches to global ethics as divided into two broad categories: rationalist approaches and alternative approaches. A key distinction between these two categories pertains to the ways in which they conceive of difference, and the significance of difference, for moral deliberation. Relatedly, these two approaches also differ in their stance over the (im)possibility of universality. On the one hand, rationalist approaches in Global Ethics assert some universal foundation for ethics, be it in the form of an appeal to a transcendent authority, such as 'natural law', or to a more immanent rationality, which is seen as common to all of humanity. For the rationalists, then, difference does not go 'all the way down', as there is always something common or universal on which to ground moral claims. The alternative approaches, on the other hand, reject the possibility of universal truths, and foreground the moral salience of differences, be they cultural, economic, religious, political, and so on.

The pluriverse, however, casts difference in a deeper and more pervasive way than has been previously conceived of in the Global Ethics literature. In the pluriverse, differences are at their most robust; pluriversal difference refers to different worlds and worldings and operates at an ontological and, as has been argued, by extension, a co-constitutive epistemological, level. The notion of the pluriverse thus opens up space for radical difference in the fullest sense. Difference as ontological – 'as a matter of what things, including alterity itself, may *be*' (Holbraad, 2013, p. 563, emphasis in original) – leaves open the question of what may in fact be different in any particular situation. This means that difference in the pluriverse may 'appear' in surprising forms, forms which exceed the limits of the categories used to capture difference in Global Ethics today.

Furthermore, but again, relatedly, while these multiple worlds, or what I have called onto-epistemologies, exceed one another due to their radical differences, they are also intertwined and connected. The pluriverse has been described as more than one and less than many (de la Cadena, 2015), or as 'the partially connected unfolding of worlds' (Blaser, 2013, p. 552). The notion of 'partial connections' (Strathern, 2004), presented briefly in Chapter 1, is particularly useful for understanding the pluriverse, and is mobilized extensively throughout this chapter. As Marilyn Strathern (2004, p. 26) argues, we need to problematize the very idea of 'wholes' and 'parts'. The logic of wholes and parts traps us between an 'atomistic view (a totality is constituted by the aggregation of independent elements) and a holistic one (where elements have no existence apart from a total structure or system).' The pluriverse cannot be conceived of along such lines; multiple worlds are not independent of one another but they also 'do not share an overarching principle that would make their entanglement a universe' (Blaser, 2013, p. 553). Because of this, the pluriverse also recasts the very idea of 'universality'. Each world may have its own ontological and epistemological premises/practices, but it is not an independent unit. Neither is the constellation of worlds – which are connected but often in excess of each other – a universal whole. In contrast, the pluriverse entreats us to begin to think about multiple universals (worlds that exist as universals in their own right) that are connected, but that never come together to form a cohesive universal (or universal-universality).

The notion of the pluriverse thereby fundamentally challenges the ways in which difference and universality have been conceived of in/by the Global Ethics literature. Grappling with this challenge is an important task for Global Ethics for several reasons which have, to varying degrees, already been discussed throughout this argument thus far. First, in offering new conceptualizations of difference, the pluriverse opens theoretical space to think about the challenge of ethical contemplation and action in and across differences that are radical and that cannot be presumed. What is 'different' and which 'differences' are significant in an ethical dilemma cannot be taken for granted, and disagreements themselves may not be easy to recognize (Blaser, 2016). Difference itself must instead be approached with openness and seen as a possible source of contestation. This both complicates and enriches the very idea of ethical dilemmas and conflicts, and the ways in which such dilemmas are constituted in/by difference, and thus merits attention in the Global Ethics literature. Second, the pluriverse, as a world of multiple particular and actually existing worlds or universals, also moves beyond, or perhaps thoroughly displaces, the antinomy of 'universality' and 'particularity' that currently characterizes, and limits, much thinking in Global Ethics. Theoretical work is required to think about global ethics in a way that does not reproduce this binary. Third, there are a growing number of ethnographies, including those drawn upon in this book, which make visible ontological differences and conflicts – that is, ethical conflicts between/across worlds (see, for example, Salmond, 2012; Green, 2013b; de la Cadena, 2015; Blaser, 2018; Omura *et al.*, 2019; Oslender, 2019). Global Ethics, as the field of study that is concerned with addressing the ethical dilemmas that arise out of our interconnectedness, cannot ignore such conflicts and moral quandaries.

Lastly, as described in Chapter 1, the pluriverse is also a critical decolonial project, which seeks to destabilize the relations of power that currently uphold the modern world as the entirety of reality and, in so doing, make space for different life projects and worlds to flourish. I believe that there is a growing concern with the colonial legacies of our field and a growing normative commitment to moving towards addressing and amending these legacies (see, for example, Blaney and Tickner, 2017b). In thinking in/through/with the pluriverse, the field of Global Ethics would make important strides towards such a goal, in part by giving ontological weight to different ways of being in and seeing the world (different onto-epistemologies) and in part by casting, or perhaps more accurately, acknowledging, certain ethical dilemmas as ethical conflicts across worlds. For these reasons, this book argues that Global Ethics must engage with the idea of the pluriverse and begin to think through the pluriversal challenge to the ways in which we currently think and do global ethics.

At the same time, I also wish to assert that the pluriversal literature must begin to contend seriously with the ethical dimensions of the pluriversal project. The purpose of this chapter is to develop this point by demonstrating that the pluriversal project is a normative, moral, and ethical project all the way down. In developing this line of thinking, this chapter also begins to draw lines of connection between the pluriversal project and the ethics of care and emphasizes why reading these literatures together will mutually expand and enhance our understandings of the pluriverse, global ethics, and a critical and political ethics of care. I suggest that this, in turn, will allow us to commit more fully to building the pluriverse.

To demonstrate this line of thinking, this chapter begins with a brief reiteration of the notion of the pluriverse. Specifically, this section builds on the existing pluriversal literature to argue that the pluriverse can fruitfully be conceived of as a world, or more accurately, a meta-world, defined by a co-constitutive relational ontology, situated epistemology, and axiology of partial connections. Thinking of the pluriverse in this way is important, it is argued, because it holds together the ontological, epistemological, and normative components of the pluriverse without privileging one at the expense of the other, as tends to happen when the discussion is overly focused on ontology, or when ontology is divorced from epistemology. Further, in explicitly emphasizing the normative dimensions of the pluriverse (which are, to be sure, already implicit in the pluriversal literature), I argue that the pluriversal project must also be concerned with normativity, morality, and ethics. Rethinking global ethics in the image of the pluriverse, as well as rethinking the pluriverse such that the normative dimensions of the pluriverse are foregrounded, would, as previously noted, mutually benefit and expand both the pluriversal and Global Ethics literatures.

This chapter then shows how the ethics of care aligns with, and usefully expands, thinking about the pluriverse as a meta-world defined by a co-constitutive relational ontology, situated epistemology, and axiology of partial connections. More exactly, the ethics of care, defined by a relational ontology and situated epistemology, is well positioned to serve as a lens for understanding the pluriverse, which shares these same ontological and epistemological premises. Furthermore, the ethics of care normatively values repairing and maintaining our relations of care that allow us to produce and reproduce ourselves and our worlds as well as is reasonably possible. This normative vantage point, I assert, amends the pluriversal axiology of valuing partial connections by encouraging us to consider critically which connections are worth maintaining and extending, and which ones are not. Subsequently, I contend that thinking about the pluriverse as a meta-world, from an ethics of care perspective, involves rethinking the normative commitment implicit in the pluriversal project so that it is focused on valuing *partial relations of care*, where care in the most general sense contributes to a world's ability to flourish as a world. In undertaking this rethinking, and in drawing out these partial connections, this chapter ultimately illustrates how the pluriversal project, care, and ethics are deeply and inescapably intertwined.

Worlding the pluriverse: ontology, epistemology, and axiology

The central argument of Chapter 2 is that modernity is a world characterized by a particular ontology, epistemology, and axiology, which are themselves co-constituting. Here, I suggest that it is similarly useful to conceive of the pluriverse – the world in which many worlds are possible[1] – as a meta-world defined by a particular ontology, epistemology, and axiology. Notably, while this discussion attends to the ontological and epistemological aspects of the pluriverse here, this section aims to foreground the axiological and normative aspects of the pluriverse. More precisely, it is argued that the pluriverse, as a concept, implicitly involves a variety of axiological questions. Axiology, as an umbrella term for what is of value, therefore also points to moral and ethical concerns, particularly when morality is understood in the care ethical sense, which (as developed in Chapter 4) conceives of morality as

---

[1] This paraphrases the well-known project of the Zapatistas.

the practices and values that constitute, repair, and maintain different forms of life. Because of these axiological dimensions, this section suggests that the literature on the pluriverse needs to engage with moral questions and moral philosophy. Indeed, while this book begins with the premise that the Global Ethics literature needs to begin thinking in/through/with the pluriverse, it is equally important that the pluriversal research programme includes ongoing engagement with ethical and moral questions.

To begin this argument, I propose that the pluriverse is a meta-world defined by a relational ontology, a situated epistemology, and an axiology that values partial connections. It is characterized by a relational ontology, because multiple worlds are connected through relations of power, which themselves emerge and exist only in and through relations and practices. Significantly, relationships here are not things that 'somehow exist outside or between' (Strathern, 2004, p. 53) worlds, connecting pre-existing 'units'. The worlds that constitute the pluriverse are, in contrast, enacted, as is the pluriverse itself, through relations all the way down. A world is not connected to other pre-existing worlds; worlds, and the pluriverse, emerge in and through relations. The pluriverse is thus an 'animated world' (Blaser, 2012, p. 49), a world*ing* (Blaser, 2013, p. 552), and particular worlds come in to being, in part, through their relations with other worlds (as well as through the 'internal' relations and practices that enact a particular world). This ontology stands in stark contrast to the modern ontology, premised on a strong Human/Nature divide, in which Nature is an external world 'out there', separate from atomistic Man.

The pluriverse is, I suggest, also constituted by a situated epistemology, as knowledge claims and knowledge practices always emerge from some place, from particular ways of life; knowledge (practices) and worlding practices emerge in and through each other. How we (meaning any 'we') know, and how we know that we know, is always 'partial [and] locatable' (Haraway, 1991, p. 191), emerging in and through our relational lives. From this perspective, how we know that we know must always involve taking responsibility for the generative components of knowledge – that which is enacted in/through/by our knowledge claims and practices. Again, this epistemology differs from the modernist rationalist epistemology, which prioritizes transcending context, splitting subject and object, and appealing to universal truth claims.

Lastly, the pluriverse, I contend, is a world that is also constituted by an axiological commitment to partial connections. This commitment to partial connections is partial not in the sense of some sort of 'negative' bias or flawed 'incompleteness' – certainly, conceiving of partiality in negative terms only makes sense when tied to the modernist celebration of completeness, totalization, and objectivity. On the contrary, an axiology of partial connections means that we value the necessarily incomplete connections between worlds. Partial connections are indispensable and inevitable; learning to live well together – in and across all our radical and unknowable differences – requires multiplying connection in non-hierarchical ways. At the same time, however, these connections are always only partial, in the sense that worlds can never wholly 'know' one another or be reduced to one another. Valuing partial connections in this way means that one world can never appropriate another world in full, reduce it to its own, or – and this is crucially important – capture other worlds in a singular hierarchy constituted by one onto-epistemology. 'Partial connections create no single entity; the entity that results is more than one, yet less than two' (de la Cadena, 2010, p. 347).

The term partial is also important here because it helps us avoid the uncritical valorisation of all relations; some relations are harmful, and it may be desirable to change these. Partial connections are themselves evolving and animated, and resist closure. Once again, this illustrates how the pluriverse differs from the modern world, as the modernist axiology values totalizing order. Modernity seeks completion and closure via the ordering of nature. This ordering can only ever result in hierarchy, as subject/object distinctions (pre)determine who/what can be ordered and who/what can do the ordering. The pluriverse, instead, is premised on an axiology which rejects closure, and therefore resists hierarchy. An axiology of partial connections emphasizes the impossibility of closure and thus necessarily implies openness to new partial connections that are yet to emerge.

Before proceeding further, however, I would like to address a possible critique of this assertion that the pluriverse is a meta-world. Perhaps, one might argue, that in making such a claim, I am falling into the modernist trap of a one-world ontology. From this perspective, 'the claim of multiple ontologies is turned into a sort of meta-ontology, the statement of fact, the really real ultimate nature of reality' (Blaser, 2012, p. 52). Mario Blaser (2012; 2013) raises this concern about different work in the ontological turn literature, arguing that some assert the pluriverse as a new foundational claim (Blaser singles out Philippe Descola (2005) in particular). This strikes me as a challenging problem. In asserting the pluriverse, are we just replacing one ontology with another, even if it is a meta-ontology? Blaser's own attempt to avoid this dilemma is to emphasize that ontology is a worlding, a reality in the making. He emphasizes the fluidity of worlds, the ways in which they are storied, and therefore aims to avoid making more foundational claims about multiple worlds. However, as Martin Holbraad (2013, p. 564) points out, it is unclear 'how this is not ultimately yet another argument that operates by grounding the possibility of difference in a prior story of how the world(s) must work, namely, in this case, the world(s) as a terrain in which ontological differences are ever-emerging, fluid, and tentative.' Even the assertion that the pluriverse is fluid and emerging is an ontological and grounding claim.

To further complicate this, at other times, Blaser also speaks of actually existing multiple ontologies; for instance, his ethnographic work with the Yshiro people of the Paraguayan Chaco (2010; 2013) and the Innu Nation (2016; 2018) articulates multiple worlds as worlds. There is a bit of a tension, then, between the assertion that there are multiple '*actual* worlds' (Blaney and Tickner, 2017b, p. 298, emphasis in original) – as evidenced by ethnographies of different onto-epistemologies – and the hesitation to assert that there are multiple worlds as some sort of ontological claim. This tension is evident in other writings on the pluriverse. For instance, Arturo Escobar (2016, 22, emphasis in original) writes:

> For the pluriverse proposal, there are multiple reals, yet it is not intended to 'correct' the view on a single real on the grounds of being a truer account of 'reality.' *The pluriverse is a tool to first, make alternatives to the one world plausible to one-worlders, and, second, provide resonance to those other worlds that interrupt the one-world story.*

There are other worlds that interrupt the one-world story, but acknowledging these other worlds is not meant to provide a truer account of 'reality'. Perhaps, then, the point of this distinction is to trouble the notion of 'reality', such that reality is not to be taken as an externally given 'out there' but rather as socially constructed. So while we can point to other worlds that interrupt modernity's one-world story, we are not asserting any of this as transcendental or prior to the relations in and through which they emerge. But this leads to another issue, especially if and when the pluriversal literature makes a distinction between epistemology and ontology. In particular, as outlined briefly in Chapter 1, the ontological turn emerged as a response to the prioritization of epistemology as a way to contemplate difference. When one begins with epistemology, according to scholars like Blaser (2013), difference is conceived of as different perspectives (knowledges, paradigms) on one world or reality. The problem with this is that some perspectives are more likely to be judged as right/truer/or better than others; this judgement is, of course, shaped by relations of power that marginalize certain ways of knowing as culture, belief, or tradition, while other ways of knowing – namely, rationalism and science – are 'true'. Asserting other worlds as worlds, and focusing on ontology over epistemology, is meant to provide a better way to conceptualize difference, one which does not depend on hierarchies of knowledge, and one which 'interrupts the one-world story' which holds up such hierarchies.

However, there is an epistemological problem that remains here. How do we know that there are other worlds interrupting the one-world story? On what epistemological grounds do we come to see or know these worlds? In bracketing epistemology, or perhaps more softly, in prioritizing ontology over epistemology, certain claims by pluriversal scholars become difficult to absorb. For instance, Blaser writes that the pluriverse is not meant as a meta-ontology but is instead concerned with new pluriversal possibilities that may emerge to address political problems. 'Central among these problems,' he writes (2013, p. 554) 'is the extent to which those of us (person and institutions) who have been shaped by an ontology that postulates/performs a "one-world world" are ill prepared to grapple with its increasing implausibility.' On what epistemological grounds is Blaser asserting that a one-world world is implausible? It seems to me that some subjects of a one-world world (like my world, modernity) will likely have strong arguments that the one-world world is plausible in part because their epistemology provides criteria – and therefore constructs evidence and knowledge claims – that support its plausibility. As Claudio Briones (2013, p. 560, citing Blaser, 2013, p. 551) writes:

> Is the awareness of the ways in which 'peoples distribute what exists and conceive their constitutive relations' (ontology) divorced from acknowledging the means by which they acquire and approve such conceptualizations (epistemology)? ... Can we grasp ontological differences by using our modern epistemology or must we also consider epistemological differences?

This is a complicated issue that seems to always end where we start. On the one hand, pluriversal scholars are not willing to assert that there are multiple worlds as a primary ontological claim. On the other hand, they also point to and evidence multiple worlds based on ethnographic data, which are meant to affirm the implausibility of a one-world world, and the fact that 'the hegemony of the story of modernity (or the modern ontology) is in crisis' (Blaser, 2013, p. 554). At the same time, they often fail to attend meaningfully to epistemological issues, the ways in which they *come to know* that there are these multiple worlds (as opposed to just different perspectives on a single reality 'out there'), and by extension, the ways in which they know that the one-world world story is implausible. It is for this reason that I insist it is more fruitful to conceive of worlds – including the worlds which produce pluriversal scholars – as onto-epistemologies, as co-constitutive ontologies and epistemologies. Our practices and our knowledges emerge together, and asserting there are multiple ontologies requires, at the very least, a situated epistemology or a sincere acknowledgement of the vulnerability of all judgement (Hutchings, 2013). Otherwise, one's commitment to a particular epistemology may prevent one from contemplating ontological difference other than that which is already acknowledged in and by said epistemology.

But what, then, of the original problem which sparked this discussion? Is the pluriverse as world simply a (meta-)ontological claim to replace the modern one-world world? The assertion here is that explicitly bringing axiology to the fore of this discussion, and thereby foregrounding questions of what we value, what is right, and what is beautiful, can help provide a way to navigate this conundrum. More acutely, conceiving of the pluriverse as a world defined by a co-constitutive relational ontology, situated epistemology, *and* an axiology of partial connections allows the pluriverse as world to emerge as a meta-ontological claim, albeit a weak one. Stephen White's (2000, pp. 6, 8) distinction between strong and weak ontologies is useful here:

> Strong are those ontologies that claim to show us 'the way the world is,' or how God's being stands to human being, or what human nature is. It is by reference to this external ground that ethical and political life gain their sense of what is right; moreover, this foundation's validity is unchanging and of universal reach.
>
> Weak ontologies respond to two pressing concerns. First, there is the acceptance of the idea that all fundamental conceptualization of self, other, and world are contestable. Second, there is the sense that such conceptualizations are nevertheless necessary or unavoidable for an adequately reflective ethical and political life.

Conceptualizations of ontologies in the weak sense are, for White, necessary to live a meaningful ethical and political life. It is clear from the pluriversal literature that the pluriversal project is committed to 'the partially connected unfolding of worlds' (Blaser, 2012, p. 55). This axiology of partial connections, as I have called it, is a normative commitment to a particular type of ethical and political life in which many worlds as worlds can flourish. Thinking about the axiology of the pluriverse foregrounds the pluriverse as a world in the making, a normative commitment to something other than the modern world as the whole of the real.

For this reason, while this argument asserts that the pluriverse is a meta-world, this claim is not a strong ontological claim about an external reality. The pluriverse as meta-world is a weak ontology. As a weak ontology, thinking about the pluriverse as meta-world does not attempt to locate some transcendental reality 'out there'; weak ontologies accept the radical contingency of all claims. At the same time, as White points out, weak ontological claims are necessary to manifest ethical and political life adequately and reflectively. If the pluriverse is the type of ethical and political meta-world we are committed to building/enacting/performing/storying, then this project will require some ontological and epistemological premises. The argument put forth here, then, is that by explicitly identifying this axiological aspect of the pluriverse – one which is certainly already inherent in pluriversal literature, but perhaps not identified with such strongly normative language – the justification for asserting such claims is unambiguously brought to the fore. As a result, the 'pluriverse as world' is a (weak) meta-onto-epistemic claim that does suggest a 'one-world' (meta-)ontology, but one that is very different from the strong one-world ontology of modernity. The axiology which in part constitutes the pluriverse keeps the ontological and epistemological premises of the pluriverse from slipping into some sort of transcendental grounding *because it is the normative goal of valuing partial connections, as opposed to some sort of transcendental truth, that justifies making such claims.* Relatedly, it seems unlikely that this normative goal can be achieved without making such weak ontological and epistemological statements.

At the same time, the relational ontology and the situated epistemology of the pluriverse means that this axiology is not transcendental either. As worlds continue to interact, different value claims will be asserted, different practices will confront each other, and different understandings will clash; indeed, different difference will be revealed. A situated epistemology, as is characteristic of the ethics of care, and which I believe is implicit to the very notion of the pluriverse, means that we must continually pursue the difficult and messy task of looking at these different value claims and the practices they are constituted in/by in order to justify – and if necessary, revise – any and all normative goals, including the normative goal of the pluriverse.

In sum, then, the pluriverse as a concept which foregrounds ontological multiplicity – and as this book has argued, therefore also epistemological multiplicity – is always normative; more precisely, this ontology, epistemology, and axiology are co-constitutive, with each justifying/constructing the other, albeit in a way that is open to revision. A central argument in this chapter is that the axiological aspect of the pluriverse must therefore be attended to and foregrounded; questions of what we value, what is normatively desirable or good, and how to enact a vision of multiple worlds are at the heart of the very notion of the pluriverse. As this chapter illuminates, ethical and moral tools and concepts will not just help us navigate actual conflicts between worlds; they also provide us with language, concepts and tools for contemplating – and crucially, committing to the building of – the pluriverse itself.

On moral practices and ethical conflicts

I believe that the concept of the pluriverse is normative, ethical, and moral in other ways as well, particularly when morality is again understood in the care ethical sense. That is, in the last chapter, I argued that from the perspective of the ethics of care, *morality is now understood as practices – both knowledge practices and actions – which make up the very fabric of our everyday lives.* As Susan Hekman (1995, pp. 115–16) elaborates, morality is 'inseparably linked to our conception of ourselves as subjects and our conceptions of the world in which we live'.[2] What we know, what we do, and what is moral, together constitute 'forms of life' (Hekman, 1995, p. 125). For this reason, morality cannot be separated from the world of which it is apart and in which it is enacted. Morality is so fundamental to a world that a change in moral beliefs would entail 'inhabiting a new world'; 'I cannot fully understand what my form of life would be if I had a different set of moral beliefs, because moral beliefs are so central to who I am' (Hekman, 1995, p. 128). Similarly, 'moral values and practices are inseparable from the broader social and political context within which they operate' (Hutchings, 2003, p. 130).

By extension, the care ethical understanding of morality implies that particular worlds are also fundamentally moral; to speak of forms of life is to speak of 'forms of moral life' (Walker, 2007, p. 105). Just as this book has argued that contemplating ontological differences and different ontologies requires thinking about epistemology, thinking of morality as a form of life means that moral contemplation is also inherent to and necessary for understanding, exploring, and engaging with multiple worlds. To be sure, some of the types of fundamental differences that emerge in the pluriverse – and that the pluriversal literature attempts to grapple with – might, in fact, be moral. Neglecting to investigate the morality of worlds (or more exactly, worlds as moral forms of life) and moral difference(s) may obfuscate some of the deep and pervasive difference that the pluriversal project seeks to take seriously. Drawing upon moral philosophy, like the ethics of care, and engaging with the literature on global ethics more broadly, can help conceptualize these dynamics and possibilities and broaden the scope of the pluriversal research project.

Second, understanding worlds as inherently moral also means that conflicts between worlds fundamentally involve morality and ethics in at least two senses. First, the moral practices and understandings that enact particular worlds form, at minimum, part of the background in and through which conflicts between worlds emerge and unfold. 'Critical moral ethnography' (Walker, 2007, p. 246) becomes an important task for understanding the moral worlds in and through which conflicts emerge, and the ways in which these moral forms of life shape the conflict itself. Second, and related to this, conflicts between worlds very often tend to be moral and ethical. For instance, in Marisol de la Cadena's (2015) account of her protest with

---

[2] It is worth highlighting that while this section draws extensively upon Susan Hekman's work (1995), Hekman would not likely identify as a care ethicist, although she did see Carol Gilligan's work as revolutionary. In her book, *Moral Voices, Moral Selves* (1995), Hekman undertakes an extensive examination of Gilligan's work on the ethics of care to deconstruct rationalist approaches to moral theory and to draw out in detail the ways in which the ethics of care necessitates a reconceptualization of the moral self as a relational subject.

Nazario to protect Ausangate, the difference that she focuses on pertains to the ontological status of Ausangate (as mountain and earth-being). However, I believe that the political protest that she and Nazario participate in to protect Ausangate also points to a clear moral problem. Nazario is not protesting the mine to assert that Ausangate is an earth-being (and therefore participate in an ontological contestation); he is protesting the mine to avoid harming Ausangate, who might then harm his people and his world out of anger. In this way, Nazario is contesting the proper treatment of Ausangate, or, to use the language of the ethics of care, he is concerned with how to care best for, and maintain good relation with, Ausangate (where what it means to care is, again, not predetermined). Of course, Nazario's ontological relationship with Ausangate deeply shapes his motivation for participating in this contestation – and in no way do I mean to diminish the significance of the fact that an ontological difference shapes this entire situation (or, as I described it at the beginning of this paragraph, this ontological difference in part forms the 'background' in and through which the conflict emerges). My aim is rather to emphasize that often ontological difference only becomes meaningful across worlds *when there is an ethical dilemma regarding what ought to be done in any given situation*. Engaging more thoroughly with and drawing upon tools in moral philosophy, and especially the ethics of care as I argue here, would again allow pluriversal scholars to attend more fully and explicitly to these moral and ethical dynamics.

As a final point, the pluriversal literature also frequently emphasizes the importance of 'world-making effects' (Blaser, 2013, p. 552). In so doing, this literature often points to the fact that sometimes judgements regarding such world-making effects need to be made. Blaser's development of ontology, which by now has been well rehearsed, is again useful to demonstrate this. Ontology, for Blaser (2013, p. 552, emphasis added), can be conceived of as 'storied performativity', sets of practices and narratives which enact worlds, and therefore are world-making (as opposed to claims about what exists 'out there'):

> One implication of this is that the stories being told cannot be fully grasped without reference to their world-making effects, for different stories imply different worldings; they do not 'float' over some ultimate (real) world. The corollary is that, indeed, some ethnographic subjects (or stories/worldings/ontologies) can be wrong, not in the sense of a lack of coincidence with an external or ultimate reality, *but in the sense that they perform wrong: they are/enact worlds in which or with which we do not want to live.*

Judging which worlds 'in which or with which we do not want to live', I believe, is a key part of the pluriversal project – although perhaps the term 'judge' connotes a stronger and more decisive stance than I intend for two reasons. First, in the context of the pluriverse, what it means 'to judge' is an enormously complicated and nuanced task because of the differences that are at play. Onto-epistemologies involve their own sets of practices and knowledge claims that limit our ability to access and therefore deliberate on other onto-epistemologies; it is the very complexity of such normative deliberation across worlds that motivates the investigation at hand in the first place. Second, as the ethics of care foregrounds, moral judgement itself is always vulnerable, difficult, and messy. As relational beings, moral agents and moral judges are produced in and through relations that sustain various worlds, and that are deeply intertwined with complex values systems, norms, institutions, and systems of power. Accordingly, moral judgement does not stand on some sort of transcendental and authoritative ground; moral judgement can only ever be vulnerable, risky, and revisable, as outlined in more detail in the discussion that follows.

At the same time, questions of what it means to live well and to live well together despite these very differences are central to the pluriversal project (both as a research programme, and relatedly, as a project that seeks to foster continually a world in which many worlds may flourish). Investigating such questions, considering what kind of world(s) we want to build (Escobar, 2018), being accountable for the world(s) we already enact, and reflecting on which worlds we do not want to live in/with are pressing questions in the context of the pluriverse. Exploring these questions inherently involves critically interrogating our own worlds in an ongoing way, as well as coming to know (as well as possible, but always imperfectly) other worlds and moral forms of life so as to scrutinize collectively and collaboratively what types of worlds we want to live in and with. Judgement, albeit a thin, tentative, deeply contextual, and revisable judgement (like the type of judgement espoused by the ethics of care), is unavoidable here, as 'actual moralities, or parts of them, are indeed comparable, if only piecemeal, for purposes of reflective testing and comparative justification' (Walker, 2007, p. 260). In turning our attention to these types of concerns, I suggest that the notion of the pluriverse and the pluriversal project is, again, intimately intertwined with moral and ethical questions, and specifically, the moral and ethical questions that emerge from an ethics of care understanding of morality.

Connecting the pluriverse and the ethics of care: preliminary steps

The previous discussion is, first and foremost, meant to demonstrate that the pluriverse is already a moral landscape; as such, the pluriversal literature needs to begin to contemplate explicitly moral questions. At the same time, this discussion also aims to develop some partial connections between the pluriverse and the ethics of care, and further illustrate how the ethics of care provides a useful starting point for contemplating the moral and ethical dimensions of the pluriverse. In particular, thinking of the pluriverse as a meta-world, defined by a relational ontology, situated epistemology, and an axiology of partial connections, draws out important lines of connection between the pluriversal vision and the ethics of care. First, the ethics of care, as described in the previous chapter, is premised upon a relational social ontology, and conceives of moral subjects as constituted in and by their relations. As such, the ethics of care is well positioned to theorize and contemplate the relations that constitute (not simply connect) worlds in the pluriverse. Moral theories underpinned by an atomistic and individualist ontology, on the other hand, are unable to attend to the political and ethical nature and consequences of the deep relationality of the pluriverse, because the ontological premise of individualism means that such approaches either deal with 'ones' or with 'a multiplicity of ones brought together for some purpose. Relationships [from this vantage point] must somehow exist outside or between these phenomena, for it is gathering the phenomena together that makes the connections' (Strathern, 2004, p. 53). More simply, beginning with 'ones' 'creates problems for the conceptualization of relationships' (Strathern, 2004, p. 53), which are primary in the pluriverse. The ethics of care does not begin with 'ones'; its relational social ontology attunes the ethics of care to relations all the way down. Such an orientation is necessary for a pluriversal ethics, where different onto-epistemologies, and the ethical conflicts that arise between them, emerge in and through (are constituted by) complex sets of relations.

Second, the ethics of care also implies a situated epistemology; this is another connection with the pluriverse. As moral selves are constituted in and through relations, their epistemologies and knowledge claims are likewise constituted in and through relations and context (and equally, their knowledge claims, and particularly moral knowledge claims, constitute moral selves). As Hekman (1995, p. 130) writes:

> Moral voices are constitutive of, not peripheral to, subjects. Each subject will possess a particular moral voice, a voice rooted in her social, historical, linguistic, and cultural situation. Although she may be able to employ other moral voices for specific purposes, forcing her to adopt a moral voice not her own, a voice that is not a product of her situatedness, would be like forcing her to speak a foreign language.

Knowledge, from an ethics of care perspective, can only be situated. Claims about what is known, including moral and ethical judgements and values, cannot be deliberated in abstraction from the world in which they arise and unfold. Instead, the ethics of care requires that any and all moral judgements be understood as contextualized and situated, and therefore vulnerable. 'Truth' does not exist 'out there'; it can only be found within the sets of relations and practices from which particular knowledge claims, and particular moral selves, emerge. For this reason, the ethics of care asserts that all moral judgement is vulnerable.[3] Care ethics understands that there is a plurality of moral voices and contends that moral deliberation will only be meaningful if subjects are allowed 'to speak in the moral voices that define them as subjects' (Hekman, 1995, p. 130). Relatedly, the ethics of care also emphasizes that there are multiple forms of moral life, which, like moral subjects, are intrinsically tied to and produced through 'the complex of values, practices, relations and institutions which sustain collective experience' (Hutchings, 2003, p. 129). As a result, moral judgement, including the moral judgement of the global ethicist, can only be a tentative, difficult, and risky undertaking, which is understood to emerge from a unique moral self who is embedded in a particular form of moral life. And understanding, as best as possible, different forms of moral life, which serve as the 'bedrock' that justifies any given moral claim, becomes an ongoing and pressing ethical task for moral philosophy. From this vantage point,

> the crucial question [must] not be how we know what is ethically necessary, but how certain values or practices come to be seen or experienced as ethically necessary. The point is not to establish in advance what is to count as moral, but to gain a deeper knowledge of the 'forms of moral life'. This deeper knowledge does not take any

---

[3] Two points should be noted here. First, this discussion draws heavily upon the work of Kimberly Hutchings (2001; 2003; 2013) and Margaret Urban Walker (2007). It is important to note that both Hutchings and Walker are writing about a broader approach to moral philosophy – what Walker calls 'the expressive-collaborative model' – and their respective discussions are not directly in relation to the ethics of care. That said, both do include the ethics of care in this broader approach to moral philosophy, and as such, their description of this broader approach can apply specifically to the ethics of care also, particularly given the way in which care ethics is understood in this book.

Second, the idea that moral judgement is vulnerable has been articulated by other theorists, albeit in different terminology. For instance, as reviewed in the section 'The Ch'ixi realm and Rivera's decolonial praxis' in Chapter 3, Silvia Rivera Cusicanqui's 'profession of faith' involves drawing momentary boundaries and making assertions that are always revisable and without transcendental groundings – they are, in this sense, vulnerable. Cecelia Lynch's (2020, p. 19) wonderful text on 'ethical precarity' also discusses the import of a 'moral and political humility', particularly in the context of Christianity. I see the ethics of care, with its emphasis on vulnerable moral judgement, as an ally to other approaches, like these two, which think about ethics and politics in a way that emphasizes the situatedness of all moral claims, the inherent struggle and riskiness that is involved in asserting such claims, and the necessity of committing to reflecting on and revising these claims when necessary.

manifestation of moral values and relations as simply given, but looks at how it has come to be and, crucially, at how interests are constructed and served by the 'bedrock' character of any particular moral practice. (Hutchings, 2003, p. 130)

At the same time, in focusing on the ways in which certain practices come to be seen as ethically necessary, and prioritizing the vulnerability of all moral judgement, the ethics of care also does not suggest that we abandon all ethical prescription. We cannot 'allow the acknowledgement of vulnerability to let [our]selves off the hook of judgement' (Hutchings, 2013, p. 26). Vulnerable moral judgement rather means that we must take responsibility for the worlds we create through our moral judgements and prioritize 'the reflective articulation of ethical prescriptions which acknowledge the conditions of their own meaningfulness' (Hutchings, 2003, p. 130). In acknowledging the assumptions underpinning ethical judgement, indicating clearly the 'explanatory benefits and costs' (Hutchings, 2001, p. 87) of a position, and recognizing the taken-for-granted moral imaginary that a moral agent operates within, moral agents can assert (vulnerable) moral claims, although they must always include a reflective articulation of 'the conditions of their own meaningfulness' (Hutchings, 2003, p. 130). Such articulation increases the likelihood that a given claim will 'become intelligible and persuasive to others' (Hutchings, 2003, p. 130).

This latter point is significant, in that it again demonstrates why morality is a collective undertaking from an ethics of care perspective. Not only is morality a form of life (as in, a socially situated and enacted part of living together), but it is also social and collective in that the very significance of a moral claim lies in the ways in which a moral judgement speaks to the experiences of the moral actors to whom the judgement is presented. To put it differently, the ethics of care understands that moral judgement is only authoritative 'within existing forms of ethical life' or if its authority is 'collaboratively built' (Hutchings, 2003, p. 129). As either already existing within forms of ethical life, or as something to be collaboratively built, the assertion, critique, and justification of a moral claim is always a collective undertaking. And as collective, moral philosophizing and moral judgement 'must make explicit the fundamental assumption[s] on which it rests' (Hutchings, 2001, p. 90) so that the moral agents we are engaging with can assess, as best as possible, the claim, the conditions of possibility for that claim, and the world(s) that claim (re)produces. Reflectively specifying the conditions in and through which we produce ethical knowledge, and the conditions in and through which ethical knowledge becomes meaningful, 'expands possibilities of engagement and critique, and holds the theorist to account beyond the world of his/her own epistemic community and historical present' (Hutchings, 2013, p. 40). Collectively engaging in this ongoing, messy, and to some extent impossible task of attempting to understand different forms of moral life, and the different claims to moral authority therein, while always foregrounding the ways in which one's own contingent moral form of life constitutes one's moral knowledge and judgement is, from a care ethical perspective, the iterative and challenging process in and through which (vulnerable) moral judgements are agonized.

It is because of this understanding of moral judgement that the ethics of care is also able to deal with the particular epistemic challenge of the pluriverse regarding the limits to knowing. As demonstrated through my discussion of discourse ethics in Chapter 3, communicating across worlds can sometimes involve an excess – something that cannot be translated across worlds, and something that therefore points to the limits of one's epistemic resources, which are themselves 'bounded' by the onto-epistemology of the moral subject. The ethics of care, premised upon a situated epistemology, inherently understands such limitations, particularly as they apply to moral claims:

> When I make a moral argument, I am making a claim to correctness; I am asserting that my moral statements are not arbitrary. This claim is rooted in the centrality of my moral beliefs to my status as a person: I am the kind of person I am because I have certain moral beliefs. Neither my subjectivity nor my morality is arbitrary; both are my way of being in the world. But they are not 'correct' in a universalist sense, because, quite obviously, other kinds of persons and other kinds of moral beliefs exist in the world. My understanding of my own world, however, is substantially constituted by my necessary moral subjectivity; I cannot fully understand any other kind of world. (Hekman, 1995, p. 129)

For the ethics of care, the inherent limitations involved in understanding the knowledge claims that constitute/arise in and through another world are foregrounded; as subjects of one world, we cannot ever fully understand a different world. At the same time, however, the ethics of care does not descend into moral relativism. Moral claims are not arbitrary, even when they cannot be made fully comprehensible across worlds. Instead, moral understandings are fundamental to the (re)production of worlds and ways of being and knowing. They may be plural, but they provide 'standards of truth' (Hekman, 1995, p. 139) within the worlds in which they are enacted and emerge. More to the point, 'the justification of the moral understandings that are woven through a particular lifeway rests on the goods to be found in living it' (Walker, 2007, p. 7).

For this reason, moral judgement across worlds, it is worth repeating, must attend as well as possible to understanding where certain moral values and claims come from, while acknowledging that comprehending these values and claims fully may not be possible. The ethics of care, with its relational social ontology and situated epistemology, thereby recasts moral deliberation as the difficult and messy task of attempting to decentre one's own judgement (never fully possible) in an attempt to know the other (never fully possible) in an ongoing and iterative way. This understanding of morality, and the continual recognition of the vulnerability of all moral judgement, is amenable to building a pluriversal ethics, and to attending to the normative and moral tasks inherent in the pluriversal project. More forcefully, given the deep and pervasive differences in the pluriverse, I believe that pluriversal moral deliberation, particularly for those in the modern world, can proceed no other way.

Lastly, as I have argued earlier, the pluriverse is constituted by an axiology of partial connections. While in the previous chapter I did not describe an 'axiology' for the ethics of care, I did discuss how the ethics of care is premised upon a normative valuation of care – that is, the maintenance and reparation of relations so as to live as well as reasonably possible (Fisher and Tronto, 1990, p. 40), given our vulnerable embodiment and relational subjectivity. This 'axiology of care' serves as an 'organizing trajectory around attentive/responsive living' (Hamington, 2015b, p. 287). This 'organizing trajectory' is, to be sure, only thinly normative; how to be attentive and respond to a plurality of situated needs and heterogenous vulnerable moral selves cannot be predetermined or prescribed, only gleaned through tentative, and sometimes agonistic, practices of care which are continually assessed and revised. Nonetheless, what is of moral value from an ethics of care perspective is care, and the substance of moral practices is found in the ways in which we attempt, often through many iterations, to live well, to respond to needs, and to minimize harm and suffering.

This axiology of care, I suggest, aligns with, and perhaps even amends, the axiology of partial connections in the pluriverse. As described at the beginning of this chapter, an axiology of partial connections in the pluriverse is a commitment to multiplying the partial connections between worlds. As has also been emphasized, these connections, however, are not to be multiplied at all costs: some connections will be harmful and prevent certain worlds from flourishing. Or, to borrow from Blaser (2013), there will be some worlds, and some connections between worlds, that are not worlds/ connections with which we want to live. The ethics of care, I suggest, thereby amends, or perhaps articulates more accurately, the pluriversal commitment to partial connections in a small but significant way. From an ethics of care perspective, a pluriversal ethics must be attuned not simply to 'connections' and relations more broadly, but rather, to *partial relations of care*, where care refers in the most general sense to a world's ability to flourish as a world. Crucially, the 'content' of this care (what, exactly, a world needs to maintain and repair itself as best as possible) is open for contestation. Debates and possibly conflicts will necessarily result as worlds require different – and sometimes directly competing – practices and resources in order to assert and maintain themselves as worlds. In fact, I suspect that ethical conflicts in the pluriverse will frequently take this form (as evidenced in Chapter 8 of this book); this is, in part, why I believe that we need pluriversal ethics, and why I believe that conceiving of 'connections' as the more precise 'relations of care' articulates more fully the normative project of the pluriverse.

At the same time, while amending the word 'connection' to the more specific 'relations of care' provides a clearer articulation of the normative project of the pluriverse, maintaining the word 'partial' is equally important. Maintaining the term 'partial' emphasizes that valuing relations of care – while necessary if we are to enact a pluriverse in which multiple worlds can coexist, in which 'the world is more than one socionatural formation' (de la Cadena, 2010, p. 361) – does not mean building a common 'care' world. Practices of care are 'partial' in that they are not meant to homogenize or totalize the worlds that comprise the pluriverse; they will be multiple, heterogeneous, and they will at times conflict and other times align. Care ethics, with its situated epistemology and relational ontology, foregrounds radical difference and the futility – and dangers – of attempting to homogenize this difference. Indeed, Carol Gilligan's (1993) work, in which she heard the different 'care' voice, illustrates this forcefully. Defining the moral realm as constituted by only one moral voice (for instance, the rationalist voice that dominates modern moral philosophy) limits the dimensions of moral discourse, silences the care voice as well as other moral voices, and renders the issues raised by other voices as outside the concerns of morality.

The ethics of care does not seek to homogenize or totalize the world into a singular care community. Rather, it is by engaging with difference, and importantly, engaging with difference in a non-hierarchical way, that varied caring practices can be enacted, evaluated, and revised when necessary. It is by engaging with difference, and by understanding how different forms of moral life give rise to different values and ways of being, that conflicts between caring practices can be investigated, weighed, and modified if needed. The ethics of care sees difference as integral to a relational ontology, as opposed to something that must be overcome to live in relations together. As a result, attending to and deliberating on different forms of life, different moral voices, different practices, and different knowledge claims becomes the means by which we can reflect on whether or not the ways in which we organize and live our lives align with our stated values. Dwelling in difference becomes the means by which we can work through ethical conflicts regarding how to live well, that is, how to care. For these many reasons, the ethics of care is well situated to attend to ethical dilemmas across radically different but partially connected worlds, to build a pluriversal ethics.

Finally, it is also by foregrounding difference that the ethics of care again reminds us of the importance of acknowledging the vulnerability of all moral judgement, and, in so doing, holds the moral judge accountable for the claims they make. Because care ethics conceives of morality as practices that unfold and enact forms of life, and moral knowledge as situated and emerging in/through such forms of life, the care ethicist is always inherently responsible for the effects of their claims, for the world(s) their (vulnerable) ethical judgements enact. As Hutchings (2003, p. 131, emphasis added) summarizes:

> In so far as any moral theorist articulates ethical prescriptions, he or she must take responsibility for also articulating the conditions within which those prescriptions are meaningful and *therefore the kind of world[(s)] they imply*. Acknowledging that judgement is a risky business, and being honest about its partiality, enables judgement to be oriented to the present and future rather than to preoccupation with its anterior conditions. The meaningfulness of moral judgement and prescription is not in the hands of the moral judge, but in the degree to which the judgment speaks to the experience of the audience to which the judgement is addressed.

In short, an ethics of care for the pluriverse is not about constructing a single world structured by a singular set of caring practices. The ethics of care, as conceived of here, provides a reconceptualization of morality that is amenable to the pluriversal project as it foregrounds the moral salience of our everyday practices and relations of care that comprise our moral lives and moral selves, and that allow for the continuation and repair of worlds. The ethics of care provides important tools with which to think about how to connect worlds via partial relations of care, and from which to deliberate on conflicts that emerge through these partial relations of care. And of equal significance, the ethics of care also holds the ethicist responsible for the connections they make (or do not make), and the worlds they enact (or do not enact). Vulnerable moral judgement, for the ethics of care, is a complicated business that we must always take responsibility for, but that we also cannot ultimately control. The actual effects of our moral philosophizing cannot be known in advance; the best we can do is return to our moral judgements and scrutinize them collectively time and time again.

For these reasons, the ethics of care does not just provide us with tools for contemplating ethical dilemmas in the pluriverse; more fundamentally, it provides us with an orientation from which to build a pluriversal ethics. More simply, as this chapter shows, the pluriverse, care, and ethics are deeply intertwined. For the remainder of this book, I further develop my argument supporting this claim, and demonstrate how the ethics of care can help us enhance partial relations of care – and attend to ethical conflicts between worlds in a way that likewise enhances partial relations of care – across different onto-epistemologies in the pluriversal matrix.

6

Vulnerable and Precarious Worlds: A Meta-Theoretical Orientation

One of the great challenges for thinking about ethics in the pluriverse, or building a pluriversal ethics, is understanding the ways in which relations of power between worlds shape ethical dilemmas across worlds in every way. What, exactly, counts as moral and ethical knowledge and practices; what differences are at play in a given interaction between worlds; how an ethical dilemma is framed, understood, or ignored; what resources are available to moral agents and how these resources are unevenly distributed; and the consequences of various responses to ethical dilemmas are all deeply shaped by relations of power between worlds. Further, as scholars like Arturo Escobar (2016) and Mario Blaser (2010) note, power relations between worlds are not symmetrical; worlds must 'strive to sustain their own existence in their interaction with other worlds' (Escobar, 2016, p. 21) and relations of power will render such sustenance more difficult for some worlds than for others.

That is, while of course every interaction between/across worlds may mean that all worlds involved are susceptible to change due to the influence of another (or many others), asymmetrical relations of power better position some worlds to reproduce and sustain themselves as worlds. As argued in Chapter 2, the current configuration of the pluriversal matrix is shaped fundamentally by the hegemony of the modern world, which sees itself as the one-world, and which, through colonial relations of power, is able to convert modern 'realities into *the* reality and demote "other" realities to differing representations of the world the colonisers have made' (Blaney and Tickner, 2017b, pp. 298–9, emphasis in original). The '(corpo)realization of modernity' and the subsequent invisibilisation of other ways of being, or the invisibilisation of other worlds as worlds, narrows the space in which these other lives can unfold (Blaser, 2010, p. 79). By corollary, the ways in which ethical dilemmas unfold across worlds is also narrowed, or perhaps more accurately, flattened; ethical dilemmas are often only deemed dilemmas from the 'point of view' of the hegemon, modernity. Modernity (and by this, I mean, the onto-epistemic framework of modernity) also often then dictates which moral responses are legitimate or possible. The ways in which ethical dilemmas may unfold in many dimensions and directions and involve actors and issues unknowable to the modern world are obfuscated by the relations of power that allow modernity to claim the whole of the real.

As a result, if we are to build a pluriversal ethics, attention must be paid to the relations of power which configure the pluriverse, and that relegate certain worlds – and their moral knowledges, practices, and concerns – to the margins for two reasons. First, as the decolonial project underpinning the entire pluriversal scholarship foregrounds, the ethical question of why some worlds are rendered invisible as worlds, while other worlds (in this case, modernity) are taken as a given, is pressing. The pluriversal project, as argued in Chapter 5, involves normative questions regarding how worlds connect *all the way down*. Or to put it more simply, I believe that, from a pluriversal perspective, attentiveness to the ways in which certain worlds are disparaged emerges as a critical, pressing, and ongoing ethical concern. Second, as the ethics of care reminds us, moral deliberation can only begin by paying attention to the contexts in and through which ethical quandaries emerge. In the pluriverse, the relations between worlds form the very background conditions in and through which ethical issues arise, are attended to, or alternatively, are ignored. In order to understand ethical dilemmas across worlds, it is thus necessary to also understand the relations between the worlds involved, and to investigate critically how uneven relations of power are at play in constructing and responding to any given moral dilemma.

The purpose of this chapter is to develop a care ethical meta-theoretical orientation from which to analyse and explore the relations of power between worlds that always implicitly, and often explicitly, shape ethical conflicts in the pluriverse. In particular, drawing upon the ethics of care, this chapter argues that a relational ontology inherently implies vulnerability. Given the relational ontology of the pluriverse, and of particular worlds in the pluriverse, I claim that, by extension, both the pluriversal matrix and the worlds therein are vulnerable. I then mobilize a conceptual distinction between vulnerability and precarity in order to highlight the processes and the ideational and material relations of power that shape the configuration of the pluriverse and render certain worlds or onto-epistemologies more vulnerable – that is, precarious – than others. This provides a useful framework for contemplating the pluriverse, because the ontological assumption of vulnerability allows us to focus on the simultaneous contingency of all worlds while also pointing to the possibility of new pluriversal configurations. At the same time, the lens of precarity attunes us to the ways in which material relations of power also affect the configuration of worlds, often with the effect of marginalizing certain worlds and stabilizing others. Together, these two lenses of vulnerability and precarity, I suggest, foreground the interplay between stability and instability that is central to the configuration of the pluriverse, and better orients a critical political ethics of care to understand the nature of the pluriverse and the ethical issues that arise as onto-epistemologies evolve and conflict.

Relational ontology and vulnerability

As I have shown in the preceding discussion, the relational social ontology of the ethics of care implies vulnerability. If moral selves are constituted in and through relations, then our very subjectivity is vulnerable and inextricably dependent on those relations. We are the product of relations; should those relations change, our vulnerable subjectivity would also change. There is not some transcendental self that can traverse different relations and contexts; 'individuals are no longer seen as atomistic units with a pre-determined identity, who meet each other in the public sphere to create social ties' (Sevenhuijsen, 1998, p. 55). The self rather *emerges in and through* relations and contexts, and is susceptible to changes in these relations and contexts. Our subjectivity is vulnerable in that it must constantly be (re)produced in and by the relations that constitute it. Moral subjectivity, from this vantage point, is vulnerable because the moral self is

> a processual self, a self which is continually in the process of being formed; moral identity is continually being developed and revised through this process. The construing of moral identities is thus, in this sense, inherently a social practice, something which we do and make within human relations and within specific social and political contexts, and the narrative conventions reflected in these. (Sevenhuijsen, 1998, p. 56)

A relational ontology, as espoused by the ethics of care, implies vulnerability in the sense that the moral subject is never complete or whole, but always a relational becoming.

Conversely, vulnerability, and particularly our corporeal vulnerability, also points to relationality. Our embodiment, and our embodied needs, mean that we are vulnerable. As Tiina Vaittinen (2015, p. 104) writes in her article in which she theorizes about the 'body rather than the subject', 'corporeal vulnerability is part of our very embodiment'. We are finite beings, 'a living organism that is internally and persistently *vulnerable to life itself*: to aging and decay and, ultimately, to death' (Vaittinen, 2015, p. 104, emphasis in original). This vulnerability implies – or perhaps more accurately, demands – relatedness. 'There are no autonomous subjects without needs, only degrees of embodied vulnerability that continue to elicit political relatedness' (Vaittinen, 2015, p. 104). Relations, including political relations, arise from (or fail to arise from) and respond to (or fail to respond to) our vulnerable embodiment and the fact that bodies need care. Thus, just as relationality implies vulnerability, vulnerability necessarily implies relationality. The two are inextricably intertwined. Our lives are vulnerable and relational in terms of both our selfhood and our embodied being, which are themselves inextricably intertwined, as our vulnerable embodiment, and the relations that result from that, shape our vulnerable subjectivity, and vice versa.

As Estelle Ferrarese (2016a, p. 150) points out, however, 'what is vulnerable is not only our lives [or our "selves"] but also our world and our links with others, which have to be repaired and supported continuously'. That is, if, as the pluriversal literature suggests, worlds are enacted and performed through practices and relations, then worlds themselves are vulnerable too. Practices, enacted by relational and vulnerable subjects, are processual; they are ongoing, shifting, and fluid. The worlds enacted by vulnerable subjects may shift as these subjects change; when worlds come to be enacted differently, vulnerable subjects of those worlds will likely also change. The relational ontology of worlds in the pluriverse means that worlds are also not transcendental or invincible. Worlds, as ongoing sets of practices and relations must be vulnerable too, as such relations and practices require either constant tending to, or at least always hold the possibility of being changed. Lastly, this same logic applies, then, to the structure of the pluriverse itself, and the connections between worlds. As Ferrarese (2016a) again points out, links with others – to which I would add, links with other worlds – are also vulnerable and require continuous support and attention. Connections between worlds, like worlds themselves, are not monolithic or indestructible. They are shifting and vulnerable to be other than they are. Because of this, I suggest that the relational ontology of the pluriverse, and the relational ontology of the worlds that comprise the pluriverse, also inherently implies that the pluriverse, and the multiple worlds therein, are vulnerable.

But what of the political? Can vulnerability serve as a fruitful concept for contemplating the political? And if not, is it useful for the pluriverse, which, as I have argued, operates at the level of the political? While I discuss the political in the context of the pluriverse in a more fulsome way in the next chapter, the relationship between vulnerability and the political merits some attention here. For, as Ferrarese (2016a, p. 152) highlights, 'the political scope of vulnerability is almost unanimously denied … vulnerability seems inevitably to be relegated to the sphere of "good sentiments"', and therefore cannot be ascribed any real political role. More specifically, Ferrarese (2016a) reviews several reasons as to why vulnerability often appears to fail to provide a useful vantage point from which to think about the political. First, she notes that some scholars see vulnerability as a private and individual concern that does not merit political deliberation in the public sphere. Second, and relatedly, it is argued that vulnerability is incompatible with the political grammars that comprise the political sphere as we know it today. Third, Ferrarese notes that there appears to be a tension in asserting a 'vulnerable political subject', as vulnerability implies powerlessness. And finally, vulnerability is associated with the body, which is deemed unworthy of consideration as a political object. At the heart of this critique is the notion that our vulnerable embodiment is an obstacle to freedom (that is, a finiteness that cannot be overcome), and the reality that there is a 'repetition that characterizes the needs of the vulnerable body' (Ferrarese, 2016a, p. 152). Such repetition is antithetical to the political, as the political is concerned with initiating something new, that is, a moment of instantiation of something that had not existed before, an unexpected beginning or new socio-symbolic order. The body, in many ways, has consistent needs that, at base, vary little through time-space (thereby evading political change), and that cannot be overcome (thereby impeding freedom).

The first of these two critiques are easily addressed. As outlined in great detail in Chapter 4, conceiving of vulnerability, as well as need and care, as a private concern, or as incompatible with our political discourse, only makes sense if a series of related binaries hold: a distinction between public/private, morality/ethics, mind/body and so on. It is only within such moral boundaries, as Joan Tronto (1993) calls them, that vulnerability, need, and care can be relegated to the private sphere, or deemed outside the scope of the political. Further, by beginning with relationality, vulnerability, and care, the ethics of care highlights the detrimental effects of these boundaries and shows how whole sections of common life are systematically ignored and devalued in political discourse and life as a result (Laugier, 2016, p. 216). In pointing this out, the ethics of care, and vulnerability, 'implies the invention of new categories, and a new way of doing politics' and in this way, 'the discourse of vulnerability has already shown itself to be fully political' (Ferrarese, 2016a, p. 157) – vulnerability itself challenges the dominant socio-symbolic order of modernity that suppresses relationality and slices the world into hierarchicalized binaries.

The third concern, which relates to the idea that vulnerability implies powerlessness or a lack of autonomy, is also important to address, particularly in the context of the pluriverse. To assert that worlds are vulnerable, as I do here, is not to assert that they are powerless. Tiina Vaittinen's (2015, p. 104) discussion of the power of vulnerable bodies is instructive on this point: 'the body in itself is politically powerful, even when incapable of articulating itself as a subject.'

> Care and its need constantly draw bodies towards each other. This latent movement creates unavoidable relations between human bodies, and

these relations are political. ... The political relations of care derive from human vulnerability and our concrete, corporeal need of care from embodied others. ...

Within the structures of political economy, however, the corporeal relations of care are never only about the two persons directly involved in the practices of care. Care always cuts through entire institutional structures ... it is constrained by the structures, but also challenges and shapes them. Thereby, through corporeal relations of care, the allegedly apolitical 'bare life' influences, challenges and shapes the structures of the political economy. (Vaittinen, 2015, p. 112)

In other words, our corporeal vulnerabilities – our bodily limitations and finiteness – draw us together and demand response; moral practices and political relations are mobilized to address our bodily needs. Global social arrangements arise in response to bodily vulnerabilities, and global political decisions can lead to bodily harm or, alternatively, can address such harms. Even in its 'barest' corporeal form, vulnerability exerts power. As argued in Chapter 4, this power of the vulnerable body, and our untameable caring needs, is so great that it confronts and resists the logic of control and mastery that is so fundamental to modern capitalism. In so doing, vulnerable bodies point to the limits of the modern order and vulnerability thus shows itself to be properly political. There is always the possibility of a political moment in which the dominant order is ruptured by that which it cannot totalize or overcome: the vulnerability of our existence.

Similarly, it is also clear that vulnerability does not prevent autonomy; instead, autonomy – the ability to act, to say and do, to exert power – only comes in and through our relations of dependency (Clement, 1996). Judith Butler (1997, p. 2) refers to this as an 'enabling vulnerability', in which we come to be in and through our dependencies on others and the ways in which they address our needs. Vulnerability, and the 'supports' it demands (Castel, 2016, p. 165), is empowering. Lastly, in understanding that all subjects are vulnerable (or, as I argue in this chapter, that all worlds are vulnerable), 'it is worth insisting not only on the fact that exposure to another's power does not signify one's own powerlessness, but also on the idea that a large part of our capacities are deployed *against*, or set out from, a vulnerability' (Ferrarese, 2016a, p. 158, emphasis in original). Our own vulnerabilities, and the vulnerabilities of those that we are in relations with, motivate us to act as political subjects. The political subject cannot be anything other than vulnerable and conceiving of worlds as vulnerable does not void them of power.

The final critique noted by Ferrarese (2016a) pertains to the vulnerable body and its repetitive needs that cannot be overcome. These repetitive and constant needs that cannot be conquered seem to be at fundamental odds with the political moment, which suggests newness and a different socio-symbolic order. How can a socio-symbolic order radically change if always tethered to a constant fragile body? Once again, I suggest – and this follows Ferrarese (2016a) – that this framing of the relationship between vulnerability and the political only makes sense if certain binaries are upheld. Locating the vulnerable body outside the political requires a distinction between the social world (the socio-symbolic), which is seen as susceptible to change, and nature, which is conceived of as timeless (unable to be overcome or altered). As a political theory which rejects such boundaries, the ethics of care and its emphasis on vulnerability insists that

> the task of theories of vulnerability is to recall the inseparability of the two levels [the socio-symbolic and nature]. It is worth dwelling on the fact that it is the nature-social circle, and the impossibility of opening it, which makes it possible to grasp the stakes of vulnerability. Nature and society can no longer constitute explanatory terms, but instead presume a conjoint explanation each time anew. It is just as necessary to shed light on what the perpetual erection and shoring up of that boundary enables, forgets and dissimulates, as it is to perform a displacement. Social world and ontological vulnerability must be thought of conjointly in order to show how they engender and co-produce each other. (Ferrarese, 2016a, p. 154)

Vulnerability requires us to hold on to the inseparability of the socio-symbolic order and nature; the ways in which embodied and organic vulnerabilities are understood, distributed, dialogued, addressed, and therefore experienced, cannot be separated from the socio-symbolic order in which they exist and unfold. Likewise, socio-symbolic orders have always been established in intimate relation to vulnerabilities and nature. The question of knowing how to live – including how to live in and with vulnerabilities, which cannot be escaped – 'cannot be addressed without taking into account the fact that any social formation always has already responded to it, whether implicitly or explicitly, and its response is embedded in an extremely material and concrete reality' (Ferrarese, 2016b, p. 236). A particular distribution of care, a specific taking charge of vulnerabilities, is always the result of a socio-symbolic order and social-political relations of power. A focus on vulnerability implores us to (re)engage with questions regarding the efficacy of how such socio-symbolic orders respond to and address vulnerabilities; such questions will also involve exploring and perhaps rethinking what it is to be vulnerable in the first place.

In this way, a focus on vulnerability as political implicitly critiques the literature on 'the political', which tends to privilege the discursive and socio-symbolic above nature. In this privileging, this literature also upholds an ontological split between Human/Nature which, as Chapter 2 argues, is key to the modern world and which has proven so problematic for contemplating the pluriverse and ontological difference. Contrarily, in starting with relationality and vulnerability, the ethics of care recasts the political so as to foreground the inseparability of our finite and material being (nature) and the ways in which we socially come to understand and meet our collective needs (social). More fundamentally, the ethics of care locates understanding the ways in which our ontological vulnerability materializes in unique vulnerable states (Ferrarese, 2016a, p. 153) through a complex interplay between nature and the social as a task of great political import, one which can point to the limitations of existing socio-symbolic orders and possibilities for new ones. Indeed, worlds or onto-epistemologies themselves are, in many ways, the outcome of this complex interplay, of organizing and structuring social life to respond to our material and vulnerable existence. Claiming that worlds are vulnerable, then, does not negate the political nature of the pluriverse. Rather, thinking about vulnerable worlds in the context of the pluriverse is useful because, on the one hand, it captures the relationality between worlds and the fluidity (that is, vulnerability) of worldings – the fact that a political moment is always possible as worlds interact and conflict. On the other hand, the claim that all worlds are vulnerable also allows us to see how the political in the context of the pluriverse – that is, the establishment of a world or onto-epistemology – is not simply the establishment of a socio-symbolic order; nature is fundamentally implicated too.

Precarity

The concept of precarity has also gained currency in the last decade.[1] Coming from the Latin root *prex* or *precis*, meaning 'to pray or to plead' (Casas-Cortés, 2014, p. 207), 'precarity' has been used in a growing literature on precarious labour and work to mean 'insecure, dependent on the favour of another, unstable, exposed to danger; with uncertain tenure' (Breman, 2013, p. 134), particularly in relation to recent changes in the economic relations of production (see, for example, Fudge and Owens, 2006; Vosko, 2006; Kalleberg, 2009). Kathleen Millar (2017) describes two main trends in this literature: first, drawing particularly on the work of Pierre Bourdieu (1998), Millar discusses precarity as a labour condition (insecure, unregulated, flexible, and low paying), and second, drawing upon the work of Guy Standing (2011), Millar points to the related literature which views

---

[1] It is beyond the breadth of this text to give a complete genealogy of the term precarity; instead, this section focuses on two broad themes in the precarity literature. For a more detailed overview of the concept, see Ronaldo Munck (2013).

precarity as a class category (the precariat). These two literatures, while differing in the object of analysis (the labour activity or the labouring subject), both focus on the particular characteristics of labour under neoliberal capitalism. For instance, Standing (2011) emphasizes that the contingency of work and employment in the current neoliberal order has created a new class, 'the precariat'. The precariat is, according to Standing, largely feminized and racialized, comprised in particular of migrants, and 'can be defined in three dimensions: distinctive relations of production (patterns of labour and work), distinctive relations of distribution (sources of social income), and distinctive relations to the state (loss of citizenship rights)' (Standing, 2018, pp. 4–5). The insecure and fluid nature of work for the precariat means that those in this 'class in the making' are left with 'a feeling of being in a diffuse, unstable international community of people struggling usually in vain to give their working lives an occupational identity' (Standing, 2011, p. 23).

As Millar notes (2017, p. 3), however, several scholars have criticized this class and labour centric approach to precarity. Brett Neilson and Ned Rossiter (2008, p. 54), for instance, argue that precarity only 'appears as an irregular phenomenon', apparently unique to this historical neoliberal moment, when set against a particular modern norm of a robust welfare state and strong citizen rights – a norm that is tied to the valorisation of waged work as a social and ethical good. This understanding of precarity, as Franco Barchiesi (2012) argues, fails to problematize the centrality of work in our neoliberal order; discussions of the 'new' precarity of labour relations (re)produce a nostalgia for a better time, when labour relations were apparently 'secure' and 'stable'. Further, as scholars like Ben Scully (2016) and Ronaldo Munck (2013) highlight, such a narrative is decidedly modern. On the one hand, conceiving of 'stable' wage labour as the norm against which precarious work is measured fails to engage meaningfully with the ways in which the forceful imposition of the capitalist system (and therefore, of so called 'decent work') on other ways of being through colonial and imperial expansion was, in no way, 'decent' to those that were colonized. As Munck (2013, p. 758) succinctly writes, 'there was nothing liberatory about being torn from traditional communal modes of production to become a "wage slave"'.

On the other hand, casting precarity as negative simultaneously masks the ways in which precarious work has allowed certain people, particularly in the Global South, to continue to resist or evade full capture by capitalism. For example, in an ethnographic study of *catadores*, those who collect and sell recyclables from a dump in Rio de Janeiro, Brazil, Millar (2014, p. 34) demonstrates that 'paradoxically, the deeply painful and precarious work that *catadores* continually return to on the dump enable them to contend with insecurities in other dimensions of their lives'. Without romanticizing the very challenging work of scavenging these landscapes, Millar demonstrates that the precarity of this work provides a relational autonomy for these workers. The flexibility of the precarious labour gives these workers control over their schedule, allows them to meet important caring and community needs, manage everyday emergencies, and 'pursue life projects amidst these disruptions' (Millar, 2014, p. 46). Many other ethnographies tell similar stories from other parts of the Global South, including Africa (Barchiesi, 2012), China (Zhan and Huang, 2012) and Guatemala (Goldín, 2011). Standing's articulation of precarity fails to attend to the ways in which precarity, from these vantage points, also offers and maintains a challenge to capitalist hegemony (in no small part, by reminding us that subsumption into the wage relation is not necessarily desirable).

It is also notable that Standing's (2011) schematic maintains a distinction between work and labour, where work can be thought of as social reproduction, and labour is work that is done for wages; in so doing, Standing (2011, p. 207) aims to demonstrate how the precariat class must spend many hours doing work in order to labour:

> As welfare systems are restructured in ways that force claimants to go through ever more complex procedures to gain and to retain entitlement to modest benefits, the demands on the time of the precariat are large and fraught with tension. Queuing, commuting to queue, form filling, answering questions, answering more questions, obtaining certificates to prove something or other, all these are painfully time consuming yet are usually ignored. A flexible labour market that makes labour mobility the mainstream way of life, and that creates a web of moral and immoral hazards in the flurry of rules to determine benefit entitlement, forces the precariat into using time in ways that are bound to leave people enervated and less able to undertake other activities.

However, these hours of work spent to undertake labour only appear as a 'new' phenomenon when the gendered division of labour is ignored. As feminist political economists have long pointed out, 'productive' labour is only made possible by continual, and most often invisibilized, socially reproductive labour, largely done by women in the household (see, for example, Hennessy and Ingraham, 1997; James, 2012). Hours of work to prepare for labour is not a new feature of precarity, but rather a key element of the functioning of the capitalist system. Evidently, Standing's work also fails to engage meaningfully with feminist insights regarding labour relations more broadly.

Given these critiques, I believe it is fair to assert that in the literature focusing on the precariat, precarity as a concept does little to challenge the centrality of labour already constitutive of capitalism, including in its neoliberal manifestation. This concept of precarity also fails to challenge patriarchal and colonial systems of oppression, and the ways in which these systems interact with capitalism. Instead, this literature tends to reproduce uncritically masculinist and modernist norms and understandings of capitalism and work. For this reason, I contend that the concept of precariousness in these literatures can be thought of as pertaining to politics – that which is already incorporated in the existing social order – and provides little inspiration for thinking through the political, the negative effects of the current social order, and the possible social orders that are yet to be.

In contrast to these understandings of precarity (that is, precarity in relation to the labour activity or the labouring subject), Millar (2017, p. 4) also identifies a third literature which focuses on precarity as an ontological experience. While the word 'precarity' does not appear in her collection of essays, this literature is most often traced back to Butler's book *Precarious Life* (2004).[2] This book, and the growing research that has picked up on the idea of 'precarious lives', mobilize precarity as a term to capture the inherent vulnerability of our being that stems from a relational social ontology. In starting with the notion that humans are fundamentally constituted through relations, this conceptualization of precarity foregrounds interdependency and the vulnerability that arises through our exposure to others (Han, 2018, p. 337). This notion of precarity therefore operates at the level of the political because it is concerned with the ways in which certain sociosymbolic orders create the conditions of different experiences of precarity. Butler (2009, p. ii) writes:

> [Precarity] describes a few different conditions that pertain to living beings. Anything living can be expunged at will or by accident; and its persistence is in no sense guaranteed. As a result, social and political institutions are designed in part to minimize conditions of precarity, especially within the nation-state. ... Political orders, including economic and social institutions, are to some extent designed to address those very needs, not only to make sure that housing and food are available, but that populations have the means available by which life can be secured. And yet, 'precarity' designates that politically induced condition in which certain populations suffer from failing social and economic networks of support and become differentially exposed to injury, violence, and death. ... Precarity also characterizes that politically induced condition of maximized vulnerability and exposure

---

[2] Notably, Butler does employ these terms in subsequent related work (Butler, 2009; 2011; 2016; Butler and Athanasiou, 2013).

for populations exposed to arbitrary state violence and to other forms of aggression that are not enacted by states and against which states do not offer adequate protection.

Precarity, according to Butler, is so intimately shaped by a given social order that it is always operating at the level of the political. As such, I suggest that the notion of precarious life à la Butler parallels the social ontological assumption underpinning the ethics of care. Constituted in and by our relations, we are all mutually vulnerable. As discussed earlier, this vulnerability cannot be conceived of as only pertaining to the 'natural' world and therefore outside the scope of the political. Instead, vulnerability/precarity in the ontological sense are analytically useful concepts because of the ways in which they foreground that basic vulnerability always shapes an existing order (given that social organization is, at base, created to respond to needs). At the same time, that order likewise shapes the experience of our particular vulnerabilities and distributes vulnerabilities in different ways by determining caring arrangements, and by responding to certain vulnerabilities and vulnerable bodies while neglecting others.

From vulnerability to precarity

While the emphasis on mutual vulnerability in the ethics of care literature, or ontological precarity in the 'precarious lives' literature, operates at the level of the political – and as I show later, can therefore be usefully applied to the context of the pluriverse – some scholars note that this emphasis can lead to some conceptual muddiness. Kelly Oliver (2015), for example, argues that conceiving of ethics as premised on shared vulnerability is limited because it does not provide us with much guidance on how to recognize and foreground the ways in which social and political conditions and relations of power render some more vulnerable than others. Put differently, in the ontological claim that all subjects are vulnerable, it can become easy to conflate this basic ontological premise with the ways in which the uneven distribution of material relations of power shapes lived experiences of vulnerability. Similarly, Neilson and Rossiter (2005) criticize Butler's discussion of precarious life (2004) for failing to provide tools to analyse the uneven distribution of basic ontological human vulnerability. Speaking only of vulnerability (or precarity) can make it challenging to interrogate how 'our constitutive vulnerability materializes in differentiated vulnerable states' (Ferrarese, 2016a, p. 153).

To help overcome this limitation, and to provide greater conceptual clarity, I wish to put forth a conceptual distinction between vulnerability and precarity, whereby precarity is *intensified* vulnerability resulting from unequal distributions of power that render certain subjects more vulnerable than others. Vulnerability is therefore a necessary but not sufficient condition for precarity.

This distinction, I suggest, is particularly useful in the context of the pluriverse, where we are faced with the significant task of understanding how and why certain worlds or onto-epistemologies are marginalized. It is here that I think the ethics of care, when combined with the distinction between vulnerability and precariousness, can make a contribution toward building a meta-theoretical orientation for contemplating ethical issues in the pluriverse. As care ethics emphasizes, all subjects are vulnerable. I believe that this ontological claim, as suggested previously, can be applied to worlds more broadly, given that worlds are themselves constituted by relations and enacted by relational practices, and given the relationality between worlds. As argued previously, the pluriverse is characterized by a relational ontology, and a relational ontology necessarily implies an ontological vulnerability. Worlds are vulnerable in that they must be reproduced; changes in the relations and practices that reproduce a world will change that world, and such changes may be the consequence of internal dynamics (as worlds 'evolve') or external dynamics (interactions with other worlds). By foregrounding that relationality necessarily implies vulnerability, the ethics of care highlights the mutual vulnerability of all worlds. By extension, the ethics of care also reminds us that the hierarchy of worlds (that is, the pluriverse) is contingent. The relations between worlds are necessarily unstable, open to change, and vulnerable. Of particular significance, in emphasizing the contingency of the pluriversal hierarchy, a care ethics lens also opens space for a critique of the current configuration of the pluriversal matrix: if all worlds are inherently vulnerable, why do we give credence to some and not others? Why are certain onto-epistemologies relegated to the margins of the global political economy, currently dominated by modernity?

Although this opening is an important first step, I assert that we also need a lens of precarity to then answer these questions, and to investigate the practices and relations of power that render certain worlds more vulnerable – that is, precarious – than others.

Therefore, the distinction put forth here between vulnerability and precarity is meant to bolster both the literatures on the pluriverse and the ethics of care in a mutually supporting way. If the ethics of care is to serve as a truly global political ethic, it must contend with the political landscape that is the pluriverse, a landscape where differences are deep and pervasive, operating at the onto-epistemological level. The distinction between vulnerable and precarious worlds helps with this task and facilitates a more robust political ethics of care by focusing on the ways in which vulnerabilities – and relations of power shaping, or more acutely, intensifying, these vulnerabilities into precarity – operate at the onto-epistemological level in the political landscape that is the pluriverse. The uneven distribution of vulnerability – that is, the differentiated precariousness of various worlds – is the ever-present backdrop against which ethical dilemmas in the pluriverse unfold. As a potential ethics for the pluriverse, the ethics of care must therefore contemplate this backdrop. The ethics of care understands the importance of context in all ethical deliberation; the notion of vulnerable and precarious worlds is an analytical tool for contemplating the pluriversal context. At the same time, conceiving of the pluriversal landscape as one of vulnerability and precarity demonstrates how the ethics of care provides important ways to think about relations of power in the pluriverse, and therefore contributes to the pluriversal literature. The next section turns to a more robust discussion of what I mean by precarity and demonstrates the analytical usefulness of this meta-theoretical ethical orientation for the pluriverse.

Expanding precarity through the pluriverse

Even though Standing's (2014) conceptualization of precarity focuses on wage labour – and thereby offers us a criticism of 'politics' instead of a site of 'the political', as argued earlier – I maintain that his articulation of three dimensions of precarious work nonetheless provides a fruitful starting point to think about the configuration of the pluriverse given its materialist focus on the relation between precarity and the means of production. First, Standing (2014, p. 969) argues that precarity is marked by particular relations of production. Those involved in precarious work experience a condition of insecure labour, are 'in and out' of jobs, and must continually contend with a sense of insecurity. Second, precarity is marked by distinctive relations of distribution. The flexibility of the wage in precarious work, and the instability of economic resources, 'means that [members of the precariat] have chronic income insecurity, experiencing volatile earnings and chronic economic uncertainty' (Standing, 2014, p. 970). Finally, for Standing, (2014, p. 971) precarity also involves particular relations to the state, characterized by a lack of citizen rights, including the right to a secure economic, social, cultural, political, and civil existence. These three dimensions of precarious labour, I advance, can be usefully applied to the pluriverse as they point to a broader understanding of precarity when reconsidered at the level of onto-epistemologies. That is, if we rethink this articulation of precarity at the level of being-in-the-world, as opposed to focusing on labour relations alone, we can see that a precarious existence is characterized by unstable subjectivities, unequal and insecure material well-being, and diminished political potentiality.

My decision to draw upon Standing's notion of precarity – despite the aforementioned critiques of his concept as engaging only with 'politics' – is therefore purposeful. Precarity, as developed here, is meant to capture the ways in which certain worlds are rendered more vulnerable than others in the global political economy. Thus, on the one hand, this analysis operates at the level of ontology and the enactment of worlds. On the other hand, this analysis also operates at the level of the global political economy, as it is concerned with the ways in which material and ideational relations of power shape the configuration of worlds in the pluriverse. Retaining Standing's (2014) understanding of precarity, rooted in material relations of work, while rethinking it at a more fundamental ontological level, is amenable to both of these tasks: this expanded understanding of precarity captures the relationship 'between precarity as a socio-economic condition and precarity as an ontological experience' (Millar, 2014, p. 35). The understanding of precarity developed and mobilized here is meant to link the study of the global political economy with questions of subjectivity, existence, and experience.

This linkage also amends Standing's work such that it no longer contributes to the invisibilisation of social reproduction and the gendered relations which constitute the global political economy. Rethinking precarity at the onto-epistemological level emphasizes that 'production and reproduction are so interwoven that it is no longer possible to speak just about precarious labour, but rather *precarious life*' (Casas-Cortés, 2014, p. 220, emphasis in original). Reconceptualizing Standing's precarity in this way is thus significant because it also moves this concept from the realm of 'politics' to 'the political'. The concept of precarity is untethered from a nostalgic notion of labour relations that upholds and reproduces the centrality of masculinist labour in the neoliberal socio-symbolic order, and instead is reoriented towards interrogating the relations of power that position worlds in hierarchical relations in the pluriverse. This reorientation thereby locates precarity as a tool to critique the political order, as opposed to a tool that serves to reform a given order.

To demonstrate this more fully, consider Standing's first dimension, the precariousness of relations of production. If we begin with the concept of onto-epistemologies, the idea of precarious relations of production, as described by Standing, can be expanded to include not just the relations of material production, but rather the relations through which worlds are produced. Certain worlds face greater instability than others. The existence of these worlds relies upon practices that are marginalized by relations of power and knowledge that legitimize some acts and relations while rendering others 'outside' what is acceptable or reasonable politically (Blaser, 2016). For instance, as Cristina Rojas (2016) illustrates, the division between the modern and non-modern renders some things thinkable and others unthinkable (that a river could be living kin, or that a mountain could have agency, for example). The relations of power which shape the modern/non-modern binary create limits to what is considered valid, to which practices and ways of being are legitimate. These limits point to the precariousness of the production of certain worlds.

The idea of precarious relations of distribution can similarly be expanded to refer to the uneven distribution of resources across worlds. This includes material resources, which, due to colonialism, primitive accumulation (see, for example, Federici, 2004), and ongoing dispossession of land have been unevenly and violently redistributed across worlds. Importantly, however, from a pluriversal perspective, the relations of distribution must also refer to the distribution of more intangible resources, like political power, and the dignity of having one's epistemic and ontological stance seen as valid. Political potentiality is also unevenly distributed across worlds, as some worlds are able to mark the boundaries of 'legitimate' politics, rendering the politics of other worlds invisible (de Sousa Santos, 2007).

Finally, precarious relations to the state, when confined to a discussion of precarious labour, are linked to the modern idea that citizenship, and citizen rights, should be, or are, linked primarily to employment and market relations. Social safety nets, membership in political collectivities, and access to political and economic rights are deeply tied to employment status and participation in the labour market in a variety of ways (Esping-Anderson, 1985). However, if we begin with the idea of onto-epistemologies as opposed to labour, we can move to a broader analysis of the ways in which citizen rights, and the relation between people and the state, are shaped far beyond the relations of production. Rather, members of certain groups are denied rights simply because of their onto-epistemological status.[3]

To help illustrate this broadened notion of precariousness, consider again the example of the Whanganui River which has been revisited throughout this book. Using the lens of precarious onto-epistemologies, the three dimensions of precariousness just discussed can be located in the Whanganui Iwi's struggle to protect Whanganui. First, throughout the struggle to gain meaningful recognition of the Whanganui River as still-living kin, the Māori world experienced precarity in terms of the relations of production necessary to produce their world. The river, as co-constitutive of the community, is

---

[3] When I use words like 'citizen', 'rights', and even the 'state', I am not attempting to assert that other worlds would also use these words or concepts to articulate their desired forms of social and political organizing. For instance, certain worlds may not have a conceptualization of the state or may reject the state as the ideal form of social and political structuring all together. Similarly, when I say members of certain worlds are denied rights, I am not asserting that they necessarily want rights in the thick, liberal sense. Rather, I am using these words – constitutive of my modern world – as empty signifiers, meant to indicate, albeit imperfectly, whatever conceptualization of the good life is inherent to different onto-epistemologies. As noted in Chapter 1, this imperfect use of words reflects the fact that I am, to some extent, bounded by the limits of the discourse of my own world, and acknowledges that translation between worlds can never overcome equivocation (Strathern, 2004; de la Cadena, 2015).

necessary for the reproduction and resilience of the Māori world. Without protection for Whanganui, the relations of production necessary to produce and reproduce their world were rendered precarious;[4] to be sure, preventing harm to the Whanganui River was the Whanganui Iwi's motivation for initiating and sustaining a 140-year struggle with the New Zealand state. The Māori world also faced precariousness vis-à-vis the relations of distribution, as their relation to Whanganui was not validated by the logic of modernity or the government constituted by this logic.[5] The distribution of who and what was seen as a legitimate political agent and issue was uneven, such that the Māori world faced instability as a valid political standpoint. The distribution of authority across these two worlds was uneven, with the Māori onto-epistemology receiving 'less' legitimacy as a world within the pluriversal matrix, currently dominated by modernity. Finally, the Māori world was also characterized by a precarious relation to the state. For the Whanganui Iwi, the Whanganui River is an ancestor and still-living kin, and the state's 140-year-long refusal to acknowledge this further marginalized the Māori world by denying certain agents (like Whanganui) the rights that the Māori onto-epistemology deems appropriate.

Vulnerable relations and the power of precarity

Thus far, this chapter has made several conceptual moves. First, drawing upon the ethics of care, I assert that worlds, or onto-epistemologies, are vulnerable. This is an ontological claim about the nature of the worlds that comprise the pluriverse, stemming from their relationality. Second, I then develop a distinction between this understanding of vulnerability – as a basic ontological premise – and precarity, which, I suggest, can be understood in the context of the pluriverse as intensified vulnerability. More specifically, precarity refers to the ways in which the (re)production of certain worlds is rendered more insecure and unstable because of the uneven distribution

---

[4] To reiterate, what is of significance for this example is that the Māori world requires certain relations for it to be re-enacted through time-space. The world of the Whanganui Iwi is constituted by/with their relationship with Whanganui. It is the very fact that the relationship is threatened (Whanganui was not protected, and so the relationship was rendered precarious), and, equally importantly, that the terms of the relationship (whether Whanganui is acknowledged as living kin, as opposed to property) are reframed by another world, that is of moral salience. To frame the conflict as a problem because threatening Whanganui means that a certain practice, ceremony, or tradition cannot be conducted would reduce the significance of this relationality and is too instrumental of a reading of the ways in which worlds are practised, enacted, and reproduced.

[5] In particular, the relationship is either ignored all together, and Whanganui is framed as property, as opposed to still-living kin, or it is reduced to a 'belief' or 'tradition', as opposed to given ontological weight as an actually existing part of the Māori world.

of material and ideational power in the global political economy, currently dominated by modernity. Together, this framework, as I now show, opens analytical space for the study of the pluriverse and the relations between worlds. In particular, I suggest that this framework allows for a more robust analysis of the *simultaneous stability and instability* of the relations between worlds and the unknowable potentiality of the relations that comprise the pluriverse.

First, the assertion that all onto-epistemologies are vulnerable emphasizes that the pluriverse is not a static assemblage; rather, worlds co-constitute each other, albeit in complex ways, and this contentious, unequal, and fluid entwinement means that worlds are always susceptible to change. The assertion that all worlds are vulnerable highlights the relatedness of worlds, and the ways in which worlds are performative and require ongoing processes of legitimation and enactment. Second, the idea of precarious onto-epistemologies then allows us to foreground the dynamics that affect the enactment of worlds and to pay closer attention to the relations of power that allow certain worlds to be enacted more easily than others. For example, Elizabeth Povinelli (2011) demonstrates how the onto-epistemology of which the sovereign state is a central figure (what I have here called modernity) is built on the back of 'the prior', the worlds of the Indigenous as filtered through the modern lens. As Povinelli explains, the prior, as an onto-epistemology, only comes into being when the modern onto-epistemology comes into being. Indigeneity and the sovereign state – and the worlds of which these concepts are a part – were constructed together. The modern, and its corresponding system of governance, could only be delineated by simultaneously marking the 'pre-modern' or prior; these onto-epistemologies – the binary of the modern and pre-modern – only make sense relationally. If there was no pre-modern, there could be no modern, and vice versa. At the same time, however, this process of mutual construction was not equal or symmetrical; the prior (as in, pre-modern) was constructed so as to be governed by the modern (Povinelli, 2011, p. 24).

Povinelli's discussion here points to a significant analytical challenge related to the study of the pluriverse and the relations between worlds: how do we explain and understand 'the persistence of the occupying ontologies' (Escobar, 2016, p. 21) without treating this persistence as given? How do we understand the current configuration of onto-epistemologies without losing sight that this configuration is contingent? It is here that the concepts of vulnerable worlds and precarious worlds can make a contribution. The ontological claim that all worlds are vulnerable reminds us that even seemingly 'stable' worlds are dependent and insecure, and that a reconfiguration of the political is always possible; the very concept of vulnerable worlds renders current configurations of power 'unstable'. The precarity lens developed here extends this by further foregrounding the reality that the precarity of subverted worlds is directly linked to the stability of the occupying worlds, therefore pointing to the precarity (or at least, vulnerability) of the occupying worlds as well. The precarity of one world, due to the mutual dependency and vulnerability of all worlds, always renders other worlds, including the dominant world, as at least always potentially precarious as well. The idea of precarious onto-epistemologies allows us to focus on the ways in which unevenly distributed material and ideational relations of power render certain worlds precarious, while also locating power in that very precarity.

Returning once again to the example of the Whanganui Iwi and their struggle to protect the Whanganui River, one can see the power of precarity at work. As the previous section demonstrated, the configuration of the pluriverse, dominated by modernity, involved a distribution of power which rendered the Māori world precarious. At the same time, however, the precarity of the Māori world, I assert, rendered the modern world of the New Zealand state precarious, thereby illuminating the mutual vulnerability of the two worlds. That is, while in this example the Māori world faced, and perhaps continues to face, a more onerous struggle for legitimacy than the modern world, modernity was, and continues to be, fundamentally challenged by the existence of the Māori world – the very assertion of the Whanganui River as kin, the struggle for this assertion to be acknowledged, and the subsequent awarding of legal personality to the river (which prevents it from being treated as property), deeply challenge the modern onto-epistemology that is premised upon a Human/Nature (and corresponding subject/object) distinction. A focus on precarious onto-epistemologies not only helps uncover the particularities of the ways in which certain worlds are marginalized in the current order, but also keeps the relationality between onto-epistemologies at the fore of our analyses.

In other words, precarity, as developed here, highlights those worlds at the margins of the global political economy, specifically those which have been colonized, excluded, purposefully re-shaped, devalued, and even erased, while also equally emphasizing that even apparently 'stable' or 'hegemonic' worlds are vulnerable and unstable, dependent upon marginalized worlds, and susceptible to falling precarious themselves. This second point is important, for just as Vaittinen (2015) has located political power in vulnerable bodies which exert pressure on the state, a focus on the precarity of worlds also locates power in precarity: those worlds which are precarious, and therefore to some extent, not subsumed wholly by the dominant onto-epistemology, wield a particular type of power, one which, in demonstrating the limits of the dominant or occupying world, can pose a challenge to the logic of said world, and perhaps even a challenge to the hierarchy which upholds the dominant world in the pluriversal matrix.

It is because of this understanding of precarity – as both intensified vulnerability and a source of power – that this framework also avoids uncritically reproducing modern norms. Ritu Vij (2019), for instance, argues that Butler's work on ontological precariousness upholds a liberal subject as the norm. Asking 'by what measure do we apprehend equality in shared vulnerability and the unequal distribution of precarity?', Vij (2019, pp. 516–17, emphasis in original) argues that Butler's account maintains an 'unwitting (default) attachment to a liberal analytic' because the liberal subject is 'taken to be the unexamined norm against which vulnerability is *measured*' in Butler's tracking of precaritization.[6] As Vij argues, when the liberal subject is upheld as the norm, then there will be a tendency to measure precarity according to such norms, and as a result, those in the Global South, and particularly those 'living within alternative ontological landscapes' (2019, p. 517), will most frequently be seen as abjectly precarious.

However, the notion of precarity developed here does not see precarity as unidirectionally intensified vulnerability, where some worlds are rendered powerless and undignified, while other worlds are powerful and invincible. Neither is vulnerability itself seen as something that is 'bad'. Instead, vulnerability, as an ontological claim that applies to all worlds is the very condition of possibility for 'alternative ontological landscapes'; it is only through vulnerable relations that different selves and worlds emerge. At the same time, vulnerability then also implies a riskiness or a precariousness; some worlds may not be able to reproduce due to the relations in which they unfold. But these two sides of vulnerability – as condition of possibility for being and as 'threat' to being – cannot be separated. For instance, concepts like resiliency only make sense in relation to vulnerability; the ability to persevere and persist is meaningless if something is invincible or unchangeable. Because of this dual nature of vulnerability (which is intimately tied to a relational ontology), a key part of this framework, and of employing vulnerability as a political concept – as the ethics of care does – is to attend to the ways in which vulnerabilities are experienced, understood, and constructed in and through relations of power and different onto-epistemological frameworks. Vulnerability as defined by one set of norms – be they liberal or otherwise – cannot serve as a useful concept for the pluriverse, and the 'quantification' or measurement of vulnerability is not the goal here. Instead, this framework is meant to help us understand and uncover different forms, experiences, and meanings of vulnerability. In so doing, this framework allows us to attend to experiences of both instability and resiliency, as both are an inherent part of vulnerability.

---

[6] Vij in particular draws upon examples from Judith Butler and Athena Athanasiou's work (2013) that focus on things like unemployment and health insurance, which, as Vij points out, are seen as precarious in relation to particular liberal norms.

Precarity, as intensified vulnerability, can likewise move in multiple directions and complex ways; precarity can be a source of power as much as it is a source of marginalization. The previously mentioned ethnographies of precarious work in the Global South highlight this multi-directionality: precarity can be a source of relational autonomy, as certain ways of being and ways of knowing evade capture by dominant logics, and it can also be experienced as a source of insecurity and instability. The analytical framework developed here, then, is committed to 'provincializ[ing] universalizing claims about precarity' (Muehlebach, 2013, p. 298). The point of focusing on precarity, and of developing conceptual lenses to explore the ways in which vulnerabilities manifest concretely as precarity, is to engage with and understand 'the context-specific variation both in the processes that give rise to precarity and how precarity is engaged' (Ettlinger, 2007, p. 321). Understanding that precarity is something that can be engaged – as opposed to a static experience or identity category – means that precarity can be deployed in many ways, including as a source of power which points to the limits of any given onto-epistemology, or to the limits of the relations of power that uphold one onto-epistemology at the expense of others. Vulnerability and precarity in this theoretical framework are not a static condition; they are conceptual tools that help us investigate and interrogate complex relations of power that position worlds in the pluriverse, that render certain worlds more unstable, and that explain the persistence of worlds even in the face of ever-present vulnerability.

By reminding us of the interplay between the stability and instability of different worlds, the idea of vulnerable and precarious onto-epistemologies, I believe, provides analytic space not only to explore the unequal relations between worlds (that is, the relations that allow some worlds to be enacted more easily than others), but also to foster meaningful dialogue on new political configurations of the pluriverse. Vulnerability, as an analytical tool, has the potential to highlight the mutual instability of all worlds, while precarity, in the context of the pluriverse, foregrounds those worlds at the margins of the pluriversal political order. These same worlds, in part because of their marginality, have the power to expose and challenge the limits and logic of dominant worlds. Precarious worlds foreground the vulnerability of the pluriversal configuration, and thus the unknowable constellations of vulnerable worlds which may emerge as worlds conflict. These unknown constellations have the potential to 'fracture' (Rojas, 2016) current systems of power; by allowing us to focus on this potentiality, the concepts of vulnerability and precarity, when applied to the political landscape that is the pluriverse, provide a useful starting point from which to contemplate this pluriversal landscape from a care ethics perspective. This may also ultimately help us begin to move towards new configurations in which a multitude of worlds can flourish.

In closing, my argument in this chapter is that the ethics of care, when supplemented with a distinction between vulnerability and precarity, reorients Global Ethics to accommodate better the political landscape that is the pluriverse as it provides a meta-theoretical framework that helps us locate the interactions between worlds as always taking place against the backdrop of the ever-present potentiality for precarity. This allows us first to attend to the pressing ethical issue of why certain worlds are rendered more or less vulnerable (that is, precarious) than others in the current political order, in the current configuration of the pluriverse. Second, this framework also allows us to be attentive to how our ethical deliberations regarding particular dilemmas further constitute the conditions for the reproduction of specific worlds. I demonstrate this second point more fully in Chapter 8 by engaging with an example of an ethical conflict regarding how to address the problem of the decline of *atîku*/caribou in Newfoundland and Labrador, Canada. But first, I return to the notion of the political, and build on my previous discussion regarding vulnerability and the political, so as to demonstrate how the ethics of care also develops a more robust understanding of the political as it pertains to the pluriverse.

7

The Political and the Pluriverse: A (Dis)Associative Theory of Care

As developed throughout the argument thus far, the relational ontology of the pluriverse is the condition of possibility for the pluriverse to be contemplated as a meta-world (as worlds are interconnected) as well as the simultaneous condition of possibility for that meta-world to be reordered or shifted (as relations are fluid and changing). Or, to put it slightly differently, the relational ontology of the pluriverse means that the relations between worlds are the condition of possibility for evoking a political moment – a simultaneous ungrounding and grounding – which shifts the pluriversal matrix. As such, the pluriverse, as I argued in Chapter 1, is always operating at the level of the political. At the same time, however, each world comprised[1] in and by the pluriverse is also constituted by its own socio-symbolic order, its own onto-epistemology, which delimits and enables what is thinkable, doable, and speakable, and which thereby defines what counts as 'politics' within that world. And, of course, because these worlds are themselves interconnected with other worlds, the possibility of a political moment is ever-present from the vantage point of particular worlds as well.

This layered 'politicality' – by which I mean, the ever-present potential for a political reordering at multiple levels (within a world, or at the level of the pluriversal matrix) as well as across multiple worlds – has some unique implications, however, when contemplating the nature of the political in the pluriverse. That is, from an ethics of care perspective, which attunes us to relations all the way down, the pluriverse is comprised of relations upon relations upon relations; worlds themselves are sets of relations, they are

---

[1] Recall that even when I use terms like 'comprised', I do not mean to imply a totality; the pluriverse is more than one but less than many, and the worlds within the pluriverse are themselves relational unfoldings. I am, again, just working within the limitations of an imperfect language.

partially connected to other worlds, and the pluriverse itself is relationally tied and configured. From this vantage point, I suggest, the occurrence of political moments – meaning, a moment of grounding and regrounding, in which a socio-symbolic order or world is ruptured and then established anew – may unfold in complex ways. For example, it is conceivable that a shift in relations will rupture the socio-symbolic order of one world, but perhaps not radically reconfigure the pluriverse itself (that is, not result in a political moment for the pluriversal matrix). Similarly, it is plausible that a world could evoke a shift in relations in the pluriverse without resulting in a political moment of its own (for instance, one world could marginalize a different world, shifting that world's position within the pluriversal matrix, without rupturing its own socio-symbolic order). Given this, I argue that the grounding/ungrounding dimensions of the political in the pluriverse can only be conceived of as partially connected. There is no guarantee that a political moment will manifest for one world in the same ways it does for another; there is no guarantee that a reconfiguration of the pluriverse will constitute a political moment for all worlds or all worlds equally. Depending on where one is situated in the pluriverse, it is conceivable that a political moment will be experienced as either an ungrounding and grounding moment, or as nothing at all. In fact, some pluriversal reconfigurations (a political moment at the level of the pluriverse) may actually 'solidify' the existing onto-epistemic grounding or socio-symbolic order of a world. This is, in part, why maintaining a focus on epistemology is important in the pluriverse. Conceptualizing the pluriverse as constituted by a situated epistemology foregrounds how the political moment will look different – manifest different relations and practices – depending on where one is already positioned within the pluriversal matrix.

More simply, from a care ethical perspective, it is crucially important to emphasize that in the context of the pluriverse there is a scalar component – or perhaps more accurately, an issue of relations upon relations – at play. The pluriverse can be thought of as one (meta)socio-symbolic order (a meta-world), comprised of several other socio-symbolic orders (worlds or onto-epistemologies). Thinking relationally – as the ethics of care and the very concept of the pluriverse enjoins us to do – means that as relations (upon relations upon relations) change or reproduce, the political (as in, a shift in a given social order) may come about slowly or in unexpected ways and places. Equally importantly in the context of the pluriverse, the 'lack' of a political moment (by which I mean, the absence of a change in a particular social order) may still be politically significant, depending upon where one is positioned within these relations.

In this chapter, I thus seek to rethink 'the political' so that it can better accommodate analysis in the pluriverse, where there are layers of relations between, in, and across worlds at play. I also expand my argument from the prior chapters, in which I argue that vulnerability, care, and reproduction are (in addition to newness and rupture) of political significance. My claim is that in the context of the pluriverse, constituted by relations upon relations, we must attune ourselves to the possibility that political moments may come about from care and reproduction: as worlds strive to establish and (of crucial importance) re-establish themselves in and through their connections with other worlds, both rupture and reproduction can be of political significance.

To make this argument, I first review the concept of 'the political', and discuss the debate in the postfoundational political thought literature regarding whether the political is 'associative' (a collective coming together) or 'dissociative' (inherently agonistic) (Marchart, 2007). Next, I draw upon a case study which focuses on the political assertions of the Yshiro people as they strive to live well with/in *yrmo* (Blaser, 2019) to illustrate how the political, as it has been conceived of in postfoundational political thought more generally, suffers from some limitations when applied to the pluriversal context. These limitations are related to the ways in which the literature on the political overvalues rupture at the expense of care and maintenance. I then put forth a (dis)associative theory of care which seeks to address these limitations by foregrounding the political significance of both rupture and newness, on the one hand, as well as care and reproduction, on the other. Lastly, I draw upon a second case study that delineates the creative ways in which Paulatuuqmiut develop solutions to fulfil their obligations to fish while challenging colonial logics (Todd, 2014; 2016b; 2018) so as to demonstrate how this (dis)associative theory of care, and this rethinking of the political for the pluriversal context, better positions us to attend to the political in the pluriverse, where layers of relations unfold in complex and often unforeseeable ways.

The political in the pluriverse

Throughout this book, I have mobilized a distinction between politics and the political, and I have argued that the pluriverse is always operating at the level of the political. In making this point, I have followed Jenny Edkins' (1999, p. 2, emphasis in original) definitions: 'Politics' is that which can be understood as the political reality as it is already described and acknowledged, whereas ' "the political" has to do with the establishment of that very social order which sets out a particular, historically specific account of what counts as politics and defines other areas of social life as *not* politics'. This definition of the political – as having to do with the establishment of a particular sociosymbolic order – encompasses three (necessarily related) points which merit unpacking here. First, the political has to do with the groundless ground, or as Oliver Marchart (2007, p. 15) writes, 'the primordial (or ontological) absence of an ultimate ground', which is the condition of possibility for the establishment of a particular (and always contingent) social order. (This point was discussed in Chapter 3, in relation to postmodernist approaches to ethics more generally.) Second, the political also entails a moment in which a particular order is established (sometimes called 'event'). In such moments, the 'groundless ground' (the fact that there is no transcendental foundation) is made visible, as one social order is ruptured and another is grounded. As Slavoj Žižek (1991, p. 195) describes, the political thus also refers to 'the moment of openness, of undecidability, when the very structuring principle of society, the fundamental form of social pact, is called into question'. Lastly, the literature on the political is also concerned with actions that enact (or not) the political. Of course, these three components are intricately intertwined. The political, as the establishment of a social order, depends equally on the conditions of possibility for an order to emerge; the moment in which an order does emerge; and other contextual actions and factors that bring rise to a political moment (for even if we cannot determine beforehand which actions will bring rise to a political moment, a point that philosopher Jacques Rancière [1999] makes, it is undeniable that actions, practices, and relations ultimately give rise to shifts in a socio-symbolic order).

This 'last' aspect of the political (that is, action that may bring about the political) has been the focus of a debate in postfoundational political theory regarding the political as 'associative' or 'dissociative'. Marchart argues that some scholars, particularly those in the Arendtian tradition, theorize the political as 'associative', as a moment of acting in concert or acting together (2007, p. 39). From this perspective, the political moment may manifest when a plurality of people freely associate within the public realm, motivated by a sense of care, respect, and responsibility for the common life (Marchart, 2007, p. 40). This coming together, it is important to emphasize, is not 'consensual'; the goal is not to do away with the political difference (an impossibility given the endless groundings that may emerge from the abyss). Instead, associative-ness may be better understood as 'inclusive agonism': 'Inclusive agonism perceives citizens as necessarily interconnected, reliant upon others to be complete. ... Endorsing political engagements that increase the role of citizens (such as norm formulation and grassroots politics), the focus is on identifying agonistic behaviours that render society more inclusive' (Lowndes and Paxton, 2018, p. 699).

Understanding the political as associative prioritizes the interconnections between people, and values agonism in so far as it leads to a more inclusive society. On the other hand, postfoundational theorists in the Schmittian tradition emphasize the 'dissociative' trait of the political moment. The dissociative trait is premised on a distinction between 'friends and enemies' or 'us and them' and conceives of the political as antagonistic, conflictual, and/or contestatory in nature. For work in this tradition (see, for example, Mouffe, 2013), the emphasis on the dissociative aspect of the political means that the 'goal of democratic politics is not to eradicate conflict but rather to transform antagonism (enemies) into agonism (adversaries), in order that citizens can engage in legitimate contestation' (Lowndes and Paxton, 2018, p. 698).

In this chapter, I assert that devolving into debates regarding the associative and dissociative traits of the political is not fruitful in the context of the pluriverse; instead, it is more productive to conceive of the political in the pluriverse as (dis)associative. First, to think about the groundless ground and the political moment as anything other than both associative and dissociative is to lose the very potency of these concepts, which seek to hold in tension both the impossibility of finality and closure and the inescapable reality that groundings do emerge, social orders arise, and that these orders serve – at least for some finite time and space – as groundings. The political, in these two senses, is (dis)associative in that orders are never totalized (retain their dissociative character) but they also emerge and structure social life (and thus retain an associative characteristic). Thinking relationally demonstrates that these concepts only make sense by focusing on the relation that holds together the ungrounding and grounding dimensions. I believe that the third component of the political, that is, acts which bring about changes in a given socio-symbolic order, can (and must) also be thought of as (dis)associative, especially in the context of the pluriverse. Changes in the pluriversal matrix, I suggest, may come about through associative political actions (in which people – including people and more-than-human beings from different worlds – come together to care for a common and collective life) and/or through dissociative political actions which are agonistic in nature (that is, involving conflict and struggle): privileging either associative or dissociative political action is insufficient in the context of the pluriverse. Rather, both types of action must be conceived of as politically significant.

Consider again the example of de la Cadena and Nazario, and their protest to protect Ausangate (de la Cadena, 2010). Despite being from different worlds and holding very different understandings of what was at stake in their political protest, both Nazario and de la Cadena (and numerous other people, including members of the Catholic brotherhood and other Peruvians) collectively came together to oppose the mining of Ausangate. This collective coming together across onto-epistemic difference (across worlds, across ontological understandings of the mountain) did not require consensus; it did not stifle the different onto-epistemologies at play. Rather, difference was maintained while a common goal was pursued. This, I suggest, is an instance of associative political action. The example of the Whanganui Iwi, and their decades-long struggle to protect Whanganui, on the other hand, is an example of a dissociative political action; what was at stake in that case was a direct ontological conflict and struggle over the status of the river. This agonistic (and perhaps for a long time, antagonistic) conflict challenged the social order of the modern world (as represented by the New Zealand state), and eventually required that order to shift, rendering something thinkable and speakable that was not thinkable or speakable before (that a river could be kin, or merit 'subject' status).

Yet, perhaps one could argue that, in different ways, neither of these cases are examples of the political. What social order changed as a result of the protest which Nazario and de la Cadena took part in? Resource development, for example, is debated all the time *within* the modern world; is it not likely that Nazario's onto-epistemology was lost or translated into such terms and hence effectively subsumed by modern logic? It seems likely that neither Nazario's world, nor the world which is constituted in/by the Peruvian state, nor the relations between these two worlds, were fundamentally reconfigured as a result of this protest. The various socio-symbolic orders involved in this example do not appear to have shifted fundamentally. Similarly, could it not be argued that awarding the Whanganui River legal personality is not really political, in the meaning employed here, given that the modern world has given legal personality to corporations? Is the modern world's onto-epistemology fundamentally shifted or reordered as a result of this conflict, given that other non-human entities have already been acknowledged with legal personality? Is it not possible to read the Whanganui River settlement as simply an extension of modern logic, and therefore just another instantiation of 'politics'? In this case, is the modern world fundamentally restructured because of this conflict? What about the world of the Māori? Was any onto-epistemology reordered in and through this struggle? While the example of de la Cadena and Nazario's protest operates in the associative vein, and the example of the struggle to protect the Whanganui River operates in the dissociative vein, perhaps neither of these cases encompass a political moment.

This discussion brings us to two thorny points about 'the political' as it has been conceived in postfoundational political thought (see, for example, Rancière, 1999), and specifically about the political as a concept to help understand the pluriversal landscape. First, as Mario Blaser (2019, p. 78) points out, the idea that the 'properly political' refers to moments or events in which an onto-epistemology, or socio-symbolic order, is ruptured 'raises the question of how such a rupture can be perceived as properly political and not as "noise"'. A political moment can only be identified retrospectively – it is only once the socio-symbolic order has been restructured, such that something that had been unintelligible is now identified as intelligible, that the moment or event that rendered said thing intelligible (that restructured the order) can be located. However, what happens if, because of deep and pervasive differences between worlds, members of one world fail to 'hear' a political assertion – by which I mean, an assertion made by members of another world in which they attempt to make something that they know to be true knowable to the other? Is it no longer properly political?

Consider the following case study. Over the past several decades, the Yshiro territory in the Chaco region of Paraguay, called the *yrmo*, has faced aggressive advances of cattle-ranching enterprises (Blaser, 2019, p. 80, emphasis in original). Clear-cutting and parcelling the land into private property are widespread. In response to this, movements to lessen the loss of 'biodiversity' that is associated with these processes have emerged. Blaser, who has worked with the Yshiro communities for over two decades (see also Blaser, 2010), recounts that as a result of this, 'the Yshiro find themselves caught between two processes of dispossession' (2019, p. 80): on the one hand, their land is being encroached upon in material ways by the cattle industry; on the other hand, movements concerned with biodiversity loss (a modern-science understanding of the importance of nature) are also encroaching on this territory. In response to this, the Yshiro federation, Unión de las Comunidades Indígenas de la Nación Yshir (UCINY), worked with their communities to start a consultation process so as to develop a unified strategy to deal with this situation. As Blaser (2019, p. 80) explains:

> One of the first actions agreed upon by the Yshiro leaders was to attack the Paraguayan government's lack of consultation in setting up a National Park [which was established to protect biodiversity loss] in the area. They hoped that demanding and obtaining a seat on the 'planning table' would give UCINY a foothold from where to pursue its wider strategy of territorial recovery. ... The governmental response came in the form of 'participatory workshops' aimed to 'harmonize' the 'development' needs of the Yshiro with the conservation plans underway in the area.

At one of these workshops, an interesting exchange happened. A group of 45–50 stakeholders gathered, including a team of four people from a non-governmental organization who were 'leading' the consultation exercise, leaders from the Yshiro community (both women and men), a large group of community members, and Blaser, who, as just mentioned, has worked with the communities for several years in various capacities. As Blaser notes, it is important to keep in mind that about one third of the participants in the workshop had little to no knowledge of Spanish, the language used by the non-governmental organization employees to conduct the workshop. Further, the Yshiro assistant in charge of translating sometimes struggled to express the Yshiro concepts to the facilitator and vice versa (recall the limits to knowing highlighted in Chapter 3, exemplified in the case of 'translating' *pukara*).

In addition to literal translation issues, it became evident to many of the participants that the workshop facilitators were 'guiding' the workshop in certain directions – directions that were deemed 'feasible'. For example, one of the exercises involved forming groups of four to discuss topics. A spokesperson would then report back to the larger group on behalf of the sub-group after 10 or 15 minutes of dialogue. The facilitator provided prompts to foster the dialogue, such as 'Think for a moment what you would need for the community to be satisfied and happy' (Blaser 2019, p. 81). In response to this particular brief, a general consensus was reported amongst groups: what they needed to feel happy and satisfied was 'access and free movement within an extended territory' (Blaser, 2019, p. 81). The facilitator then translated this to 'General Goal = Recovery of Territory', which was written on a piece of paper and posted on the wall. The prompts continued: 'Why is territory important?' As Blaser notes (2019, p. 81), by the end of this process three labels, 'economics', 'cultural', and 'environmental', were written on pieces of paper as responses to this last question. This process continued, narrowing in on specific problems and potential 'solutions' through the exercise.

Yet, in this narrowing process, it became clear that the central issue for the Yshiro people – stopping the clear-cutting that was happening for the cattle industry –was being subtly and continually eroded and replaced with different demands:

> In effect, the recovery of territory ended up translated into, for example, alternative productive projects, promotion of Yshiro culture in school curriculum, and training Yshiro individuals as 'environmental wardens' to control land-owners' clear-cutting. ... As is usually the case, the [non-governmental organization's] mandate had a number of unspoken constraints. ... For instance, it went without saying that an expanding cattle-ranching industry was an unshakable fact and would remain such. Similarly it went without saying that different governmental schemes for the protection of natural resources were there to stay. ... When a few Yshiro started to vent their frustration as to why the government was creating protected areas instead of stopping cattle-ranchers from clear-cutting the forest in their properties, the facilitator pulled the discussion back on track: 'Guys, guys, let's keep on topic. Yes, it is true the ranchers keep cutting down trees, but we cannot do anything about this here in this workshop.' (Blaser, 2019, p. 81)

The entire direction of the process, as Blaser (2019, p. 82) notes, was therefore in line with liberal inclusionary practices more broadly: 'express your vision/difference in a way that we can work with'.

At the same time, however, Blaser foregrounds that there was also a subversive component at play in the Yshiro's participation in the workshop. The Yshiro communities had years of experience with these 'participatory methods', starting from the early 1990s (see Blaser, 2010). Yshiro participants were not 'dupes' of the process, unaware of what was unfolding. Rather, they continued to engage in 'the theatrics of the process' as a way of 'gaining a foothold from where to pursue their more ambitious goals' (Blaser, 2019, p. 82). For instance, the primary issue of gaining control of the territory was made evident to the workshop facilitators – their continued efforts to redirect away from this goal, and towards goals that were more 'feasible', attests to their awareness of the Yshiro's political demand. Indeed, reading this situation through the politics/political distinction that I am interrogating in this chapter helps highlight this subversive component. In their demand that the clear-cutting and ranching industry must be stopped, the Yshiro were posing a political demand, by which I mean, a challenge to the modern onto-epistemology, which sees Nature as something separate from Humans, and therefore something that is exploitable. The Yshiro's assertion here was political: this is evidenced, in some sense, by the very fact that this demand was 'unthinkable' from the modern perspective. As the workshop facilitators continually asserted, this demand could not be attended to, as stopping the industry was unfathomable. The workshop participants were told they had to be 'realistic' (Blaser, 2019, p. 82), meaning they had to operate within the realm of 'politics', the realm of that which is already acknowledged (specifically by the modern world of capitalist development).

This returns us to Blaser's point raised earlier, regarding the ways in which something can be identified as 'properly political'. The fact that the facilitator team translated the (political) demand of the Yshiro into terms that were deemed realistic (that is, into terms that were already acknowledged from the viewpoint of the dominant world, and that are therefore constitutive of the politics of the dominant world) would seem to render the Yshiro's actions here as un-political. The political moment was not recognized by the workshop facilitators – or at least, it was not recognized in the sustained way that seems to be needed for the political moment to continue to unfold to the point of an onto-epistemic reordering or re-defining of what is thinkable, speakable, and knowable. Does this mean that the Yshiro's actions were not political? As Holloway Sparks (2016, p. 432) shows, it seems that the political moment, then, is not just about something becoming intelligible; implicit in this is the ever-important question 'intelligible to whom?' To all members of the modern world? To just some in power? Let us continue to think through this by returning to the workshop.

As Blaser (2019, p. 83, emphasis in original) recounts, at one point in the discussion, an elder, Don Ramon Zeballos Bibi, starts to further explain why territory is important:

I am a shaman. All those animals that are there are my children. I am their child as well. If I sing, those animals come out [come into being]. If I do not sing there are no animals. When I was a child I ate *pitino* [anteater]. I was not supposed to eat it. Prohibited!! But I ate anyway. I was hardheaded. Then I got sick. And that guy came. The owner of the *pitano*. 'You are very hardheaded, you will not withstand my power. You will die now.' But I spoke to him. That guy has a daughter, she was fat, beautiful girl. I spoke to that guy to let me marry his daughter. Then I married her.

[After a brief interruption where a facilitator intervenes and says this is not the place for traditional stories, Don Ramon continues.]

Then, that *pitino* owner let me go. Now he is my father-in-law. He gives me his song, to bring about the *pitano*. If I don't sing, there are no more [anteaters]. Nobody will eat *pitino*. Nobody will be able to hunt it. Then the owner gets mad. There, around nepurich [a place within the Yshiro territory] I have to go. But now there is a *patron* [cattle rancher] that does not allow anyone to pass [through his property]. He is destroying the *yrmo*. … I have nothing for [i.e. materials to make] *peyta* [maracas]. How can I sing? All those animals are not coming out anymore, they no longer have their house, because nobody takes care of the *yrmo*.

Before unpacking this further, a brief note on the *yrmo* is needed. While the Yshiro in the workshop speak of the importance of 'territory', they do not mean territory in the sense that it is understood in the modern world. Instead, territory is intricately intertwined and constitutive of the '*yrmo* (the Yshiro reality/world)' (Blaser, 2010, p. 23, emphasis in original). The world of the Yshiro is enacted through *yrmo*-making practices; the Yshiro are a 'specific entity within this emplaced collective. … Yshiro is only in intra-relation with *yrmo*' (Blaser, 2019, p. 85, emphasis in original). As such, the political demand to regain control of the traditional territory was, for some Yshiro, to 'ensure that practices and relations that sustain the *yrmo* could be performed' (Blaser, 2019, p. 85, emphasis in original); it is to ensure the continuation of the *yrmo* collective, which can be thought of as a community that is embedded in and emerges from unique heterogeneous assemblages of entities, in various configurations, and tied to a specific place. Importantly, the entities that constitute (and that are constituted by) the *yrmo* do not follow the ontological divide that structures the modern world, where Humans are separate from Nature (Blaser, 2019, p. 84). This is an important point to dwell on, lest we succumb to the modern tendency to think of the *yrmo* as an environment. Such an understanding of the *yrmo* is not accurate.

'The *yrmo* is a "thing" that is not quite an "environment" both because it cannot be abstracted from its specificity (its placeness) and because the stuff that makes its relations is not "environment": environmental relations do not involve *bahluts* (spirit owners) instructing Yshir to sing!' (Blaser, 2019, p. 86). The *yrmo* is a different world, and the cattle industry is destroying the practices that enact the world, impeding the ability of the Yshiro to care for the *yrmo*. It is this fact that Don Ramon is highlighting in his intervention.

Predictably, however, the facilitator again translates Don Ramon's point into a language of 'cultural practices'. Territory is important because, without it, the culture of the Yshiro will be lost. But this obfuscates entirely Don Ramon's point and his concern. It is not cultural practices that will be lost, but the *yrmo*, the embedded and place-based collective, which is enacted through bonds and relations that exist between the Yshiro and other non-human entities. This, I believe, returns us to the question of to whom one is making something knowable, thinkable, or speakable. The occurrence of a political event, in postfoundational political thought, can only be identified in reference to a specific order, a specific politics. Retroactively, an event is identified which prompted a reordering of a socio-symbolic order, or world, a reordering which reconfigures the boundaries of said world, rendering different things knowable. And such identification requires, at least to some extent, that a 'political sequence' builds, in which an initial moment of recognition of the political assertion is expanded and repeated to the point of a larger socio-symbolic shift (Blaser, 2019, p. 88). However, what happens when those in the modern world fail to hear, or recognize, the political assertions of those from other worlds? Do these assertions no longer count at all? It seems like the possibility that a political assertion from another world will be identified, gain momentum, and carry forward to the point of rupturing the modern order might be extraordinarily small in the pluriverse, given the excesses between worlds, the limits to knowing, and the fact that the modern world occupies a privileged position from which it can easily refuse to listen to claims from other worlds. From this vantage point, it also then seems that political assertions that occur when actors affirm their own worlds, as Don Ramon did in the workshop, will not ever be conceived of as 'properly political' (Blaser, 2019) from the standpoint of the literature on postfoundational political thought.

Postfoundational political thought therefore almost sets up a self-fulfilling prophecy. Other than examples of extreme violence or force that demands recognition (for instance, a revolt), the political assertions of other worlds become all too easy to ignore from the perspective of the modern world, and are thus likely to be downgraded as 'not political'. (I suspect that it is, in part, for this reason that 'rupture' and 'change', and dissociative political action that is agonistic in nature, has been emphasized in the postfoundational political thought literature, at the expense of 'care' and 'maintenance', and associative action.) And in this downgrading, a fidelity to the modern world's socio-symbolic is re-affirmed, as the very act of downgrading these political assertions as 'not political' cuts off the sequence that is needed for such assertions to 'expand' to the point of shifting the modern world's onto-epistemology. In other words, to deem these political assertions as 'un-political' because an order was not immediately ruptured is to preclude the possibility that such assertions might ever result in a political event – our refusal to hear them, and stick with them, undercuts their political potentiality from the beginning.

This brings me to my second, but related point. It is crucially important to recall that in the context of the pluriverse there is a scalar component – or perhaps more accurately, an issue of relations upon relations – at play. The pluriverse, as a meta-world, is one socio-symbolic order, comprised of several other socio-symbolic orders (that is, worlds or onto-epistemologies). Because of this, I suggest that within the pluriverse, the (dis)associative effects of the political (in all three senses of the term used in the previous discussion) may not be evenly distributed across worlds, and they may not be instantaneous. Thinking relationally, as the ethics of care and the very concept of the pluriverse implores us to do, means that we must abandon the approach that only identifies the political based upon newness and rupture (that is, a moment when an order is fractured and re-established anew). Instead, I contend that in the pluriverse, comprised of complex sets of relations (upon relations upon relations), the political, meaning a shift in a given onto-epistemology, may come about slowly or in unexpected ways and places. Equally important in the context of the pluriverse, the 'lack' of a political moment (by which I mean, the absence of a change in a particular order) may still be politically significant through time and depending on where one is positioned within these relations.

Let us again return to the example of de la Cadena and Nazario's protest to stop the mining of Ausangate. While perhaps neither the modern world nor Nazario's world is reordered as a (direct) result of the protest, protecting Ausangate allows Nazario's world to reproduce and maintain itself more easily. This collective and associative political action of protesting the mining development, and protecting Ausangate, can enable the reproduction of Nazario's world (his onto-epistemology, his socio-symbolic order). At first glance, this reproduction seems antithetical to notions of the political which focus on a ruptural moment of change in which one order is fractured and a new order emerges, and by extension, which valorizes 'newness' and 'change' uncritically. But in the context of the pluriverse, where (as I show in the previous chapter) certain worlds are rendered precarious through relations of power, the ability to reproduce a given order can be deeply meaningful, ethically desirable, and I would argue, political. If struggling to maintain a multiplicity of partial connections is the goal of the pluriverse, *then acts which allow relations to reproduce are as important as acts which change relations that are preventing other sets of relations from flourishing.* Or to put it differently, if we conceive of worlds as vulnerable, then the reproduction of a world (the re-establishment of an order) is as political(ly significant) as a shift in that world/order. Moreover, because these vulnerable worlds are relationally tied, the maintenance and reproduction of a world may eventually result in a rupture and restructuring of a world elsewhere.

For instance, because of the partial connections between worlds, various practices that preserve the relations which allow for the continuation of Nazario's world may later prove politically significant as Nazario's world – in its precarity and corresponding resiliency – poses a challenge to the very limits and logics of the modern world, which is currently hegemonic in the pluriverse matrix. In persisting in/through its precarity, Nazario's world may bring about a political moment, in that a reordering of the pluriversal matrix may eventually occur as modernity's hegemony is continually challenged by the existence and persistence of other worlds. And of course, this political moment may not reorder and re-structure Nazario's world at all. The deep relationality of the pluriverse means that there are scales of change (of political rupture and regrounding) that are not necessarily aligned or equally distributed, but that are nonetheless significant. While the political will always be both associative and dissociative, the distribution of these traits may not be equal; as a result of protecting Ausangate, Nazario's world may experience a greater associative effect – as this world is able to come together and reproduce more easily – while (eventually, if not instantaneously), this same 'regrounding' of Nazario's world may result in a greater dissociative effect from the vantage point of the pluriverse. The maintenance of Nazario's world, perhaps now more easily enacted as a result of the associative political protest, may eventually come to disrupt the hegemony of modernity so fundamentally that modernity experiences a more disruptive and dissociative political moment, and/or the configuration of the order of the pluriverse itself may be shifted. In this way, the associative political act that is the protest can be thought of as political in the other two meanings of the term as well. The preservation of Nazario's world in spite of the dominating forces of modernity reminds us that a multiplicity of grounds is always possible (the political as the groundless ground). At the same time, the continued reproduction of Nazario's world points to the limitations of the modern world, and in so doing, poses a challenge to modernity's narrative as the one-world, a challenge that may one day manifest in a shift in the social order of modernity or the order that is the pluriverse (a political moment).

I suggest that a similar conclusion can be drawn regarding the political implications of the recognition of the Whanganui River as a legal person. For instance, as James D. K. Morris and Jacinta Ruru (2010, pp. 50, 54) argue, the act of awarding legal personality to rivers creates 'an exciting link between the Māori legal system and the state legal system':

> The legal personality concept aligns with the Māori legal concept of a personified natural world. By regarding the river as having its own standing, the mana (authority) and mauri (life force) of the river would be recognised, and importantly, that river would be more likely to be regarded as a holistic being rather than a fragmented entity of flowing water, river bed and river bank.

Or as Gerrard Albert, the lead negotiator for the Whanganui Iwi, says:

> We have fought to find an approximation in law so that all others can understand that from our perspective treating the river as a living entity is the correct way to approach it, as in indivisible whole, instead of the traditional model for the last 100 years of treating it from a perspective of ownership and management. (Roy, 2017)

With legal personality, the Whanganui River cannot be owned, nor can it be divided into parcels of property. The very concept of nature that is not, and cannot be, property, I suggest, poses a fundamental challenge to the modern onto-epistemology, defined by a strong ontological distinction between Humans and Nature (as outlined in Chapter 2). I also assert that failing to foreground the seriousness of this challenge precludes the possibility of *political ramifications that may yet arise* as a consequence of the outcome of the Whanganui River settlement. As Elaine Hsiao (2012) notes, while the river's standing could be likened to the legal status of a corporation, it also has the potential to extend further. The ways in which this development may create openings that can further destabilize the modern world's hegemony while centring Māori law is a hopeful possibility, one with political significance.

Finally, a similar reading of the Yshiro communities' participation in the workshop, recounted earlier, draws comparable conclusions. Through this workshop participation, the Yshiro might develop better capacity to 'maneuver and later recover control of the territory' (Blaser, 2019, p. 83), where territory, for the Yshiro, is a much more fulsome part of the *yrmo*. In the associative act of coming together with the workshop participants to try and recover this territory, the Yshiro's participation in the workshop can still maintain a properly political quality (even if this political action is translated by the modern world into 'politics'), in that if it allows the *yrmo* to be enacted, and thus the world of the Yshiro to reproduce, it has the potential to continue to confront the modern world, pointing to its limits, and revealing the contingency of the modern world's own foundations. Eventually, this may result in a political moment from the perspective of the modern world (a moment in which, being confronted with the ongoing enactment of other worlds, the modern world finally sees that, despite its self-narrative, it is but one world amongst many).

The point I am trying to make here might be most easily grasped by returning again to Edkins' definition: the political has to do with the very establishment of a social order (a world, or an onto-epistemology). But in the pluriverse, where there are multiple vulnerable worlds co-existing and interacting, the notion of 'establishment' needs to be expanded. If we begin from the premise of a single world or social order, then establishment can be singular and momentary: an order is established, and then all other practices reproduce that order (until that order is ruptured and regrounded anew). However, if we begin with a care ethical reading of the pluriverse, the partial connections between vulnerable worlds means that related, and perhaps competing, vulnerable worlds must constantly *be re-established in the face of each other*. The political, as such, can no longer be conceived of as only a moment (although we can still talk of a moment in which a particular order shifts), nor can it be thought of only in terms of newness. Instead, the political must be thought of relationally and as a process: an ongoing relational becoming, in which the order of the pluriverse and particular vulnerable worlds are constantly enacted and/or disrupted. Indeed, vulnerability points to both the possibility of rupture and to the value of repair and maintenance. As vulnerable, a world is always potentially susceptible to change and rupture; simultaneously, as vulnerable, a world must be re-enacted, repaired, and maintained. Understanding the pluriverse as comprised of partially connected vulnerable worlds, as I have suggested in Chapter 5 by drawing upon an ethics of care, allows us to reconceptualize the political as a relational process in which vulnerable worlds, and the pluriverse, are *continually becoming*.

Furthermore, such a relational becoming will always be both associative and dissociative, although the associative and dissociative effects may not be evenly distributed; in any given context, some orders will be relatively regrounded, others will be relatively ungrounded. These ungroundings and regroundings may come from agonistic conflicts, or from meaningful collective action and working together, or both. A key task for thinking about the political in the pluriversal context, then, is developing tools that can tend to both facets of the *ongoing establishment of worlds* in the pluriverse. On the one hand, vulnerable worlds are vulnerable – they are subject to change and rupture – and particularly so given that they are intertwined and interacting with other worlds. This side of vulnerability (the side that cannot be mastered or overcome) highlights the dissociative nature of the political, and the fact that the establishment of worlds can never be totalizing or complete. On the other hand, vulnerability also means that worlds must be maintained; worlds are continually re-established and reproduced, often in spite of their interrelatedness with other worlds. This side of vulnerability (the side that demands care) highlights the associative nature of the political, the fact that worlds are established and re-established, and that this always involves a 'coming together' so as to enact particular visions of the good life. As the next section argues, the ethics of care can provide tools to contemplate the (dis)associative nature of the political, that is, the establishment of worlds as a continual reproduction that is also always vulnerable to change.

A (dis)associative theory of care

To help us contemplate this reconceptualized notion of the political – in which the 'establishment of a given order' refers to either the establishment of a new order or the re-establishment of an existing order in/through/despite its connections with others – I would like to put forth the ethics of care as a (dis)associative theory of care. It is associative because it starts from a relational social ontology and understands that moral selves only emerge in and through relations. Consequently, the ethics of care foregrounds the ethical significance of being attentive and responsive to the mutual interdependency and vulnerability of all. Significantly, as discussed in Chapter 4, the ethics of care sees such attentiveness – attending to and seeking to understand the needs of others – and responsiveness – responding to and addressing these needs as well as reasonably possible – as a collective and political activity. (Re)distributing caring responsibilities, ensuring caring needs are met as well as possible, and maintaining, continuing, and repairing our worlds (to paraphrase Fisher and Tronto, 1990, p. 40) is a collective task that arises because of our fundamental interconnectedness and mutual vulnerability. Meeting needs also requires an 'acting in common' because needs (and the ways in which we address them or not) are fundamentally shaped by the political order (the world, or the onto-epistemology) in which they arise. Even if or when the actual practice of care is done by an individual or group of individuals, the social meaning, significance, and organization of care is inescapably collective and political, and shaped by the complex interaction of nature and the social.

Accordingly, care is necessarily 'a form of political relatedness' (Hoppania and Vaittinen, 2015, p. 87). Every world inherently organizes care, and has already responded to the demands of vulnerability. For the ethics of care, coming together to deliberate on care, its meaning, and how is has been (and could be) organized, is politically meaningful. In fact, it is in such coming togethers that the establishment of an onto-epistemology is possible (recalling that establishment in the context of the pluriverse refers to both the establishment of a new order or world, as well as to the re-establishment and constantly enacted continuation of a world as it interacts with other worlds). Shifts in the political may be possible through associative political acts, as new social orders may emerge as we work together to respond to and address caring needs and enact different versions of what it means to live well. Likewise, existing orders or worlds may be able to reproduce more easily through associative political action (as is the case of Nazario and de la Cadena's protest to protect Ausangate). Care as a collective and political activity therefore clearly aligns with the understanding of the political as associative. For instance, Sheldon Wolin (1996, p. 31; quoted in Marchart, 2007, p. 40), whom Marchart locates in the associative paradigm, describes the political as 'the idea that a free society composed of diversities can nonetheless enjoy moments of commonality when, through public deliberations, collective power is used to promote or protect the well-being of the collectivity'. This associative aspect of the political is clearly in line with the ethics of care.

At the same time, the ethics of care understands care as dissociative and agonistic. Again as described in Chapter 4, the relations which constitute infinitely different moral selves and the perpetual neediness of our corporeal vulnerable bodies mean that care is an ongoing process that can never be completed. At the same time, however, our particular caring needs will shift and change throughout our lives, and they will differ greatly across differently constituted and situated moral selves. In acknowledging this, the ethics of care emphasizes differences all the way down (Robinson, 2019), as relational moral selves are always unique, and therefore have unique needs which arise from their relational complexity. The continuity of our caring needs, held in tension with the ways in which our caring needs shift and change, and the differences that emerge through our relationality (thereby constituting a multiplicity of moral selves), points to care as dissociative in two ways.

First, care cannot be controlled (Hoppania and Vaittinen, 2015) and it is never 'complete'; it is a continual unfolding that evades closure or finality. Because of this, care ceaselessly confronts the 'endlessly totalizing tendencies' (Hoppania and Vaittinen, 2015, p. 87) of a social order. As Hanna-Kaisa Hoppania and Tiina Vaittinen (2015, p. 78) argue, the 'latent forces of disruption that are imbued in the corporeal character of care relations' point to the limits of, and thereby challenge, a given social order. This challenge is agonistic, that is, dissociative, in character, as it involves the disruption of the existing order which cannot ever tame in full our caring needs. In other words, the ways in which vulnerability can never be mastered fully confronts and disrupts the tendencies of a social order toward closure and completeness in an ongoing way, and thereby points to the dissociative aspects of the political. The establishment of a world will never be totalizing or complete – this is precisely why we must think about the political as it pertains to maintenance and reproduction in the context of multiple vulnerable worlds.

Second, because 'we are all constituted as selves through a multitude of different historical and contemporary relations on a variety of scales that work together to construct our subjectivities, there is no limit to the scope or nature of how these relations will shape our moral voices' (Robinson, 2019, p. 4). The radical and infinite differences that emerge through relational selves, by extension, imply radically different and infinite versions of 'care', types of needs, moral voices, and forms of life. These differences will unavoidably confront each other in agonistic ways – particularly in the pluriverse – both because they are by nature different (and perhaps irreconcilable) and because the relations that constitute moral selves and forms of life are themselves rife with power. These power dynamics and the inescapable differences that emerge through our relationality mean that 'care' will be agonistic; competing claims of how to care and the relations of power that shape how we meet caring needs (or not) will at times conflict and confront each other. The situated epistemology of the ethics of care, which understands all knowledge claims to be contextual and partial, is committed to such agonism. As noted previously, a central task for a critical political ethics of care is to attend carefully to the different versions of care at stake, to consider the ways in which varying practices of care constitute particular moral subjects and their ways of life, and to be open to the possibility that one's vision of 'good' care may need to be revised in light of the needs and ways of life of the other. Such deliberation must also be attuned to the power relations at play in our (agonistic) interactions. For the ethics of care, the ever-present potential for conflicting moral understandings and visions of living well, and the commitment to confronting these conflicts in a way that foregrounds the vulnerability of one's own judgement (one's own moral voice, one's own onto-epistemology), points to the dissociative and agonistic aspects of the political. The establishment and ongoing re-establishment of a world may involve (often will involve) agonism; dissociative political action may bring about a 'new' world or may allow an existing world to reproduce itself more easily (as is the case of the Whanganui Iwi and their struggle to protect Whanganui).

Put differently, because the ethics of care is premised upon a relational social ontology and situated epistemology, it implies a (dis)associative theory of care. The relational ontology of the ethics of care points towards the associative aspect of care: our mutual vulnerabilities and interdependencies emphasize that we only emerge through our relations, and in this emergence, we are a political collective. In its thin normativity regarding care, the ethics of care additionally foregrounds the political and ethical significance of responding to others via attentive and responsive practices of care. The ethics of care departs from the thin normative premise that where relational and vulnerable beings – and in the case of the pluriverse, relational and vulnerable worlds – are concerned, maintaining and repairing relations is a very important moral task, one which can be thought of as associative, and one which is crucial for the (re)establishment of worlds (the political). At the same time, it is also through our relationality that deep and pervasive differences emerge. Sets of relations construct different moral voices and different forms of life, different onto-epistemologies. These differences will, at times, confront each other agonistically. Our different caring needs will disrupt a particular order and organization of care; our different moral voices will involve conflicting moral understandings; our different visions of care, of living well, will be at odds. The ethics of care, with its situated epistemology, does not shy away from such agonistic encounters, or from agonizing what it means to live well, to care. Instead, the ethics of care notes the impossibility of a singular truth or singular moral voice, and 'challenges the disciplinary power that circumscribes those [other] voices by denying the moral legitimacy of relationality' (Robinson, 2019, p. 4). By extension, the ethics of care demonstrates its commitment to agonizing care, agonizing different versions of living well, and to the revisability of all judgement. Through such agonism, the dissociative aspect of the political is evident, as agonistic encounters between worlds may result in the reconfiguration or reordering of certain onto-epistemologies.

This argument regarding care as (dis)associative can be articulated with a different set of terms (which are more common in the care ethics literature). The ethics of care, I suggest, can be understood as simultaneously *critical and productive*. It is *critical*, in that it is an ethic which seeks to uncover critically the relations of power, norms, and exclusionary social practices which oppress groups of people and cause harm and suffering. It is also critical because the ethics of care is committed to the revisability of all (moral) judgement and knowledge claims. Departing from a relational ontology, the ethics of care foregrounds difference, and the ways in which these differences manifest varied notions of and practices of care. Living well together means taking these differences seriously, understanding the situatedness of one's own knowledge claims, and thereby maintaining an openness to revising moral judgements, and correspondingly, our caring practices. The critical aspect of the ethics of care is well positioned to attend to the dissociative aspect of the political in the context of the pluriverse, where multiple, relational, and therefore, vulnerable worlds are susceptible to conflict, agonism, and rupture. On the other hand, the ethics of care is a 'reconstructive' or *productive* theory, because 'care claims a tangible moral idea': 'rather than concluding in a deconstructed state, care provides an organizing trajectory around attentive/responsive living' (Hamington, 2015b, pp. 286–7). Of course, this 'organizing trajectory' is only thinly normative – how to be attentive and respond to heterogenous, complex, shifting, and situated needs cannot be predetermined or prescribed, only gleaned through tentative (and sometimes agonistic) practices of care which are continually assessed and revised. Yet, this thin normativity nonetheless renders the ethics of care productive and constructive because 'claims about what ought to be the case are never abandoned entirely' (Robinson, 2011b, p. 28). Care provides us with a normative orientation from which to understand and address harms and sufferings. This aspect of care is therefore well suited to attend to the associative aspects of the political in the pluriverse, in which vulnerable and interacting worlds must also be reproduced and maintained. In short, the messy moral life of care renounces the thick normativity of universal and transcendental morality but – and this is crucial – it also does not leave us in the 'void'. Instead, the ethics of care locates the moral subject with 'both feet in the real world' (Sevenhuijsen, 1998, p. 59) and orients us towards the (always political) task of attempting to live well together given our (paradoxical) interconnectedness and radical differences.

Putting the pieces together

As both a productive and critical theory, the ethics of care, I argue, conceives of care as (dis)associative; as a result, care ethics can provide a framework from which to analyse the (dis)associative nature of the political in the context of the pluriverse. Specifically, I assert that in the pluriverse, the political must be thought of as having to do with the establishment – and, crucially, the ongoing establishment – of (vulnerable) worlds or onto-epistemologies as they interact in various ways. In the pluriverse, it does not make sense to speak of the establishment of a world as a singular moment; because worlds are vulnerable, they must continually 'strive to sustain their own existence as they interact and mingle with each other' (Blaser, 2009, p. 877). Simply put, the establishment of a world is ongoing and requires reproduction and re-establishment. Of course, in this ongoing re-establishment, the possibility of a 'new' world, or an onto-epistemic reordering, is also always present: because worlds are vulnerable, interactions between worlds (be they conflictual or cooperative) can cause the relations of one world (or multiple worlds, or the relational symmetry between worlds) to shift. The political – as in the (ongoing) establishment of a world or onto-epistemology – cannot a priori prioritize either the grounding (associative) or ungrounding (dissociative) aspect of the establishment of worlds, nor can the political be conceived of as singular or momentary. The political must rather be conceptualized as an ongoing process in which worlds are established over and over again, sometimes in ways that reproduce their onto-epistemic frameworks and other times in ways that alter these frameworks. And because of the partial connections between worlds, the 'regrounding' of one world may fundamentally disrupt the order of another world or shift the entire pluriversal matrix (and vice versa). The dissociative (disruptive, ungrounding) and associative (coming-together, regrounding) traits of the political may be unevenly distributed across worlds as they interact in the pluriversal matrix.

The political, in the pluriverse, can only be conceived of as (dis)associative, in which neither trait is abstractly nor theoretically prioritized above the other.

By the same line of thinking, political action – by which I mean action that brings about the political – can also only ever be thought of as (dis)associative. Establishing and re-establishing a world (that is, the political, the establishment of an onto-epistemology) may happen through agonistic conflict or through associative cooperation and action. Likewise, agonistic political action and/or associative political action may allow one world to re-establish itself, while it disrupts another, leading to a political moment elsewhere (or perhaps even a shift in the pluriversal matrix more broadly). If we are committed to the pluriversal project of a world of partial connections in which many worlds are possible as worlds, then both conflict and cooperation may prove fruitful means by which to change the relations between worlds, establish new worlds, and maintain existing ones. The key analytical challenge to understanding the political in the pluriversal sense, then, is to be able to hold both the associative and dissociative traits of the political at the fore, and to analyse how both agonistic political action and cooperative and collective political action can contribute to the pluriversal project.

For instance, in some cases, the key task for enacting the pluriverse will be ensuring the maintenance of a world. Precarious worlds, as defined in the previous chapter, struggle to maintain their own existence in the pluriversal matrix. In this case, we do not want these worlds to experience the political as rupture; the goal is *to reproduce that which already is*, to make the *ongoing re-establishment* of that onto-epistemology easier. On the other side of the coin, a key task for enacting the pluriverse will be disrupting certain worlds (here I am thinking of modernity, which has asserted itself as the whole of the real). In this case, we may require an onto-epistemology to rupture and shift, to think and be differently. Working to achieve these tasks may involve deconstructing and disrupting relations of power that render some worlds precarious (indeed, the meta-theoretical orientation towards vulnerable and precarious worlds developed in the previous chapter is meant in part to provide a framework for this very task). At the same time, working to facilitate the maintenance of precarious worlds may also involve associative political action that involves working together without overcoming or subsuming the differences at play. To move towards a symmetrical, dehierarchicalized pluriverse, will likely require both of these things, although in different ways in different times and places.

Consider a final example for this chapter, drawing upon the work of Zoe Todd (2014; 2016b; 2018).[2] From January to October 2012, Todd

---

[2] Importantly, Todd does not use the language of the pluriverse in her ethnographic work, although I have translated this case into those terms to some degree here.

conducted field work in Paulatuuq, a hamlet in the Northwest Territories, Canada, focusing on human–fish relationships so as to 'develop a more nuanced understanding of the dynamic strategies that northern Indigenous people, including the Paulatuuqmiut (people from Paulatuuq), use to navigate shifting environmental, political, legal, social, cultural, and economic realities in Canada's North' (2014, pp. 217–18). Paulatuuq is a small Inuvialuit community with 321 residents located on the Beauford Sea, at the base of Darnley Bay, and 400 km east of Inuvik, the town that serves as the administrative centre for the Inuvik region (Todd, 2014, p. 219). As Todd explains, the 'human movements and occupation of the land around Paulatuuq' extend both 'far into the past' and continue today. The community relies on a diverse set of strategies to meet local needs, including 'strong local involvement in harvesting activity', as well as other opportunities in wage labour, resource exploration, guiding for sports hunters, wildlife monitoring and relationships with researchers, and the private sector (Todd, 2014, pp. 219–20). Todd's research focuses on the role fishing plays in the community. In her rich ethnographic account, Todd explains how, through the teachings of important community interlocutors (2016b) and by participating in 'jiggling' (the local term for the style of ice fishing used in the community) (2014), she came to know fish as 'more than food' (2016b, np):

> Fish are simultaneously many things: food, sentient beings with whom humans share territory; specimens of study and regulation in wildlife co-management regimes; [and] citizens and agents in legal-governance relationships. ... Across these sites, human–fish relations inform and capture memory, stories, teaching, and philosophies. I also learned that human–fish relations can act as 'micro-sites' across which fish and people, together, actively resist and shape colonial logics and processes within Inuvialuit territories. Just as humans can shape and experience the colonial encounter, so too can animals. Human–fish relations in Paulatuuq therefore present a plurality of meanings, strategies and principles for those enmeshed within them. As a result, fish pluralities in Paulatuuq deeply inform a vibrant and creative set of local strategies through which some community members have refracted colonial State formations of human–animal and human–environmental relations.

Just as fish themselves are an ontological multiplicity, so too is the relationship between fish and fisherman:

> The relationship between fish and fishermen is more than a physical or utilitarian one; working with fish and water is also deeply bound to social relations and Paulatuuq articulations of Inuvialuit legal orders.

In other words, to engage with fish in Paulatuuq is also to engage with, refract, and disperse the complex layers or territorial and federal understandings of how to treat fish. (Todd, 2018, p. 64)

As Todd shows (2018, p. 61, emphasis in original), following these human–fish relations reveals a rich diversity of ways in which the Paulatuuqmiut 'and fish, together, work to disrupt, refuse and challenge the ways in which the Canadian state imposes *its* understanding of land, property, conservation, and law'. More precisely, the Paulatuuqmiut, motivated by their deep relations with fish pluralities, use a 'principled pragmatism' strategy which in part employs science (an epistemology key for the modern world, as argued in Chapter 2) to honour and protect their relationship with fish (Todd, 2014, p. 226).

For example, the Hornaday River, which drains into Darnley Bay, is accessible from Paulatuuq by a road east of the community; as Todd notes (2014, p. 227), the Paulatuuqmiut have accessed Hornaday char regularly since the 1940s. In the 1960s, however, government actors developed a commercial fishery on the Hornaday to promote local economic development. This fishery ran from 1968 to 1986, alongside a small sport fishery that emerged in the area in the 1970s. These industries were encouraged by government officials despite a lack of scientific knowledge regarding the potential impact of these activities on the fish populations; not surprisingly, the result of this was over-fishing. Yet, as Todd (2014, p. 227) writes, 'It is here that an interesting local strategy emerged':

> With the signing of the Inuvialuit Final Agreement (comprehensive land claim) in 1984, a host of wildlife co-management bodies were established. Paulatuuqmiut turned to the co-management bodies of the Inuvialuit Final Agreement to mobilize scientific responses as one prong of a dynamic and pragmatic local strategy to shut down the commercial fishery on the Hornaday River. As a result, commercial fishing was stopped on the Hornaday in 1986, although subsistence harvesting continued. However, in 1995 a peak of 3,851 char were harvested for subsistence (versus the 1,700 allowed under current quotas), and renewed local concerns emerged about the number and size of char in the river and lasting damage from the government's commercial enterprise.

In response to the over-fishing, a diverse group of actors, such as the co-management body that interfaces between the Inuvialuit Game Council (the Inuvialuit self-government body) and the Federal Department of Fisheries and Oceans, and the Hunters and Trappers Committee (which represented the Paulatuuq harvesters), formed the Hornaday River Char Management

Project (Todd, 2014, p. 228). Quoting John Max Muffa Kudlak, who worked with the Hornaday River Char Management Project since its creation, Todd (2014, p. 228) shows how local actors employed a 'dynamic recovery strategy' that drew upon a diverse set of understandings of/relationships with fish to resolve this conflict over how to care for the fish. In Kudlak's words:

> [In] 1997 we came up with a plan for the community to decide if they [Paulatuuqmiut] can live with 1,700 char for the winter, which will be monitored by the harvest study coordinator. They found out they could live with it, 1,700 – so in 1998 we signed the first char management plan for Paulatuuq.

As Todd (2014, p. 228, emphasis added) foregrounds, this statement reveals how fish is mobilized in a variety of ways – as food, as a site of engagement for different stakeholders, as scientific specimens and as population estimates. In this mobilization, local harvesters negotiated and defined 'their relationships to fish *alongside* scientific-bureaucratic understandings and concepts of fish'. While this pragmatic approach thus facilitated scientific study and co-management (an approach to 'knowing' nature that is decidedly modern), 'it also paradoxically enabled local actors to challenge colonial impulses to turn local fish into economic outputs' (Todd, 2014, p. 228).

Dominant approaches to understanding the political would not, I believe, read the ways in which this community came to care for fish and sustain their human–fish relations by mobilizing a variety of logics as political. It would appear that neither the modern world nor the world of the Paulatuuqmiut are altered by this pragmatic approach to caring for fish: there is no ruptural moment of restructuring. Moreover, perhaps one could even argue that the use of science to 'manage' the fish population extends and entrenches the modern world's onto-epistemological framework, and thereby serves as an extension of modern 'politics'. I suspect that for many in the modern world, this would be the most obvious way to understand this case. However, a (dis)associative theory of care perspective encourages us to pause and press back on such a conclusion. This act could be read as political in that the principled pragmatism strategy employed by the Paulatuuqmiut allows them to reproduce their world, their legal orders which rest on their relations of responsibility with fish (Todd, 2018, p. 67), and their deep and layered relations with the more-than-human fish, in and through an ongoing colonial confrontation with the modern world. As the Paulatuuqmiut world must be established, maintained, and reproduced in the face of violent colonial logics and practices, the fact of this reproduction is, as I have argued earlier, political. The associative aspects of the creation of the Hornaday River Char Management Project, which involved diverse actors coming together to care for the char, facilitated the ongoing reproduction of the Paulatuuqmiut world. This care, and the reproduction it manifests, is decidedly political from a pluriversal vantage point, in which intricately connected worlds must continually be re-established in the face of one another.

At the same time, as Todd points out (albeit not in these terms), there is a dissociative quality at play here too. The strategic mobilization of the modern logic of science paradoxically disrupts the mobilization of the modern logic that fish are economic products. Further, this mobilization could provide a moment for subjects of the modern world to agonize over these different logics, and to consider what each offers us (or not) in terms of living well in the world. And lastly, as I have asserted at length in this chapter, because of the complex layers of relations that comprise the pluriverse, the reverberations of this disruption may yet manifest in significant ways. While the modern world has perhaps not yet been fundamentally restructured as a result of the Paulatuuqmiut's principled pragmatism, to say that this action is not 'properly political' (Blaser, 2019) is to preclude the possibilities implicit in the relational intertwinement of worlds and to discount political interventions that may work 'by slow accretion, reiteration, and citation rather than surprising rupture' (Sparks, 2016, p. 430). It is also, I suggest, to turn away from the opening that this associative political action (the collective coming together to protect fish and human–fish relations) offers for a dissociative exchange, in which we dwell in this example, the different onto-epistemologies at play here, and commit to agonizing the ethical merits of different care practices and the worlds that these practices alternatively reproduce and disrupt. A (dis)associative theory of care, which holds together the political significance of both associative and dissociative actions – of rupture and repair, as well as change and maintenance – entreats us instead to linger in this scenario in a way that is both critical (reflexive, open to revisability, to the possibility that certain grounds will need to be shifted) and productive (committed to caring for worlds as best as possible, in all the various iterations of what that care may be).

As a final note, I wish to reiterate a point I made about the possibility of pragmatism as a pluriversal ethics for the modern world (see Chapter 3), as I think it is especially pertinent in this rethinking of the political in the context of the pluriverse. As Todd (2018, pp. 62–3) compellingly shows, 'principled pragmatism' (Kuptana, 2014) served as an effective and creative strategy by which the Paulatuuqmiut apply 'their own governance practices and Indigenous legal order vis-à-vis fish and humans in the face of complex and cumulative and intertwined colonial and environmental challenges'. However, as I have emphasized throughout this book, I am most primarily concerned with how subjects of the modern world can better contemplate ethical horizons in the pluriverse. As I hope this discussion of the political illustrates, such horizons, I believe, require the modern world to commit to an ongoing awareness and examination of its onto-epistemic commitments and the ways in which these commitments render other onto-epistemologies unthinkable. Bracketing ontological and epistemological concerns, as is characteristic of a pragmatic approach, will prevent such critical examination. As Todd (2018, p. 62) writes:

> We have a responsibility to pay attention to the ways that communities and collectives of people tend to, care for, and work reciprocally with fish to build and sustain relationships which disrupt the State's attempts to 'command and control' the terms upon which Indigenous peoples, and Canada more broadly, interacts with the lands, waters and atmospheres within its reach.

I fear that a pragmatic approach to a pluriversal ethics for the modern world would make it all too easy for the modern world to eschew this responsibility, which implicitly, I believe, requires a commitment by the modern world to examine critically the different onto-epistemic biases it brings to the table, and the different forms of life that are unfolding in the scenario. A consequence of such eschewing, as this chapter has sought to demonstrate, is that it becomes all too easy for the ongoing reproduction and care of non-modern worlds to be viewed as 'unpolitical'. First and most obviously, this is problematic because, as I have argued, the re-establishment of a world that has been rendered precarious given the current configuration of the pluriverse, is, in fact, political (where the political has been rethought in the context of multiple distinct yet interconnected worlds). Second and relatedly, as Blaser (2019) points out, deeming such acts as not 'properly political' then greatly reduces the chance that they will have substantive ruptural consequences for the modern world, and the current configuration of the pluriverse. In dismissing the political nature and significance of caring for worlds, we preclude the possibility that the challenge posed by the continual resiliency of non-modern worlds will grow and expand into something that may, at some point, bring about a fundamental reordering of the modern onto-epistemology.

The ethics of care, as a critical and productive theory, prioritizes the (dis)associative nature of the political in the pluriverse, and avoids this danger. The ethics of care is attuned to both the dissociative (the ruptural, the deconstructive, the revisable, the contingent, the situated) and associative (the collective, the connected, the continuous, the common, the caring, the reproductive) aspects of the establishment and ongoing re-establishment of multiple worlds as they interact in and through power-laden partial connections. As Fiona Robinson (2018, p. 331) summarizes, 'a caring moral life is never decided, never finished, never tidy – it is a life of impossible decisions and constant struggle to know, understand and respond to others'. Care is never complete, never totalizing, always revisable, always difficult, but nonetheless focused on response, attentiveness, repair, maintenance, and living well. For these reasons, care provides us with tools to contemplate the political, rethought in the context of multiple partially connected vulnerable worlds, as (dis)associative, involving relational layers of onto-epistemic rupture and conflict, on the one hand, and onto-epistemic continuity and cooperation, on the other.

8

Building the Pluriverse with Care

In this final substantive chapter, I draw upon another example from the pluriversal literature, regarding a conflict over caring for what the modern world calls caribou and the Innu Nation calls *atîku* (Blaser, 2016; 2018), to demonstrate how the meta-theory developed in the previous chapters orients us to contemplate this ethical conflict. In so doing, this chapter also draws out other ways in which the ethics of care can help build a pluriversal ethics. Notably, the example mobilized here is particularly useful for the broader argument of this book because it involves a conflict which centres on a more-than-human being. The existence of more-than-human beings or earth-beings – non-human living beings or subjects (de la Cadena, 2014) – is one of the most prevalent claims demonstrating ontological multiplicity in the pluriversal literature. Indeed, many such beings have been introduced in the pluriversal examples woven throughout this book so far: Gyack, the Whanganui River, Ausangate, and the ontological plurality that is fish. Illustrating how the ethics of care can orient those in the modern world to contemplate ethical dilemmas involving more-than-human beings is necessary if the ethics of care is going to help build a fruitful ethics for the pluriverse.

Lastly, in addition to showing how the preceding meta-theoretical tools and orientations, based on a critical and political ethics of care, can help us contemplate a specific pluriversal ethical conflict, this chapter also aims to bring the argument of this book full circle: by starting with the understanding of morality inherent in a critical, political ethics of care, it becomes clear that the pluriverse is always and already a moral landscape. An ethics of care for the pluriverse thereby reveals that building a pluriversal ethics is much more than the 'application' of ethics to this 'new' pluriversal context. Instead, building a pluriversal ethics is the very means by which the pluriverse may flourish.

The case of *atîku*/caribou: a political, ontological, and ethical conflict

Newfoundland and Labrador is the most easternly province in Canada, comprised of both an island (Newfoundland) and an area of land (Labrador) that is connected to the main portion of the continent, specifically bordering Quebec and, less expansively, Nunavut. The George River caribou herd migrates an area that covers both Labrador and Northern Quebec. On 28 January 2013, the Government of Newfoundland and Labrador imposed a five-year hunting ban on caribou (Blaser, 2016). This ban was meant to help address the decline in the George River caribou population, which had decreased by over 96 per cent in just over a decade, from approximately 800,000 individuals in 1990 to 27,000 in 2012 (Blaser, 2016, p. 545). While the reasons for the decline of the herd's population were unclear, the provincial government was sure 'that a continued caribou harvest was not sustainable, even for the Innu and Inuit [I]ndigenous communities that live in Labrador' (Blaser, 2016, p. 545). Immediately after the ban was announced, however, the Innu Nation grand chief, Prote Poker, said that the ban was a threat to the Innu way of life; the Innu would continue their hunting practices as they always had. As Mario Blaser (2016, pp. 545–6) explains:

> Among other concerns, the Innu refusal to accept the ban was based on the insistence of knowledgeable hunters and elders who saw the decline in population as a symptom of the deteriorating relationship between the Innu and Kanipinikassikueu, the master of *atîku* (the word Innu use to refer to what Euro-Canadians call caribou). The extent to which established protocols for hunting are followed – such as the treatment of bones and the sharing of meat, among other prescriptions – determines the health of that relationship and the willingness of Kanipinikassikueu to keep giving animals to, and generally bless, the Innu. Hunters and elders had been complaining for several years by then that younger generations of Innu were not following these protocols, calling on the young people to recommit to them. In this context, for hunters and elders, the hunting ban would make it impossible to repair the relationship with *atîku* and its spirit master. In short, while for the wildlife managers in the provincial government hunting could mean the disappearance of the caribou, for the Innu hunters and elders, being prevented from hunting according to protocol almost assuredly would mean the disappearance of *atîku*.

A common reading of this scenario, informed deeply by the modern onto-epistemology, would cast this conflict as one that involves respecting traditional Innu beliefs and practices while trying to manage (master, control) caribou, which is treated as a passive material resource. In such a reading, it is clear 'who' has the hold on the real: caribou is what actually exists, while *atîku* is downgraded to a belief or tradition that is part of Innu culture. However, thinking pluriversally recasts this conflict as an ontological conflict. As Blaser (2016; 2018) argues, this conflict is not about competing understandings of *atîku*/caribou and divergent perspectives on how to manage *atîku*/caribou. Instead, the very ontology (the being) of *atîku*/caribou is at stake, as *atîku*/caribou is, itself, the product of different relations and practices. '*Atîku* emerges from an assemblage that involves *atanukan*, hunters, the sharing of meat, generosity, a spirit master, and so on; caribou emerges from an assemblage that involves the discipline of biology, wildlife managers, predictive modeling, calculations to balance environmental and economic concerns, and so on' (Blaser, 2016, p. 558). While there is, of course, a being, that being is multiple; 'various practices associated with caribou and *atîku* encounter each other in the flesh of a being (so to speak)' (Blaser, 2018, p. 56, emphasis added). More simply, *atîku*/caribou 'is more than one and less than many' (Blaser, 2016, p. 557). Both *atîku* and caribou are real; accordingly, *atîku*/caribou is in some ways the literal embodiment of the entanglement of two worlds.

Undoubtedly, then, this is an ontological conflict – a conflict over *what is*. By extension (or perhaps co-terminously), it is also a political conflict. Reading *atîku*/caribou as the embodiment of the entanglement of worlds, it is clear that this conflict is unfolding and located at the level of the political and has to do with the ongoing establishment and reproduction or disruption of worlds. The Innu world – co-constituted by its relationship with *atîku* – and the modern world – represented here by the Government of Newfoundland and Labrador – are struggling over which world-enacting should be continued, and which world-enacting may be impeded as a result. Put differently, these two worlds, which are themselves vulnerable and in need of continual re-enactment, are engaged in a conflict regarding which re-enactment/re-establishment should prevail, and which world(ing) will be rendered precarious as a result.

Lastly, however, I believe it is crucial to foreground that this is equally an ethical conflict. While there are ontological and political disagreements at play here (Blaser, 2016, p. 551), it is the normative question of how to care appropriately for the declining *atîku*/caribou population that draws out these ontological and political disagreements, that makes it necessary to contemplate and tend to these disagreements. The ontological difference between *atîku*/caribou, and the competing re-establishment of the Innu world and the modern world that lies at the heart of this conflict, are not meaningful in the abstract or as theoretical and conceptual debates. These ontological and political conflicts gain meaning because of the moral stakes involved in addressing the moral dilemma of caring for *atîku*/caribou. It is the competing understandings and practices of caring for *atîku*/caribou in this example that draw out the ontological multiplicity of *atîku*/caribou and the ways in which *atîku*/caribou is enacted through different forms of (moral) life.

Caring for *atîku*/caribou

How can we approach this moral dilemma using the ethics of care? First, as described in detail in Chapter 4, the ethics of care understands morality as the very practices of care that form the fabric of our lives. The purpose of moral philosophy, from a care ethical perspective, is not to locate abstract and transcendental rules in order to apply them to a given scenario; the purpose of moral thinking is to look at our practices of care, and to use these practices to engage in an ongoing critical dialogue regarding how we wish to organize our lives so as to live as well as reasonably possible. However, understanding concrete moral practices involves paying attention to the context in and through which our moral practices emerge and unfold. In the pluriverse, understanding context involves foregrounding continually the relations between worlds. The distinction between vulnerable and precarious onto-epistemologies, developed in Chapter 6, provides a meta-theoretical orientation from which to begin this task.

To return to the case study at hand, one can mobilize the vulnerable framework to argue that the relations of power that connect the world of the Government of Newfoundland and Labrador (modernity) and the Innu world are asymmetrical, such that the Innu world is rendered precarious. That is, while both the modern world and the Innu world are vulnerable (as all worlds are, in that they require continual enactment and maintenance), the history of colonialism and relations of power therein make the continuation and/or revitalization of the Innu world more precarious than the reproduction of the modern world. This can be evidenced in the three dimensions of precarity outlined previously: precarious relations of production, precarious relations of distribution, and precarious relations to the state. First, the relations of production for the Innu world are precarious; the Innu articulate that the relationship with *atîku* and its spirit master Kanipinikassikueu needs repair (Blaser, 2016, p. 546). This relationship, as a key relation in the Innu world, is required for the continuation of the Innu way of being and knowing. Yet, as Blaser notes, the relationship had been rendered precarious due to several factors. For instance, when asked about the declining herd, Innu elders and hunters explained that the 'decrease in the frequency of *atîku* giving themselves to hunters is a symptom that [indicates that] Kanipinikassikueu is angry':

> Elders and hunters said that the disrespect of younger generations for *atîku* was rampant. They spoke of *atîku* remains being carried away

by dogs, of the people selling meat, and of a general lack of interest about life on the land by younger people. But they were not angry; they were worried. For most of them the consequences of all this were obvious not only in the decline of the herds but also in the epidemic of addiction, suicide and diabetes that has plagued younger generations of Innu for the last twenty years. ... The elder Ponas Nuke expressed the problem thus: 'Without *atîku* we are nothing. If we are not in the land, hunting, it will come the day Kanipinikassikueu will not know us, it will ask "who are you people?" ... and if we do not have its blessing, things will get worse.' (Blaser, 2018, pp. 54–5, emphasis added)

The disrespect of younger generations towards *atîku*,[1] and most acutely, the hunting ban (implemented and enforced by another world), make the Innu relationship with *atîku* precarious, and therefore, as the elder Ponas Nuke points out, renders precarious the Innu's entire way of being and knowing. The relations necessary to produce the Innu world are more vulnerable due to the hunting ban, which comes from the entanglement between the Innu world and modernity, the world of the Government of Newfoundland and Labrador.

Second, the Innu world also faces increased vulnerability, that is, precariousness, vis-à-vis the relations of distribution, as their relation to *atîku* is not validated by the dominant logic of modernity, or the Government of Newfoundland and Labrador which operates in/through this logic. The latter casts the Innu's relationship with *atîku*, in accordance with the terms of the 'modernist assumption of one world with multiple perspectives on it' (Blaser, 2016, p. 549), as 'mere' belief. And as a belief, the Innu's 'claims are automatically disqualified as being unreasonable or unrealistic' (Blaser, 2016, p. 550). The distribution of political authority across the worlds implicated in this political-ethical conflict is uneven as a result. The Innu's

---

[1] Without speculating too much, it seems plausible that the 'lack of respect' for *atîku* by younger generations of Innu likely can be linked to colonial relations in Canada, in which the disruption of Indigenous ways of life were violent and have had ongoing consequences. However, I believe it is useful to include this point as part of the explanation for the precarity of relations of production of the Innu world because it emphasizes that worlds must be reproduced; when members of a world no longer reproduce and maintain said world, that world can be rendered as precarious as when a confrontation with another world is forceful and violent. To put it differently, 'politics' (the practices within an established socio-symbolic order) is also important in the pluriverse, as politics inherently forms part of the ways in which a world is reproduced or not. Furthermore, noting that some members of the Innu world do not participate in Innu practices also highlights that worlds are not complete and consistent wholes; 'ontological inconsistency' (Salmond, 2012, p. 125) is to be expected because of the partial relations between worlds, and the ways in which worlds have interacted and shaped each other historically.

knowledge is translated into and thereby mutilated by the discourse of modernity; government consultations re-write Innu concerns, splitting them 'according to supposedly common sense criteria that distinguish reliable environmental information from cultural beliefs' (Blaser, 2016, p. 560). The relations of distribution are asymmetrical between worlds, such that the modern world determines what counts as 'reasonable politics' (Blaser, 2016) and the knowledge and political stance of the Innu is granted less (if any) legitimacy. As a result, the Innu world is, again, rendered precarious.

Lastly, the Innu world is characterized by a precarious relation to the state. Neither the Innu nor *atîku* are recognized meaningfully by the state. While Innu leaders and hunters were consulted about how to respond to the declining numbers of *atîku*/caribou, the Government of Newfoundland and Labrador translated and recodified their knowledge and concerns and made it clear that such knowledge and concerns were less valuable than scientific knowledge (Blaser, 2016). This, in effect, downgraded their contributions and insights on the moral dilemma at hand. Furthermore, *atîku* is not recognized by the state; *atîku* can only ever be contemplated as caribou by the Government of Newfoundland and Labrador. Consider the following recollection from a related ethnography:

> One day, while I was in the Innu Nation office, a very experienced hunter who had been recently charged with illegal hunting came to the office where I was working and told me 'they found a Red Wine [protected herd] collar close to lake Kamistastin; see, caribou *wants* to go there.' Lake Kamistastin is located about 400 kilometers north of Sheshatshiu, very far from the Red Wine mountains caribou range, and right in the migration area of George River herd. This information, as he and other Innu argue, shows that the Red Wine woodland herd and the George River migratory herd intermingle. Therefore there is no point in declaring the hunt illegal on the basis of the assumption upheld by government scientists that the herds are different: for the Innu, there is only *atîku*. Furthermore, the words of this hunter obliquely indicate differences in how the collar information is used. The government uses it to obtain the information the scientists need to learn about caribou behavior, such as their whereabouts, while the Innu use this information to show *what atîku wants*. In other words, while the government administer the collars to satisfy its will to learn, the Innu use it to learn the will of *atîku*. Like human beings, *atîku* has will. (Castro, 2015, pp. 54–5, emphasis in original)

Atîku's relationship to the state is precarious, as the state cannot contemplate *atîku* at all. For the Government of Newfoundland and Labrador, *atîku* can only ever be caribou, something to be studied through science. *Atîku* is not thinkable as having 'full person-hood and will of their own' (Blaser, 2018, p. 54) from the vantage point of the modern world. As unthinkable, *atîku* is made precarious by the state, and by extension, so is the Innu world which is reliant upon its relationship with *atîku*.

In mobilizing the meta-theoretical framework developed in Chapter 6, this analysis illustrates how the ethical dilemma of how to care for *atîku*/caribou unfolds within a particular context that is already deeply shaped by relations of power between the worlds involved. These relations of power render, in particular, the Innu world precarious; the Innu world faces a more formidable struggle to be seen as a world, and to reproduce and sustain itself, than the modern world. In order to understand this ethical dilemma, these dynamics, as the ethics of care emphasizes, need to be brought to the fore. Moral dilemmas have to be understood within the contexts in which they emerge. The specific and contextual histories in and through which moral dilemmas unfold are key to understanding the dilemma itself.

At the same time, understanding the contexts in/through which moral dilemmas unfold also helps orient us to the ways in which power relations come to frame the dilemma and our responses to it. The meta-theoretical orientation proposed here, which traces the vulnerability and precarity of the worlds implicated in any given ethical dilemma, not only helps to reveal the material relations of power that shape the ethical conflict itself (thereby providing us with important details and information regarding the moral issue), it also illuminates the relations of power that shape whether we actually recognize the conflict (at all, as ethical, as political, as worthy of moral concern), the ways in which we then frame the conflict, and, equally significantly, the horizon of possibilities for responding to and addressing the issue at hand. Without paying attention to the relations of power between these worlds, and without understanding the mutual vulnerability of both these worlds, it becomes easy for those from the dominant world to construct the moral dilemma along modern terms only. Yet, the care ethical framework proposed here, while perhaps still of the modern world, decentres this tendency: by starting with the notion that all worlds are vulnerable, the ethics of care foregrounds the impossibility of a single truth or reality. Just as the relational social ontology of the ethics of care points to multiple different moral selves, understanding worlds as relational and therefore vulnerable means that multiple onto-epistemologies – different ways of being in and seeing the world – are possible; accordingly, one's own world may be fallible. And, of course, acknowledging the vulnerability of one's own world means acknowledging the vulnerability of the knowledge and practices that emerge through that world. Prioritizing the vulnerability of judgement creates space to consider seriously other onto-epistemologies. It creates space for us to attempt to decentre our own assumptions and reflect on how they shape our very acknowledgement and understanding of the ethical quandary.

Furthermore, the notion of precarity as intensified vulnerability due to relations of power draws attention to the fact that not only is one's own world vulnerable (and therefore contestable and revisable), but also that relations of power already shape the contestations and conflicts between worlds. Using precarity as a lens to uncover these relations of power, and to bring them to the fore of the ethical discussion, is an important way to see how unexamined hierarchies and moral understandings shape the terms of the ethical dialogue, often in asymmetrical ways. Taken together, vulnerability and precarity, as conceptual tools, can help attune us to two types of epistemic injustices that often discredit certain knowledges and practices:

> testimonial injustice [which] occurs when prejudice causes a hearer to give a deflated level of credibility to a speaker's word: [and] hermeneutical injustice [which] occurs at a prior stage, when a gap in collective interpretive resources puts someone at an unfair disadvantage when it comes to making sense of their social experiences. (Fricker, 2007, p. 1)

Acknowledging the vulnerability of our onto-epistemology, and the multiplicity of worlds that exist, helps us foreground the possibility, and likelihood, of hermeneutical injustice. Because of the differences between worlds, and because we are products of a particular world with a particular socio-symbolic order, ethical dilemmas across worlds will involve gaps in collective interpretive resources. The limits of knowing, or the impossibility of knowing another world fully, have already been described throughout this book, and are again evident in the example of how to care for *atîku*/ caribou. The modern world, premised on a thick distinction between Human and Nature, in which nature can only ever be an object, does not have the epistemic resources to understand the will of *atîku*. However, understanding one's own world as vulnerable and, by extension, one's practices and judgements as vulnerable, as the ethics of care proposes, orients moral actors towards the ongoing task of decentring their assumptions and beliefs so as to try to learn the other's needs while also foregrounding the *vulnerability of this very task*. Vulnerable moral thinking does not attempt to gloss over difference, nor does it involve a hubristic assuredness that difference can be translated; instead, vulnerable moral thinking involves acknowledging the vulnerability of one's own judgement (including acknowledging the vulnerability of asserting a particular understanding of 'vulnerability' itself) and the riskiness and difficulty of attempting to dialogue across difference.

A lens of precarity likewise helps attune us to the possibility of testimonial injustice, which occurs when prejudice allows some to discredit, or give less credit to, the knowledges and practices of others. To be certain, the precarity of the Innu world, as outlined here, points to such prejudices in the example at hand. Because the modern world fails to acknowledge its own vulnerability,[2] and because of prejudices and relations of power that render the Innu world precarious vis-à-vis modernity, the Innu knowledge, Innu hunting practices, and Innu relationship with *atîku* are discredited as 'not real', downgraded to belief or tradition, and seen as less valuable than the knowledges and practices of science. However, by orienting the moral actor to these pre-existing relations of power and revealing the ways in which these power dynamics shape the ethical dilemma, the conceptual tools of vulnerability and precarity can together position the moral actor to contemplate the vulnerability of their own world and judgement in order to try and suspend, or even amend, their prejudices. This move, while never totalizing or complete, would greatly reduce the likelihood and severity of testimonial injustice.

In other words, in addition to providing a conceptual lens from which to understand the relations between worlds – and therefore understand the context in and through which any given ethical dilemma is unfolding – thinking about vulnerability and precarity allows moral actors to emphasize continually their own vulnerability while also interrogating critically how relations of power mask the vulnerability of some worlds/practices/judgements by discrediting other worlds/practices/judgements. As a meta-ethical orientation, understanding the pluriversal landscape as vulnerable and precarious serves as both a critical tool, in that it uncovers relations of power between worlds and investigates how these relations of power shape the ways in which the moral quandary is understood and discussed, and a reflexive tool, in that vulnerability and precarity urge the moral subject to critique and destabilize the biases and assumptions that shape their moral judgements and response. In so doing, vulnerable ethical dialogue and judgement aims to de-hierarchicalize the relations of power that shape the ethical dilemma; vulnerability and precarity, as critical concepts, allow moral subjects to identify and interrogate relations of power and then seek to address those relations of power, and how they shape the construction and response to the ethical problem, through reflection, through vulnerable and revisable judgement. Vulnerable judgement rejects pre-existing moral hierarchies that render some moral voices precarious and allows for a more symmetrical relation between moral selves, and moral forms of life, to develop.

---

[2] To some extent, the modern world may be acknowledging vulnerability in this case, in that it is acknowledging the vulnerability of the caribou herd (a sort of ecological vulnerability). However, it does not acknowledge that its own understanding of vulnerability (in terms of biodiversity and sustainability, for instance) is vulnerable (that is, one understanding of vulnerability amongst many, including the Innu's understanding of vulnerability, which relates to the ways in which their relationship with *atîku* has been rendered precarious).

Of course, engaging in vulnerable judgement is difficult. It requires a constant decentring of the self to try and contemplate the needs of the other. It requires an ongoing commitment to moral judgements and practices as iterative processes. It is often characterized by agon and may require contestation and conflict. For instance, given the limits of knowing, I believe it is impossible for the subjects of the modern world *to know atîku*. As Susan Hekman (1995) reminds us, we are constituted by our onto-epistemologies, our moral forms of life; as such, to know *atîku*, I suggest, would entail the modern subject inhabiting a new world (and thus, the subject would not in fact be modern). Yet, in deciding how to care for *atîku*/caribou, the ethics of care would suggest that the actors representing the Government of Newfoundland and Labrador must try to decentre their assumptions and biases and learn about the world of the Innu.

At the same time, it must be emphasized that this is not meant to suggest some sort of romanticized adoption (co-optation) of Innu knowledge and practice. In contrast, I believe that the ethics of care is also a generative approach to ethics for the modern world in the pluriversal context because care provides a language that can help us with the great task of translating across worlds without losing sight of the difference(s) at stake. As Mary Louise Pratt (2002, p. 29) notes, one of the most interesting things in terms of translation is the ways in which worlds[3] 'can at one and the same time be so deeply, utterly, and particularly distinctive and yet be comprehensible to those outside them'. Care shares this same attribute; what, exactly, constitutes good care is contextual, rooted in a particular moral form of life, and therefore, heterogeneous and changing. At the same time, we often (although not always) recognize care when we see it; care can be comprehensible to those outside the caring relation, and we can find connections of understanding when we talk about care, even if 'care' itself means something different to the moral subjects involved in the discussion.

Because of these paradoxical qualities, I believe that care can provide a language to talk about moral concerns even when differences are at play, particularly because, as the ethics of care requires, care itself must be agonized. To return again to the case study, Blaser (2016, p. 561) notes that because the 'spiritual connection with caribou did not translate into what Euro-Canadians would recognize as care, then there was no such connection'. If care was instead agonized, if the modern subjects involved in this dilemma were willing to acknowledge their own vulnerable judgements and the ways in which relations of power rendered the care of *atîku* precarious (precarious as in difficult to conceive at all, and precarious as in making the practices

---

[3] Pratt actually writes this quote in reference to 'cultures'. However, substituting 'world' for 'culture' is appropriate because her understanding of culture and irrepressible difference aligns with the concept of worlds in the pluriversal literature.

of care deemed necessary by the Innu world difficult to reproduce), the Innu practices of care would not be erased. Inversely, care itself would be expanded, and the ethical dialogue would be enriched as other possible solutions for caring for *atîku*/caribou are put forward and contemplated in meaningful ways. For this reason, the language of care can prove useful in the pursuit of 'translation as a process of controlled equivocation' (Viveiros de Castro, 2004, p. 5). Translation in this vein is not about reaching equivalence through either an existing or new referent. Instead, the goal of translation as a process of controlled equivocation is to address multiple things/achieve multiple goals simultaneously (Blaser, 2016).

For example, Blaser (2016, pp. 564–5) describes how his research team worked to build a proposal to intervene in the dilemma of how to care for *atîku*/caribou. In particular, the team proposed, and continues to propose, that the Government of Newfoundland and Labrador support a limited hunt, 'allowed to the Innu communities under their strict "traditional" protocols' (Blaser, 2018, p. 61). This, the researchers suggest, would likely generate support from the Innu community, and as a result, they would take fewer animals, therefore decreasing hunting without stopping it fully. As a result, both *atîku* and caribou are cared for: 'Promoting and enforcing proper *nataun* protocol (caring for *atîku*) also meant hunting for fewer animals (caring for caribou); neither the Innu hunters nor the wildlife managers had to subordinate their own practices of caring. In fact, in this translation, caring for caribou and *atîku* would have reinforced each other' (Blaser, 2016, p. 565). In this solution, the language of care provides a way to address the moral problem of the declining population of *atîku*/caribou without requiring that *atîku* be translated to caribou or vice versa.

Relational thinking – a key part of moral deliberation from an ethics of care perspective – is also evident in this solution; the goal is to preserve the relations with both *atîku* and caribou that are at the heart of this ethical dilemma, and to meet everyone's caring goals. This type of solution is, I believe, central to the type of moral thinking/doing inherent in the ethics of care. The ethics of care prioritizes the enhancement and preservation of relationships as a moral good; resolving moral dilemmas is to attend to the relationships involved, to engage with them critically, and to respond to the ways in which the relationships are rendered precarious. The point is not to get it perfect. Care can never be finished, it can only be engaged in over and over again to the best of our abilities and revised when necessary.

As may now be evident, it is also for these reasons that I suggest that the language of care and relational thinking makes the ethics of care a particularly useful lens for modern subjects when deliberating on ethical dilemmas involving more-than-human entities and earth-beings, which are not part of the onto-epistemic framework of modernity. María Puig de la Bellacasa (2017) attests to this when she uses an ethics of care approach to analyse the ethical practices involved in composting. She argues that the ethics of care, with its relational ontology, decentres morality from human subjects by focusing on *relations* of care, like the relation between soil and humans, by which people contribute to the maintenance and rejuvenation of the soil via composting, and by which soil provides nourishment for the food which sustains people. This decentring 'de-objectifies' non-human worlds and entities 'by exposing their liveliness and agency' in the relationship, and 'de-subjectifies' humans 'by trying to think of [human moral] agency as a form of ontological agency among others' (Puig de la Bellacasa, 2017, p. 141). The ethics of care, by prioritizing relations – and particularly, caring relations – can *contemplate more-than-human beings without knowing more-than-human beings.*

For instance, as pointed out earlier, modern subjects, such as the wildlife agents involved in the management of the caribou herd, cannot know *atîku*; they are not constituted by the relational onto-epistemology in and through which *atîku* is (re)produced, and which, in turn, reproduces the Innu world. However, they can think relationally, and understand that the relationship between the Innu people and *atîku* is of great importance to the maintenance and continuation of the Innu world. They can contemplate how to enhance that relationship, and grapple with how their own relationship with caribou interacts with the Innu relationship with *atîku*. They can understand that agency comes from our various relations, even if they cannot conceive of agential more-than-human beings in the most robust sense; preserving these relations is therefore of moral value. In this way, the ethics of care avoids a romanticized engagement with more-than-human beings, in which modern subjects now 'know' or 'revere' these entities, while also centring their significance, existence, and onto-epistemic importance for different forms of moral life. A language of care, and relational thinking, helps provide both discursive tools and different vantage points to account for many different types of subjects, relations, forms of agency, and practices of care that comprise heterogeneous worlds.

Ultimately, the Government of Newfoundland and Labrador did not accept the researchers' proposal (Blaser, 2016); they implemented and maintained the hunting ban. This moral dilemma was addressed by a rationalist approach to morality, so very characteristic of the modern onto-epistemology: the caribou population was declining, 'science' indicates that banning hunting will stop the decline, so the solution is to implement a hunting ban universally, thereby suppressing other knowledges about how to care for *atîku*/caribou. It is also worth highlighting that the ban has proven largely ineffective. As of 2018, the herd population had dropped significantly again, to a low of 5,500 individuals (CBC News, 2018).

The ethics of care, I suggest, provides a useful vantage point from which to contemplate this aspect of this dilemma as well, as a critical and political ethics of care requires moral actors to pay attention continually to how an ethical conflict unfolds and evolves in light of different interventions. In particular, the ethics of care, as an iterative and materialist ethics, would compel us to revisit this situation given the consequences of the hunting ban.

> A material ethics entails ... that we can compare the very real material consequences of ethical positions and draw conclusions from those comparisons. We can, for example, argue that the material consequences of one ethics [are] more conducive to human and nonhuman flourishing than that of another. Furthermore, material ethics allows us to shift the focus from ethical principles to ethical practices. ... Ethical practices – as opposed to ethical principles – do not seek to extend themselves over and above material realities, but instead emerge from them, taking into account multiple material consequences. (Alaimo and Hekman, 2008, pp. 7–8)

For the ethics of care, applying a principle cannot resolve an ethical dilemma, because the ethics of care sees ethics as an ongoing task of tending to care responsibilities. For the ethics of care, we must be attentive to the outcomes of our moral practices of care and take account of whether or not caring needs are addressed. In this case, the continuing decline of the caribou herd would suggest that the ethical practice (the hunting ban) is insufficient; it fails to address the needs of the herd. Consequently, the ethics of care would demand that we revisit the question of how to care for *atîku*/caribou, pay attention to how *atîku*/caribou have responded to the first intervention (the hunting ban), and revise this intervention given the results. Again, the ethics of care reminds us that care is never complete or over with; we cannot shed our caring responsibilities, nor can we ignore them. The ethics of care orients us towards the ongoing and iterative process of responding to vulnerability and precarity through revisable and contestable practices of care. This is, in fact, how our worlds are maintained and made better.

There is a second reason, however, that the ethics of care would demand that we revisit the question of how to care for *atîku*/caribou. First and foremost, as just noted, it is evident that the caring needs of the herd have not been met; the way in which we have addressed the caring need has not been effective. Second, and of particular import in the pluriversal context, understanding vulnerable and precarious worlds is ethically significant because the unequal distribution of precarity across worlds operates at two registers when contemplating particular moral issues. On the one hand, a focus on vulnerable and precarious worlds, as has been well rehearsed by now, allows us to attend to the pressing ethical issue of why certain worlds are rendered more or less vulnerable (that is, precarious) than others in the pluriversal matrix, which in turn helps us understand how the unequal vulnerability (that is, precarity) of worlds shapes the ways in which we construct, understand,

and address moral dilemmas between worlds. By the same token, however, this framework also allows us to be attentive to how our ethical deliberations regarding particular dilemmas further constitute the conditions for the reproduction of specific worlds. The ways in which we address and respond to moral dilemmas also (re)create the conditions in and through which worlds (re)produce, in and through which the configuration of the pluriverse along hierarchical lines is sustained or disrupted. Accordingly, the ethics of care would thus also demand that we revisit this moral conflict because of the ways in which caring for *atîku*/caribou is implicated in the reproduction of both the modern world and the Innu world. As Blaser (2016, p. 564) writes, 'what the *atîku*/caribou case shows us is that worlding a common world does not always produce just an externality; sometimes it interrupts and destroys other worldings: caring for caribou in certain ways endangers the existence of *atîku*' and the world of which *atîku* is a part. The modern world's enactment of a common world, via the enactment of a common caring practice for *atîku*/caribou, disproportionally impacts, and renders precarious, the reproduction of the Innu world, and thereby upholds the pluriversal matrix in its current configuration, with the modern world dominating and marginalizing other worlds. It is for this reason that this ethical dilemma, like all ethical dilemmas across multiple worlds, is also a political dilemma. The political in the pluriverse is about the ongoing re-establishment of onto-epistemologies as they interact, conflict, and confront one another; the ways in which a given ethical dilemma is understood and addressed (or not) further forms the conditions of possibility for a world to establish and re-establish itself. More simply, how we address ethical dilemmas in the pluriverse has political implications for the production and reproduction of worlds.

This can be seen clearly in the case of *atîku*/caribou. The ways in which the ethical dilemma of caring for *atîku*/caribou has been resolved (a hunting ban) is insufficient in a least two ways: first, *atîku*/caribou have not responded well to the intervention, and the herd continues to deplete;[4] second, the world which requires a particular relationship with *atîku* is rendered (more) precarious by the intervention. That is, even though caring for *atîku*/caribou has been associative (if not symmetrical), as both groups have dialogued on the issue and recognize that *atîku*/caribou need to be cared for, the outcome of the ways in which this issue has been addressed is

---

[4] The Government of Newfoundland and Labrador maintains that the herd's decline is generally related to 'deterioration in habitat and food resources, predation and climate change' (MacEachern, 2016, np). One could posit, based on this, that the reason for the continuing decrease in the herd's population suggests that the other factors – habitat and food resources depletion and climate change – are having a much more significant impact on the herd's overall health than 'predation', which was meant to be addressed through the ban.

dissociative and destablizing for the Innu world. The hunting ban interrupts and destroys the Innu worlding practices and renders their world (more) precarious. The ethics of care, as attuned to both the efficacy of specific caring relations as well as to the ways in which caring relations reproduce vulnerable/precarious worlds, would demand that these caring practices be revised, as they not only fail to meet the direct caring need, but they also hinder the reproduction of the Innu world.

(On the other hand, I would be remiss not to point out that the fact that the modern intervention has continued to fail to address the problem sufficiently may yet come to destabilize the modern world and point to the limits of modern science – thereby also rendering the modern world relatively precarious. The pluriverse, as I argued in the previous chapter, is always unfolding through complex (dis)associative practices and relations. Practices of care and caring knowledge can alternatively deconstruct and produce relations and worlds in surprising ways.)

Lastly, thinking about this ethical dilemma of how to care for *atîku/* caribou also illustrates why I believe that building a pluriversal ethics with the ethics of care and thinking ethical horizons in the pluriverse along the lines of vulnerability and precarity is a more fruitful pluriversal project than the 'cosmopolitical proposal' (Stengers, 2005), which is oft cited in the pluriversal literature. The cosmopolitical proposal is a commitment to building a common world *more slowly*. As Isabelle Stengers (2005, p. 995) explains, 'The idea is precisely to slow down the construction of this common world, to create a space for hesitation regarding what it means to say "good"'. In this way, the cosmopolitical project is a normative and axiological project that is committed to building a common world or vision of the good, although what that vision may be is undecided beforehand. The cosmopolitical proposal focuses on two mechanisms for building this common world: slowing down reasoning and equality. Slowing down reasoning means discarding or suspending one's onto-epistemic commitments as best as possible so as to focus on whatever exists in common. Equality means that 'all have to be present in the mode that makes the decision as difficult as possible, that precludes any shortcut or simplification, any differentiation a priori between that which counts and that which does not' (Stengers, 2005, p. 1003). Given this, 'cosmopolitics remains oriented to the composition of the common world, even [as] it insist[s] on the lack of guarantees for such a project' (Blaser, 2016, p. 548).

However, as Blaser (2016, p. 563) argues:

> sometimes different worldings may coexist – enabling each other or without noticing each other – but at other times they interrupt each other. Not being reducible to each other's terms, when and where worldings interrupt each other, the multiplicity at stake might not be

amenable to the kind of singularization that ... the constitution of the common world seems to require.

Indeed, in the case of *atíku*/caribou, the hunting ban interrupts the Innu world and renders their relationship with *atíku*, and hence their worlding practices, precarious. As Blaser (2016; 2018) argues, when different worlding practices are not amenable to singularization (that is, stringing together in common; in this case, the impossibility of simultaneously hunting and not-hunting *atíku*/caribou), and given the colonial relations of power that already constitute relations between worlds, relying solely on building a common world may end up reproducing the power hierarchies that already exist. The more powerful world can more easily dictate what, exactly, is 'common', and thereby erase differences that are not comprehensible to its logic. This is, in many ways, what has happened in the case of the Government of Newfoundland and Labrador's 'consultation' with the Innu Nation, as outlined in the preceding discussion.

An ethics of care for the pluriverse, as presented here, is not premised on, nor committed to the prospect of, such a common world. Instead, the ethics of care is an open-ended and continually unfolding project, which orients us to the 'ethico-political significance of doings of care that make the substrate of everyday life' (Puig de la Bellacasa, 2017, p. 204). These doings of care require continual attentiveness to the other and to difference; they are ongoing, iterative, and revisable. Care is not a theory for building a common world based on thick prescriptive caring practices; care does not seek 'a separate cozy realm where "nice" relations can thrive' (Puig de la Bellacasa, 2017, p. 204). The ethics of care, conversely, orients us to the difficult task of challenging relations of power that impede relations of care while simultaneously fostering relations that maintain lives in and across worlds as well as reasonably possible. Of course, there will be competing caring needs; vulnerabilities do not neatly align, and often require unique responses. The ethics of care does not shy away from such conflicts. Rather, the ethics of care demands that we dwell in the messiness of care and acknowledges that while we must always respond to vulnerable needs, such response will never be ideal. Eduardo Viveiros de Castro writes (2013, p. 37, emphasis in original), 'the "good life" is a good *enough* life. There is no better than enough.' The ethics of care, which understands that responding to caring needs, repairing relations, and living as well as reasonably possible, is a difficult, messy, and often conflictual business, would agree.

Building an ethics for the pluriverse/building the pluriverse

This final chapter – in which I use the example of *atíku*/caribou to demonstrate how the ethics of care, and specifically the care ethical meta-theoretical framework of vulnerable and precarious worlds developed in this book, provides a useful vantage point from which to contemplate an ethical dilemma across worlds – therefore brings my argument full circle. By starting with the ethics of care, I argue that the pluriverse is constituted by morality, understood as the practices of care by which we reproduce and maintain our lives and our worlds as well as reasonably possible. Moreover, the ways in which we attend to ethical dilemmas in the pluriverse further constitutes the very political conditions for the reproduction (or not) of the multiple vulnerable worlds that comprise the pluriversal matrix. Thinking about the ethics of care, and employing key concepts such as vulnerability and precarity, helps us to understand better the ethical conflicts between worlds, the relations that partially connect worlds and the ways in which power permeates these relations, situating worlds differently, and shaping the ethical conflicts and consequences that emerge as worlds co-mingle.

To recapitulate, the notion of vulnerable worlds reminds us that all worlds – even seemingly stable ones – are contingent and vulnerable to change. At the same time, certain worlds are rendered more vulnerable, that is precarious, by relations of power that legitimize certain onto-epistemologies while devaluing others. Of course, there is also always a modicum of empowerment in this precarity; precarious worlds are not wholly subsumed by the logic of the dominant onto-epistemology, and therefore point to the limits and vulnerability of that occupying world. In tracing the ways in which certain worlds are rendered precarious, this meta-theoretical orientation towards vulnerable and precarious worlds allows us to attend to several pressing ethical tasks in the context of the pluriverse.

First, the pluriverse, as I have described it from a care ethical perspective, is characterized by an axiological commitment to partial relations of care and to the multiplication of worlds as worlds. Given this, a pressing ethical concern for the pluriverse is attending to the ways in which certain worlds face a greater struggle to reproduce than others. Investigating precarious worlds, and the ways in which certain worlds experience precarious relations of production, precarious relations of distribution, and/or precarious relations to the state, helps with this ethical task. Second, understanding the relations between worlds, and the ways in which some worlds are rendered precarious, helps to foreground the background conditions which shape particular ethical dilemmas across worlds. Looking at the relations between vulnerable and precarious worlds helps to uncover how power dynamics and moral-epistemic hierarchies operate to shape the ethical issue itself, as well as the ways in which ethical dilemmas are understood, debated, and addressed. This is a crucially important task because, as the ethics of care emphasizes, moral dilemmas always emerge in and through some context; they cannot be abstracted from the relations of power in and through which they unfold. Addressing any concrete ethical conflict will require understanding the power-laden relations in and through which it arises and transpires. Relatedly, understanding the relations of power that uphold some worlds in hegemonic positions while relegating others to the margins of the global political economy encourages moral subjects, and particularly modern moral subjects, to interrogate their own onto-epistemic assumptions and biases, and to be open to revising their own (vulnerable) moral judgement when necessary. This allows other moral voices to be heard, and different moral forms of life to stand on equal footing. In so doing, I believe we can begin to move towards a de-hierarchicalized pluriverse, in which worlds are, of course, partially connected, but not necessarily configured according to one-sided power differentials. Lastly, an orientation towards vulnerable and precarious worlds also orients moral selves towards the fact that in the pluriverse, the ways in which we deal with ethical conflicts across worlds is implicated in the very production or disruption of worlds. Moral practices and moral understandings are intimately intertwined with the reproduction of particular forms of (moral) life and must be attended to carefully if we are to build the pluriverse, and repair, sustain, and care for the many worlds therein.

As a final point, and to return specifically to my own world, the implications of this care ethical approach to pluriversal ethics are radical for modernity. In opening space for other moral knowledges/practices to be taken seriously as valid and meaningful forms of moral life, and in attending to the ways in which addressing ethical dilemmas across worlds is always implicated in the production and reproduction of worlds (often in unequal ways), the meta-theoretical orientation developed here destabilizes modernity's hegemonic position in the pluriverse, and thereby works, as just noted, to de-hierarchicalize the pluriverse itself. De-hierarchicalizing the pluriverse in this manner, I believe, also renders modernity a more liveable world in the most fulsome sense. On the one hand, modernity will be better able to co-exist with other worlds, worlds that are inextricably intertwined and co-constitutive of it, and which have often been rendered precarious in and through modernity's domination. On the other hand, modernity's own moral epistemic resources and moral practices will be enriched: the horizons of possibility for addressing moral and ethical dilemmas will be expanded in productive and generative ways as the modern world better cultivates tools for meaningful consideration of the good to be found in living a variety of forms of moral life. In engaging in such deliberation – which will, of course, always be difficult, messy, iterative, and vulnerable – modernity can come to critique, and change, its moral landscapes that have been found wanting, and perhaps begin to foster a different form of moral life that is more liveable for those in and of the modern world as well. The care ethical pluriversal ethics developed in this book positions modernity to enact the pluriversal project, which is normatively defined (as I have put forth here) by a commitment to valuing (partial) relations of care, including those relations of care which minimize harm and suffering and allow life to flourish in the modern world.

In these ways, my hope is that this book demonstrates that rethinking global ethics in the context of the pluriverse is a much greater task than 'applying' a particular approach to ethics to this 'new' landscape. Instead, this book uses the ethics of care to rethink the pluriverse as a meta-world, to rethink ethics as practices that constitute and emerge from forms of life, and to demonstrate that the pluriversal project is ethical all the way down. An ethics for the pluriverse is not something to be 'added' to pluriversal considerations. Building a pluriversal ethics, from an ethics of care perspective, is to build the pluriverse itself.

9

Rethinking Global Ethics with Care and the Pluriverse

As a final reflection, I would like to offer some closing thoughts on what the argument of this book implies more generally for the field of Global Ethics. As noted in the introductory chapter, the field of Global Ethics strives to address the ethical questions, issues and concerns that inevitably result from our relatedness and interconnectedness, on the one hand, and our divergent needs, interests, views, and practices, on the other. Yet, the pluriverse – which foregrounds multiple ways of being in and seeing the world, and thereby illuminates both our inextricable interconnectedness and our radical differences – poses a fundamental challenge to the ways in which the field of Global Ethics approaches ethical questions. In the pluriverse, differences are at their most robust; the onto-epistemic differences across worlds can manifest in surprising places and in surprising ways, and they may not be translatable or fully conceivable to subjects from different worlds. Concomitantly, worlds – as relational unfoldings and enactments – are also deeply interconnected and enmeshed. We share a material reality, and our onto-epistemologies are inescapably intertwined through 'partial connections' (Strathern, 2004).

This apparent paradox, in which worlds are at once intimately intertwined and also radically different, constitutes a particular political landscape with unique implications for conceiving of global ethics and deliberating and addressing global ethical dilemmas. Addressing global ethical questions cannot rely on universal grounds and principles, à la the rationalist approaches in Global Ethics, as the pluriverse orients us to multiple universals, that is, a multiplicity of heterogeneous worlds which are 'true' in their own right. There is not an ultimate foundation, structuring principle, or common trait that we can assume will ground and unite moral thinking across these multiple worlds. Differences in the pluriverse are onto-epistemic, and cannot be subsumed, circumvented or made commensurable. Relying on transcendental and universal truths, accessed by a particular form of rationalism, is not efficacious when contemplating ethical dilemmas where such deep and pervasive differences are at play. Indeed, the ways in which rationalist approaches purport one right approach to moral thinking often smuggle in unexamined hierarchies (Beattie and Schick, 2013) which reflect and reproduce existing relations of power; in so doing, rationalist approaches in the field of Global Ethics fail to engage seriously with different ways of being in and seeing the world, different 'forms of moral life' (Walker, 2007, p. 105).

At the same time, neither can global ethical issues in the pluriverse be contemplated purely by emphasizing the contingency of all grounds – as is the case with some alternative approaches in the field of Global Ethics, like postmodernist ethics – as worlds exist, and persist, through time, although perhaps not evenly so. Focusing on radical contingency alone does not provide much guidance when attempting to theorize and address ethical dilemmas across actually existing worlds. A primary goal in the pluriversal context, which is firmly rooted in the decolonial project, is to create space, or reorder relations of power, so as to allow multiple worlds to flourish. Deconstructing worlds – while useful for challenging any specific world's claim to be the only world – is not amenable to the task of treating worlds as real. Navigating ethical issues in the context of the pluriverse in part requires giving weight to the groundings of multiple particular worlds, as opposed to undermining such groundings. Worlds, as enacted and unfolding and as co-constitutive of subjects, are actually existing, and a key part of the pluriversal project is to treat them as such.

Because of this, the pluriverse poses a particular challenge to Global Ethics, in that the pluriverse asks *how can we rethink global ethics in the pluriverse, where differences are at their most deep and pervasive? How might we build a pluriversal ethics? How can we live well with other worlds? How can we care for worlds that are not our own?* Such a challenge requires displacing several of the binaries that shape many approaches in the field of Global Ethics; it demands that we, as global ethicists, undertake a different kind of theorizing project.

For instance, the antinomy of universality versus particularity is an insufficient theoretical space for thinking pluriversally: the pluriverse is neither a universal nor is it composed of multiple contingent particularities. The pluriverse asks us to contemplate a different landscape composed of temporally simultaneous actually existing onto-epistemologies, and to consider the ethical-political conflicts that arise as these actually existing worlds interact. These worlds exist – and are therefore unique 'universals' in their own right – but they are also vulnerable, and susceptible to change, as the relations and practices that constitute a world may shift, evolve, or even be rendered precarious through relations of power. Holding on to either end of the universal-contingency pole is untenable for contemplating ethical horizons in the pluriverse, which requires focusing on the unfolding relations that make and remake worlds time and time again. To be sure, it is these very unfolding relations that make worlds both real and enacted and, somewhat paradoxically, particular, contingent, and vulnerable.

Relatedly, the pluriverse requires moving beyond epistemic binaries like objective/subjective, impartial/biased, and absolute/relative. In the pluriverse, all knowledge is situated: all knowledge is partial and subjective in that it comes from a particular world, a particular co-constitutive and enacted ontology and epistemology. At the same time, however, this situatedness does not mean that we descend into relativism, a scenario in which we can never contemplate right or wrong. In contrast, it is the very situatedness of all knowledge that allows us to pursue moral criticism and debate, although this is a very different kind of moral philosophizing than that which is found in many dominant approaches in Global Ethics. Rather, this type of moral thinking involves detailed examination of worlds, critical moral ethnography (Walker, 2007, p. 246), and the investigation of moral forms of life that are co-constitutive of worlds, so as to understand as best as possible (although never perfectly) where moral knowledge, ethical practices, and different sets of values come from. And of course, this task equally involves critically examining one's own world, one's own onto-epistemology, and the situatedness of one's own moral claims. The pluriverse demands an approach to global ethics that rejects attempts to find universal and 'objective' moral truths, on the one hand, and moral apathy, on the other. In contrast, as I have argued, building a pluriversal ethics requires that we pursue the relentless task of examining over and over again the ways in which different moral voices, and different moral knowledges, are formed, the conditions in and through which certain moral claims and judgements gain authority and meaning, and the good to be found in living different forms of moral life.

The pluriverse also challenges the understanding of the political as either associative (cooperative, collaborative) or dissociative (agonistic, ruptural). Instead, the political in the context of the pluriverse can only be conceived of as (dis)associative. As worlds intermingle and interact, and as worlds maintain or break partial connections, certain worlds will experience degroundings and ruptures more impactfully than others, who may in fact experience regroundings, and thus greater stability of their onto-epistemic orders. By extension, dissociative and associative political action can both lead to the political in the pluriverse; sometimes collective coming together to care for a common world will result in a political moment (for some but perhaps not all of the worlds involved), while at other times the political moment will be brought about by conflict and agonism. Worlds are both established and continually re-established *and* sometimes ruptured and regrounded anew as they interact in complex, and often unforeseeable, ways. The importance of deconstructing relations of power that suppress certain relational practices and knowledges as well as the value of maintaining and reproducing relations of care that allow us to live well are relationally tied from a pluriversal perspective (frequently, these two tasks are two sides of the same coin).

And lastly, the binary of wholes and parts, in which we are either talking about a part of a whole, or the whole as formed by all the parts, is not a useful framework for contemplating a pluriversal ethics. The pluriverse is not a totalizing whole, comprised of units that come together to form a structure; it is a partially connected matrix of worlds that both overlap and exceed each other in meaningful ways. Yet, Global Ethics is again often trapped by this kind of thinking. Commonly, approaches to global ethics begin with a conception of individuals (atomistic units) who come together to form political-ethical communities (perhaps in the cosmopolitan vision of a global community and common humanity, or in the form of states or other political communities, which themselves are treated as individual units that together comprise the international sphere or some other whole). It is very difficult to think pluriversally from such a conceptual space. In contradistinction to conceptualizing pre-existing parts that seamlessly come together via relationships to form a totalizing whole, the pluriverse, which I have argued is premised upon a relational ontology, demands that we focus on the continually enacted, (re)produced, and unfolding relations which bring worlds in to existence.

Thinking through this challenge, thinking in/through/with the pluriverse, and attempting to contemplate global ethics in a way that does not rely on or reproduce such binaries – which so very often keep us from caring – has been the core task of this book. More specifically, I have sought to develop theoretical tools, drawing upon the ethics of care, to understand better this pluriversal landscape, and to develop an orientation from which to build a pluriversal ethics.

The ethics of care, as presented here, is a critical political moral theory which starts from a relational social ontology, and which conceives of moral subjects as constituted in and by their particular relations. As a result, moral subjects are both heterogenous – emerging from unique sets of relations – and vulnerable. The moral subject, for the ethics of care, is not an atomistic individual, but rather a vulnerable processual self (Sevenhuijsen, 1998), who is always a relational becoming. Because of this relational ontology, the ethics of care is normatively oriented towards repairing relations of care, by which I mean relations that minimize harm and suffering, meet the needs of vulnerable moral subjects, and allow us to reproduce our worlds as well as is reasonably possible. From this vantage point, morality does not refer to principles that can be applied to a given context in order to know what the right thing is to do; morality is instead recast as moral practices, in and through which we repair and maintain our vulnerable selves, and our vulnerable worlds. It is also through these moral practices, and our forms of (moral) life, that moral knowledge emerges. The ethics of care sees moral knowledge as embedded in the complex sets of relations that constitute our lives and our practices of care which allow us to respond to the needs of others iteratively and in an ongoing way. As such, the ethics of care also understands all moral judgement to be situated, vulnerable, and therefore open to revision; our particular moral voices, our particular moral practices, and our particular moral knowledge emerge in and through our co-constitutive relations. As these relations change and evolve, and as other moral practices are brought to the fore, the ethics of care contends that moral selves must continually pursue the messy and difficult task of attempting to decentre themselves (never fully possible) so as to learn attentively about other forms of moral life and other moral selves (again, never fully possible). In so doing, moral selves come to agonize their moral response and revise their moral practices when necessary.

For these reasons, the ethics of care critiques and rejects binary thinking – including the universal/particular, objective/subjective, absolutist/relativist, associative/dissociative, and whole/part binaries mentioned just now – and positions the ethicist to think relationally, to focus on relations and practices of care that repair and maintain vulnerable moral selves and vulnerable worlds, and to understand that all knowledge is uncertain, and thus open to revision. I argue that the ethics of care is therefore well positioned to serve as a starting point from which to build a pluriversal ethics, particularly for the modern world. The care ethical premises presented here reorient Global Ethics to contemplate better the political landscape that is the pluriverse because the ethics of care foregrounds how a pluriversal ethics is an ethics of vulnerability and precarity. An ethics of care perspective, I have suggested, implies that worlds, as relational sets of practices that are in need of continual reproduction, maintenance, and repair, are vulnerable: they are contingent, and open to change and restructuring as relations of power (re)shape worlding practices. The implications of conceiving of worlds as vulnerable, for a pluriversal ethics, are threefold.

First, understanding how certain worlds are rendered more vulnerable – that is, precarious – as worlds conflict and co-mingle emerges as a pressing ethical task for the pluriverse, which is, itself, a normative commitment to building a world in which multiple worlds as worlds can flourish. 'Multiplying' worlds, in this sense, means that we must attend to the ways in which the reproduction of certain worlds is made precarious (rendered more vulnerable by relations of power). It is to foreground the co-constitutive existence of these multiple yet distinct worlds, and to focus continually on the ways in which this co-constitutive existence is often structured by relations of domination, violence, and oppression. Interrogating critically the relations of power which impede the maintenance and reproduction of particular worlds and striving to amend those relations so that many worlds can co-exist in a de-hierarchicalized way is a primary ethical task in the pluriverse – one which is made visible by understanding that, as the ethics of care with its relational social ontology suggests, worlds are vulnerable.

At the same time, it is also against this background of vulnerable and precarious worlds that specific ethical quandaries unfold and are addressed. Again, understanding this background is of moral import here, as it forms the very conditions in and through which ethical issues across worlds emerge and are understood. The ethics of care emphasizes the moral salience of context; all moral dilemmas and ethical practices stem from and unfold within particular sets of complex relations. A pluriversal ethics, from an ethics of care perspective, must likewise be attuned to context, where the context of the pluriverse, as explicated in this book, is one of vulnerable and precarious worlds which are striving to sustain their existence as they confront each other continually.

Lastly, the ethics of care, by understanding the configuration of the pluriverse (and the multiplication of worlds within) as inescapably vulnerable, also highlights the importance of paying attention to how the specific practices that constitute particular ethical deliberations in the pluriverse can render some worlds more vulnerable – that is, precarious – than others. The ways in which we address and respond (or do not address and respond) to moral problems constitutes further the conditions of possibility for worlds to reproduce. The ethics of care, as both a materialist and revisable ethic, positions us to pay attention to the ways in which our moral practices and moral responses impact the reproduction of certain worlds in a given context.

In these ways, an ethics of care for the pluriverse, as developed here, is not simply the application of care ethics to the pluriversal context. Rather, building a pluriversal ethics, from an ethics of care perspective, is building the pluriverse itself. It is through our moral practices of care that we can agonize our different values and forms of moral life, as well as collectively strive to maintain, repair, and reproduce our different onto-epistemologies (including those we cannot know, such as entities in different onto-epistemologies that are inaccessible to us). It is also from this care orientation that we can begin the collective and collaborative task of moral philosophy, which is reflecting on the moral orders we participate in, asking when certain practices stand scrutiny, when they are worth reproducing, and under which conditions and limitations one can claim to have made a sound moral judgement. Such an approach to moral philosophy 'sets an agenda for moral criticism to lead or guide us in slow, often puzzling, and sometimes painful and costly tasks of mutual correction' (Walker, 2007, p. 257). It is by thinking relationally, thinking 'with care', and recognizing the vulnerability of our judgement that we can engage with others – including others who may be very different from ourselves – so as to pursue the collective task of moral philosophy: contemplating whether our values are the values which we want to live by, scrutinizing whether our moral forms of life reflect the ways in which we want to live, and in so doing, collectively enlarging the 'possibilities and the goods of shared lives' (Walker, 2007, p. 258). And as I emphasized throughout this discussion, enlarging these possibilities must include interrogating, revising, and, of significant import in the context of the pluriverse, *expanding* our understandings of 'care' as well. For example, in putting the feminist ethics of care in conversation with the pluriversal literature, forms of care that have largely been rendered invisible by the colonial logic of modernity – and here I am specifically thinking about care for earth-beings and more-than-human entities – are brought to the fore. Continuing to nurture this 'partial connection' between the ethics of care and the pluriversal literature, and continuing to expand and explore different understandings of/practices of care so as to broaden the horizons of possibilities for our shared lives, is an important task for future research.

As a final reflection, in Chapter 1 I noted that while I here focus on building a pluriversal ethics using the ethics of care, taking the pluriverse seriously suggests that pluriversal ethics is most likely plural in the fullest sense: just as there are multiple worlds in the pluriverse, there will be a multiplicity of pluriversal ethics, of moral understandings that can help build the pluriverse and navigate ethical dilemmas across worlds. For this reason, I wish to end this book with a call for Global Ethics to think pluriversally and grapple with the challenge of multiple distinct yet intimately interconnected worlds. Despite certain limitations, including those outlined here, I believe that the field of Global Ethics has much to offer in terms of thinking about the pluriverse, and for enriching the dialogue I have tried to foster here between moral philosophy and the pluriversal literature. Many different approaches to global ethics, for instance, may provide additional partial knowledges for contemplating ethical horizons in the pluriverse. Global Ethics has the potential to enhance our webs of partial ethical knowledges and to help us pursue the type of agonizing philosophizing required to deliberate on what it means to live well in a world of many worlds. Recent work by scholars like Cecelia Lynch (2020), who writes about ethical precarity in Christianity and its significance for International Relations, and Marcos Scauso (2021), who draws upon Silvia Rivera Cusicanqui's 'profession of faith' to rethink the problem of difference in International Relations, are, I believe, already developing fruitful avenues towards such aims.

At the same time, however, there is one thing that global ethicists can no longer do. We can no longer claim to be outside of the worlds we study, outside of the ethical dilemmas we contemplate, or outside relations of responsibility. Arturo Escobar (2018, p. 33) asks us to consider 'What world[s] do we want to build?' To commit to building a pluriversal ethics requires that we confront this question head on, time and time again. In this sense, global ethicists *must* care. We are complicit in the building of the pluriverse; we must take responsibility for the worlds we choose to enact and disrupt, for the fallibility of our moral knowledge, and for the consequences of our theorizing. Ethics in and for the pluriverse can proceed no other way.

References

Adorno, T. and Horkheimer, M. (2002) *Dialectic of Enlightenment: Philosophical Fragments* (Stanford, CA: Stanford University Press).

Agathangelou, A.M. and Ling, L.H.M. (2009) *Transforming World Politics: From Empire to Multiple Worlds* (London: Routledge).

Alaimo, S. and Hekman, S. (2008) 'Introduction: emerging models of materiality in feminist theory', in S. Alaimo and S. Hekman (eds) *Material Feminism* (Bloomington, IN: Indiana University Press), pp. 1–19.

Alfred, T. (2005) *Wasáse: Indigenous Pathways of Action and Freedom* (Toronto: University of Toronto Press).

Amin, S. (2009) *Eurocentrism* (2nd edn) (New York: Monthly Review Press).

Anghie, A. (1996) 'Francisco de Vitoria and the colonial origins of international law', *Social & Legal Studies,* 5, 3, pp. 321–36.

Anievas, A. (2005) 'Critical dialogues: Habermasian social theory and international relations', *Politics,* 25, 3, pp. 135–43.

Appiah, K.A. (1998) 'Cosmopolitan patriots', in P. Cheah and B. Robbins (eds) *Cosmopolitics* (Minneapolis: University of Minnesota Press), pp. 91–114.

Appiah, K.A. (2006) *Cosmopolitanism: Ethics in a World of Strangers* (New York: W. W. Norton & Company).

Aradau, C. and Huysmans, J. (2014) 'Critical methods in international relations: the politics of techniques, devices and acts', *European Journal of International Relations,* 20, 3, pp. 596–619.

Arrighi, G. (2010) *The Long Twentieth Century: Money, Power and the Origins of Our Times* (London: Verso).

Arruzza, C. (2017) 'Capitalism and the conflict over universality: a feminist perspective', *Philosophy Today,* 61, 4, pp. 847–61.

Asher, K. (2017) 'Spivak and Rivera Cusicanqui on the dilemmas of representation in postcolonial and decolonial feminisms', *Feminist Studies,* 43, 3, pp. 512–24.

Balibar, É. (2011) *Politics and the Other Scene* (London: Verso).

Barad, K. (2008) 'Posthumanist performativity: toward an understanding of how matter comes to matter', in S. Alaimo and S. Hekman (eds) *Material Feminism* (Bloomington, IN: Indiana University Press), pp. 120–54.

Barchiesi, F. (2012) 'Liberation of, through, or from work? Postcolonial Africa and the problem of "job creation" in the global crisis', *Interface: A Journal for and about Social Movements*, 4, 2, pp. 230–53.

Barnes, M., Brannelly, T., Ward, L. and Ward, N. (eds) (2015) 'Introduction: the critical significance of care', in M. Barnes, T. Brannelly, L. Ward and N. Ward (eds) *Ethics of Care: Critical Advances in International Perspective* (Bristol: Policy Press), pp. 3–20.

Baynes, K. (2004) 'The transcendental turn: Habermas's "Kantian pragmatism"', in F. Rush (ed.) *The Cambridge Companion to Critical Theory* (Cambridge: Cambridge University Press).

Beattie, A.R. (2013) 'Vulnerability, moral luck and the morality of natural law', in A.R. Beattie and K. Schick (eds) *The Vulnerable Subject: Beyond Rationalism in International Relations* (Basingstoke: Palgrave Macmillan).

Beattie, A.R. and Schick, K. (2013) 'Introduction', in A.R. Beattie and K. Schick (eds) *The Vulnerable Subject: Beyond Rationalism in International Relations* (Houndmills, Basingstoke, Hampshire: Palgrave Macmillan), pp. 1–21.

Benhabib, S. (1987) 'The generalized and the concrete other: the Kohlberg-Gilligan controversy and moral theory', in E.F. Kittay and D.T. Meyers (eds) *Women and Moral Theory* (Totowa, NJ: Rowman & Littlefield), pp. 154–77.

Benhabib, S. (1992) *Situating the Self: Gender, Community, and Postmodernism in Contemporary Ethics* (Cambridge, MA: Blackwell Press).

Bennett, J. (2009) 'Modernity and its critics', in R.E. Goodin (ed.) *The Oxford Handbook of Political Science* (Oxford: Oxford University Press), pp. 127–38.

Blaney, D. and Tickner, A. (2017a) 'International relations in the prison of colonial modernity', *International Relations*, 31, 1, pp. 71–5.

Blaney, D. and Tickner, A. (2017b) 'Worlding, ontological politics and the possibility of a decolonial IR', *Millennium: Journal of International Studies*, 45, 3, pp. 293–311.

Blaser, M. (2009) 'Political ontology: cultural studies without "cultures"?', *Cultural Studies*, 23, 5–6, pp. 873–96.

Blaser, M. (2010) *Storytelling Globalization from the Chaco and Beyond* (Durham, NC: Duke University Press).

Blaser, M. (2012) 'Ontology and indigeneity: on the political ontology of heterogeneous assemblages', *Cultural Geographies*, 21, 1, pp. 49–58.

Blaser, M. (2013) 'Notes towards a political ontology of "environmental" conflicts', in L. Green (ed.) *Contested Ecologies: Dialogues in the South on Nature and Knowledge* (Cape Town: HSRC Press), pp. 13–27.

Blaser, M. (2016) 'Is another cosmopolitics possible?', *Cultural Anthropology*, 31, 4, pp. 545–70.

Blaser, M. (2018) 'Doing and undoing caribou/atiku: diffractive and divergent multiplicities and their cosmopolitical orientations', *Tapuya: Latin American Science, Technology and Society*, 1, 1, pp. 47–64.

Blaser, M. (2019) 'On the properly political (disposition for the) Anthropocene', *Anthropological Theory*, 19, 1, pp. 74–94.

Blaser, M. and de la Cadena, M. (2021) 'Pluriverse: proposals for a world of many worlds', in M. de la Cadena and M. Blaser (eds) *A World of Many Worlds* (Durham, NC: Duke University Press), pp. 1–22.

Bleiker, R. (2006) 'Searching for difference in a homogenous discipline', *International Studies Review*, 8, pp. 128–30.

Bohman, J. (1999) 'International regimes and democratic governance: political equality and influence in global institutions', *International Affairs*, 75, 3, pp. 499–513.

Bohman, J. and Rehg, W. (2017) 'Jürgen Habermas', in E.N. Zalta (ed.) *The Stanford Encyclopaedia of Philosophy*, Available from: https://plato.stanford.edu/archives/fall2017/entries/habermas/ [Accessed 10 June 2021].

Borrows, J. (2009) 'Physical philosophy: mobility and the future of indigenous rights', in B. Richardson, I. Shin and K. McNeil (eds) *Indigenous Peoples and the Law: Comparative and Critical Perspectives* (Portland, OR: Hart Publishing), pp. 403–20.

Boulton, A. and Brannelly, T. (2015) 'Care ethics and Indigenous values: political, tribal and personal', in M. Barnes, T. Brannelly, L. Ward and N. Ward (eds) *Ethics of Care: Critical Advances in International Perspective* (Bristol: Policy Press), pp. 69–82.

Bourdieu, P. (1998) *Acts of Resistance; Against the Tyranny of the Market* (New York: The New York Press).

Bourgault, S. (2014) 'Beyond the saint and the red virgin: Simone Weil as feminist theorist of care', *Frontiers: A Journal of Women Studies*, 35, 2, pp. 1–27.

Breman, J. (2013) 'A bogus concept?', *New Left Review*, 84, pp. 130–8.

Briones, C. (2013) 'Comments', *Current Anthropology*, 54, 5, pp. 559–60.

Broughton, J.M. (1983) 'Women's rationality and men's virtues: a critique of gender dualism in Gilligan's theory of moral development', *Social Research*, 50, 3, pp. 597–642.

Brown, G.W. (2009) *Grounding Cosmopolitanism: From Kant to the Idea of a Cosmopolitan Constitution* (Edinburgh: Edinburgh University Press).

Brown, G.W. and Held, D. (2010) 'Editor's introduction', in G.W. Brown and D. Held (eds) *The Cosmopolitanism Reader* (Cambridge: Polity Press), pp. 1–14.

Burke, A. (2013) 'The good state, from a cosmic point of view', *International Politics*, 50, 1, pp. 57–76.

Butler, J. (1992) 'Contingent foundations: feminism and the question of "postmodernism"', in J. Butler and J. Scott (eds) *Feminists Theorize the Political* (New York: Routledge), pp. 3–21.

Butler, J. (1997) *Excitable Speech* (New York: Routledge).

Butler, J. (2004) *Precarious Life* (London: Verso).

Butler, J. (2009) 'Performativity, precarity and sexual politics', *Revista de Antropología Iberoamericana*, 4, 3, pp. i–xii.

Butler, J. (2011) 'For and against precarity', *Tidal: Occupy Theory, Occupy Strategy*, 1, pp. 12–13.

Butler, J. (2016) *Frames of War: When Is Life Grievable?* (London: Verso).

Butler, J. and Athanasiou, A. (2013) *Dispossession: The Performative in the Political* (Cambridge: Polity Press).

Campbell, C. (2004) 'I shop therefore I know that I am: the metaphysical basis of modern consumerism', in K.M. Ekstrom and H. Brembeck (eds) *Elusive Consumption* (Oxford: Berg Publishers), pp. 27–44.

Caraus, T. (2015) 'Introduction: cosmopolitanism of dissent', in T. Camil and A. Pârvu (eds) *Cosmopolitanism and the Legacies of Dissent* (London: Routledge), pp. 1–27.

Caraus, T. (2016a) 'Cosmopolitan ontology or the cosmopolitical', in T. Caraus and E. Paris (eds) *Re-Grounding Cosmopolitanism: Towards a Post-Foundational Cosmopolitanism* (London: Routledge), pp. 103–22.

Caraus, T. (2016b) 'Introduction: re-grounding cosmopolitanism – towards a post-foundational cosmopolitanism', in T. Caraus and E. Paris (eds) *Re-Grounding Cosmopolitanism: Towards a Post-Foundational Cosmopolitanism* (London: Routledge), pp. 1–26.

Caraus, T. and Paris, E. (eds) (2016) *Re-Grounding Cosmopolitanism: Towards a Post-Foundational Cosmopolitanism* (London: Routledge).

Caraus, T. and Pârvu, C.A. (eds) (2015*) Cosmopolitanism and the Legacies of Dissent* (London: Routledge).

Casas-Cortés, M. (2014) 'A genealogy of precarity: a toolbox for rearticulating fragmented social realities in and out of the workplace', *Rethinking Marxism: A Journal of Economics, Culture & Society*, 26, 2, pp. 206–26.

Castel, R. (2016) 'The rise of uncertainties', *Critical Horizons: A Journal of Philosophy and Social Theory*, 17, 2, pp. 160–7.

Castro, D. (2015) 'Meating the social: caribou hunting and distribution in Shshatshiu, Labrador', PhD dissertation, Memorial University of Newfoundland, Canada.

Castro-Gómez, S. (2007) 'The missing chapter of empire', *Cultural Studies*, 21, 2–3, pp. 428–48.

CBC News (2018) 'How much has this caribou herd dropped since 2001? 99 per cent', *CBC News* September 24, Available from: https://www.cbc.ca/news/canada/newfoundland-labrador/george-river-caribou-critical-1.4833339 [Accessed 10 June 2021].

Chakrabarty, D. (2008) *Provincialising Europe: Postcolonial Thought and Historical Difference* (Princeton, NJ: Princeton University Press).

Champagne, D. (2005) 'Rethinking native relations with contemporary nation-states', in D. Champagne, K.J. Torjesen and S. Steiner (eds) *Indigenous Peoples and the Modern State* (Landham, MD: Rowman & Littlefield Publishers), pp. 3–25.

Chang, K.A. and Ling, L.H.M. (2011) 'Globalisation and its intimate other: Filipina domestic workers in Hong Kong', in M. Marchand and A.S. Runyan (eds) *Gender and Global Restructuring: Sightings, Sites and Resistances* (2nd edn) (New York: Routledge), pp. 27–43.

Chatterjee, P. (1990) 'The nationalist resolution of the women's question', in K. Sangari and S. Vaid (eds) *Recasting Women: Essays in Indian Colonial History* (New Brunswick, NJ: Rutgers University Press), pp. 233–53.

Cheah, P. (1998) 'Introduction part II: the cosmopolitical today', in P. Cheah and B. Robbins (eds) *Cosmopolitics* (Minneapolis: University of Minnesota Press), pp. 20–41.

Clement, G. (1996) *Care, Autonomy, and Justice: Feminism and the Ethic of Care* (New York: Routledge).

Cloyes, K.G. (2002) 'Agonizing care: care ethics, agonistic feminism and a political theory of care', *Nursing Inquiry*, 9, 3, pp. 203–14.

Code, L. (1991) *What Can She Know? Feminist Theory and the Construction of Knowledge* (Ithaca: Cornell University Press).

Code, L. (2002) 'Narratives of responsibility and agency: reading Margaret Urban Walker's *Moral Understandings*', *Hypatia*, 17, 1, pp. 156–73.

Confortini, C.C. and Ruane, A.E. (2013) 'Sara Ruddick's *Maternal Thinking* as weaving epistemology for *justpeace*', *Journal of International Political Theory*, 10, 1, pp. 70–93.

Connell, R. (2016) 'Masculinities in global perspective: hegemony, contestation, and changing structures of power', *Theory and Society*, 45, pp. 303–18.

Conway, J. (2011) 'Cosmopolitan or colonial? The world social forum as "contact zone"', *Third World Quarterly*, 32, 2, pp. 217–36.

Conway, J. (2013) *Edges of Global Justice: The World Social Forum and Its 'Others'* (New York: Routledge).

Coole, D. (1996) 'Habermas and the question of alterity', in M.P. d'Entrèves and S. Benhabib (eds) *Habermas and the Unfinished Project of Modernity: Critical Essays on the Philosophical Discourse of Modernity* (Cambridge, MA: The MIT Press), pp. 221–44.

Cooper, D. (2007) '"Well, you go there to get off:" vising feminist care ethics through a women's bathhouse', *Feminist Theory*, 8, 3, pp. 243–62.

Coulthard, G. (2014) *Red Skins, White Masks: Rejecting the Colonial Politics of Recognition* (Minneapolis: University of Minnesota Press).

Crawford, N. (2002) *Argument and Change in World Politics: Ethics, Decolonization, and Humanitarian Intervention* (Cambridge: Cambridge University Press).

Crawford, N. (2009) 'Homo politicus and argument (nearly) all the way down: persuasion in politics', *Perspectives on Politics*, 7, 1, pp. 103–24.

Dallmayr, F. (2001) 'Conversation across boundaries: political theory and global diversity', *Millennium: Journal of International Studies*, 30, 2, pp. 331–47.

Dallmayr, F. (2012) 'Cosmopolitanism: in search of cosmos', *Ethics and Global Politics*, 5, 3, pp. 171–86.

Deitelhoff, N. and Müller, H. (2005) 'Theoretical paradise – empirically lost? Arguing with Habermas', *Review of International Studies*, 31, pp. 167–79.

de la Cadena, M. (2010) 'Indigenous cosmopolitics in the Andes: conceptual reflections beyond "politics"', *Cultural Anthropology*, 25, 2, pp. 334–70.

de la Cadena, M. (2014) 'Runa: human but *not only*', *HAU: Journal of Ethnographic Theory*, 4, 2, pp. 253–9.

de la Cadena, M. (2015) *Earth Beings: Ecologies of Practice across Andean Worlds* (Durham, NC: Duke University Press).

de Meriche, D. (2015) 'Empathy in pursuit of a caring ethic in international development', in M. Barnes, T. Brannelly, L. Ward and N. Ward (eds) *Ethics of Care: Critical Advances in International Perspective* (Bristol: Policy Press), pp. 95–107.

Dennis, R.M. (1995) 'Social Darwinism, scientific racism, and the metaphysics of race', *The Journal of Negro Education*, 64, 3, pp. 243–52.

Descola, P. (2005) *Par-delà Nature et Culture* (Paris: Gallimard).

de Sousa Santos, B. (2006) 'Globalizations', *Theory, Culture & Society*, 23, 2–3, pp. 393–9.

de Sousa Santos, B. (2007) 'Beyond abyssal thinking: from global lines to ecologies of knowledge', *Review*, 30, 1, pp. 45–89.

Diez, T. and Steans, J. (2005) 'A useful dialogue? Habermas and international relations', *Review of International Studies*, 31, pp. 127–40.

Donald, D. (2009) 'Forts, curriculum, and Indigenous metissage: imagining decolonization of Aboriginal-Canadian relations in educational contexts', *First Nations Perspectives*, 2, 1, pp. 1–24.

Donnelly, J. (2007) 'The relative universality of human rights', *Human Rights Quarterly*, 29, 2, pp. 281–306.

Duffy, M. (2011) *Making Care Count* (London: Rutgers University Press).

Dussel, E. (1993) 'Eurocentrism and modernity (introduction to the Frankfurt lectures)', *boundary*, 220, 3, pp. 65–76.

Dussel, E. (2000) 'Europe, modernity, and eurocentrism', *Nepantla: Views from South*, 1, 3, pp. 465–78.

Dussel, E. (2009) 'A new age in the history of philosophy: the world dialogue between philosophical traditions', *Philosophy & Social Criticism*, 35, 5, pp. 499–516.

Edkins, J. (1999) *Poststructuralism and International Relations: Bringing the Political Back In* (Boulder, CO: Lynne Rienner).

Edkins, J. (2003) 'Humanitarianism, humanity, human', *Journal of Human Rights*, 2, 2, pp. 253–8.

Ehrenreich, B. (2001) *Nickel and Dimed: On (Not) Getting By in America* (New York: Metropolitan Books).

Ellis, J. (2002) 'International regimes and the legitimacy of rules: a discourse-ethical approach', *Alternatives: Global, Local, Political*, 27, pp. 273–300.

Engster, D. and Hamington, M. (2015) 'Introduction', in D. Engster and M. Hamington (eds) *Care Ethics and Political Theory* (Oxford: Oxford University Press), pp. 1–16.

Escobar, A. (2007) 'Worlds and knowledges otherwise: the Latin American modernity/coloniality research program', *Cultural Studies*, 21, 2–3, pp. 179–210.

Escobar, A. (2008) *Territories of Difference: Place, Movements, Life, Redes* (Durham, NC: Duke University Press).

Escobar, A. (2010) 'Worlds and knowledges otherwise: the Latin American modernity/coloniality research program', in W.D. Mignolo and A. Escobar (eds) *Globalization and the Decolonial Option* (London: Routledge), pp. 33–64.

Escobar, A. (2016) 'Thinking-feeling with the earth: territorial struggles and the ontological dimension of the epistemologies of the South', *Revista de Antropología Iberoamericana*, 11, 1, pp. 11–32.

Escobar, A. (2018) *Designs for the Pluriverse: Radical Interdependence, Autonomy, and the Making of Worlds* (Durham, NC: Duke University Press).

Esping-Anderson, G. (1985) 'Power and distributional regimes', *Politics & Society*, 14, 2, pp. 223–56.

Ettlinger, N. (2007) 'Precarity unbound', *Alternatives: Global, Local, Political*, 32, 3, pp. 319–40.

Evans, T. (1998) 'Introduction: power, hegemony and the universalization of human rights', in T. Evans (ed.) *Human Rights Fifty Years On: A Reappraisal* (Manchester: Manchester University Press), pp. 2–22.

Fanon, F. (2008) *Black Skin, White Masks*, Translated by R. Philcox (New York: Grove Press).

Faur, E. and Tizziani, A. (2018) 'Towards a situated ethics of care: some moral dilemmas around aspects of care in an unequal society', *International Journal of Care and Caring*, 2, 3, pp. 389–404.

Federici, S. (2004) *Caliban and the Witch: Women, the Body and Primitive Accumulation* (Brooklyn, NY: Autonomedia).

REFERENCES

Federici, S. (2012) *Revolution at Point Zero: Housework, Reproduction, and Feminist Struggle* (Oakland, CA: PM Press).

Ferrarese, E. (2016a) 'Vulnerability: a concept with which to undo the world as it is?', *Critical Horizons: A Journal of Philosophy and Social Theory*, 17, 2, pp. 149–59.

Ferrarese, E. (2016b) 'The vulnerable and the political: on the seeming impossibility of thinking vulnerability and the political together and its consequences', *Critical Horizons: A Journal of Philosophy and Social Theory*, 17, 2, pp. 224–39.

Fisher, B. and Tronto, J. (1990) 'Toward a feminist theory of caring', in E.K. Abel and M.K. Nelson (eds) *Circles of Care: Work and Identity in Women's Lives* (Albany, NY: State University of New York Press), pp. 35–62.

Flikschuh, K. (2000) 'Metaphysics and the boundaries of justice', *Global Society*, 14, 4, pp. 487–505.

Foucault, M. (1970) *The Order of Things* (New York: Pantheon).

Foucault, M. (1972) *The Archaeology of Knowledge*, Translated by A.M.S. Smith (New York: Pantheon).

Fraser, N. and Nicholson, L. (1989) 'Social criticism without philosophy: an encounter between feminism and postmodernism', *Social Text*, 21, pp. 83–104.

Fricker, M. (2007) *Epistemic Injustice: Power and the Ethics of Knowing* (Oxford: Oxford University Press).

Fudge, J. and Owens, R. (2006) *Precarious Work, Women, and the New Economy* (Oxford: Hart Publishing).

Gaonkar, D.P. (ed.) (2001) *Alternative Modernities* (Durham, NC: Duke University Press).

Geras, N. (1999) 'The view from everywhere', *Review of International Studies*, 25, pp. 157–63.

Gilligan, C. (1993) *In a Different Voice* (Cambridge, MA: Harvard University Press).

Gilligan, C. and Snider, N. (2018) *Why Does Patriarchy Persist?* (Cambridge: Polity Press).

Goldín, L. (2011) 'Labour turnover among maquiladora workers of highland Guatemala: resistance and semiproletarianization in global capitalism', *Latin American Research Review*, 46, 3, pp. 133–56.

Goodey, C. (2012) 'Learning disability – from the devil to DSM-IV', *The Psychologist*, 25, 4, pp. 326–7.

Green, J. (ed.) (2007) *Making Space for Indigenous Feminisms* (Winnipeg, MB: Fernwood Publishing).

Green, L. (2013a) 'Comments', *Current Anthropology*, 54, 5, pp. 562–3.

Green, L. (ed.) (2013b) *Contested Ecologies: Dialogues in the South on Nature and Knowledge* (Cape Town: HSRC Press).

Haacke, J. (1996) 'Theory and praxis in international relations: Habermas, self-reflection, relational argumentation', *Millennium: Journal of International Studies*, 25, 2, pp. 255–89.

Haacke, J. (2005) 'The Frankfurt school and international relations: on the centrality of recognition', *Review of International Studies*, 31, pp. 181–94.

Habermas, J. (1987) *The Theory of Communicative Action* (vol. 2), Translated by T. McCarthy (Boston, MA: Beacon Press).

Habermas, J. (1990) *Moral Consciousness and Communicative Action*, Translated by C. Lenhardt and S. Weber Nicholsen (Cambridge: Polity Press).

Hamington, M. (2015a) 'Care ethics and engaging intersectional difference through the body', *Critical Philosophy of Race*, 3, 1, pp. 79–100.

Hamington, M. (2015b) 'Politics is not a game: the radical potential of care', in D. Engster and M. Hamington (eds) *Care Ethics and Political Theory* (Oxford: Oxford University Press), pp. 272–92.

Hamington, M. (2018) 'The care ethics moment: international innovations', *International Journal of Care and Caring*, 2, 3, pp. 309–18.

Han, C. (2018) 'Precarity, precariousness, and vulnerability', *Annual Review of Anthropology*, 47, pp. 331–43.

Hankivsky, O. (2004) *Social Policy and the Ethic of Care* (Vancouver, BC: UBC Press).

Haraway, D. (1991) *Simians, Cyborgs, and Women: The Reinvention of Nature* (London: Free Association Books).

Harvey, D. (2004) 'The "new" imperialism: accumulation by dispossession', *Socialist Register*, 40, pp. 63–87.

Hayden, P. (2005) *Cosmopolitan Global Politics* (Farnham, Hampshire: Ashgate).

Hegel, G.W.F. (1977) *Phenomenology of Spirit*, Translated by A.V. Miller (Oxford: Oxford University Press).

Hegel, G.W.F. (1988) *Introduction to the Philosophy of History*, Translated by L. Rauch (Indianapolis, IN: Hackett Publishing Co).

Hegel, G.W.F. (1991) *Elements of the Philosophy of Right*, Edited by A.W. Wood, Translated by H.B. Nisbet (Cambridge: Cambridge University Press).

Heidegger, M. (1977) *The Question Concerning Technology and Other Essays*, Translated by W. Lovitt (New York: Garland Publishing, Inc).

Heinrich, M. (2004) *An Introduction to the Three Volumes of Karl Marx's Capital*, Translated by A. Locascio (New York: Monthly Review Press).

Hekman, S. (1995) *Moral Voices, Moral Selves: Carol Gilligan and Feminist Moral Theory* (University Park, PA: The Pennsylvania State University Press).

Held, D. (2003) 'Cosmopolitanism: globalisation tamed?', *Review of International Studies* 29, pp. 465–80.

Hennessy, R. and Ingraham, C. (eds) (1997) *Materialist Feminism: A Reader in Class, Difference, and Women's Lives* (New York: Routledge).

Hobbes, T. (1985) *Leviathan* (London: Penguin).

Hobson, J.M. (2012) *The Eurocentric Conception of World Politics: Western International Theory, 1760–2010* (Cambridge: Cambridge University Press).

Hochschild, A. (2000) 'Global care chains and emotional surplus value', in W. Hutton and A. Giddens (eds) *On the Edge: Living with Global Capitalism* (London: Jonathan Cape), pp. 130–46.

Holbraad, M. (2013) 'Comments', *Current Anthropology*, 54, 5, pp. 563–4.

Holbraad, M., Pedersen, M.A. and Viveiros de Castro, E. (2014) 'The politics of ontology: anthropological positions', *Cultural Anthropology*, January 13, Available from: https://culanth.org/fieldsights/the-politics-of-ontology-anthropological-positions [Accessed 10 June 2021].

Hopgood, S. (2000) 'Reading the small print in global civil society: the inexorable hegemony of the liberal self', *Millennium: Journal of International Studies*, 29, 1, pp. 1–25.

Hoppania. H.-K. and Vaittinen, T. (2015) 'A household full of bodies: neoliberalism, care and "the political"', *Global Society*, 29, 1, pp. 70–88.

Hsiao, E. (2012) 'Whanganui River agreement – Indigenous rights and rights of nature', *Environmental Policy and Law*, 42, 6, pp. 371–5.

Hunt, S. (2014) 'Ontologies of indigeneity: the politics of embodying a concept', *Cultural Geographies*, 21, 1, pp. 27–32.

Hutchings, K. (2001) 'The nature of critique in critical international theory', in R.W. Jones (ed.) *Critical Theory and World Politics* (Boulder, CO: Lynne Rienner), pp. 79–90.

Hutchings, K. (2003) *Hegel and Feminist Philosophy* (Cambridge: Polity Press).

Hutchings, K. (2005) '"Speaking and hearing": Habermasian discourse ethics, feminism, and IR', *Review of International Studies*, 31, pp. 155–65.

Hutchings, K. (2010) *Global Ethics: An Introduction* (Cambridge: Polity Press).

Hutchings, K. (2013) 'A place of greater safety? Securing judgements in international ethics', in A.R. Beattie and K. Schick (eds) *The Vulnerable Subject: Beyond Rationalism in International Relations* (Basingstoke: Palgrave Macmillan), pp. 25–42.

Hutchings, K. (2018) *Global Ethics: An Introduction*, Vol 2 (Cambridge: Polity Press).

Hutchings, K. (2019) 'Decolonizing global ethics: thinking with the pluriverse', *Ethics & International Affairs*, 33, 2, pp. 115–25.

Ingram, J.D. (2013) *Radical Cosmopolitics* (New York: Columbia University Press).

Jaeger, H.-M. (2018) 'Political ontology and international relations: politics, self-estrangement, and void universalism in a pluriverse', in M. Jackson (ed.) *Coloniality, Ontology, and the Question of the Posthuman* (London: Routledge), pp. 227–45.

Jahn, B. (1998) 'One step forward, two steps back: critical theory as the latest edition of liberal idealism', *Millennium: Journal of International Studies*, 27, 3, pp. 613–41.

James, S. (2012) *Sex Race and Class* (Oakland, CA: PM Press).

Kalleberg, A.L. (2009) 'Precarious work, insecure workers: employment relations in transition', *American Sociological Review*, 74, pp. 1–22.

Kant, I. (1998) *Critique of Pure Reason*, Edited and Translated by P. Guyer and A.W. Wood (Cambridge: Cambridge University Press).

Kant, I. (2005) *Groundwork for the Metaphysics of Morals*, Edited by L. Denis, Translated by T.K. Abbott (New York: Broadview).

Kayaoglu, T. (2010) 'Westphalian eurocentrism in international relations theory', *International Studies Review* 12, pp. 193–217.

Kelly, C. (2020) 'Direct funded home care for older adults: exploring the legacies of disability activism', in C. Kelly, K. Aubrecht and C. Rice (eds) *The Aging/Disability Nexus* (Vancouver, BC: University of British Columbia Press), pp. 97–113.

Kerber, L. (1986) 'Some cautionary words for historians', *Signs: Journal of Women in Culture and Society*, 11, 2, pp. 304–10.

King. H. (2017) 'The erasure of Indigenous thought in foreign policy', *Open Canada*. Available from: https://opencanada.org/erasure-indigenous-thought-foreign-policy/ [Accessed on 15 November 2021].

Kittay, E.F. (2002) 'When caring is just and justice is caring: justice and mental retardation', in E.F. Kittay and E.K. Feder (eds) *The Subject of Care: Feminist Perspectives on Dependency* (London: Rowman & Littlefield Publishers), pp. 257–76.

Kittay, E.F. (2015) 'A theory of justice as fair terms of social life given our inevitable dependency and our inextricable interdependency', in D. Engster and M. Hamington (eds) *Care Ethics and Political Theory* (Oxford: Oxford University Press), pp. 52–71.

Kittay, E.F., Jennings, B. and Wasunna, A.A. (2005) 'Dependency, difference and the global ethic of longterm care', *The Journal of Political Philosophy*, 13, 4, pp. 443–69.

Kröger, T. (2009) 'Care research and disability studies: nothing in common?', *Critical Social Policy*, 29, 3, pp. 398–420.

Kuokkanen, R. (2008) 'Globalization as racialized, sexualized violence: the case of Indigenous women', *International Feminist Journal of Politics*, 10, 2, pp. 216–33.

Kuokkanen, R. (2009) 'Achievements of Indigenous self-determination: the case of Sami parliaments in Finland and Norway', in J.M. Beier (ed.) *Indigenous Diplomacies* (London: Palgrave Macmillan), pp. 97–114.

Kuptana, R. (2014) 'Indigenous peoples in Canada: politics, policy and human rights-based approaches to development and relationship building', Lecture, Trent University, Nottingham, 8 August 2014.

Ladner, K. (2001) 'When buffalo speaks: creating an alternative understanding of traditional blackfoot governance', PhD dissertation, Carleton University, Canada.

Ladner, K. (2009) 'Gendering decolonization, decolonizing gender', *Australian Indigenous Law Review*, 13, 1, pp. 62–77.

Laugier, S. (2016) 'Politics of vulnerability and responsibility for ordinary others', *Critical Horizons: A Journal of Philosophy and Social Theory*, 17 2, pp. 207–23.

Law, J. (2015) 'What's wrong with a one-world world?' *Distinktion: Scandinavian Journal of Social Theory*, 16, 1, pp. 126–39.

Lawrence, B. (2003) 'Gender, race, and the regulation of native identity in Canada and the United States: an overview', *Hypatia*, 18, 2, pp. 3–31.

Leget, C., van Nistelrooij, I. and Visse, M. (2019) 'Beyond demarcation: care ethics as an interdisciplinary field of inquiry', *Nursing Ethics*, 26, 1, pp. 17–25.

Leinius, J. (2014) 'Decolonizing cosmopolitanism in practice: from universalizing monologue to intercultural dialogue?' in L. Kaunonen (ed.) *Cosmopolitanism and Transnationalism: Visions, Ethics and Practices* (Helsinki: Helsinki Collegium for Advanced Studies), pp. 39–65.

Li, C. (1994) 'The Confucian concept of jen and the feminist ethics of care: a comparative study', *Hypatia*, 9, 1, pp. 70–89.

Lightfoot, S. (2016) *Global Indigenous Politics: A Subtle Revolution* (New York: Routledge).

Linklater, A. (1996a) 'Citizenship and sovereignty in the post-Westphalian state', *European Journal of International Relations*, 2, 1, pp. 77–103.

Linklater, A. (1996b) 'The achievements of critical theory', in S. Smith, K. Booth and M. Zalewski (eds) *International Theory: Positivism and Beyond* (Cambridge: Cambridge University Press), pp. 279–98.

Linklater, A. (1998) *The Transformation of Political Community* (Columbia, SC: University of South Carolina Press).

Linklater, A. (1999) 'Transforming political community: a response to the critics', *Review of International Studies*, 25, pp. 165–75.

Linklater, A. (2005) 'Dialogic politics and the civilising process', *Review of International Studies*, 31, pp. 141–54.

Locke, J. (1980) *Second Treatise of Government*, Edited by C.B. Macpherson (Indianapolis: Hackett Publishing Co.).

Locke, J. (2009) 'Essay concerning human understanding', in R. Ariew and E. Watkins (eds) *Modern Philosophy: An Anthology of Primary Sources* (2nd edn) (Indianapolis: Hackett Publishing Co.), pp. 316–420.

Lowndes, V. and Paxton, M. (2018) 'Can agonism be institutionalised? Can institutions be agonized? Prospects for democratic design', *The British Journal of Politics and International Relations*, 20, 3, pp. 693–710.

Lugones, M. (2007) 'Heterosexualisms and the colonial/modern gender system', *Hypatia*, 22, 1, pp. 186–209.
Lugones, M. (2010) 'Toward a decolonial feminism', *Hypatia*, 25, 4, pp. 742–59.
Lugones, M. (2012) 'Methodological notes toward a decolonial feminism', in A.M Isasi-Diaz and E. Mendieta (eds) *Decolonizing Epistemologies: Latina/o Theology and Philosophy* (New York, NY: Fordham University Press), pp. 68–86.
Lynch, C. (2020) *Wrestling with God: Ethical Precarity in Christianity and International Relations* (Cambridge: Cambridge University Press).
MacEachern, D. (2016) 'George River caribou herd could be wiped out in 5 years, says province', *CBC News*, 29 August, Available from: https://www.cbc.ca/news/canada/newfoundland-labrador/george-river-caribou-herd-drastic-drop-1.3568316 [Accessed 10 June 2021].
Machiavelli, N. (1998) *The Prince* (2nd edn), Translated by H.C. Mansfield (Chicago: The University of Chicago Press).
Macpherson, C.B. (1985) 'Introduction', in Thomas Hobbes, *Leviathan* (London: Penguin Books), pp. 9–63.
Marks, S. (2009) 'False contingency', *Current Legal Problems*, 62, 1, pp. 1–21.
Marx, K. (1977) *Capital, Volume One* (New York: Vintage House).
McClintock, A. (1995) *Imperial Leather: Race, Gender and Sexuality in the Colonial Context* (London: Routledge).
McNay, L. (2000) *Gender and Agency: Reconfiguring the Subject in Feminist and Social Theory* (Cambridge: Polity Press).
McNay, L. (2008) *Against Recognition* (Cambridge: Polity Press).
Marchart, O. (2007) *Post-foundational Political Thought: Political Difference in Nancy, Lefort, Badiou and Laclau* (Edinburgh: Edinburgh University Press).
Marchart, O. (2016) 'The political, the ethical, the global: towards a post-foundational theory of cosmopolitan democracy', in T. Caraus and E. Paris (eds) *Re-grounding Cosmopolitanism: Towards a Post-foundational Cosmopolitanism* (London: Routledge), pp. 181–202.
Meyers, D.T. and Kittay, E.F. (1987) 'Introduction', in E.F. Kittay and D.T. Meyers (eds) *Women and Moral Theory* (Totowa, NJ: Rowman & Littlefield), pp. 3–33.
Mignolo, W. (2002) 'The many faces of cosmo-polis: border thinking and critical cosmopolitanism', in C.A. Breckenridge, S. Pollock, H.K. Bhabha and D. Chakrabarty (eds) *Cosmopolitanism* (Durham, NC: Duke University Press), pp. 157–87.
Mignolo, W. (2010) 'Cosmopolitanism and the de-colonial option', *Studies in Philosophy and Education*, 29, pp. 111–27.
Mignolo, W. (2011) *The Darker Side of Western Modernity: Global Futures, Decolonial Options* (Durham, NC: Duke University Press).

Mignolo, W. (2012a) 'Decolonizing western epistemology/building decolonial epistemologies', in A.M. Isasi-Diaz and E. Mendieta (eds) *Decolonizing Epistemologies: Latina/o Theology and Philosophy* (New York: Fordham University Press), pp. 19–43.

Mignolo, W. (2012b) *Local Histories/Global Designs: Coloniality, Subaltern Knowledges, and Border Thinking* (Princeton, NJ: Princeton University Press).

Mignolo, W. (2013) 'On pluriversality'. Available from: http://waltermignolo.com/on-pluriversality/ [Accessed 10 June 2021].

Mignolo, W. (2018) 'Foreword: on pluriversality and multipolarity', in B. Reiter (ed.) *Pluriverse: The Geopolitics of Knowledge* (Durham, NC: Duke University Press), pp. ix–xv.

Millar, K. (2014) 'The precarious present: wageless labor and disrupted life in Rio de Janeiro, Brazil', *Cultural Anthropology*, 29, 1, pp. 32–53.

Millar, K. (2017) 'Toward a critical politics of precarity', *Sociology Compass*, 11, 6, p. e12483.

Mohanty, C.T. (2003) *Feminism without Borders: Decolonizing Theory, Practicing Solidarity* (Durham, NC: Duke University Press).

Morris, J.D.K. and Ruru, J. (2010) 'Giving voice to rivers: legal personality as a vehicle for recognising Indigenous peoples' relationship to water?' *Australian Indigenous Law Review*, 14, 2, pp. 49–62.

Mouffe, C. (2013) *Agonistics: Thinking the World Politically* (London: Verso).

Muehlebach, A. (2013) 'On precariousness and the ethical imagination: the year 2012 in sociocultural anthropology', *American Anthropologist*, 115, 2, pp. 297–311.

Munck, R. (2013) 'The precariat: a view from the south', *Third World Quarterly*, 34, 5, pp. 747–62.

Nadasdy, P. (2007) 'The gift in the animal: the ontology of hunting and human-animal sociality', *American Ethnologist*, 34, 1, pp. 25–43.

Najmabadi, A. (2005) *Women with Mustaches and Men without Beards: Gender and Sexual Anxieties of Iranian Modernity* (Berkeley, CA: University of California Press).

Narayan, U. (1995) 'Colonialism and its others: consideration on rights and care discourses', *Hypatia*, 10, 2, pp. 133–40.

Neilson, B. and Rossiter, N. (2005) 'From precarity to precariousness and back again: labour, life and unstable networks', *The Fibreculture Journal*, 5, 3, pp. 10–13.

Neilson, B. and Rossiter, N. (2008) 'Precarity as a political concept, or, Fordism as exception', *Theory, Culture & Society*, 25, 7–8, pp. 51–72.

New South Wales Government (2019) 'Northern corroboree frog – profile'. Available from: https://www.environment.nsw.gov.au/threatenedspeciesapp/profile.aspx?id=10694 [Accessed 23 November 2021].

Ngā Tāngata Tiaki (2021) 'Te Pou Tupua'. Available from: https://www.ngatangatatiaki.co.nz/our-story/ruruku-whakatupua/te-pou-tupua/ [Accessed 15 November 2021].

Noddings, N. (2002) *Starting at Home: Caring and Social Policy* (Berkeley, CA: University of California Press).

Noddings, N. (2003) *Caring: A Feminine Approach to Ethics and Moral Education* (2nd edn) (Berkeley, CA: University of California Press).

Noddings, N. (2015) 'Care ethics and "caring" organizations', in D. Engster and M. Hamington (eds) *Care Ethics and Political Theory* (Oxford: Oxford University Press), pp. 72–84.

Oliver, K. (2001) *Witnessing: Beyond Recognition* (Minneapolis: University of Minnesota Press).

Oliver, K. (2002) 'Subjectivity as responsivity: the ethical implications of dependency', in E.F. Kittay and E.K. Feder (eds) *The Subject of Care: Feminist Perspectives on Dependency* (Lanham, MD: Rowman & Littlefield), pp. 322–33.

Oliver, K. (2015) 'Witnessing, recognition, and response ethics', *Philosophy & Rhetoric*, 48, 4, pp. 473–94.

Omura, K., Otsuki, G.J., Satsuka, S. and Morita, A. (eds) (2019) *The World Multiple: The Quotidian Politics of Knowing and Generating Entangled Worlds* (London: Routledge).

O'Neill, O. (2000) *Bounds of Justice* (Cambridge: Cambridge University Press).

O'Neill, O. (2010) 'A Kantian approach to transnational justice', in G.W. Brown and D. Held (eds) *The Cosmopolitanism Reader* (Cambridge: Polity Press), pp. 61–80.

Oslender, U. (2019) 'Geographies of the pluriverse: decolonial thinking and ontological conflict on Colombia's pacific coast', *Annals of the American Association of Geographers*, 109, 6, pp. 1691–705.

Pagden, A. (1982) *The Fall of Natural Man: The American Indian and the Origins of Comparative Ethnology* (Cambridge: Cambridge University Press).

Pagden, A. (2003) 'Human rights, natural rights and Europe's imperial legacy', *Political Theory*, 31, 2, pp. 171–99.

Parreñas, R.S. (2015) *Servants of Globalization: Migration and Domestic Work* (2nd edn) (Redwood City, CA: Stanford University Press).

Pârvu, C.A. (2016) 'Contingency and contestability: questioning cosmopolitan foundations', in T. Caraus and E. Paris (eds) *Re-Grounding Cosmopolitanism: Towards a Post-Foundational Cosmopolitanism* (London: Routledge), pp. 86–99.

Peterson, V.S. (2003) *A Critical Re-writing of Global Political Economy: Integrating Reproductive, Productive and Virtual Economies* (London: Routledge).

Pin-Fat, V. (2000) '(Im)possible universalism: reading human rights in world politics', *Review of International Studies*, 26, pp. 663–74.

Piketty, T. (2017) *Capital in the Twenty-First Century*, Translated by A. Goldhammer (Cambridge, MA: Belknap Press).

Pogge, T. (1994) 'Cosmopolitanism and sovereignty', in C. Brown (ed.) *Political Restructuring in Europe: Ethical Perspectives* (London: Routledge), pp. 89–122.

Povinelli, E. (2011) 'The governance of the prior', *interventions*, 13, 1, pp. 13–30.

Povinelli, E. (2016) *Geontologies: A Requiem to Late Liberalism* (Durham, NC: Duke University Press).

Puig de la Bellacasa, M. (2017) *Matters of Care: Speculative Ethics in More Than Human Worlds* (Minneapolis: University of Minnesota Press).

Pratt, M.L. (2002) 'The traffic in meaning: translation, contagion, infiltration', *Profession*, 2002, 1, pp. 25–36.

Prattes, R. (2020) '"I don't clean up after myself": epistemic ignorance, responsibility and the politics of the outsourcing of domestic cleaning', *Feminist Theory*, 21, 1, pp. 25–45.

Prozorov, S. (2014) *Ontology and World Politics: Void Universalism I* (New York: Routledge).

Quijano, A. (2000) 'Coloniality of power and eurocentrism in Latin America', *International Sociology*, 15, 2, pp. 215–32.

Raghuram, P. (2012) 'Global care, local configurations – challenges to conceptualizations of care', *Global Networks*, 12, 2, pp. 155–74.

Raghuram, P. (2016) 'Locating care ethics beyond the global north', *ACME: An International Journal for Critical Geographies*, 15, 3, pp. 511–33.

Raghuram, P. (2019) 'Race and feminist care ethics: intersectionality as method', *Gender, Place & Culture*, 26, 5, pp. 613–37.

Rancière, J. (1999) *Dis-agreement: Politics and Philosophy*, Translated by J. Rose (Minneapolis: University of Minnesota Press).

Rawley, J.A. (2005) *The Transatlantic Slave Trade* (Lincoln, NE: University of Nebraska Press).

Reinaga, F. (2014) *Fausto Reinaga: Obras Completas*, Vol. 6 (La Paz: Vice-presidencia del Estado Plurinacional).

Rieff, D. (2002) *A Bed for the Night: Humanitarianism in Crisis* (New York: Simon & Schuster).

Risse, T. (2000) '"Let's argue!": communicative action in world politics', *International Organization*, 54, 1, pp. 1–39.

Rivera Cusicanqui, S. (2010) 'The notion of "rights" and the paradoxes of postcolonial modernity: indigenous peoples and women in Bolivia', *Qui Parle*, 18, 2, pp. 29–54.

Rivera Cusicanqui, S. (2012) '*Ch'ixinakax utxiwa*: a reflection on the practices and discourses of decolonization', *The South Atlantic Quarterly*, 111, 1, pp. 95–109.

Rivera Cusicanqui, S. (2015) *Sociología de la Imagen: Miradas Ch'ixi Desde La Historia Andina* (Buenos Aires: Tinta Limón).

Rivera Cusicanqui, S. (2018) *El Mundo Ch'ixi Es Posible: Ensayos Desde un Presente en Crisis* (La Paz: Talleres Gráficos Hisbol).

Robbins, B. (1998) 'Introduction, part I: actually existing cosmopolitanism', in P. Cheah and B. Robbins (eds) *Cosmopolitics* (Minneapolis: University of Minnesota Press), pp. 1–20.

Robinson, F. (1999) *Globalizing Care: Ethics, Feminist Theory, and International Relations* (Boulder, CO: Westview Press).

Robinson, F. (2006) 'Methods of feminist normative theory: a political ethic of care for international relations', in B. Ackerly, M. Stern and J. True (eds) *Feminist Methodologies for International Relations* (Cambridge: Cambridge University Press), pp. 221–40.

Robinson, F. (2011a) 'Care ethics and the transnationalization of care: reflections on autonomy, hegemonic masculinities, and globalization', in R. Mahon and F. Robinson (eds) *Feminist Ethics and Social Policy: Towards a New Global Political Economy of Care* (Vancouver: University of British Columbia Press), pp. 127–44.

Robinson, F. (2011b) *The Ethics of Care: A Feminist Approach to Human Security* (Philadelphia: Temple University Press).

Robinson, F. (2011c) 'Stop talking and listen: discourse ethics and feminist care ethics in international political theory', *Millennium: Journal of International Studies*, 39, 3, pp. 845–60.

Robinson, F. (2013) 'Global care ethics: beyond distribution, beyond justice', *Journal of Global Ethics*, 9, 2, pp. 131–43.

Robinson, F. (2015) 'Care ethics, political theory, and the future of feminism', in D. Engster and M. Hamington (eds) *Care Ethics and Political Theory* (Oxford: Oxford University Press), pp. 293–311.

Robinson, F. (2018) 'Care ethics and international relations: challenging rationalism in global ethics', *International Journal of Care and Caring*, 2, 3, pp. 319–32.

Robinson, F. (2019) 'Resisting hierarchies through relationality in the ethics of care', *International Journal of Care and Caring*, 4, 1, pp. 11–23.

Rodríguez-García, J.M. (2001) 'Scientia potestas est – knowledge is power: Francis Bacon to Michel Foucault', *Neohelicon*, XXVIII, I, pp. 109–22.

Rojas, C. (2016) 'Contesting the colonial logics of the international: toward a relational politics for the pluriverse', *International Political Sociology*, 10, 4, pp. 369–82.

Rorty, R. (2010) 'From logic to language play', in C.J. Voparil and R.J. Bernstein (eds) *The Rorty Reader* (Malden, MA: Wiley-Blackwell), pp. 145–51.

Roy, E.A. (2017) 'New Zealand river granted same legal rights as human being', *The Guardian*, 16 March, Available from: https://www.theguardian.com/world/2017/mar/16/new-zealand-river-granted-same-legal-rights-as-human-being [Accessed 10 June 2021].

Ruddick, S. (1987) 'Remarks on the sexual politics of reason', in E.F. Kittay and D.T. Meyers (eds) *Women and Moral Theory* (Totowa, NJ: Rowman & Littlefield), pp. 237–60.

Ruddick, S. (1989) *Maternal Thinking: Towards a Politics of Peace* (Boston, MA: Beacon Press).

Rustin, C. (1999) 'Habermas, discourse ethics, and international justice', *Alternatives: Global, Local, Political*, 24, 2, pp. 167–92.

Ruti, M. (2015) 'The posthumanist quest for the universal', *Angelaki: Journal of the Theoretical Humanities*, 20, 4, pp. 193–210.

Said, E. (1979) *Orientalism* (New York: Vintage Books).

Salmond, A. (2012) 'Ontological quarrels: indigeneity, exclusion and citizenship in a relational world', *Anthropological Theory*, 12, 2, pp. 115–41.

Sandel, M.J. (1998) *Liberalism and the Limits of Justice* (2nd edn) (Cambridge: Cambridge University Press).

Scauso, M. (2021) *Intersectional Decoloniality: Reimagining International Relations and the Problem of Difference* (New York: Routledge).

Schroeder, M. (2016) 'Value theory', in E.N. Zalta (ed.) *The Stanford Encyclopedia of Philosophy* (Stanford, CA: Stanford University). Available from: https://plato.stanford.edu/archives/fall2016/entries/value-theory/ [Accessed 10 June 2021].

Schulenberg, U. (2017) 'From finding to making: Jacques Rancière, Richard Rorty, and the antifoundationalist story of progress', *Culture, Theory and Critique*, 58, 3, pp. 275–93.

Scott, J. and Marshall, G. (2005) 'Ontology', in J. Scott and G. Marshall (eds) *A Dictionary of Sociology* (Oxford: Oxford University Press).

Scully, B. (2016) 'Precarity north and south: a southern critique of Guy Standing', *Global Labour Journal*, 7, 2, pp. 160–73.

Segato, R.L. (2003) 'Género, política y hibridismo en la transnacionalización de la cultura Yoruba', *Estudos Afro-Asiáticos*, 25, 2, pp. 333–63.

Senchuk, D.M. (1990) 'Listening to a different voice: a feminist critique of Gilligan', *Studies in Philosophy and Education*, 10, 3, pp. 233–49.

Seth, S. (2013) '"Once was blind but now can see": modernity and the social sciences', *International Political Sociology*, 7, pp. 136–51.

Sevenhuijsen, S. (1998) *Citizenship and the Ethics of Care: Feminist Considerations on Justice, Morality, and Politics* (London: Routledge).

Shapcott, R. (2002) 'Cosmopolitan conversations: justice, dialogue, and the cosmopolitan project', *Global Society*, 16, 3, pp. 221–43.

Shilliam, R. (2015) *The Black Pacific: Anti-Colonial Struggles and Oceanic Connections* (London: Bloomsbury).

Sil, R. and Katzenstein, P.J. (2010) 'Analytic eclecticism in the study of world politics: reconfiguring problems and mechanisms across research traditions', *Perspectives on Politics*, 8, 2, pp. 411–28.

Simplican, S.C. (2015) 'Care, disability, and violence: theorizing complex dependency in Eva Kittay and Judith Butler', *Hypatia*, 30, 1, pp. 217–33.

Simpson, A. (2014) *Mohawk Interruptus: Political Life across the Borders of Settler States* (Durham, NC: Duke University Press).

Simpson, L.B. (2014) 'Land as pedagogy: Nishnaabeg intelligence and rebellious transformation', *Decolonization: Indigeneity, Education & Society*, 3, 3, pp. 1–25.

Slater, L. (2021) 'Learning to stand with gyack: a practice of thinking with non-innocent care', *Australian Feminist Studies*, 1–12.

Sloan, P.R. (1973) 'The idea of racial degeneracy in Buffon's *Histoire Naturelle*', in H.E. Pagliaro (ed.) *Studies in Eighteenth Century Culture: Racism in the Eighteenth Century* (Vol. III) (Cleveland: Case Western Reserve University Press), pp. 293–321.

Slote, M. (2007) *The Ethics of Care and Empathy* (New York: Routledge).

Slote, M. (2015) 'Care ethics and liberalism', in D. Engster and M. Hamington (eds) *Care Ethics and Political Theory* (Oxford: Oxford University Press), pp. 37–50.

Smith, L.T. (2012) *Decolonizing Methodologies: Research and Indigenous Peoples* (2nd edn) (London: Zed Books).

Sparks, H. (2016) 'Quarreling with Rancière: race, gender, and the politics of democratic disruption', *Philosophy & Rhetoric,* 49, 4, pp. 420–37.

Spelman, E. (1988) *Inessential Woman: Problems of Exclusion in Feminist Thought* (Boston, MA: Beacon Press).

Stack, C.B. (1986) 'The culture of gender: women and men of color', *Signs: Journal of Women in Culture and Society*, 11, 2, pp. 321–4.

Stammers, N. (1993) 'Human rights and power', *Political Studies* 41, pp. 70–82.

Stammers, N. (1995) 'A critique of social approaches to human rights', *Human Rights Quarterly*, 17, 3, pp. 488–508.

Standing, G. (2011) *The Precariat: The New Dangerous Class* (London: Bloomsbury Academic).

Standing, G. (2014) 'Understanding the precariat through labour and work', *Development and Change*, 45, 5, pp. 963–80.

Standing, G. (2018) 'The precariat: today's transformative class?' *Great Transition Initiative* (October). Available from: https://greattransition.org/images/Standing-The-Precariat.pdf [Accessed 8 April 2022].

Stengers, I. (2005) 'A cosmopolitical proposal', in B. Latour and P. Weibel (eds) *Making Things Public: Athmospheres of Democracy* (Cambridge, MA: MIT Press), pp. 994–1003.

Strathern, M. (1987) 'Out of context: the persuasive fictions of anthropology', *Current Anthropology*, 28, 3, pp. 251–70.

Strathern, M. (2004) *Partial Connections* (Lanham, MD: AltaMira Press).

Taylor, C. (1991) *The Malaise of Modernity* (Toronto: House of Anansi Press).

Taylor, C. (1992) 'The politics of recognition', in A. Gutmann (ed.) *Multiculturalism and the Politics of Recognition* (Princeton, NJ: Princeton University Press), pp. 25–74.

Tlostanova, M.V. and Mignolo, W.D. (2009) 'On pluritopic hermeneutics, trans-modern thinking, and decolonial philosophy', *encounters*, 1, 1, pp. 11–27.

Todd, Z. (2014) 'Fish pluralities: human-animal relations and the sites of engagement in Paulatuuq, Arctic Canada', *Études/Inuit/Studies*, 38, 1–2, pp. 217–38.

Todd, Z. (2016a) 'An indigenous feminist's take on the ontological turn: "ontology" is just another word for colonialism', *Journal of Historical Sociology*, 29, 1, pp. 4–22.

Todd, Z. (2016b) 'From fish lives to fish law: learning to see Indigenous legal orders in Canada', *Science, Medicine, and Anthropology*. Available from: http://somatosphere.net/2016/from-fish-lives-to-fish-law-learning-to-see-indigenous-legal-orders-in-canada.html/ [Accessed 17 November 2021].

Todd, Z. (2018) 'Refracting the state through human-fish relations: fishing, Indigenous legal orders and colonialism in north/western Canada', *Decolonization: Indigeneity, Education & Society*, 7, 1, pp. 60–75.

Towns, A. (2013) *Women and States: Norms and Hierarchies in International Society* (Cambridge: Cambridge University Press).

Tronto, J. (1993) *Moral Boundaries: A Political Argument for an Ethic of Care* (New York: Routledge).

Tronto, J. (2013) *Caring Democracy: Markets, Equality, and Justice* (New York: New York University Press).

Tronto, J. (2017) 'There is an alternative: *homines curans* and the limits of neoliberalism', *International Journal of Care and Caring*, 1, 1, pp. 27–43.

Turpel-Lafond, M.E. (1997) 'Patriarchy and paternalism: the legacy of the Canadian state for First Nations Women', in C. Andrew and S. Rogers (eds) *Women and the Canadian State* (Montreal: McGill-Queen's University Press), pp. 174–92.

Tynan, L. (2021) 'What is relationality? Indigenous knowledges, practices and responsibilities with kin', *Cultural Geographies*, 28, 4, pp. 597–610.

Vaittinen, T. (2015) 'The power of the vulnerable body', *International Feminist Journal of Politics*, 17, 1, pp. 100–18.

van Dijke, J., van Nistelrooij, I., Bos, P. and Duyndam, J. (2019) 'Care ethics: an ethics of empathy?', *Nursing Ethics*, 26, 5, pp. 1282–91.

Vaughan-Williams, N. (2005) 'Protesting against citizenship', *Citizenship Studies*, 9, 2, pp. 167–79.

Vázquez, R. (2012) 'Towards a decolonial critique of modernity: buen vivir, relationality and the task of listening', in R. Fornet-Betancourt (ed.) *Capital, Poverty, Development* (Aachen: Wissenschaftsverlag Mainz), pp. 241–52.

Verran, H. (2013) 'Engagements between disparate knowledge traditions: toward doing difference generatively and in good faith', in L. Green (ed.) *Contested Ecologies: Dialogues in the South on Nature and Knowledge* (Cape Town: HSRC Press), pp. 141–61.

Vij, R. (2019) 'The global subject of precarity', *Globalizations*, 16, 4, pp. 506–24.

Vitalis, R. (2015) *White World Order, Black Power Politics: The Birth of American International Relations* (Ithaca, NY: Cornell University Press).

Viveiros de Castro, E. (2004) 'Perspectival anthropology and the method of controlled equivocation', *Tipití: Journal of the Society for the Anthropology of Lowland South America*, 2, 1, pp. 3–22.

Viveiros de Castro, E. (2013) 'Economic development and cosmopolitical re-involvement: from necessity to sufficiency', in L. Green (ed.) *Contested Ecologies: Dialogues in the South on Nature and Knowledge* (Cape Town: HSRC Press), pp. 28–41.

Vosko, L.F. (ed.) (2006) *Precarious Employment: Understanding Labour Market Insecurity in Canada* (Montreal: McGill-Queen's University Press).

WAI 167 (1999) *The Whanganui River Report* (Wellington: Waitangi Tribunal).

Walker, K. (2021) 'Okâwîmâwaskiy: regenerating a wholistic ethics', PhD dissertation, University of British Columbia, Canada.

Walker, M.U. (2007) *Moral Understandings: A Feminist Study in Ethics* (2nd edn) (New York: Routledge).

Waring, M. (1999) *Counting for Nothing: What Men Value and What Women Are Worth* (Toronto: University of Toronto Press).

Warnke, G. (1995) 'Communicative rationality and cultural values', in S.K. White (ed.) *The Cambridge Companion to Habermas* (Cambridge: Cambridge University Press), pp. 120–42.

Watson, N., McKie, L., Hughes, B., Hopkins, D. and Gregory, S. (2004) '(Inter)dependence, needs and care: the potential for disability and feminist theorists to develop on emancipatory model', *Sociology*, 38, 2, pp. 331–50.

Watts, V. (2013) 'Indigenous place-thought and agency amongst humans and non-humans (First Woman and Sky Woman go on a European world tour!)', *Decolonization: Indigeneity, Education & Society*, 2, 1, pp. 20–34.

Weber, M. (1981) *From Max Weber: Essays in Sociology*, Edited and Translated by H.H. Gerth and C.W. Mills (Oxford: Oxford University Press).

Weber, M. (2005) 'The critical social theory of the Frankfurt school, and the "social turn" in IR', *Review of International Studies*, 31, pp. 195–209.

Whanganui River Māori Trust Board. (2010) 'Timeline'. Available from: http://www.wrmtb.co.nz/assets/rivertime.html [Accessed 22 February 2022].

White, S. (2000) *Sustaining Affirmation: The Strengths of Weak Ontology in Political Theory* (Princeton, NJ: Princeton University Press).

Williams, F. (2001) 'In and beyond new labour: towards a new political ethics of care', *Critical Social Policy*, 21, 4, pp. 467–93.

Wolin, S. (1996) 'Fugitive democracy', in S. Benhabib (ed.) *Democracy and Difference: Contesting the Boundaries of the Political* (Princeton, NJ: Princeton University Press), pp. 31–45.

Ylä-Anttila, T. (2005) 'The world social forum and the globalization of social movements and public spheres', *ephemera: theory and politics in organization*, 5, 2, pp. 423–42.

Young, I.M. (1997) *Intersecting Voices: Dilemmas of Gender, Political Philosophy, and Policy* (Princeton, NJ: Princeton University Press).

Young, I.M. (2006) 'Responsibility and global justice: a social connection model', *Social Philosophy and Policy*, 23, 1, pp. 102–30.

Zhan, S. and Huang, L. (2012) 'Rural roots of current migrant labor shortage in China: development and labor empowerment in a situation of incomplete proletarianization', *Studies in Comparative International Development*, 48, 1, pp. 81–111.

Žižek, S. (1991) *For They Know Not What They Do: Enjoyment as a Political Factor* (London: Verso).

Index

References to footnotes show both the page number and the note number (83n1).

A
abstract other 107
accountability 122, 138
aesthetics 31
Agathangelou, A.M. 7
agency 63, 99, 107, 120, 141, 162, 206
agonistic action 143, 171, 172, 185–6, 188, 192, 204, 216
agonizing care 121–2, 124, 143, 185, 186
Alaimo, S. 111, 207
Albert, G. 181
Alfred, T. 64
Amin, S. 37
Andean cosmology 93–102
Anghie, A. 51, 52
Anievas, A. 69, 70
anthropocentrism 65, 66, 67
anthropology 19, 89, 91, 102
anti-essentialism 113–17, 124
antifoundationalists 78, 90–3
Aotearoa/New Zealand 8–10, 40, 64, 66, 93, 162, 164, 173
Appiah, K.A. 57, 60, 80
appropriation 25, 53, 59, 101
Aradau, C. 6, 18
Arrighi, G. 38, 41n3
Arruzza, C. 117
Asher, K. 97
associative, care as 184–94
associative, political as 27, 171–9, 184, 185, 186, 216
Athanasiou, A. 165n6
atíku 27, 195–213
attentiveness 116–17, 123, 183, 194
Ausangate 4–5, 73, 75, 87–8, 137, 172–3, 179–80, 184
autonomy 45, 60, 105, 107, 148–51, 155
axiology 31–2, 34, 48, 129–35, 143, 209
ayllu 73–5
Aymara 96

B
Bacon, F. 34
Barad, K. 7n1
Barchiesi, F. 154, 155
Barnes, M. 108n2
Baynes, K. 69
Beattie, A.R. 12–14, 35, 45, 122, 215
Benhabib, S. 104, 105, 106, 111
Bennett, J. 32
binaries
  binary thinking 28, 106, 108n2, 114, 218
  Human/Nature binary 9–10, 33–6, 48, 53, 105, 130, 153, 164, 177, 181, 202
  Human/Non-human binary 52
  living/non-living binary 9–10
  Man/Nature 105, 130
  masculine/feminine binary 105–6, 107
  mind/body binary 116
  in modernity 104–7, 115, 150, 152
  moving beyond 216–18
  patriarchy 43
  public/private binary 105–6
  rationalism 124
  Right/Good binary 106
  Subject/Object binary 33, 38, 39, 43, 73, 131, 164
  Us/Them binary 39
Blaney, S. 56, 128, 132, 146
Blaser, M. 5–6, 7, 10, 17–18, 19, 27, 127, 128, 130–4, 137, 143, 146, 160, 170, 173–8, 181, 187, 192, 193, 195–8, 200, 204–6, 208–10
bodily needs 107, 150, 184
Borrows, J. 100
Bourdieu, P. 153
Bourgault, S. 107
Breman, J. 153
Briones, C. 133
Brown, G.W. 57, 60
Butler, J. 78, 79, 82, 89, 151, 156–7, 165

C
Campbell, C. 42
Canada 68, 188–93, 196
capitalism
  and the body 45
  and care 122–3
  hidden work 155
  intersection with other power systems 45–7

INDEX

and modernity 38, 41–2
power systems in the modern world 22
precarity 154
surplus-value production 41–2
technomuscular capitalism 118
Caraus, T. 80, 82–6
care ethics *see* ethics of care
care work
  coded as feminine 44–5
  feminization of 20–1
  global nature of 117–20
caribou 27, 195–213
Castel, R. 151
Castro, D. 200
Castro-Gómez, S. 42
catadores 154
Chakrabarty, D. 47, 54
Champagne, D. 38–9
Chang, K.A. 118, 119
Chatterjee, P. 43
Cheah, P. 80
China 155
ch'ixi 92, 93–102
citizen rights 154, 159, 161
class 42, 114, 118, 122, 154
Cloyes, K.G. 121
Code, L. 110, 113
coercion 61, 62
collaboration 3, 22, 138, 140, 141, 219
collective activity, care as 183–4
colonialism
  as 'civilizing' 52
  colonized subjects 68
  and democratic states 39
  and the ethics of care 120
  and gender 43, 44
  and humanitarian aid 39
  and international law 51
  intersection with other power systems 45–7
  and modernity 37–8
  modernity/coloniality/decoloniality (MCD) 10–12, 29–55
  power systems in the modern world 22
  progress as history 49
commodification of care 122–3
common humanity 57, 68, 217
common world, building 209–10
commonality 82, 94, 183
complementarity 96–7, 98
concrete other 106–7
Confortini, C. 111
context
  ch'ixi realm 97
  ethics of care 110, 115, 121, 159
  moral cosmopolitanism 61, 80
  moral dilemmas 201
  moral salience of 13
  situated epistemology 140

contingency 8, 15, 54, 79, 84–9, 103, 121, 163, 215
continuous nature of care 184, 193–4, 205, 210
contractualist ethics 13
convergences of meaning 59, 96, 97, 100, 101–2
Cooper, D. 121
corroboree frog 1–3, 28, 101
cosmopolitanism
  cosmopolitans from below 80–2
  cosmopolitical proposal 209
  critical cosmopolitanism 81
  cultural cosmopolitanism 60
  decolonial cosmopolitanism 74, 81
  difference 61
  equality 84
  freedom 84
  insurgent cosmopolitanism 81
  justice 61–2, 84
  moral cosmopolitanism 24, 57, 60–9, 80, 83, 102
  multicultural dialogical cosmopolitanism 70, 103
  postfoundational cosmopolitanism 58, 59, 78–90, 103
Coulthard, G. 38, 68
Crawford, N. 39
critical cosmopolitanism 81
critical moral ethnography 136–7
critical theory 24, 31, 54
cultural cosmopolitanism 60
cultural relativism 7

D

de la Cadena, M. 3–5, 7, 10, 19, 24, 72–3, 75–7, 92, 97, 127, 128, 131, 136–7, 144, 161n3, 172–3, 179–80, 184, 195–213
de Meriche, D. 116
de Sousa Santos, B. 53, 81, 86, 161
de Vitoria, F. 51–2
decolonialism
  ch'ixi realm 94–7
  decolonial cosmopolitanism 74, 81
  and ethnography 19
  Global Ethics 59
  and modernity 24, 29–55
  modernity/coloniality/decoloniality (MCD) 10–12, 29–55
  pluriversal scholarship embedded in 10–12
  and the pluriverse 128
decolonization 96
deconstructivism 78, 98, 215
de-hierarchicalization 20, 188, 203, 212, 219
democracy 39, 86–7, 88, 172
deontological moral approaches 13
dependency 44–5, 109–10, 151, 164
  see also interdependency
development 49, 97

dialogue 76–7, 95
difference
  complementarity 96–7
  different ways of being/knowing 3
  ethical significance of 62
  ethics of care 124, 144, 186
  and the global 8
  incommensurability across difference 25, 77, 95
  moral cosmopolitanism 57, 68–9
  onto-epistemology 7
  and the pluriverse 126, 127
  pluriverse as meta-world 131
  radical difference 68–9, 98, 185
discourse ethics 24, 57–8, 69–77, 87–8, 102
dissociative, care as 183–7
dissociative, political as 27, 170, 171–9, 184, 185, 186, 216
distance 117, 119
diversity 95, 174, 184, 203n2
domestic work 155
Donald, D. 108n2
Donnelly, J. 64
Dussel, E. 31, 38, 47, 49, 54

E
earth-beings 4, 66–7, 73, 75, 77, 87–8, 93, 99, 137, 195
Edkins, J. 8, 10, 39, 80, 85, 182
Ehrenreich, B. 42
emancipation 69, 70, 71, 74, 75, 82
embodied other 107
embodied stories 99
embodied vulnerability 148–9, 150–2, 164, 184
embodiment of care practices 112
emotion
  coded as feminine 45, 48, 107
  concrete other 107
  senti-pensar 95
empathy 116
empiricism 34
enlightenment 37–8, 69
enquiry, care as form of 111
entanglement of worlds 7, 59, 77, 117, 127, 197, 199
epistemology
  definition 5–6
  empiricism 34
  epistemic communities 110
  epistemic humility 122, 123
  epistemic injustices 202
  epistemic precarity 96
  intersubjectvist epistemology 69
  versus ontology 132–3
  pluriverse as meta-world 129–35
  situated epistemology 110–11, 130, 135, 139, 142, 169, 185, 186, 216
  see also knowledge
equality 60, 64, 84, 86, 165

Escobar, A. 30, 32, 37, 132, 138, 146, 163, 220
Esping-Anderson, G. 161
essentialism 113–14, 121
establishment of a social order 182
establishment of onto-epistemologies 187–8
ethical compasses 96, 98
ethical conflicts/ethical dilemmas
  atíku/caribou 195–213
  gaps in collective interpretive resources 202
  ontological difference 136–7
  as political dilemmas 208
  uneven distribution of vulnerability 158–9
ethical necessity 140–1
ethical precarity 140n3, 220
ethical relationality 108n2
ethics of care
  (dis)associative theory of 183–7
  caring for *atíku*/caribou 198–210
  as critical 113, 122, 186–94
  feminist ethics of care 15–17, 25, 37, 220
  in Global Ethics 217–21
  meta-theoretical framework 146–67
  outline of critical, political ethics of care 101–2, 104–25
  pluriversal ethics 15–17, 138–45
  political and the pluriverse 168–94
  power 17, 121, 122, 124, 210
  productive ethics of care 186–94
ethnography 5, 19, 27, 127–8, 132, 133, 136–7, 155, 189–90, 200
Ettlinger, N. 166
Eurocentrism 31, 37, 49, 54, 56, 74
exclusion 70, 86, 106
exploitation 30, 46, 47, 119, 176

F
false contingencies 85
Fanon, F. 40–1, 68
Federici, S. 45, 46–7
feminist ethics 13, 104
feminist philosophy 107
feminist political economics 155
feminist relational ontology 25
Ferrarese, E. 149–50, 151–3, 157
fish 189–93
Fisher, B. 2, 111, 143, 183
Flikschuh, K. 61
'forms of moral life' 20
Foucault, M. 32, 54
foundational thought 78
foundations, ontological status of 79
French Revolution 38
Fricker, M. 202

G
Gaonkar, D.P. 47
gender 43, 61
gender relations 43–5

gender roles 113–14
generalized other versus the concrete other 106–7
generative potentials 26
George River 196
Gilligan, C. 16, 21, 25, 45, 108, 136n2, 144
global, care as 117–20, 124
global capitalism 118
global care chains 118
Global Ethics 12–15, 18, 23, 24, 28, 56–103, 126–8, 167, 214–21
global justice 83, 85
Global South 118–19, 154, 155, 165, 166
globalization 47
globalized localism 81
'good' care 121–2, 185, 204
good life 70, 104–6, 113, 138, 185, 186, 209, 210
Green, L. 18
Grotius, H. 51
groundings 79, 83, 84, 89–91, 101, 103, 131, 168, 170–2, 215
grounding/ungrounding 169
groundless ground 170–2, 180
Guatemala 155
Gyack 1–3, 28, 101

H
Haacke, J. 69, 74
Habermas, J. 57–8, 69, 70, 72, 74, 75, 87
Hamington, M. 111–13, 143, 186
Han, C. 156
Hankivsky, O. 109, 110
Haraway, D. 115, 130
harm, minimization of 111, 143, 213
Hegel, G.W.F. 35–7, 49, 50
Heinrich, M. 41
Hekman, S. 16, 25, 111, 114, 115, 135–6, 136n2, 139, 140, 142, 204, 207
Held, D. 57, 60
hierarchies 8, 14, 24, 38–40, 50, 59, 86, 105, 131
   see also de-hierarchicalization
historicism 36, 49
Hobbes, T. 33, 39, 48, 49, 50, 105
Holbraad, M. 15, 126, 131
Hopgood, S. 71
Hoppania, H.-K. 118, 122–3, 183, 184
Hornaday River 190–2
Hsiao, E. 9, 181
human rights 57, 63–8, 105
humanitarian aid 39, 120n4
Hunt, S. 55, 98, 99, 100
Hutchings, K. 12, 13, 16, 24, 35, 57, 58, 60, 71, 72, 77, 91–4, 104, 110, 126, 133, 136, 140–1, 145
Huysmans, J. 6, 18

I
ignorance 112
immanence 126
in-*ayllu* 73–5
inclusion 39, 82, 175
inclusive agonism 171
incommensurability across difference 25, 77, 95
independence 45, 109–10
Indigenous peoples
   building the pluriverse with care 188–93
   ch'ixi realm 93–102
   human rights 64–6
   modernity and decolonialism 38, 39, 43–4, 47
individualism 60, 139, 148, 217
Industrial Revolution 42
inequality 42, 50, 100, 161
Ingram, J. 82–4, 86
Innu Nation 27, 132, 195–213
insurgent cosmopolitanism 81
interconnectedness 12, 14, 22, 38, 94, 117, 119, 124
interdependency 109, 120, 156, 183
International Relations 39, 56, 70, 220
intersectionality 114–15
intersubjectivity 63, 69, 71, 110
Intra-European Modernity 30, 37
Inuit people 92, 196
invisibilization of worlds 146, 147, 155
Iran 44

J
Jaeger, H-M. 11
Jahn, B. 75–6
justice 61–2, 84, 104–6, 119, 202

K
Kanipinikassikueu 196, 198–9
Kant, I. 34–6, 48, 50, 60, 61, 69, 105
King, H. 39
Kittay, E.F. 105, 107, 109
knowledge
   collaborative building of 141–2
   equality of 95–6
   ethics of care 110
   Eurocentric ways of knowing 74
   feminine knowledge coded as inferior 107
   generative components of 130
   legitimacy of 200–3
   limits to knowing 72–7, 142
   moral knowledge 112, 114, 218
   pragmatism 92
   situated epistemology 110–11, 130, 135, 139, 142, 169, 185, 186, 216
   translation 174–5, 200
   unknowable worlds 3, 74, 77, 102, 103, 131, 147
   see also epistemology

Kudlak, J.M.M. 191
Kuokkanen, R. 47, 64
Kuptana, R. 92, 192

L

labour
  globalized care labour 118
  modernity and decolonialism 40–3, 45–6, 47, 50
  and precarity 154, 159
Ladner, K. 43–4
land 161, 174, 175, 181, 189, 190
language 18–19, 174–5, 204–5
  see also translation
Laugier, S. 150
law 9, 50, 181
Law, J. 55
Leclerc, G.-L. 40
legal personhood for non-human actors 8–9, 65–6, 164, 173, 180–1, 201
Leget, C. 108
Leinius, J. 81–2
liberalism 38–9, 64, 72, 120n4, 165, 175
lifeworlds (*Lebenswelt*) 58, 70, 71, 73–4
Lightfoot, S. 64–6
limits to knowing 72–7, 202
linear time 35–6, 49
Ling, L.H.M. 7, 118, 119
Linklater, A. 58, 70–1, 72, 75, 76
Locke, J. 34, 35, 48–50, 105
Lowndes, V. 171–2
Lynch, C. 140n3, 220

M

Machiavelli, N. 33, 50
Macpherson, C.B. 33
magic 45–6
Māori world 8–10, 40, 108n2, 161–2, 164, 181
Marchart, O. 27, 78–80, 86–7, 88, 170, 171, 184
Marks, S. 85
Marx, K. 41, 42, 50
Marxism 37, 45
masculinity 62, 118
material ethics 111–12, 159, 207
McClintock, A. 40
McNay, L. 62–3, 68
meta-ethical tools 15, 19–21, 124–5, 203
metaphor 4–5, 98–100
meta-theoretical framework 26, 102, 146–67, 188, 195, 198, 201, 211
meta-worlds 26, 129–35, 168, 179, 213
methodology 17–23
Meyers, D.T. 105, 107
Mignolo, W. 3, 7, 10–11, 15, 37, 59, 80, 81, 89
migrant care labour 118
Millar, K. 153–6, 160
misrecognition 67–8

modernity
  'birth' of 38
  caring for *atíku*/caribou 199
  ch'ixi realm 97–8
  decentring of 54–5
  definition 23, 29–55
  as doing 29–31, 37–49, 51
  ethics of care 108n2, 212
  and Global Ethics 24
  modernity-centric research in Global Ethics 56
  and non-modern worlds 193
  precarity 160
  as thinking 29–37, 48–9, 51
  and understandings of morality 105
  as world 19–20, 48–9, 50–4
modernity/coloniality/decoloniality (MCD) 10–12, 29–55
Mohanty, C.T. 54
moral boundaries 107
moral cosmopolitanism 24, 57, 60–9, 80, 83, 102
moral judgement 110, 115, 138, 140–5
moral knowledge 111–12, 114, 218
moral philosophy 19, 34, 104, 106, 136, 140, 141, 198, 219–20
moral practices 111–12, 135–8
moral psychology 15, 75, 108
moral selves 16, 115, 140, 148, 184, 218
moral voices 140, 144, 185, 212
more-than-human beings 1, 66, 93, 99, 172, 191, 195–213, 220
Morris, J.D.K. 180–1
Mouffe, C. 83n1, 84–5, 171
Muehlebach, A. 166
multicultural dialogical cosmopolitanism 70, 103
multiple worlds 132–3, 136, 144, 187, 220
Munck, R. 153n1, 154

N

Nadasdy, P. 11
Najmabadi, A. 44
Narayan, U. 120
natural law 51, 126
Nature 30, 99, 152, 177, 181, 202
Nazario 3–5, 24, 72–7, 87–8, 92, 97, 137, 172–3, 179–80, 184
needs, meeting 107, 148–9, 183, 207
Neilson, B. 154, 157
neo-colonialism 87
neoliberalism 118, 154, 156
'new' worlds 136, 185, 187, 188, 204
New Zealand/Aotearoa 8–10, 40, 64, 66, 93, 162, 164, 173
Noddings, N. 112, 116, 122
non-humans 52, 65–6, 77, 111, 172–3, 195–213
  see also more-than-human beings

normativity
  care 113, 120–3, 128–9, 138, 143–4, 147, 185–7, 197
  colonialism 49, 52, 128
  discourse ethics 58, 69, 70, 74
  Nature 33–5, 105
  partial connections 134–5
  and pluriversality 11, 24, 25, 55, 59, 134–5, 138, 143, 212–13, 217–18
  postmodernist ethics 78–80, 83–4, 87–9, 90
Nuke, P. 199

O
objectivity 107, 113
Oliver, K. 68, 109, 157
O'Neill, O. 57, 60–2, 63
one-world metaphysics 55, 57, 69, 103, 131, 132–4, 135
onto-epistemology
  definition 6–7, 18
  and difference 126–7
  methodology 17–23
  modernity 30, 53–5
  performativity of 18–19
  politics versus the political 8
  and research 56
ontological turn 10, 11, 31, 53–5, 132
ontology
  definition 5–6
  enactment of ontologies 6
  modernity 98
  pluriverse as meta-world 129–35
  strong versus weak 134
'order' 32–6
Oslender, U. 19
otherness 59, 97, 102, 106, 119, 160

P
Pachamama 94, 95, 98–101
Pagden, A. 48, 51
Paraguay 132, 174–8
partial connections 7, 22, 77, 126–45, 180, 182, 188, 211–12, 214, 220
partial relations of care 26, 129, 143, 145, 211, 213
Pârvu, C.A. 80, 84
paternalism 120n4
patient struggle 116–17
patriarchy
  and the body 45
  essentialism 114
  and feminist ethics 104, 107
  intersection with other power systems 45–7
  and modernity 42–3
  power systems in the modern world 22, 82
  stifling relational ethics 113
Paulatuuqmiut 27, 170, 188–93

Paxton, M. 171–2
performativity 112, 137
Peru 3–5
Peterson, V. S. 43
philosophy 32, 33
  see also moral philosophy
Piketty, T. 42
Place-Thought frames 98
pluriverse
  building the pluriverse with care 195–213
  connecting with the ethics of care: preliminary steps 138–45
  definition 3, 7, 127
  fluid entwinement of worlds 163
  in Global Ethics 214–21
  meta-worlds 26, 129–35, 168, 179, 213
  modernity as world 51
  ongoing establishment of worlds 182
  pluriversal ethics 218–20
  and the political 3, 4–10, 27, 168
  reconfigurations of 169
  scalar components 169
  and vulnerability 166
  world of many worlds 3
Pogge, T. 60
Poker, P. 196
political, the
  (dis)associative 172–3, 216
  (dis)associative theory of care 183–94
  care as political 120–4, 183–4
  and the pluriverse 3, 4–10, 27, 168–94
  versus politics 8–10, 170–1
  and precarity 160
political economy 118, 160
political ontology 5–6, 17–18
politicality 168–9
politics
  versus the political 8–10, 170–1
  postfoundational cosmopolitanism 85–6
  postmodernist ethics 78
  and precarity 156, 159–60
  and vulnerability 149–50, 152–3
politics versus the political 8–10
postcolonial scholarship 24, 31, 54, 120
postfoundational cosmopolitanism 58, 59, 78–90, 103
postfoundational political theory 170, 171, 173, 178
postmodernist ethics 13, 24, 57–9, 77–93, 94n8, 102, 103, 171, 215
Povinelli, E. 9, 163
power
  asymmetries of 146, 198
  capitalism 38
  colonialism 38
  deconstruction 188
  de-hierarchicalization 20, 188, 203, 212, 219
  and difference 185
  erasure of moral voices 114

ethics of care 17, 121, 122, 124, 210
and gender 42–3
and modernity 22, 24
pluriversal ethics 146–67, 218–19
and the pluriverse 7, 128
pluriverse as meta-world 130
and politics 50–3
politics versus the political 8–10
and precarity 160, 204–5
racism 40
and recognition 68
unequal distribution 161
and vulnerability 151, 163–5, 201–4
women 61
powerlessness 150, 151
practices, morality as 16, 111–12, 135–8
pragmatism 58, 59, 78, 90–3, 190, 192–3
Pratt, M.L. 77, 204
Prattes, R. 111, 112, 118
precarity
    caring for atíku/caribou 198–202, 207–8, 210
    ethical conflicts/ethical dilemmas 211
    as intensified vulnerability 26–7, 157–9, 164–6, 202, 218–19
    meta-theoretical framework 153–67, 188, 193
    pluriversal ethics 218–19
primitive accumulation 42, 45, 46
principled pragmatism 92, 190, 192
private property 48, 49, 181
procedural ethics 58, 70–1
'profession of faith' 96–7, 140, 220
Prozorov, S. 88, 89
Puig de la Bellacasa, M. 205–6, 210
pukara 72–3, 74, 174

Q
Quechua people 4, 72–3, 87
Quijano, A. 38, 39–40

R
race 39–40, 114, 118, 122
racism 22, 40–1, 45–7, 82
radical alterity 11, 17, 52
radical contingency 87, 89
radical difference 68–9, 98, 185
Raghuram, P. 121
Rancière, J. 10, 75, 82, 171, 173
rationalism
    approaches to global ethics 12–15, 20, 57
    conquering nature with reason 33
    discourse ethics 58
    and the 'generalized other' 106
    and modernity 30
    modernity as world 48
    moral cosmopolitanism 62–3
    moral epistemology 35
    rationalist/alternative framework 24
    and science 34

separation of morality 112
rationality/reason
    coded as masculine 45, 107
    difference 126
    discourse ethics 70
    language as rationality 76
    moral cosmopolitanism 60
    ways of knowing 74–5
Rawley, J.A. 40
recognition 38, 67–8, 178
regrounding 169, 180, 187
Reinaga, F. 94
relational ontologies 108–10
relational selves 16–17, 114, 116
relationality
    and agency 206
    (dis)associative theory of care 185–6
    and difference 186
    emergence of the self through 148
    ethics of care 109–10, 117, 120, 121, 144, 205, 217
    grounding/ungrounding 172
    modernity 22, 24
    moral selves 184
    partial connections 131
    and patriarchy 21
    and the pluriverse 139
    pluriverse as meta-world 130, 168
    and power systems 211–12
    and precarity 157, 211
    relational ontology and vulnerability 148–53
    'relations of care' 144–5
    stability/instability 163–7
    and vulnerability 148–53, 158
relativism 36, 76–7, 79, 115
repair of the world 2, 111, 143, 145, 182, 183, 192, 198
reproduction 45–7, 61, 118, 155, 170, 199n1, 211
research
    enactment of ontologies 6, 56
    methodology 17–23
    modernity/ coloniality/ decoloniality (MCD) 11–12
    as worlding 56
resiliency 165
responsibility 111–13, 119, 122, 183
Rieff, D. 39
Rivera Cusicanqui, S. 24, 59, 92, 93–102, 108n2, 140n3, 220
Robbins, B. 80
Robinson, F. 14, 16, 19, 25, 72, 109–14, 116–18, 120, 184–7, 193
Rojas, C. 7, 10, 11, 48, 160, 166
Rorty, R. 59, 78
Rossiter, N. 154, 157
Rousseau, J.-J. 105
Roy, E.A. 9, 66
Ruane, A. 111

Ruddick, S. 115, 117
Ruru, J. 180–1
Ruti, M. 90

S
Salmond, A. 66, 199n1
Scauso, M. 24, 59, 93–8, 220
Schick, K. 12–14, 35, 45, 122, 215
Schroeder, M. 31
Schulenberg, U. 91
science
  collapsing of thinking and doing 48
  Human/Nature binary 33, 53
  limits of 209
  and modernity 34, 190, 192, 200
  normativity 34
  pragmatism 191
  and racism 40
Scully, B. 154
self
  de-centring of 111, 143, 204
  inextricable link with morality 111, 114
  self-alienation 86, 87
  self-consciousness 36, 37, 49
  self-legislation 50, 60
  self-narratives 37
  self-reflection 69
sensory perception 34, 35
senti-pensar 95
Seth, S. 35–6
Sevenhuijsen, S. 110, 111, 116, 148, 187, 217
sexism 47
Shapcott, R. 70, 71
Shilliam, R. 40
Simpson, A. 64
Simpson, L.B. 64–5
situated epistemology 110–11, 130, 135, 139, 142, 169, 185, 186, 216
Slater, L. 1, 2, 3, 99
slavery 40, 45–7, 65
Slote, M. 116
Smith, L.T. 39
Snider, N. 21
social class 42, 114, 118, 122, 154
social contract 105
social order
  care 122, 124
  changes in 157, 171–3
  cosmopolitanism 84
  establishment of a social order 8, 182, 183
  justice 105
  and the political 170–1
  precarity 156, 157
  radical contingency 89
social relationships *see* relationality
socio-symbolic order
  dissociative theory of care 168, 169, 172

modernity 179
  and the pluriverse 27
  and the political 8
  postmodernist ethics 80, 84, 85
  precarity 156
  relational ontologies 150, 152, 153
  and the subject 85
solidarity 81, 85, 96, 101–2
sovereignty 33, 50, 99, 163
Spain 38, 51, 52
Sparks, H. 176, 192
speech acts 69–70
spiritual domain 65, 99, 204
Stammers, N. 67
Standing, G. 153–5, 159, 160
state
  and the body 45
  ch'ixi realm 97
  and modernity 36, 38–9
  power of 50
  and precarity 159, 161, 164
Stengers, I. 209
stories 98–9, 137, 177
Strathern, M. 7, 101, 127, 130, 139, 161n3, 214
structural injustices 119
subalterns 81–2
subjectivity 85, 109, 110, 139, 148, 160, 187, 206
suffering, minimization of 111, 143, 213

T
Taylor, C. 32, 34, 67–8
Te Awa Tupua/Whanganui River 8–10, 24, 27, 64, 66, 93, 161–2, 164, 172–3, 180–1
Te Pou Tupua 66
territory 176–8, 181
testimonial injustice 202–3
Tickner, A. 56, 128, 132, 146
time 35–6
Tlostanova, M.V. 89
Todd, Z. 11, 19, 22, 27, 92, 98–100, 188–93
totalization 115, 144, 168n1, 184, 217
Towns, A. 43
transcendence 12–14, 35–6, 77–8, 87, 111, 117, 130, 135, 171
translation 76, 174–5, 200, 202, 204–5
transnational care relations 118
Tronto, J. 2, 12, 16, 20, 21, 107, 110–13, 116, 122, 143, 150, 183
Turpel-Lafond, M.E. 44
Tynan, L. 2

U
ungrounding 8, 79, 84, 86, 168, 169, 182, 187
Unión de las Comunidades Indígenas de la Nación Yshir (UCINY) 174

universalism
  assimilative 72
  discourse ethics 70
  and ethics 13, 14
  moral universalism 60
  postfoundational cosmopolitanism 82, 89
  void universalism 88, 103
  Western universalism 10–11
universality
  difference 126
  moral cosmopolitanism 60
  versus particularity 215
  versus pluriversality 127
  postfoundational cosmopolitanism 89
  as reality 117
universals
  alternative universals 89
  discourse ethics 71
  Global Ethics 214–15
  global order 54
  pluriversality 10–11, 25
  postfoundational cosmopolitanism 90
  void universalism 88
unknowable worlds 3, 74, 77, 102, 103, 131, 147
unthinkable, thinking the 160, 175–6

V
Vaittinen, T. 118, 122–3, 148–51, 164, 183, 184
values 22, 31–2
  see also axiology
Vázquez, R. 53
Verran, H. 112
Vij, R. 165
violence 42, 48, 52, 61, 99, 178
Viveiros de Castro, E. 205, 210
void universalism 88, 103
vulnerability
  care as political 122
  caring for *atîku*/caribou 198, 199, 201–2, 207–8
  coded as feminine 45
  ethics of care 16, 109, 110
  modernity 19–21
  moral cosmopolitanism 60–2
  of moral judgements 21, 22
  pluriversal ethics 218–19
  and the pluriverse 182, 184
  and precarity 156–9, 162–7
  precarity as intensified vulnerability 26–7, 157–9, 164–6, 202, 218–19

  relational ontologies 148–53
  vulnerable bodies 118

W
wage labour 154, 159
Walker, K. 65, 108n2, 110
Walker, M.U. 16, 19, 20, 22–3, 107, 111–13, 115, 136, 138, 140n3, 142, 215, 216, 219, 220
Wallace Brown, G. 60
Warnke, G. 58
Watts, V. 98, 99
weak ontologies 134–5
Weber, M. 32, 34, 69
Western philosophical tradition 32
Western universalism 10–11
Western-centric research 56
Whanganui River/Te Awa Tupua 8–10, 24, 27, 64, 66, 93, 161–2, 164, 172–3, 180–1
White, S. 134
white Western approaches to ethics 13–14
wholes/parts 127, 217
Williams, F. 120
witch hunts 45–7
Wolgalu/ Wiradjuri community 1–3
Wolin, S. 184
women
  and capitalism 45–6
  essentialism 114
  exclusion 106
  female migrant workers 118
  heterogeneity of 115
  legal personhood 65
  moral cosmopolitanism 61
  moral philosophy 107
  and the 'private sphere' 43
work versus labour 155
worldings 130, 208–10
world-making effects 137
worlds *see* onto-epistemology

Y
Young, I.M. 22, 117, 119
yrmo 27, 170, 174–8, 181
Yshiro people 27, 132, 170, 174–8, 181

Z
Zapatistas 129n1
Žižek, S. 171

www.ingramcontent.com/pod-product-compliance
Lightning Source LLC
Chambersburg PA
CBHW071155070526
44584CB00019B/2793